10/24/79

A Salut !

Mox & Gou

THE GAME OF WINE

The Game of Wine

 Forrest Wallace and Gilbert Cross

Illustrated with maps of wine regions
by Rafael Palacios

HARPER & ROW, PUBLISHERS

NEW YORK, HAGERSTOWN,

SAN FRANCISCO, LONDON

Specified list of wines of the Côte d'Or Burgundy from *Alexis Lichine's New Encyclopedia of Wines,* copyright © 1967, 1974 by Alexis Lichine. Reprinted by permission of Alfred A. Knopf, Inc.

"A Good Wine Cellar for $2,000," by Craig Claiborne, from *Travel & Leisure,* February 1974 issue, reprinted from *Travel & Leisure.* Copyright © 1974 by American Express Publishing Corporation. Reprinted by permission of the author and publisher.

"Braised Bass in Red Wine" recipe from October 24, 1971, issue of the New York *Times.* Copyright © 1971 by the New York Times Company. Reprinted by permission of the New York *Times.*

Excerpt from Elizabeth David, *A Book of Mediterranean Food* (Penguin Handbook, 2nd rev. ed., 1965), pp. 118–20. Copyright © 1958, 1965 by Elizabeth David. Reprinted by permission of the author and Penguin Books Ltd.

There is but one thing better in life.

Hans Joachim Guntrum
GERMAN WINEGROWER.

Foreword

Perhaps more than any book now in print *The Game of Wine* talks directly to the needs and problems, the interests and concerns, of the man who wants to go out and buy a bottle of wine intelligently and then to use it gracefully when it reaches his table. It is the most original approach to this vastly popular subject of any book in memory—the only totally fresh approach, so far as I know. There is no novice so innocent he cannot follow its guidance; no connoisseur so jaded he cannot learn from its explorations. This is a serious book in its effort to provide a broader understanding and a better working knowledge of its subject, yet at no point does it lose sight of the fact that one of the chief rewards of wine is the fun and fascination of the game.

The Game of Wine has as much to say about fine foods and how to serve them as about fine wines and how to enjoy them, and gives particular and welcome stress to the art and pleasure of blending and "orchestrating" wines and foods and people. The examination here of the mysteries and perils of the wine trade is by long odds the best I have seen, and the strategies offered for outwitting the trade in the purchase of a single bottle or a dozen cases are both funny and sound—and eminently timely.

The authors of *The Game of Wine* have made a remarkably wise, witty, amusing, original, and above all practical and useful contribution to what someone has called "the most beguiling of the minor pleasures."

CLIFFORD T. WEIHMAN, Grand Maître
Commanderie d'Amérique
Confrérie des Chevaliers du Tastevin

Acknowledgments

The Game of Wine has been the work of many hands over many years (more years than anybody imagined at the start). It had its beginnings in 1959, in a conversation over dinner, presumably with wine, between Forrest Wallace and Samuel Vaughan, then a junior editor at Doubleday, now president of all of Doubleday's publishing operations. An early participant in the project was Martin Mayer. Coauthor Gilbert Cross joined in 1964. Further research and editing were contributed by Marc Haefle. Final editorial responsibility at Doubleday fell to Louise Gault. Karen Van Westering played a key role in helping to pull together the many parts of a complex project. The brunt of typing the final draft was borne with patient good will by Kathy Abele.

The authors wish to express appreciation to a great many members of the wine and restaurant trades in France, Germany, Switzerland, New York, Chicago, and northern California for their advice and assistance in the research and illustration of this book. Particular thanks are also due to William Leedom, Frank Schoonmaker, Michael Aaron, and Craig Claiborne of New York, to Don and Elmer Singewald of Norwalk, Connecticut, to Paul Child of Cambridge, Massachusetts, and to Alex Gotfryd, Barbara Rasmussen, and Bill Betts of Doubleday.

Contents

APPENDIX

Maps

THE GAME OF WINE

PLAYING THE GAME OF WINE

In any line of work the mind develops a kind of shorthand. In searching for the reason why you have a pain in your belly, a doctor, while he pokes and thumps, is riffling consciously or semiconsciously through the categories of possibility. By the second thump he has eliminated whole vast areas of indisposition, including beriberi, hydrophobia, and the jungle rot. Two pokes and a temperature reading later he has narrowed it down to perhaps three general alternatives. After one or two moderately embarrassing questions and a reflective, impressively professional-looking glance at a tree outside the window, he has settled on one, not with dogmatic certainty but with the educated tentativeness of a civilized man.

A woodsman on strange terrain follows a similar procedure. The pitch of the sun, the run of the rivers, the moss on the trees, may not tell him where he *is,* but they give him useful indications of where he is *not.* The lay of a ridge line, the pattern of vegetation, the "logic" of a pass will narrow the uncertainty a trifle more. Other clues and indicators contribute gradually to a sort of subliminal calculus which in the normal course brings him out of the woods in fairly good time and in fairly good shape.

The game of wine, in all its many aspects, employs the same kind of shorthand.

Is there leg of lamb on the menu tonight? Then obviously we must enjoy its classic accompaniment, red Bordeaux. But look at the wine list. The vineyards are not first-rate and the bottles appear overpriced. Then what else looks good? *Filet de sole Véronique.* Haut-Brion Blanc is perfect with that, of course. But it is not on this list (and if it were they would charge too much for it). What about Montrachet? They have one, but it is suspiciously hyphenated and of uncertain sponsorship. The Chablis? Too light for that sauce, and in any case, Chablis would also be risky in a place like this. Well, then, what wine? Pouilly-Fumé. Pouilly-Fumé from de Ladoucette. You can count on de Ladoucette.

Would *sole Véronique* go with the Fumé? It could, but it is not an inspired solution. Then how about crab meat, sautéed in butter? Perfection. A simple wine of medium body, a simple dish that is medium-full.

Some decisions about wine are more complicated than that. Most are less so. But the story shows the method. The business of deciding on the "right" wine to go with your dinner and then of appraising it after you have bought it is a process of diagnosis very similar to the one a doctor uses. The procedure for actually buying a bottle of the chosen beverage or a satisfactory equivalent among the trackless intricacies and nameless perils of the wine trade bears a close parallel to the means by which a woodsman finds his way. When the two processes intertwine, as they so often do, that in very essence is the game of wine.

To the novice either of these procedures seems infinitely mysterious and complex—and in their application they can be. Perhaps one reason the subject of wine holds such fascination to skilled professionals in any field is that its strategies and complexities give leisure-time employment to highly developed faculties. But in broad outline they are very simple, as good military or business strategy in its essentials is nearly always simple.

However, in wine more than most fields the broad outlines of practice are clouded and cluttered with a profusion of specifics: villages, vineyards, vintages; growers, shippers, and merchants; etiquette, protocol, and nonsense, most of it in a foreign language. The root of the difficulty lies in the fact that wine is an infinitely variable product. It can vary not only from year to year but from hour to hour, depending on when the grapes were picked and whether or not it rained at harvest time. It varies not only from region to region or vineyard to vineyard but from acre to acre, from barrel to barrel, from vine to vine, almost from grape to grape in some areas, depending on slight nuances of location and exposure. And a tiny difference in time or place can make an enormous difference in quality and therefore in price. This means that dishonesty—the changing of a label or dilution of a batch—can be highly profitable. So the profusion of detail which would be confusing and deceptive in any case is made immensely more so by dishonest wine practices, and by the legal measures—and their evasions—brought about by these dishonest practices.

The result of all this is that a great deal of the literature in the field of wine has to do primarily with the sort of detail that would be useful to a merchant or collector, along with supporting detail relating to its history and folklore. This is of little enough use to the average man attempting to purchase an ordinary bottle in a typical situation. It is of no use at all in helping him to figure out the kind of wine he wants to drink in the first place, and then to handle it properly.

In the face of this bewildering profusion of specifics there has grown up a formidable subliterature of wine, the simplistic "Now-dearie-just-don't-you-bother-your-little-head" approach. The argument here is that the subject of wine isn't complicated at all. It is just those grubby Europeans who want it to seem that way, and if you will ignore all those silly details, you will get along fine.

To the extent that this approach helps people to enjoy the game of wine who would otherwise not do it, it is certainly not all bad. But the fact is that wine, at the level of day-to-day purchase, is indeed very complicated, and all those details are not merely important, they are useful, interesting, and fun, *provided* you learn how to handle them.

It is the purpose of this book to help you do precisely that: to lay out and explain as clearly as possible the broad, general principles that underlie not merely the great mass of detail that relates to buying wine, but also the necessary, challenging, and too often neglected art of deciding what wine you want to drink in the first place, and then of handling it with assurance after it is in your hands. (This is thus not a competitor to the more detailed books on wine, but rather a companion and guide, making their contributions more understandable and useful—and fun.)

It is worth pointing out that the famous Harvard Business School "decision-making process" is really no more than an effort to reduce to super-organized form this very same business of making up one's mind, while the art and science of computers merely goes the Harvard Business School one step further, attempting to counterfeit the process in electronic circuitry and a mathematical "language." Thus, in its effort to organize and systematize a body of fact and a method of working with it, this could be called "a Harvard Business School approach to wine"—as long as it is understood that it is done for fun and not for money. It is also very much the sort of careful organization of material a systems analyst might do in attempting to write a computer program by means of which an IBM Systems/360 computer could in three fifths of a second select the correct wine for a party of six eating tournedos Rossini on the expense account at Twenty-one—although no one would *dream* of suggesting that a machine could ever fully supplant the workings of human imagination and taste.

The elements of a sound approach to wine, as to most other areas of human life and commerce, are three: Know what you want, know how to get it, know what to do with it after you have it.

To know what you want you must first "program" into your thinking the options, the alternatives, of what you can get.

How many wines are available to the man who wants a bottle to go with his dinner? It can be said that there are three: red, white, and pink.

Or it can be said that there are, as a conservative estimate, twenty thousand, counting different vintages, different vineyards, different areas within the same vineyard, different growers within the same area, different shippers dealing with the same grower, different importers dealing with the same shipper.

But neither list is useful. Three categories is too crude. Twenty thousand is not a manageable list. For purposes of the mental shorthand necessary to do a job of choosing wine it is necessary to remember five categories: light and delicate white wine, fuller-bodied white, rosé, light red, and fuller-bodied red. This range of options, which is fundamental to any use of wine, we shall call the Spectrum of Possibility.

Our Spectrum does not include Champagne, which is primarily useful as an appetizer wine or party drink. It does not include the other appetizer wines such as dry Sherry or Vermouth, nor the sweet dessert wines—Sauternes and the sweet wines of the Rhine Basin, along with Madeira, Marsala, Malaga, sweet Sherry, and Port—whose function is so narrow it is obvious. Thus we are considering only *still* (nonsparkling) *table wines.*

The table wines on our list are dry or moderately dry, since that is what people are drinking nowadays. But for someone who likes them, sweet or moderately sweet wines can be substituted in each category. Anyone who prefers sweet Concord Grape wine, however, had better read some other book. This one is not for him. However, it is worth noting that even the Concord Grape people are now producing drier wines in response to current trends of taste.

To lump all still, dry table wines into five categories is obviously a thundering oversimplification. Any connoisseur worthy of the name would immediately point to exceptions and refinements—for that is the name of the game of wine. But the same connoisseur, when choosing a wine to go with a meal, will unconsciously work with a list that is very similar.

However, to classify all wine by physical characteristics is not enough. Little if any wine is sold as "light and delicate white," "fuller-bodied red," and so on. In general, wine is named for real estate, since, as we have pointed out, the location and exposure of a vineyard are prime determinants, along with the weather, of the quality and character of the wine it grows. As Frank Schoonmaker notes in his *Encyclopedia of Wine,* the smaller the piece of real estate noted on the label, the better the wine is likely to be, for if they were not proud of it they would not mention it.

For purposes of the American buyer the five general categories of wine in the Spectrum of Possibility come from seven geographic areas: from Bordeaux, Burgundy, and the valleys of the Loire and Rhône in France; from the Rhine Basin in Germany; from Italy; and from California. This generalization would also naturally start an argument, with devotees of wines from other parts of France, from Switzerland, Spain, Portugal, Greece, Sicily, Yugoslavia, South Africa, Chile, and Australia. But most of the drinkable wine in most of the wine shops and restaurants in America come from the seven areas noted. Furthermore, while each of the wines of the other countries has its own distinctive character, it can generally be described by comparison with the wines of the major European areas (as can the wines of California*).

It would be nice for purposes of simplicity if each of the seven areas mentioned above produced only one of the five basic categories of wine listed. This, of course, is not true. For purposes of the American buyer, and again to oversimplify, one of the areas, Burgundy, produces wines in four of the five categories; three others, Bordeaux, northern Italy, and the Loire, produce three; the Rhône and the Rhine produce two each; and the Golden State of California, needless to say, produces all of them.

Moreover, in each area the wine in each category is produced under more than one name. In Burgundy, for example, both Chablis and Pouilly-Fuissé are reasonably delicate white wines, while Meursault and Montrachet fall into the category of fuller-bodied white.

Thus at a minimum—and it is a difficult minimum to maintain—the mind has to retain the names of about thirty wines, broken into five categories, before the mental shorthand required for selection can begin. The best of the California wines, fortunately or unfortunately, require another parallel list of names. In an effort to declare their independence of the names of European pieces of real estate, the California winegrowers have named their better wines not for the points of origin of their European grape varieties, but for the grape varieties themselves. For example, the California wines made from the great grape of Bordeaux are called Cabernet Sauvignon after that variety, and those that are made from the grape that produces such famous white Burgundies as Chablis and Montrachet are called Pinot Chardonnay for that species.

It is the function of the first five chapters of this book to develop in a systematic way this basic list of wines, and to show in broad outline the business institutions, reflected in labeling practices, that have grown up around them. Chapter I, "A General Theory of Wines," explains how physical factors—location, topography, composition of the soil—largely determine the quality and other characteristics of the wine a given plot of land will produce. It also explores both the temptation and the opportu-

---

* Limiting the American wines discussed to the California ones will cause anguish to the growers and drinkers of the wines of New York State, which have a substantial and loyal following in this country. But the fact is that the curious fruity (called foxy) taste of American wines grown east of the Rockies is not pleasant to a palate tuned to European wines. Only on the Pacific Coast have weather conditions permitted wine to be grown in volume from European grape varieties. However, as in the case of the sweet wines, the five categories of the Spectrum can also be used to classify the wines of New York State, along with those of Ohio, South Carolina, Maryland, Arkansas, Virginia, Michigan, and a surprising number of other states. All that is necessary is to learn some odd grape names like Catawba, Niagara, and scuppernong.

nity for human tampering the same factors create. Chapter II applies these principles to Bordeaux and its environs, the greatest winegrowing area in the world, to show why it is what it is, and what are the chief entries on the Spectrum that result.

Chapter III applies the same principles to Burgundy, where the wines are less plentiful and over-all less reliable, but no less famous. Chapter IV, "The Other Wines of Europe," surveys the remaining districts of major importance to the Spectrum on that side of the Atlantic. Chapter V reviews the interesting and promising if somewhat perplexing wines of California.

Anyone who wants to gain a working mastery of wines should memorize the Spectrum of Possibility, or at least become very familiar with it, and try to understand the various commercial institutions as they are reflected in labeling practices. If he will do this, it can safely be said that he will know everything he needs to know to begin acquiring a mastery of the art of using wines, and will *understand* more than most people who know —or pretend to know—much more than he does. He will also achieve a general grasp of a very substantial proportion of the merchandise actually worth buying on any wine card or in any wine shop in Europe or North America.

But even when you have mastered the Spectrum of Possibility, you are not ready to announce with assurance what wine you want for dinner. Except on the rarest occasions, wine is obviously not drunk in isolation, at least table wine is not. It is consumed with food, ordinarily in the company of people. A great part of the pleasure of wine is not simply gulping it, but "arranging" it, orchestrating it into the culinary and human elements of a meal.

The variables that govern the selection of wines to go with food occur in three overlapping and interdependent stages. First are the natural affinities between the broad classes of wine and comparable categories of food. These affinities are the source of the old rule of "red wine with red meat, white wine with white meat"—although that is oversimplified and not very helpful. Essentially, they are products not of etiquette or snobbery or superstition or tradition, but of the physiology of human taste, and are explained in Chapter VI, "The Categories of Affinity."

Once a person understands these general relationships he is prepared to do a rudimentary, garden-variety job of picking wine for any occasion. He can stay out of trouble and it will taste good. But he will still miss a lot.

The next set of issues, the next level up, is the "human level." Influencing your choice will be the obvious but often overlooked questions: the age, sex, sophistication, interests, and background of your guests, along with the occasion and your motives for entertaining them, how well you like them, how much you want to spend, and not least important, what you yourself like to drink. This all is explored in Chapter VII, "The Human Variable."

At this point the selection process becomes less a science or a discipline than a sport or an art. We have escaped the certitudes of geology, meteorology, and physiology and entered into the subtleties of strategy, diplomacy, chicanery, and romance.

Interacting in turn with the human variable, but still rooted in the physiology of taste, is the third and culminating set of elements, the most subtle and complex of all. This is the influence on the selection process of sauces and seasonings.

There are probably not as many different dishes in existence in the world as there are wines, but gaining a working knowledge of them is in some respects more difficult than gaining a comparable knowledge of the wines. As we have noted, the *general* characteristics of the wine produced on a given piece of land are constant, despite year-to-year variations in quality and price. And while the name of a particular vineyard may reflect nothing more than its ownership, past or present, or a local landmark or legend or saint, the name of the village, region, or district in which the vineyard is located (usually appearing on the label) gives at least a rough indication of the character and quality of the wine. By contrast, new dishes are developed by the dozen every year, and the name by which a dish is known may or may not give any clue to its ingredients. Let us take as an example the famous dish called lobster thermidor. Thermidor, as some readers of this book may not be aware, was the name given during the French Revolution to the eleventh month of the year in the Republican calendar, which fell during the hottest season, beginning on July 19 or 20 and ending August 18 or 19. The revolution of 9 Thermidor year II (July 27, 1794), which resulted in the fall of Robespierre and the collapse of the Terror, came to be known as the Revolution of Thermidor. In 1894 a play opened in Paris dealing with these events, and it was entitled *Thermidor*. In honor of the opening, the owner of the famous Paris restaurant Chez Maire created a new lobster dish called, naturally, Thermidor.

The play closed after the first night. Chez Maire is long since gone. But lobster thermidor goes on and on. However, there is nothing in all of this to suggest that lobster thermidor is made with white wine, cream, eggs, and cheese, flavored with tarragon, shallots, and mustard, and goes best with a white wine of relatively full body, with perhaps a trace of sweetness.

Happily, it is possible to do with sauces as we did with wines: develop a General Theory, or in this case we might call it a Science of Sauce, to cover the principal contingencies, and to provide clues and indicators to help out with the rest. This we do in Chapter VIII, "Cherchez la Sauce." Understanding the influence of sauces and seasonings on the choice of wine will not only greatly expand your knowledge, understanding, and confidence in the art of matching, but will also take away much of the mystery and terror from the whole subject of elegant cooking and eating.

If knowing the Spectrum of Possibility gives a major advantage in the art of choosing wines, and learning the Categories of Affinity consolidates it, and appreciating the importance of the Human Variable reinforces it, then understanding the Science of Sauce will add the capstone. Few people ever approach this degree of competence. You could easily stop here.

But growing capability in matching *wines with foods* brings the beginning of a curiosity about matching *foods with wines*—the occasion when you acquire a particularly fine bottle and plan a meal to show it off. An appreciation of good wines brings a desire to try the great ones. And once you become skillful at working with one wine it becomes tempting to serve two, three, or even more wines at a single sitting.

However, at this point the problem becomes not simply factual or intellectual but economic. To order a great wine in a fine restaurant, with meal to match, could easily cost three hundred dollars for a party of six. It requires no elaborate mental shorthand to understand that that is a lot of money.

Yet the same wine with a comparable meal could be served at home without great difficulty of preparation from recipes available in any reasonably good cookbook for a cost of ten to fifteen dollars a person—less, if you are careful. Assuming each couple goes Dutch, this is no more than the price of an ordinary evening out. And there is no better means—none —for developing a palate, for increasing your appreciation of foods and wines, for learning the arts of their service and enjoyment, than the preparation and consumption of a "Great Meal." And there are few more charming pastimes.

In Chapters IX and X we explore and explain the process of creating a Great Meal in the classic tradition. In "How to Serve a Masterpiece: The Wines," we return to the wine districts of Burgundy and Bordeaux to choose four representative samples of the world's very greatest wines (with alternate selections for the thrifty). Then in "How to Serve a Masterpiece: Food and Wine," we construct, stage by stage, showing the concepts and principles involved, five Great Meals, each one orchestrated around one of our four great wines.

Here the matching process becomes no longer a calculation but a calculus. Vary the first course and it modifies the second; alter the second and it affects the third. But any tinkering with the succession of foods influences the succession of wines, not only as they relate to the foods but as they relate to each other; then, with the unavailability of a crucial wine (or food) the whole structure collapses, like twin rows of interlocking dominoes, and you start again. But with time and love a meal emerges, a great part of whose fascination has been the process of creating it.

Now we have reached not only the summit of the pleasures of wine but the pinnacle of *la haute cuisine*. All that remains is to draw the cork. But as anyone who has been in a fine restaurant knows, there is great ritual and mystery in the drawing of a cork. Like the other customs and procedures of wine, this rests not on etiquette or snobbery, but on practical considerations. Wine is not simply a variable commodity at its point of origin, it is an uncertain one by the time it reaches you. The bottle you open could, alas, be spoiled, for one of a number of excellent biochemical reasons. Or, as noted, it could be fraudulent, in a fraud that occurred years ago in the wine vat, hours ago at the liquor store, minutes ago in the pantry, or at a number of locations between. Assuming it is honest and sound, it still might be young and harsh or old and past its prime. Even if it is neither of these, it may or may not prove appropriate to the dish in question. It is your job as host to pronounce on all these matters—sometimes under the watchful eyes of your in-laws, your fiancée, your clients, or your boss, and despite the efforts of the wine steward to confuse you because he is arrogant, ignorant, dishonest, lazy, or any combination of these. The purpose of the ritual of uncorking is to enable you to deliver your judgment—or to bluff it successfully.

In Chapter XI, "The Battle of the Tastevin," we offer a moment-by-moment analysis of the rituals, stratagems, and calculations that accompany the drawing of a cork. Then in Chapter XII, "The Language of the Grape," we provide a vocabulary for delivering and discussing your verdict, whatever that might be.

The primary focus of the book to this point is on the skills of choosing your wine before you buy it and of handling it confidently after you own it, because those are the areas where the average reader is most in need of guidance and where the existing literature provides the least help. But it is of little use to know how to choose and handle wine *en principle* if you cannot then go out and lay your hands on a satisfactory bottle of the stuff. Moreover, as we indicated at the outset, it is not possible to separate the problems of matching from the hazards and uncertainties of buying. To one degree or another they occur simultaneously with and interact upon each other. The full pleasure and fascination of the game of wine lies in working gracefully with both elements as parts of a single whole.

In Chapter XIII, "Wines and Wall Street," we review the chief problems of buying that are likely to be encountered by a reader of this book, and outline the strategies required for surmounting them. It turns out, not surprisingly, that the dynamics of the wine market differ in no fundamental way from those of the stock market, and the strategies for dealing with each are about the same. Next, in Chapter XIV, "The Perils at the Point of Sale," we apply these buying strategies to a series of real-life situations: to great, less than great, and eminently ungreat restaurants, and to the same range of alternatives in wine shops and liquor stores. And then, in Chapter XV, "The View from the Cellar," we review the forces of commerce and logic (and love) that in time compel the serious amateur to establish his own personal inventory of wines, and some of the practical requirements of doing so.

Now, finally, the Appendix of the book draws together, in as immediately usable a form as possible, the high points of everything that has gone before. First, a summary listing of "The Spectrum of Possibility," for the wine world as a whole, then for individual districts, with page references to the descriptions of each wine. Then "A Guide to Matching" recapitulates the food-wine affinities, beginning at the simplest level, then making allowance for the influence of sauces and seasonings.

Next, "An Album of Labels" provides, in effect, a short course in label reading, giving examples and explanations of the varying business institutions of each of the major districts. Then an essay on "How to Choose a Wine Merchant" offers practical advice on locating a source of good wine in your own community. "The Wine Catalogue of John Walker & Co.," reprinted in full, then furnishes a real-life example of the treasures to be found in the catalogue of an outstanding merchant. And last, in "Craig Claiborne's Wine Cellar" and "The Wine Cellar of Paul and Julia Child" are given two distinguished case studies of the way the game is played.

The sponsor of this book and its prime source of expertise on the higher uses of food and wine is Forrest Wallace, a management consultant who discovered and explored the world of elegant eating and drinking during a career that has called for frequent travel and entertainment in the United States and abroad. A founding member of the Wine and Food Society of Hollywood and of the Chicago chapter of the Chevaliers du Tastevin—he is currently a *commandeur* in both the Chicago and the Los Angeles chapters—Wallace is one of the few Americans ever named to the Confrérie au Guillon, the wine society of Switzerland. Over the years he has shared in the planning and preparation of countless elegant meals, accompanied by superb wines, in famous restaurants and in his own kitchen, and has more than once eaten his way across Europe, following the stars of the *Guide Michelin*. As president of the Mid-America Club of Chicago during the early 1960s, he supervised the development of one of the finest kitchens and one of the most distinguished wine cellars on the North American continent.

The chief architect and principal draftsman of the work, and its "chief theoretician," is Gilbert Cross, a journalist and publicist who has been an associate editor of *Fortune,* a speech writer for the Secretary of State and for the White House, and a contributor on varied subjects to *Look, Holiday, Esquire,* and the *Reader's Digest*. A relative novice in wines when the work began, Cross brought to the collaboration not only the skills of a trained reporter (and a set of interests ranging from the cooking practices of the Late Stone Age to the marketing techniques of Ernest and Julio Gallo), but the point of view, the questions and concerns, of the average buyer of wines. The result has been a treatment which, the authors hope, will prove uniquely fresh and useful to anyone—novice or connoisseur—who enjoys the game of wine.

I

A GENERAL THEORY OF WINES

❧

The quality and characteristics of a given bottle of wine are determined by three interacting variables: the physical location of the vineyard in which the grapes were grown, the grape variety or varieties used, and the influence of the hand, brain, and too often the avarice of man. The governing variable is location. You cannot grow grapes at the North Pole, no matter what you do, nor can you produce a light and delicate Chablis in a place more suited to luscious, sweet Sauternes.

The vine considered merely as a berry-bearing shrub will grow almost anywhere. The vine as a source of drinkable wine is more limited. North of roughly 50° latitude (about seventy-five miles north of Paris) the grapes are so sour a bird would hesitate to eat them and the wine they yield would at best be drunk reluctantly. In fact in Germany, where this is just what happens in a bad year, such a wine is called "a three-man wine." It takes two men to force a third to drink it. It is not surprising that in the northerly latitudes beer made from barley, whiskey made from corn or rye, and vodka made from potatoes are more reliable and more commonly drunk.

South of perhaps 30° latitude (about the location of Rabat, Morocco, or Cairo, Egypt) the grape will grow and in fact does grow in the fertile, steaming valleys and parched, dusty hillsides. But the wine it makes is harsh and rough—the *vin ordinaire* that pours down the throats of thirsty Frenchmen by the millions of gallons every year. Thus in really hot places rum made from molasses, gin made from sugar cane, tequila made from cactus juice, and toddy made from coconut milk are the brew of choice.

So the practical upper and lower limits of the Wine Zone are latitudes

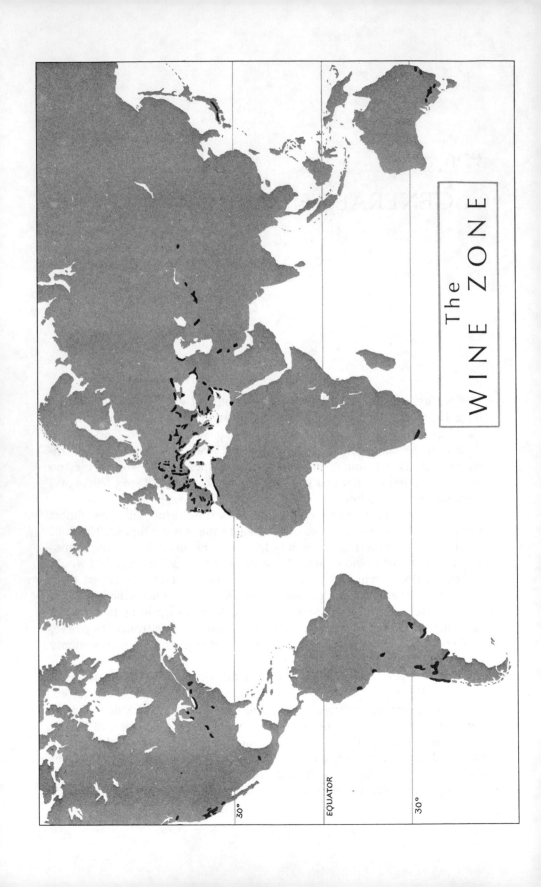

The
WINE ZONE

EQUATOR

30°

30°

50° and 30°. But to generalizations about wines there are always exceptions, and this case is no exception. The shore of the English Channel,
with its cold and fog, is not hospitable to the grape, so ordinarily no wine
occurs along the coast of France until you reach the estuary of the Loire
River, roughly 47° latitude. Moreover, as the map shows, there is a handful of vineyard regions in Central and South America which are located
closer to the equator than the normal latitudes 30° north and 30° south.
The vine was brought to Spanish America in the sixteenth century by the
missionaries who followed the Conquistadors, and descendants of some of
these early plantations linger on in the highlands of Mexico, Colombia,
Bolivia, and Peru, where the coolness of high altitude compensates for the
heat of the equatorial sun.

Most people think of the Wine Zone as primarily consisting of France,
with outriders in Italy, Germany, Spain, Portugal, California, and the
Finger Lakes district of New York. Yet the fact is that wine can be grown
and in most cases either is grown or has been grown almost anywhere in
the world between latitudes 50° and 30°. (The same is true between latitudes 30° and 40° in the Southern Hemisphere, but not to the same extent.
The grape, being indigenous to the north, has only been transplanted south
in recent centuries.) Algeria, Morocco, and Tunisia produce large amounts
of wine. There is good wine grown in Yugoslavia; an almost legendary
sweet wine, the Tokay, is grown in Hungary; the Russians are proud of the
Champagne of the Caucasus; wine has been grown for several millennia at
the central Asian oasis of Samarkand; and was grown in ancient times in
India, China, Egypt, and Mesopotamia.

There are notable wine districts in South Africa and Australia; the
wines of Chile are the best of South America, the vineyards of Argentina
the most productive. And, as noted in the Introduction, in North America
wine is grown not only in New York and California, but in Ohio, Maryland, Illinois, Washington, the Carolinas, the Ozarks, and Canada, to
name just a few places.

Within the extremes of the growing range of the grape, conditions are
by no means uniform, and as conditions vary the character of the wine
varies, too. The major variations in growing condition, and the general
differences in wines that result, provide the most important single device
for understanding and remembering the basic categories of the Spectrum
of Possibility. The upper third of the Wine Zone—in Europe, the Loire
River of France, Chablis in northern Burgundy, Champagne near Paris,
the Rhine Basin, and Switzerland—is white wine country. (In terms of latitude Switzerland is actually in the middle third of the Wine Zone. But
here again, altitude overrules latitude. The alpine situation of the Swiss
vineyards results in growing conditions more similar to those of vineyards
farther north than to those of the vineyards of the mid-zone.) White wine
(actually it is yellow or gold or pale green) is often made from "black"

grapes (actually they are purple), the same ones used to make red wine. The difference is that the skins are taken out as soon as the grapes are crushed. It is the skins of the grapes which carry the pigment that gives red wines their color. But in the cool northern areas the flavor in the skins does not usually mature well; it is too harsh and acid. So the purple skins are removed, and the wine is made from the yellow pulps alone, left naked in the vat.

In the Northern Hemisphere the sun rides in the southern portion of the sky; the farther north you go, the more southerly it slants and the more of its heat it loses in the atmosphere. Thus in these northern areas in a good year the summer days are warm but not too hot; the nights cool but not too cold.

The grape pulps and resulting wines thus develop great delicacy of flavor. Not surprisingly, they also tend to be a bit low in sugar, so the wine is "light" in alcohol. (That is why these wines are considered good lunch wines. Your head will not be as fuzzy when you get back to the office.) In a poor year, as we have noted, with too little sun, or rain at the wrong moment, the resulting wines will be hard and acid, or watery and thin. A few hours of rain during harvest time will swell the grapes with water, diluting their sugar and flavor, converting a potentially great vintage into a crop hardly worth harvesting. If there is hail or an untimely freeze, there may be no harvest at all. So vintage years are terribly important in the northern vineyards,* and winegrowing is a risky business.

In the central portion of the Wine Zone, primarily central and southwest France, the valley of the Rhône, and northern Spain and Italy, there are longer days, clearer skies, warmer nights, more direct sunshine. The skins of the grapes will thus ripen more fully, the pulps will develop a bit more sugar, a fuller, rounder flavor. This is the country of great and good reds and fuller-bodied whites. There are fewer disastrous years than in the north, but there is still a major difference between a year that is merely good and one that is great.

The southern third of the Wine Zone includes Provence in southern France, southern Spain, Portugal, southern Italy, Sicily, Sardinia, Corsica, and Algeria. (Provence is at the same latitude as northern Italy and Spain, which we have counted in the mid-zone. But as in the case of Switzerland, altitude overrules latitude. The vineyards of northern Spain are in the foot-hills of the Pyrenees, the best ones of northern Italy in the foothills of the Alps or other hilly sections, while those in Provence are on the broad plain along the Mediterranean shore.) The southern part of the Wine Zone with its warm nights and baking sun produces not only the coarse *ordinaires* of Provence and Algeria but the appetizer and dessert wines, full and rich in flavor, high in alcohol—Sherry from Spain, Port from Portugal,

---

* Unless, as in the case of Switzerland, the wine is extensively blended and treated.

and the three M's, Madeira, Marsala, and Malaga. In these areas, where the weather is usually fair, vintage years are not as a rule important, except in a reverse sort of way. In 1959, for example, when a warm, sunny autumn produced superlative wine in the middle and northern sections of the Wine Zone, there was too much sun in the south and the wine tended to burn. Even so, a bottle of southern wine with "1959" on it sold very well, because the public was uncritically aware that 1959 was a "great year." (California wines with "1959" on the label sold equally well, although weather conditions in California the summer of 1959 had no connection with those of Europe that year.)

Within these three major areas are endless minor variations in condition, and these minor variations make major differences, astonishing and crucial differences in the quality and price of a wine. At the same time it is important to note that while a slight change in soil or exposure might double or triple the price and make an indeterminable difference in your pleasure of drinking it, it will not ordinarily change its position on our Spectrum of Possibility. A light wine remains a light wine, a full wine a reasonably full one, whether the quality is superlative or horrible.

Wine that comes from sloping ground is nearly always somewhat fuller-bodied, and at the same time finer, more interesting, than that which comes from the flat; the tilt of the land allows excess water to drain away, preventing it from making the bunches too juicy and fat; the breezes on the slopes also ventilate the maturing grapes, taking away the heat of the day or killing frost at night. By the same token wine grapes usually grow best near a body of water, which functions as a sort of additional thermostat, keeping the temperature from getting too high in hot weather, too low in cold. Most if not all the great and good vineyards are found on sloping land near a river or a lake.

Direction of exposure counts. In the northern third of the Wine Zone the best vineyards are usually found on slopes that face due south, catching every precious ray of a southward-riding sun, and in some cases also collecting those reflected off the surface of a body of water. Nature likes the best of both worlds: the delicacy of flavor made possible by cool nights and mornings, the fuller maturity and higher sugar content provided by a southern exposure.

In the central section of the Wine Zone the very best wines are very often found on eastward-facing slopes. This is true from California to the Rhône. In this way the very first rays of the early sun are able to strike the vines, burning away the morning mist and providing the earliest possible start to the growing day. By afternoon, when the rays might be too hot, the sun has passed beyond the ridge crest, leaving the grapes in gentle shade to digest the warmth of the morning.

And, needless to say, in the extreme southern third of the Wine Zone —Algeria, for example—the better wine often comes from northerly-facing slopes, sheltered by the crest of the hill from the most direct rays of the southward-riding sun. However, in the south exposure is in general less important because the wine in any case is not going to be very delicate and fine.

In addition to the angle of exposure there is the soil of the vineyard itself. The exact reason why a given grape in a given spot yields the wine it does is so immemorially mysterious that great superstition has grown up about it. In almost every region of the wine country there is a tradition that the wine is fiery, let us say, because of volcanic soil, harsh because of phosphorus, and so on. In Burgundy, where one vineyard in one place will give immortal wine and another twenty feet away will give decidedly secondary stuff, the soil is considered so precious that the peasants will carefully scrape it off their shoes when they finish work for the day.

Opinions differ as to the extent of influence on the wine of the chemicals in the soil. What seems to count primarily, however, is physical properties which—like location and exposure—affect the retention of heat and water. One thing is sure. Rich soil is out of the question. It retains too much water, provides too many nutrients, makes the grape too fat and juicy and bland. The best soil for winegrowing is usually pebbly or rocky. In rain the pebbles allow the water to drain away quickly. In sun they reflect away the worst of the heat, absorbing some of the rest, to release it during the evening to warm the soft underbelly of the grape. Even the color of the pebbles counts. Light-colored ones reflect away more sunshine than darker-colored ones, and appear to produce a lighter, more delicate wine. The shape of the stones can also be important. Smooth, round pebbles appear to be more efficient for both reflection and drainage than broken bits of rock; thus, soil made up of decomposed limestone tends to produce a fuller-bodied wine, other things being equal, than river-polished gravel. A soil with more sand among the pebbles—retaining more water—produces a fuller wine than one with less.

The origin of the stones also appears to make a difference. Rock of organic origin, such as limestone, created by the deposit of millions of little dead organisms at the bottom of a prehistoric sea, appears to retain water better than that of igneous origin, such as granite, created by fire when the world was young. Thus, wine grown on granitic soil tends to be very much lighter and fresher than that grown on limestone.

Excellent wine is sometimes grown on soil that is chalky. Chalk appears to have even better qualities of drainage and heat reflection than pebbles, and the wine it yields can be exceptionally "flinty" and clean.

None of these conditions occurs pure, of course. The soil of a vineyard may be limestone mixed with chalk, or pebbles mixed with sand. And sometimes a hidden spring or a bank of cold clay under the topsoil will throw off the whole calculus and give the natives renewed basis for their superstition.

So, latitude (corrected for altitude), slope, nearness to water, direction of exposure, and the composition of the soil, these five will largely determine what if any sort of wine can be grown on a given piece of ground. It is not possible for a layman to predict in advance what kind of wine a certain plot will produce. But it is surprisingly easy to explain after the fact, or at least to speculate, why a given piece of land produced the wine it did.

The soil in which grapes will grow interacts in turn with the kind of grapes best suited to grow there, the second of our three major variables. For purposes of understanding and enjoying wine there is much less to be said about individual grape varieties than there is about location. A thousand or two years of experience have shown pragmatically that one grape produces the best wine on the soils of Burgundy, another makes the best in Bordeaux. Another is responsible for the distinctive characteristics of the finest wines of the Rhine Basin, and other wines are "made up" from as many as fifteen grape varieties blended carefully together.

The precise scientific reasons why these grapes contribute as they do is the province of agronomists and biochemists. There is little reason for a lover of wines to go into it. However, as we noted in the Introduction, in certain areas—notably California and Alsace on the Rhine—the best wines are named for the grape from which they are made. So unless you know the names and general characteristics of certain grape varieties, you will not be able to order what you want among those wines. Furthermore, at the higher levels of drinking if you hope to gain any real understanding of the subtler distinctions, you must understand the contribution certain "noble" varieties make, and a rudimentary something about the chemical reasons why.

Of course, the fact that one grape is grown on one patch of ground and another on another is no accident. They were planted: by someone. This leads us to our third major variable; the working of the hand and brain of men.

In the matter of this human variable in the growing of wines a basic distinction must be made. So long as the interests of the producers and handlers of a wine are parallel to those of the ultimate consumer—as long, that is, as it best serves the purposes of both parties for the wine to be as good as possible—the various practices are merely earthy and quaint: how the vine is trained and pruned, whether or not pregnant women are allowed to gather the grapes (in the old days they were not), whether or not men go into the vat naked to break up the crust that forms on the top of the fermenting mass (in some areas they still do), the fact that the wine bottles of Franconia are shaped like and named for the scrotum of a billy goat. Other practices are revealing of the characteristics of the end product, and provide interesting insight into the history and economics of the wine trade: how Champagne gets its bubbles, the blending of Sherry, the frank adulteration of Port.

It is when the interests of the growers and handlers of wine diverge from those of the drinker of it—when it is more profitable for the wine trade to sell you bad wine and call it good than to sell you good wine— that it is vital for the buyer to know what has been going on, and correspondingly difficult to find out.

The "noble" varieties of grape—the ones that give the best wines— are typically "shy bearers" capable of giving only a few barrels per acre, but compensating with a very high price for each bottle in a good year. Nearby is land not capable of producing really fine wine which will be planted to lesser but far more productive grapes. But who is to say the peasant grower, a thrifty crafty man, will not in the privacy of his own cellar "stretch" his few barrels of great wine by mixing them with several barrels of the lesser one, and then sell the whole batch very profitably under the better label? And if the grower does not, the shipper may, and if the shipper does not, the merchant might.

Moreover, if the name of one tiny vineyard is so famous that wine lovers everywhere will almost literally genuflect upon hearing it, and the general public will buy blindly when they merely hear that name, it is very tempting for nearby vineyards or whole areas to change their names to one very similar to the great one, and thereby enhance the marketability of all their wine.

What man's hands can do, of course, man's laws can undo, or they can try. Every major wine country in the world has laws, remarkably detailed laws, governing what grapes may be grown on a given piece of ground, how they are to be cultivated, fermented, and so on, and specifying certain geographic and other information that must appear on the label. But if this is helpful in one way, it is immensely confusing in another. In France alone there are more than two hundred *appellations contrôlées* (registered place names) for wine, and this does not count the thousands of individual vineyards. No one but an expert could remember them all, and even if he could, their usefulness has limits, for what law can do politics can undo, at least partially, and forgery and fraud can take care of the rest. The appellations contrôlées of France, as originally proposed by the experts, were quite precise in limiting a certain "superior" appellation to land which historically had been shown capable of producing a superior wine. But then the local logrolling and compromise began, and precise delimitations began to blur. Land of secondary quality was blanketed in under the superior appellations, and gained the legal right to carry the superior appellations on its labels.

But for many shippers of wine the political route has historically been too slow. There is a saying that the chief product of Beaune, the wine capital of Burgundy, is not wine but labels. As the wine pours into the bottles, fraudulent labels roll off the press. Government inspectors regularly catch the offenders, a fine is levied and cheerfully paid, like a football team accepting an off-side penalty, and the cheating goes on.

As complex as it is, furthermore, the French system of place names applies only to France. In Germany there is another system, as Germanic in its pedantic meticulousness as the French one is Gallic in its precision and evasion. And the labels are in German. In California there is another system, and in Italy until fairly recently there was hardly any system at all. Moreover, even within France, the heartland of wine, the commercial practices and institutions of Burgundy, for example, are quite different from those of Bordeaux, raising additional problems for the buyer.

In terms of our basic Shorthand of the Mind it is not necessary to remember any of this. In fact, the rank beginner is better off to forget it. Fraud, however outrageous, does not usually change the fundamental category of the wine that comes from a given region (any more than minor variations in condition will). And even if it is mislabeled, a wine at a decent price is usually drinkable. But as soon as you begin to move up the scale even slightly, attempting to order wines by names and reputation, and to match them off against the finer foods, you have to remember that there are forces in the wine trade that want you to buy a lesser wine than you had in mind for a higher price than it is worth. So a skill in the culinary uses of wine cannot rise beyond the most elementary levels without a corresponding knowledge of the commercial abuses of wine, and a degree of competence in dealing with them.

In the chapters that follow we shall examine the hills and river shores of the major districts of the Wine Zone and construct our Spectrum of the basic choices, and at the same time try to get a general sort of notion of the principal commercial institutions that have evolved in each area, and their implications to the buyer of wines.

The Wines

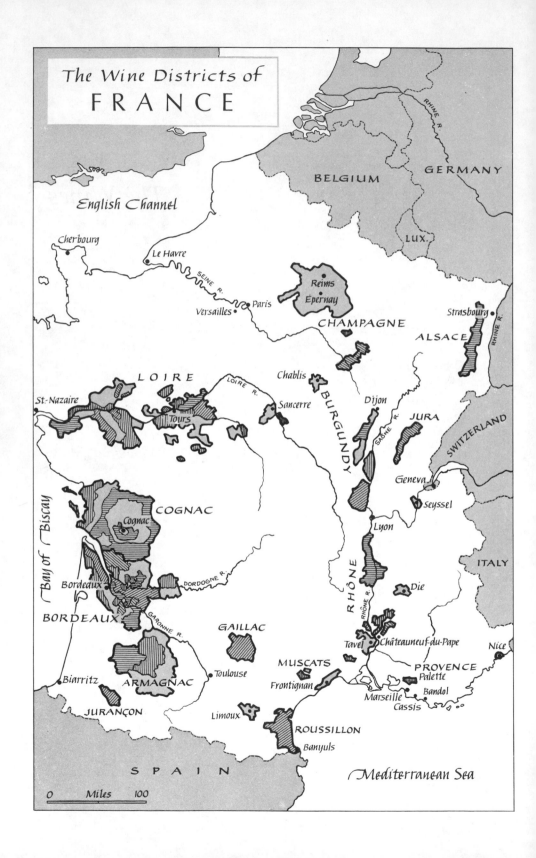

The Wine Districts of
FRANCE

English Channel

Cherbourg

Le Havre

SEINE R.

Versailles • Paris

BELGIUM

GERMANY

RHINE R.

LUX.

Reims
Épernay

CHAMPAGNE

Strasbourg •

ALSACE

RHINE R.

LOIRE

Chablis

LOIRE R.

Sancerre

Dijon

BURGUNDY

SAÔNE R.

JURA

SWITZERLAND

St.-Nazaire

Tours

Geneva •

Seyssel

Lyon

Bay of Biscay

COGNAC

Cognac

DORDOGNE R.

Bordeaux

RHÔNE

Die

RHÔNE R.

ITALY

BORDEAUX

GARONNE R.

GAILLAC

Châteauneuf-du-Pape

Tavel •

Nice

ARMAGNAC

Biarritz

Toulouse •

MUSCATS

Frontignan

Marseille

Palette

Bandol

Cassis

PROVENCE

JURANÇON

Limoux

ROUSSILLON

Banyuls

SPAIN

Mediterranean Sea

0   Miles   100

II

BORDEAUX, UNDISPUTED QUEEN

🌿

A glance at the map shows that Bordeaux is located not simply in the mid-zone of the world of wine, but in the middle of the mid-zone. It is situated not merely on the shores of two rivers, the Garonne and the Dordogne, where they meet to form a broad, tidal estuary called the Gironde: its best vineyards are located on a strip of land that lies between the rivers and the sea. With its favorable latitude and its relationship to water it is not surprising that Bordeaux produces not only more great wine but more fine and good wine than any other wine district anywhere. Taken together with the adjacent growing areas of Cognac, Armagnac, Bergerac, Gaillac, and Jurançon, you have here in southwest France the most astonishingly productive vineyard region in the world. (But still it does produce the greatest total gallonage of wine. Provence, with its hot, flat, fertile irrigated vineyards on the shore of the Mediterranean, pours out *ordinaire* by the truck-tank load; Algeria produces even more.)

No one knows just when the supreme winegrowing qualities of the Bordelais were discovered. (Bordelais means simply the region or area of Bordeaux, to distinguish it from Bordeaux city; it can also mean a resident or native of Bordeaux. The Bordelais is also sometimes called the Gironde, after its great tidal estuary.) What *is* known, on the basis of archaeological evidence, is that sometime in the Middle Bronze Age, about 2000 B.C., ships from the eastern Mediterranean were sailing to and from the Scilly Islands off Cornwall in what is now England to get the tin to make the bronze from which the Bronze Age got its name. It is hard to believe that these bold sailors would not have done some exploring along the way, or, like Ulysses, been blown off course in a storm. So at some point a party of Greeks or Phoenicians is likely to have sailed into the estuary that was later named the Gironde and recognized in the poor, scraggly moors and sparse uplands the conditions under which the grape might prosper.

By the time the Romans arrived the area was well established in winegrowing. In the fourth century A.D. the Roman poet Ausonius owned a villa on what is now the Hill of St.-Émilion, reputed to be the location of what is called the Château Ausone today.

The area that was to become the Bordelais was chiefly populated at that time by a tribe of Gauls, called the Bituriges Vivisci. Their chief town was called Burdigala, and the Romans called the whole region Aquitania. Burdigala was later corrupted to Bordeaux; Aquitania became in the Middle Ages Aquitaine and then Guyenne or Guienne. In 1152 Eleanor of Aquitaine married a boy from up north, Henry of Anjou, bringing the lands of Aquitaine with her as dowry. Two years later Henry inherited the throne of England, and Aquitaine/Guienne/Bordeaux—however you want to call it—came under the British crown. As a result the wines of Bordeaux for the next three hundred years enjoyed a great trade advantage in England, and for most of the time since have been a favorite English drink. The Bordeaux wines were then called *clairet*. This literally means "clear," and has the same favorable connotation that "pale" does in English, as in "pale ale." But in time the word came simply to mean light red wine. *Clairet* was anglicized to Claret and that is the English term for red Bordeaux wine to this day.

Within the ancient and bountiful district of Bordeaux there are well over five thousand separately delimited vineyards, distributed among two dozen or so regions, which in turn are subdivided into several score communes (villages), and carefully classified as to quality and price on a variety of lists, official and unofficial. To the novice buyer, this profusion of choice is so overwhelming he might be tempted to look for a wine from some less complicated place. But no matter how they are subdivided and classified, all red Bordeaux (red is what we are primarily talking about here) belong to one great family of wines which are relatively light, delicate, subtle, sometimes called "feminine," "intellectual," or "aristocratic" in their characteristics.

Among these red Bordeaux, moreover, those of real note can be grouped under three principal geographic headings: the Haut-Médoc, Graves, and St.-Émilion. These are the names a beginner need remember, if he remembers that many, and the only ones that appear on our basic Spectrum of Possibility. Among the white wines of Bordeaux, only Sauternes need be remembered, and this is not even a dinner wine, but a sweet white wine, drunk with dessert.

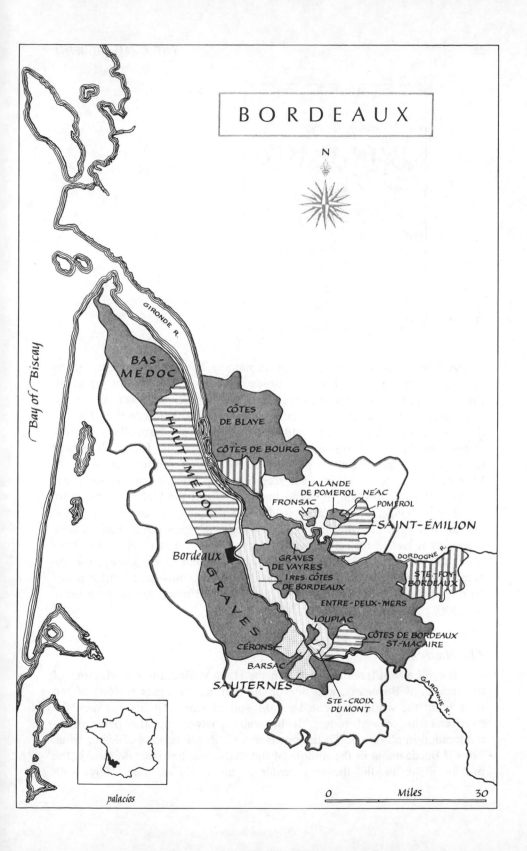

BORDEAUX

N

BAS-
MÉDOC

CÔTES
DE BLAYE

HAUT-MÉDOC

CÔTES DE BOURG

GIRONDE R.

Bay of Biscay

LALANDE
DE POMEROL NÉAC

FRONSAC

POMEROL

SAINT-ÉMILION

Bordeaux

GRAVES
DE VAYRES
Ires. CÔTES
DE BORDEAUX

DORDOGNE R.

STE.-FOY
BORDEAUX

GRAVES

ENTRE-DEUX-MERS

LOUPIAC

CÉRONS

BARSAC

SAUTERNES

CÔTES DE BORDEAUX
ST.-MACAIRE

STE.-CROIX
DU MONT

GARONNE R.

palacios

0   Miles   30

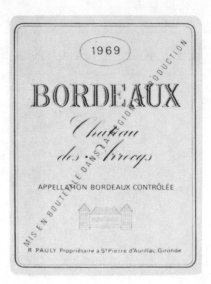

A note is needed here about place names. The four names just given are *regions* within the *district* of Bordeaux. As noted in the Introduction, the rule of geographic designation is this: The smaller the piece of real estate referred to on a label, the better the wine, and therefore the "higher" the appellation. The broadest and therefore the lowest appellation is the *district* appellation: Bordeaux, Burgundy, the Loire, the Rhône. The next higher is the *region* within a district: in the district of Bordeaux—Haut-Médoc, Graves, St.-Émilion, Sauternes. Next up on the scale is the *commune* (village or township) within the region, and the highest designation of all is the *château* (vineyard) itself—the veritable soil upon which the grapes were grown. Additionally, in the case of some large and famous vineyards it has historically become known that a given subsection produces the best wine—for the great Clos de Vougeot of Burgundy, for example, the area between the château and the back wall—and bottles noted on the label as coming from this even smaller and more special area bring an added premium.

The Haut-Médoc

It can be seen from the map that the Haut-Médoc, the most famous of the regions of Bordeaux, and one of the two most famous regions of red wine in all the world, is located on the spit of land that lies between the river and the sea. Moreover, it lies only partway up the peninsula— moderation in all things. To the north and south are regions of lesser wine. Thus if Bordeaux is in the middle of the mid-zone, the Haut-Médoc is the middle of the middle, the very center of the world of wine. Here, with water on both sides and prevailing westerlies out of the Azores blowing over the vineyards, are some of the most temperate and gradual growing conditions anywhere. Even the name of the region—Médoc—reflects its peculiar genius. It is believed to be a corruption of the Latin *in medio aquae,* "between the waters." Since the southern (and better) part of the peninsula lies upstream from the river's mouth, it is called the Haut-Médoc (Upper Médoc). It can be seen from the map that the vineyards of the Haut-Médoc are at once farther from the ocean and closer to the river than the vineyards to the north. Thus ventilation and drainage are better here than farther downstream, and there is less exposure to fog and mist. Once upon a time, the section to the north was called the Bas-Médoc (Lower Médoc), correctly reflecting its downstream situation. But the winegrowers of the Bas-Médoc did not want the customer to think their wine was lower in quality, especially since this was true. So they wrote the Gallic equivalent of their congressman and got the name of the place changed to simply "Médoc."

This necessarily creates confusion. The greatest wines of the whole peninsula are usually referred to in conversation as "Médocs," not "Haut-Médocs." But if you buy on the basis of the appellation "Médoc" on a label, you will not get what you expected. On the other hand, if you were to look for a bottle with the appellation "Haut-Médoc," you could have trouble finding one, and if you did, it might not be very good. The wine of the Haut-Médoc is so good and so sought after that it is usually more profitable for the growers to send it to market under the name of one of its communes or individual châteaux.

For anyone who has not been prepared for it, the look of the incomparable Haut-Médoc is a sharp disappointment. It might best be compared to a gravel pit, which is not surprising, since the poor, pebbly soil was once the bed of an ancient river. And with nature's perversity the terrain is not hilly, despite the fact that, as noted in the preceding chapter, nearly all great wines are grown on slopes. But conditions are somewhat equivalent. The deep, gravelly soil provides incomparable drainage; the breezes from the ocean give superb ventilation. Moreover, it is a tradition that the best wines are grown on the tops of the barely perceptible knolls—giving even better ventilation and drainage. And the very best wines of all are grown only on knoll-tops from which you can see the river, affording that crucial eastern exposure, along with closeness to the tempering influence of water. Thus a wine of the plain enjoys many of the advantages of being on a hill without entirely giving up the characteristics of a wine of the plain—nature getting the best of both worlds again.

The wines of the Haut-Médoc, grown in such delicate, temperate conditions, are, not surprisingly, known as the most delicate and temperate of all the wines of Bordeaux. (This is an overgeneralization, as we shall see a little later, but for present purposes there is no avoiding it.) The wines

from the (Bas-) Médoc to the north are a trifle rougher and coarser—just a
trifle. In an unusual year, however, when conditions in the north approximate those farther south, some of the wines can be equal or nearly so, and
provide good bargains for anyone knowing enough to seek them out. The
Médocs, Haut or Bas, are traditionally considered to taste best when
drunk with the lighter sorts of meats: veal, lamb—especially lamb; there
seems to be a particular affinity between a red Bordeaux and lamb. They
are good also with such relatively light dishes as ham, liver, sweetbreads,
and brains.

It will be seen on the map that lying to the east of the central portion
of the Médoc peninsula, between the vineyards and the sea, is a lake or
lagoon of substantial size. This protected water would obviously be
warmer than the open sea, so the westerlies blowing over it toward the
vineyards might well be more temperate. It is perhaps no coincidence that
just to the east of this lake are four little wine towns where the very best
wines of the Haut-Médoc are grown. These are the communes of Margaux,
St.-Julien, Pauillac, and St.-Estèphe (see detail map, page 42), and these
are the names to look for on a bottle of wine from the Haut-Médoc. They
appear either as the name of a "communal" wine, going to market under
the name of the commune itself, or as the commune of origin (in smaller
print) of the wine from one of the fine châteaux.

(The saints among wine names create a very unsaintly confusion, the
village of St.-Julien, for example, being all too easy to confuse with the
region of St.-Émilion, twenty-five miles to the south and east, and not
always readily distinguishable from the *village* of St.-Estèphe, five miles to
the north. Short of carrying a list around with you, which does not create
the desired impression of *savoir-faire,* there is no workable way out of this
confusion except to become familiar enough with the wines to remember
which is which. However, if you cannot tell one from the other, there is
always this solution: Let your eye travel over to the right-hand column of
the wine list, assume that the more expensive wine will usually be the better one—another unavoidable oversimplification—and then decide what
you can afford, which is what you would have had to do sooner or later in
any case.)

In two of the four principal communes of the Haut-Médoc are located
four vineyards whose names are known the world around as the four
greatest vineyards of the region, and thus four of the very greatest vineyards in the world. These are Château Margaux, in the commune of Margaux, and Châteaux Lafite, Mouton, and Latour, in the commune of
Pauillac.

One reason the prices of these four wines are so high is that their
quality is for all practical purposes guaranteed, and a list with only four
names on it is easy to remember. A man who knows relatively little about
wines can order Lafite or Mouton in the confident knowledge that he is

getting the very best. Nobody can laugh at him—except of course those antisnob snobs who laugh at those who buy on the basis of snob appeal alone.

Besides these four immortals there are several hundred other vineyards in the Haut-Médoc, many of them very fine. It is obviously among these other vineyards where the bargains lie. But it no less obviously takes a great deal more knowledge and experience to order confidently among the other vineyards than simply to bid up the prices of the very best.

We shall have more to say about the other vineyards later. But the above is all the novice really needs to know about the legendary Haut-Médoc.

Graves

Adjoining the Haut-Médoc immediately to the south is the region called Graves, whose name, appropriately enough, means "gravel." The gravel beds here—some as deep as sixty feet—were left behind by the same prehistoric river that created the gentle knolls of the Médoc. A look at the map shows, however, that the vineyards of Graves are in general farther away than those of the Médoc from both the river and the sea; and here the river is relatively narrow compared to the broad tidal flow of the Gironde. Moreover the land is almost dead flat, in contrast to the slight roll of the Médoc to the north.

Not surprisingly, there is a discernible difference in character between the red wines of Graves and those of the Médoc. Red Graves as a rule does not achieve quite the distinction, the elegance, of a fine Médoc. It has been compared to a soft print rather than a glossy one from the same negative. Even so, the greatest vineyard of Graves, the Château Haut-Brion, is considered on a par with the four immortals to the north, showing that even a soft print, under the right circumstances, can be a masterpiece. And there

MIS EN BOUTEILLES AU CHÂTEAU

CHATEAU LAFITE ROTHSCHILD
1959

DÉPOSÉ

APPELLATION PAUILLAC CONTRÔLÉE

are a number of other vineyards in Graves producing excellent red wine. Here are some of them:

Château La Mission-Haut-Brion	Château Malartic-Lagravière
Château Haut-Bailly	Château Latour-Martillac
Domaine de Chevalier	Château Latour-Haut-Brion
Château Carbonnieux	Château Smith-Haut-Lafitte
Château Bouscaut	Château Olivier

The use of the word *haut* (high) in the name of the Haut-Médoc is easy to understand since it is in fact the *upper* Médoc. The use of *haut* in Haut-Brion is harder to understand unless you pronounce it. "Oh Brion" sounds very much like someone with a French accent trying to say O'Brian, and tradition has it that the vineyard was in fact named for an Irishman who was one of its owners during the days when Bordeaux was British. (Perhaps, too, there was emulation, the feeling that the *haut* in Haut-Brion would remind potential buyers of the glories of the Haut-Médoc.)

The distinctions between red Médoc and red Graves are interesting, as all wine distinctions and their reasons are interesting. For learning the finer details of wine and in stocking your cellar you are going to need to take them into account. It can also be great fun at dinner to open a bottle of each and see whether you can spot the differences. But it cannot be stressed too often that for daily drinking, for purposes of our Spectrum of Possibility, we can simply assume that these differences are not there, and that here is another good and usable light red wine, which also goes best with the lighter sorts of meats, especially veal and lamb.

As you move southward (upstream) from the region of Graves, you move farther from the coast and into an area where the river is narrower and shallower, and therefore functions less effectively as a thermostat. Gradually, conditions fade away in which red wine of good or even adequate quality can be produced. At some point in past history an enterprising *vigneron* discovered that by taking the skins out of the just-crushed grapes he could make a white wine with better market potential than the red. Thus was born white Graves. This is a rather full-bodied wine, a bit too full for the modern palate; moreover, it has a bad reputation. For many years a high proportion of the white wine exported under the name of Graves was of only "regional" quality—a notch below a "communal" wine, two notches below a château bottling. And much of it was sloppily produced, only semidry, with too much sulfur added as preservative.

Even so, there are a few fine, interesting white wines produced in Graves, including Haut-Brion Blanc (white), from the same château that produces the great red Haut-Brion. These white Graves go best with a dish like chicken, veal, or fish in a rich, creamy white sauce. (One of the authors of this book, Forrest Wallace, is particularly fond of serving Haut-

Brion Blanc with *filet de sole Véronique*—in a cream sauce with fresh or canned white grapes.)

The white wines of Graves are not important enough to win a place on our basic Spectrum of Possibility, but they are one of the interesting minor options as your skill increases in the game of wine. Here are some of the other good ones:

Château Carbonnieux	Château Olivier
Domaine de Chevalier	Château Laville-Haut-Brion
Château Couhins	Château Bouscaut

Because of the traditional wide availability of white Graves, plus the fact that the reds have always been overshadowed by the more famous Médocs to the north, Graves has been known in the past more for white wines than for red, even though its red wines consistently sell for higher prices than the whites. But this confusion can work to the advantage of the careful buyer, since the reds of Graves tend not to be quite as sought after and expensive as those of the Haut-Médoc.

To the west and south of the vineyards of Graves the gravel bank runs out and conditions of exposure decline to the point where even an indifferent white cannot be produced. The wines from these fringe areas are entitled to only the lowest appellation, the "district" appellation: Bordeaux. (The only lower title is the generic name *vin rouge* or *vin blanc,* which is applied to *ordinaires* and means simply red wine or white wine, nothing more.)

To the east, however, the story is different.

Sauternes

The southern part of Graves, as the map shows, entirely surrounds on all but its river side the region of Sauternes, with its two little outriders Barsac and Cérons. The white wines of these three regions are rich and full.

If anything they are fuller than white Graves: they are farther from the sea with its tempering effect; the river is even narrower here; the grapes are grown on slopes. But because the slopes are generally eastward-facing and overlooking what water is left in the river, the wines of Sauternes are much finer, more elegant, by and large, than the whites of Graves. Moreover, the slopes of Sauternes form a little bowl, and according to local tradition this permits the morning mist to gather and hang there, so that in the late fall a mildew called *pourriture noble,* literally, "the noble rot," attacks the grapes.

The story of the Noble Rot has often been told. As a normal thing, every measure is taken to prevent diseases from afflicting grapes, but this mildew is a notable, not to say noble, exception. The filament of the mildew penetrates the skin of the grape, drawing off a high proportion of the moisture inside, thus greatly concentrating the sugar in the grape. When, late in the harvest season, the withered, almost raisinous grapes are finally gathered and fermented, the resulting wine is liquorous and sweet, a wine drunk not with the main body of the meal, but with certain sweet desserts, or even as a dessert course by itself.

Sweet wines are not so commonly drunk today as they once were, and that is a shame, because a sweet wine at the end of a meal is a charming, civilized custom. But in any case, no listing of great wines is complete without Sauternes.

The most famous vineyard of Sauternes is the Château d'Yquem, the only white wine that is ranked in quality with the great reds of the Haut-Médoc and Graves. The only challengers to Yquem among dessert wines are the best ones from the Rhine and Moselle in Germany. Here are some of the runners-up to Yquem:

Château La Tour-Blanche	Château Climens
Château Lafaurie-Peyraguey	Château Guiraud
Château Haut-Peyraguey	Château Rieussec
Château Rayne-Vigneau	Château Rabaud-Promis
Château Suduiraut	Château Sigalas-Rabaud
Château Coutet	

St.-Émilion

Thus most of the really notable wines of Bordeaux, in all the thousands of châteaux, can be described in a single sweep down the gravel bank from the river mouth to Sauternes. But, as always, there is an exception. Twenty miles to the west is the hill of St.-Émilion, a plateau, actually, that rises above the Dordogne River. The wines of St.-Émilion are "wines of the hill," wines grown inland, wines grown on limestone. Moreover, the vineyards that receive the wind from the sea face southwest where they are exposed to the strong afternoon sun; the others lie on the flat of the plateau, where they bake in the noonday heat. It is not surprising then that the red wines of St.-Émilion, along with those of its cousin district Pomerol, are fuller-bodied than those of Médoc or Graves.

Too much should not be made, however, of the fact that the St.-Émilions are fuller than Médoc or red Graves. They are by no means as full as the biggest Burgundies, much less the robust Rhônes. For purposes of our Spectrum we are still dealing with relatively light red wines, the heaviest of the lights or the lightest of the heavies, as you wish. If a Médoc or a Graves goes well with veal or lamb, a St.-Émilion would be considered best suited to be drunk with something a bit fuller and richer: duck, pheasant, goose; a stew, a roast rib of beef. But if you choose to have a St.-Émilion with veal or lamb, that is your business—no one will laugh at you.

These are some of the best wines of St.-Émilion:

Château Ausone	Château Canon
Château Cheval Blanc	Clos Fourtet
Château Beauséjour	Château Figeac
(Dufau-Lagarosse)	Château La Gaffelière-Naudes
Château Beauséjour	Château Magdelaine
(Dr. Fagouet)	Château Pavie
Château Bel-Air	Château Trottevieille

Within the region of St.-Émilion there is a subdistinction. The wines grown on the limestone slope are a shade fuller-bodied than those grown on the more gravelly flat of the plateau. The most famous of the vineyards of the limestone slope is the Château Ausone, previously mentioned, where the Roman poet Ausonius is supposed to have lived. The most famous wine of the plateau is Château Cheval Blanc, translated "white horse," of no known connection with the scotch whisky of the same name. The wines of neighboring Pomerol are similar in body to the St.-Émilions of the gravelly flat, lighter than the ones from the limestone slope. The most

CHATEAU AUSONE
SAINT-EMILION
APPELLATION SAINT-EMILION CONTRÔLÉE
1962
Vᵉᵉ C. VAUTHIER & J. DUBOIS-CHALLON
PROPRIÉTAIRES A SAINT-ÉMILION (GIRONDE)
MIS EN BOUTEILLES AU CHATEAU

famous vineyard of Pomerol is Petrus. Since the name Petrus is originally Latin, not French, the final "s" is sounded, even in French.

Here are others of the best growths of Pomerol:

Château Certan	Château l'Évangile
Vieux Château Certan	Château La Fleur
Château La Conseillante	Château Gazin
Château Petit-Village	Château La Fleur-Petrus
Château Trotanoy	

As the map shows, between the hill of St.-Émilion and the vineyards on the great gravel bank to the west is a veritable sea of vineyards which do not enjoy fully the advantages of either a hillside location or a gravel bank along the water. Some of the wine they produce is not worth much. Some is pretty good, and comes at a price suited to daily drinking. But when you buy these wines it is not usually on the basis of your own knowledge and judgment, but on the recommendation of a merchant you trust.

The lesser Bordeaux, red and white, go best with the same dishes as a red Médoc or a white Graves. But simpler wines would go, by and large, with simpler methods of preparation, which is eminently appropriate, since you are spending less money on them.

Thus, Bordeaux. Here is the way our Spectrum of Possibility has developed so far:

	Basic Spectrum	*Secondary Listings*
Fuller-bodied White	—	White Graves
Light-bodied Red	HAUT-MÉDOC*	(Bas-) Médoc
	RED GRAVES	
Fuller-bodied Red	ST.-ÉMILION	Pomerol
(Sweet Dessert Wines)†	SAUTERNES	Barsac
		Cérons

The Business Institutions of Bordeaux

The successful purchase of any bottle of Bordeaux wine, be it great or humble, depends on the buyer's ability to look at the label on a bottle and understand what it has to tell him (or on his ability to find a merchant or a wine steward who can do the job for him). The label in turn reflects the business institutions of the ancient and extensive *vignoble* (wine district) of Bordeaux. The institutions themselves—classification, château bottling—are well known. Less well known or understood are the economic and political reasons and the full implication of these institutions to the buying of Bordeaux wines.

---

* Oversimplification: Not all Haut-Médocs are light.

† Not actually a part of the Basic Spectrum, but essential in any listing of the major wines of Bordeaux.

As in the case of the actual wine itself, the primary force shaping the *institutions* of wine is geographic location. It was because it was reachable by water (and because it happened to lie along the sea route to the ancient tin mines of the Scillies) that a remote situation like Bordeaux was discoverable as early as the Bronze Age, and the cultivation of the grape could begin so soon. And it was not simply the marriage of Eleanor of Aquitaine to Henry of Anjou that made it possible for the vineyards of Bordeaux to prosper during the Middle Ages, when the vineyards of other areas were producing for strictly local consumption or had fallen into disuse. More basic was the fact that England was accessible by water at a time when the land routes of Europe were largely closed to trade. (And it was at least in part the propinquity of Aquitaine to Anjou that made it likely that a nice girl like Eleanor would find it politically advantageous to marry a fine boy like Henry in the first place.)

And it is a matter of geography that Bordeaux, located in a remote corner of France, with ocean on one side and wild, rough country on two others, is relatively remote from centers like Paris and Versailles. This comparative political isolation, combined with commercial access to most of the markets of the known world, combined in turn with the huge volume of good wine produced in southwestern France, and its relative year-to-year reliability—two more functions of geography—has meant that winegrowing and wine-selling have been a dominant preoccupation of the Bordelais for four thousand years, with relatively less disruption by outside events than many other winegrowing areas.

Furthermore, the location of the great port of Bordeaux, commanding the Gironde, gave the merchants in that city a stranglehold on the transport of wines from the extensive districts upriver, and thus a monopoly of the export trade. Over the centuries, this has tended to create in Bordeaux a powerful class of growers and merchants, and it was in their interest, in turn, to develop a formidable set of institutions organized around wine.

The best known institution, of course, is *classification*. The French are great classifiers. They classify chickens. They classify cheeses. They classify oysters and artichokes and truffles and cider and sardines. It is impossible, in the orderly Bordelais, at least, to conceive of their *not* classifying the wines. The wines of the Haut-Médoc, since they not only were the best but were controlled by the powerful merchant-aristocracy, were the first to be classified. The sixty-one Great Growths (vineyards) of the Haut-Médoc, along with the great Château Haut-Brion of Graves and the twenty-five best of Sauternes, were officially classified in 1855, and unofficial classifications of these wines go back at least two centuries before that. Of the sixty-one Médoc vineyards classified in 1855, fifty-nine are still in production, and the classification remains generally valid today (although experts argue about it, as they do about all things).

Below the fifty-nine Great Growths of the Haut-Médoc are seven Crus

Exceptionnels, Exceptional Growths. Below the Crus Exceptionnels are two hundred fifty Crus Bourgeois, Bourgeois Growths; divided into Crus Bourgeois Supérieurs, Superior Bourgeois Growths, and simply Bourgeois Growths. Below the Bourgeois Growths are several hundred lesser wines —Crus Artisans, Artisan Growths, and Crus Paysans, Peasant Growths.*

Lacking the political clout of the Haut-Médoc, the other regions of Bordeaux were not officially classified until much later. But they did not need to be. Reliable unofficial rankings, based on the records of average prices paid in the Bordeaux market, have been available for a long time.

Classification is certainly not an unmixed blessing. As we noted at the beginning of this chapter, there are something upward of five thousand individually named and delimited vineyards in Bordeaux, of which at least a thousand are classified in one way or another. If you walk into a wine shop or look at a wine card and want to buy a Bordeaux wine at a price level suited to daily drinking, you will very often not recognize the merchandise being offered you. And even if you do recognize a name, you may have difficulty remembering what its classification is and what the merit of its particular vintage was; so you still have no clear idea of what the wine is worth. And the names of a great many vineyards of Bordeaux—sometimes accidentally, sometimes deliberately—are confusingly similar.

The problems thus created encourage a serious drinker of wines to start his own "cellar," even if it is only a closet, in order to justify the time

---

* These classifications reflect not only a French meticulousness about gastronomic distinction, but, in the tradition of the landed gentry of Bordeaux, a keen consciousness of social distinction as well. In effect, the wines are classified as Aristocrats, Near-Aristocrats, Upper Middle Class, Middle Class, Blue Collar, and Peasants. Below the Peasants are a number of vineyards that are not even classified at all. Following the logic above they should be considered Untouchables or Undrinkables, although they are not actually that bad.

and trouble required to buy wisely. But if you do want to buy wisely, in Bordeaux, with the help of classification, you can do it.

The institution of classification depends in turn on the institution of the *château* (vineyard). The vineyards of the district of Bordeaux, even some of the finest ones, in general are big vineyards, in distinct contrast to many of the fine vineyards of other areas. To take an extreme example, Romanée-Conti, considered the greatest vineyard of Burgundy, consists of only 4½ acres, while Château Lafite, the premier vineyard of Bordeaux, consists of no less than 150 acres. Moreover, the rules of classification tend to encourage large size and stability of holdings of the high-rated vineyards. If, for example, the proprietor of a high-rated vineyard sells some of his land to his neighbor, the proprietor of a lower-rated vineyard, the wines from the transferred parcel must thereafter go to market under the lower rating. Since nobody is exactly eager to have that happen, the high-rated land tends to remain with the high-rated holdings. The resulting large and relatively stable volume of production of the high-rated vineyards means in turn that it is economically feasible to bottle the wines at the château, rather than send them to town to have a shipper do it. The institution of *château bottling* in turn means that the owner-management of a château is in position to guarantee the soundness and honesty of the wine at the time it was bottled. The rules encourage honesty and penalize dishonesty in this connection. But even if the rules did not, the institution would. The desire to protect the future reputation and market value of the wines from a large and valuable property gives powerful incentive to tell the truth. The phrases *mise du château* or *mise en bouteilles au château,* appearing on the label of a reputable château of Bordeaux, are very strong indications that the wine was sound and authentic at the time it went into bottle.*

Established classifications, reliable merchandise, and a large and stable volume of production in turn make possible *orderly markets* (and it was the existence of reasonably orderly markets over a long period which created the competitive prices and consistent price records which made the institution of classification possible in the first place). The wine market of Bordeaux City is like a combination of the New York Stock Exchange and the Chicago Commodity Exchange. The growers of the wine finance their operations by selling to shippers or speculators "futures"—contracts to deliver wines that are not yet produced, or are still maturing in barrel. Prices for futures for various vintages are quoted on a daily basis, as are prices for vintages now in bottle and held either at the château or in the warehouse of a shipper.

The result of all this for a buyer is that if he buys a château bottling of, let us say, Haut-Brion '66 and likes it, he can later go to any reasonably

---

* Cheating in wines happens in Bordeaux as it happens everywhere. But here usually affects the humbler wines, not the top-rated vineyards.

large wine shop in the country, or indeed the world, and buy another Haut-Brion '66, with the assurance that, barring some accident, it will be the same wine in the same condition (with allowance for a slight increase in age). And because the production of a given year is relatively large and the channels of trade well established, he can assume, too, that once he develops a taste for Haut-Brion '66 it will be on the market long enough for him to enjoy it. And when the '66's are gone he will know that the '70's will be coming along, reflecting a different vintage, to be sure, but the same quality of management of the same fine vineyard.

In the case of some wines from other districts—Romanée-Conti of Burgundy as a case in point—reliable bottles of a particular vineyard in an excellent year are so rare that the object of buying ahead and storing the wine is to corner some of the available supply while there is any. Price questions are secondary. In the case of a famous Bordeaux, by contrast, you can assume the wine is going to be there. The main purpose of advance buying is to put in a supply before the relentless rise in price has put a particular vintage beyond your reach.

Two remaining institutions, not unique to Bordeaux but important there as elsewhere, are the *shipper* and one of his chief offerings, the *shipper's wine.*

The shipper is in effect a wholesale buyer, usually located at the main shipping point of a vineyard area—in this case the city of Bordeaux. In the normal course of events, a shipper will buy all or part of the wine from a given year from a particular château, and in turn will sell it to importers in the United States, England, Sweden, or wherever, who in their turn sell it to the various regional wholesalers who sell it to your favorite restaurant or liquor store.

Of course, in Bordeaux, where the name of the château and the institution of château bottling are the primary guarantee of the honesty of the wine, the shipper is chiefly a physical handler and commercial broker. His name appearing on a label is unimportant. In areas where the name of the vineyard is less than a guarantee, the name of a reliable shipper (or an importer or wholesaler or retail outlet) may be your only "landmark," your only indication of whether the merchandise in question is honest and sound.

In most areas the large shippers have found it profitable to go one step further. A shipper will bottle wines of a district, a region, or a village under his own label, with no indication at all of the vineyard of origin. Usually the wine will not even come from a single vineyard, but will be a blend of the wines from different vineyards, regions, or vintage years. (And if the blending is done skillfully, this often results in a better, more balanced wine than any of its individual components.)

This is a "shipper's wine," and in this case the name of the shipper and his skill and reputation are your sole indication of the quality of the

wine. Here we see developed in rudimentary form what could be called "brand names" and the creation of "brand preference." In fact, wines from shippers such as Barton & Guestier and Drouhin and Julius Wile, and in particular the numerous shippers of Champagne, are advertised in the United States like any other branded merchandise.

A shipper's wine meets the needs of the many people who don't have the knowledge, interest, money or time to worry about all the complicated classifications and are looking for an easy way out. It can also be very helpful to the merchant or restaurateur who wants to offer his customers reliable merchandise without bothering with the expertise, the inventory, and the headaches required to maintain a good wine list on his own. The appellations most likely to appear on the label of a shipper's wine are the larger-volume, lower-priced ones. In the case of Bordeaux, these would be the "district" appellations, Bordeaux Rouge (red) and Bordeaux Blanc (white); the "regional" appellations, Médoc, Graves, St.-Émilion, Sauternes; and three of the four "communal" appellations of the Haut-Médoc: Margaux, St. Julien, and St.-Estèphe (the wines of the commune of Pauillac can often find a more profitable market under a vineyard name).

THE GLORIES OF THE HAUT-MÉDOC

Before we leave behind us the ancient *vignoble* of the Bordelais, it is essential to take a closer look at the wines and wine names of the incomparable Haut-Médoc. A relative novice, attempting to apply the Spectrum of Possibility to a simple problem of matching, is certain *not* to remember the names of these world-famous villages, much less the vineyards, and he has no need to. As we have pointed out, for everyday purposes, a Bor-

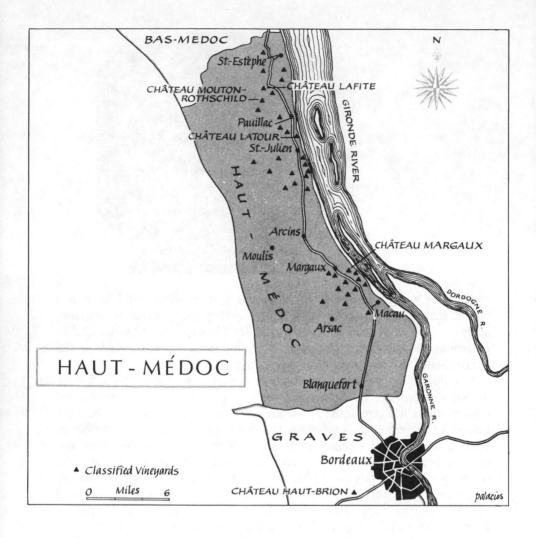

BAS-MEDOC

St.-Estèphe

CHÂTEAU MOUTON-
ROTHSCHILD

CHÂTEAU LAFITE

Pauillac

CHÂTEAU LATOUR

St.-Julien

H A U T

Arcins

Moulis

Margaux

CHÂTEAU MARGAUX

M É D O C

Macau

Arsac

Blanquefort

GIRONDE RIVER

DORDOGNE R.

GARONNE R.

N

HAUT - MÉDOC

G R A V E S

Bordeaux

▲ Classified Vineyards

0   Miles   6

CHÂTEAU HAUT-BRION ▲

palacios

deaux is a Bordeaux is a Bordeaux. Furthermore, he may not even like
them at the start. Beginners as a rule prefer the simple directness of the
lesser (and cheaper) wines to the subtlety and complexity of the fine and
great ones. But as soon as your competence in matching wines begins to
rise even slightly, and with it the discernment of your palate, you will need
to know how to deal with these famous names; until you do you cannot
fully understand, much less play, the game of wine.

Too many people for too long while they are learning are intimidated
by these near-legendary names, and either shy away entirely or reach com-
pulsively for the small group of familiar, overpriced labels.

'Tis a far, far better thing to plunge right in and take your chances, at
whatever price you can stand, learning as you go. The learning process will
be accelerated if you periodically read through the lists of the names of the

better-known châteaux, to improve your feel for them, or even take the list with you when you visit your wine merchant. Consulting a list when you are ordering in a restaurant is very bad form indeed. But at the wine merchant's it will be taken as the badge of a scholar, a connoisseur, a man of worth.

Comparative tastings of the various wines according to quality or character will educate both your palate and your memory for the names. This can be done at the dinner table or at a wine-tasting, held in lieu of a cocktail party. At such time as your interest in wine and your desire to save money on the good wines leads you to start a cellar, a "cellar book," if you want to keep one, recording what you bought and when, and when you drank it and how you liked it, can be both an educational tool and a guide to future purchase.

In the wines of the Haut-Médoc, as in all other wines, there are two principal variables: fullness and fineness. As to their relative fineness— quality—we have already noted that the wines of the Haut-Médoc are among the most classified in the world. As to fullness, we have indicated that red Bordeaux wines generally and the Médocs in particular are considered lighter and more delicate than most other fine wines. But we also noted that this is an overgeneralization. The wines of Margaux, the southernmost of the four great wine towns of the Haut-Médoc, are usually lighter, more delicate, more "feminine" than the others. As you move northward—St.-Julien, Pauillac, St.-Estèphe—the wines become progressively fuller, with those of St.-Estèphe the fullest of all, and rather full wines by any standard. (It should be noted, too, that the highest-rated wines of a given commune are usually just a shade fuller than their lower-rated neighbors.)

Let us now take a brief but respectful tour of the Haut-Médoc, to see how nature has played its variations on these two basic themes: fullness and fineness.

To reach the Médoc, you travel northward from Bordeaux (see map) along the road running across the poor, gravelly soil that connects the wine towns with the city, and along which, immemorially, the wine has moved to market. You enter the Haut-Médoc juridically when you cross a little tidal stream called Blanquefort, a convenient breaking point and perhaps in the Middle Ages considered a good line of defense against bandits or invaders. (Farther north, along the river, they once built a fence to keep the pirates out, and in the old days the *courtiers*—wine brokers—of Bordeaux used to provide protection to out-of-town wine buyers on their way to visit the châteaux.)

Yet vinologically the rivulet Blanquefort does not divide the Haut-Médoc from Graves. The gravelly land here is flat, not rolling as it is farther north; and, as the map shows, the river is narrow at this point— not an effective thermostat—and separated from the vineyards by marshland. Not many fine wines are made near the Blanquefort, and what there are bear more resemblance to the soft wines of Graves to the south than to the clearly defined ones of the Haut-Médoc. About two miles farther on, the villages of Ludon and Macau make wines similar to those of Blanquefort (Macau is also famous for artichokes). But now the river widens, the wine lands rise and begin a gentle rolling, and the marshes disappear from the shore. About a mile to the left of the road is a little village called Arsac. Arsac is too far from the tempering waters of the Gironde to produce more than a single Fifth Growth, but suddenly the wines are lighter, more fragrant, more clearly defined. The true Haut-Médoc has begun.

A few hundred yards farther on is the village of Labarde, nearer the river, producing two Classed Growths: one Third Growth and one Fifth. Just beyond is Cantenac, producing one Second Growth, four Thirds, two Fourths, and one Cru Exceptionnel. One of the Third Growths, the Château d'Issan, describes itself on its label as "for the tables of kings and the altars of the gods."*

The Commune of Margaux

With this introduction it is not surprising that in the very next village, Margaux, close by the edge of the river now, the glory of the great Château Margaux now bursts upon us, reigning atop her deep, gravelly drainage. The most delicate and feminine of the four greatest Médocs, Margaux has been described as of "truly incomparable distinction and class, delicate, velvety, suave, well balanced, and astoundingly long-lived, a bouquet unsurpassed by any red wine on earth."

This is not just wine country, this is adjective country!

Surrounding the great château are her ladies of honor, a handful of fine vineyards sharing her qualities of delicacy and grace. Within this one township there is one First Growth, Margaux itself, three Seconds, four

* To repeat, "Growth" means "château"—vineyard.

Thirds, one Fourth, and one Cru Exceptionnel. In the villages of Arsac, Labarde, Cantenac, and Margaux together we find nineteen Classed Growths of the fifty-nine of the Haut-Médoc, 32 per cent, all of surpassing delicacy and femininity. The better wines of Arsac, Labarde, and Cantenac are legally entitled to use the appellation Margaux on their labels because of the similarity of the wines. Here is a listing of the Classified Growths of the Margaux area:

First Growth

Château Margaux

Second Growth

Château Rausan-Ségla   Château Lascombes
Château Rauzan-Gassies   Château Brane-Cantenac (Cantenac)

Third Growth

Château Malescot-St.-Exupéry   Château d'Issan (Cantenac)
Château Boyd-Cantenac   Château Cantenac-Brown (Cantenac)
Château Ferrière   Château Palmer (Cantenac)
Château Marquis-d'Alesme-Becker   Château Giscours (Labarde)
Château Kirwan (Cantenac)

Fourth Growth

Château Marquis-de-Terme   Château Prieuré-Lichine (Cantenac)
Château Pouget (Cantenac)   Château Dauzac (Labarde)

Fifth Growth

Château du Tertre (Arsac)

Just past Margaux the land flattens out and there is no wine worthy of note along the shore, so the farm road swings thriftily inland to pick up other produce from villages with names like Soussans and Arcins (not to be confused with Arsac). But off to the eastward, on a little plateau, are the towns of Moulis and Listrac. There are no Classed Growths here (too far from the river again), but the sloping land and the eastward exposure have produced twenty-four Crus Bourgeois and two Crus Exceptionnels. These wines, firmly and reliably Clarets if not great ones, have traditionally been favorites on French railroad dining cars. They have been granted their own appellation (both go to market as Moulis) in order that riders on French railroads might not be deceived.

Next north are two other little towns called Lamarque and Cussac, which between them can manage only nine Crus Bourgeois. But now the land toward the river is rising again and the soil is growing sandier. Sandy soil, as noted in Chapter I, does not provide the instant drainage that deep beds of gravel do, nor does it as efficiently deflect the sun's rays by day nor hold the heat by night. Conditions, then, are not as delicate, nor are the wines.

The Commune of St.-Julien

About a mile beyond Cussac is the township of St.-Julien. The wines of St.-Julien, fuller-bodied than those of Margaux but lighter than those from the even sandier soil to the north, come as close as possible to being "typical" Médocs. Indeed St.-Julien has been called "the Claret for Claret lovers." Bordeaux is the center of the world of wines. The Haut-Médoc is the center of Bordeaux. And St.-Julien is the center of the Médoc.

Curiously, there are almost no bad wines here and at the same time none of the greatest ones. (Perhaps there is a philosophic point. There is a saying that "your faults determine your style." St.-Julien seems almost a wine without fault—no rough edges. By the same token, it does not take the risks that might have brought true greatness.)

There are five Second Growths in St.-Julien, two Thirds, five Fourths, and one Cru Exceptionnel. The *average* quality of the wines is probably the highest of the Médoc, and the "communal" wines (those carrying only the appellation of the commune on the label) command the highest prices of any in the region.

Here are the wines of St.-Julien. Between them they offer twelve of the fifty-nine Classed Growths, 20 per cent of the total:

First Growth
None

Second Growth

Château Léoville-Las-Cases	Château Gruaud-Larose
Château Léoville-Poyferré	Château Ducru-Beaucaillou
Château Léoville-Barton	

Third Growth

Château Lagrange	Château Langoa

Fourth Growth

Château St.-Pierre-Sevaistre	Château Branaire-Ducru
Château St.-Pierre-Bontemps	Château Beychevelle
Château Talbot	

Fifth Growth
None

The Commune of Pauillac

A little over two miles to the west of St.-Julien, on a rise of ground, is the village of St.-Laurent. Like Moulis and Listrac, it is too far from the water to achieve true greatness, but it does manage three Classed Growths, a Fourth and two Fifths. But about a mile north of St.-Julien, right on the

river, is the little village called Pauillac, perhaps the most remarkable wine township in the world. Here, on soil just a bit sandier, slightly closer to the river and somewhat higher above it, are grown the other three of the four greatest Médocs: incomparable Lafite, the greatest of them all, and Mouton and Latour. (The name of the great Château Lafite means "knoll." The name Latour means "tower." Since it is impossible to copyright a knoll, and the Médoc is full of ancient towers, there is a confusing variety of Lafites, Laffites, and Laffittes scattered about the Médoc, along with several dozen Latours. The name Mouton means "sheep," but in old French it means "hill," which is about the same as "knoll." It is not as widely copied as its neighbors.)

Château Lafite is owned by one branch of the Rothschild family, Château Mouton by another branch. Mouton was listed at the top of the Second Growths of the Médoc when the original classification of Great Growths was made in 1855, but it is said that only dirty politics kept it from being classified a First Growth. Ever after, like the Avis automobile rental company, it tried harder; its superb wine generally sold at a price equal to a First Growth, and finally, more than a century later, it was at last officially elevated to First Growth.

It is interesting that the very greatest Bordeaux, Lafite, and two of its runners-up, Latour and Mouton, are relatively full-bodied wines, even in a region famous for lighter, more feminine wines. This suggests that even in feminine Bordeaux for a wine to achieve the supreme pinnacle it must possess a certain level of force, of authority—a thought that would not bring pleasure to women's lib.

Because they are heavy in tannin—the ingredient that gives the wine body—the wines of Pauillac are slow to mature. A wine from an excellent vintage may not be ready to drink for fifteen years. Until the astringent tannin has had time to transmute biochemically into perfumelike esters, the wines can be rough and harsh on the tongue.

Unlike the best wines of St.-Julien, which are clustered at the center of the list of Great Growths, the best Pauillacs are classed either at the top or at the bottom of the scale. There are three First Growths, two Seconds, no Thirds, one Fourth, twelve Fifth Growths, one Cru Exceptionnel, and no fewer than fifteen Crus Bourgeois. In contrast to St.-Julien, the wines here take chances. They gamble on the quality of fullness. If the gamble succeeds, the wine rises to the pinnacle. If it doesn't, it is just a bit too full. All things in moderation, especially in Bordeaux.

Here are the Great Growths of Pauillac. It will be noted that eighteen of the fifty-nine Crus Classes, 30 per cent, come from Pauillac, compared to twelve from St.-Julien and twenty-one from the Margaux cluster.

First Growth
Château Lafite-Rothschild
Château Mouton-Rothschild
Château Latour

Second Growth
Château Pichon-Longueville
Château Pichon-Longueville-Lalande

Third Growth
None

Fourth Growth
Château Duhart-Milon

Fifth Growth

Château Pontet-Canet	Château Lynch-Moussas
Château Batailley	Château Mouton-Baron-Philippe
Château Haut-Batailley	Château Haut-Bages-Libéral
Château Grand-Puy-Lacoste	Château Pédesclaux
Château Grand-Puy-Ducasse	Château Clerc-Milon
Château Lynch-Bages	Château Croizet-Bages

The Commune of St.-Estèphe

Such sublimity is more than nature can sustain. A couple of miles beyond Pauillac, again right on the river, is St.-Estèphe. The soil here is even sandier, the elevation lower, closer to the morning mist. Now the virtue of body definitely becomes a vice. The wines of St.-Estèphe are sturdy, forthright, full-bodied, and lusty, but without the finesse and breed of the incomparable Clarets just two miles south. Not surprisingly, a St.-Estèphe can also be very rough in its youth, and by the same token will live forever. The tannin, which lends body and delays maturity, also acts as a preservative. (A few years back, Forrest Wallace happily consumed one of the last eight bottles of the St.-Estèphe of '78 in the famous French restaurant Père Bis. The other seven were consumed shortly after by a party hosted by French President Charles de Gaulle.)

In St.-Estèphe there are five of the fifty-five Classed Growths, 8 per cent of the total. There are two Second Growths, one Third, one Fourth, one Fifth, and *twenty-five* Crus Bourgeois, of which no fewer than fifteen are Bourgeois Supérieurs. Here, but for a trace of excess tannin, would have been far greater wines.

First Growth

None

Second Growth

Château Cos d'Estournel
Château Montrose

Third Growth

Château Calon-Ségur

Fourth Growth

Château Rochet

Fifth Growth

Château Cos Labory

Past St.-Estèphe the music ends, more suddenly than it began, and so does the Haut-Médoc. Now the soil is too heavy and moist, the land too low, the sea with its wind and fog too close. Most of the wines are lesser growths. Some can be excellent, and as we have pointed out, in good years when the sun and rain are just right can compare with the Classed

MIS EN BOUTEILLE AU CHATEAU

COS D'ESTOURNEL 1962
SAINT-ESTÈPHE
APPELLATION SAINT ESTÈPHE CONTROLÉE
SOCIÉTÉ DES VIGNOBLES GINESTET PROPRIÉTAIRE A SAINT-ESTÈPHE

Growths to the south. But there is no longer the near-perennial miracle that occurs along the twenty miles of shoreline of the Haut-Médoc.

Now here are all fifty-nine of the existing Great Growths of the Haut-Médoc (along with Haut-Brion of Graves) listed according to the original classification of 1855:

FIRST GROWTHS

	Township
Château Lafite	Pauillac
Château Latour	Pauillac
Château Margaux	Margaux
Château Haut-Brion	Pessac, Graves
Château Mouton-Rothschild	Pauillac

SECOND GROWTHS

Château Lascombes	Margaux
Château Rausan-Ségla	Margaux
Château Rauzan-Gassies	Margaux
Château Léoville-Las-Cases	St.-Julien
Château Léoville-Poyferré	St.-Julien
Château Léoville-Barton	St.-Julien
Château Durfort-Vivens	Margaux
Château Gruaud-Larose	St.-Julien
Château Brane-Cantenac	Cantenac
Château Pichon-Longueville	Pauillac
Château Pichon-Longueville (Comtesse de Lalande)	Pauillac
Château Ducru-Beaucaillou	St.-Julien
Château Cos d'Estournel	St.-Estèphe
Château Montrose	St.-Estèphe

THIRD GROWTHS

Château Giscours	Labarde
Château Kirwan	Cantenac
Château d'Issan	Cantenac
Château Lagrange	St.-Julien
Château Langoa	St.-Julien
Château Malescot-St.-Exupéry	Margaux
Château Cantenac-Brown	Cantenac
Château Palmer	Cantenac
Château Grand La Lagune	Ludon
Château Desmirail	Margaux
Château Calon-Ségur	St.-Estèphe
Château Ferrière	Margaux
Château Marquis-d'Alesme-Becker	Margaux
Château Boyd-Cantenac	Margaux

FOURTH GROWTHS

Château Prieuré-Lichine	Cantenac
Château St.-Pierre-Bontemps	St.-Julien
Château St.-Pierre-Sevaistre	St.-Julien
Château Branaire-Ducru	St.-Julien
Château Talbot	St.-Julien
Château Duhart-Milon	Pauillac
Château Pouget	Cantenac
Château La Tour-Carnet	St.-Laurent
Château Lafon-Rochet	St.-Estèphe
Château Beychevelle	St.-Julien
Château Marquis-de-Terme	Margaux

FIFTH GROWTHS

Château Pontet-Canet	Pauillac
Château Batailley	Pauillac
Château Grand-Puy-Lacoste	Pauillac
Château Grand-Puy-Ducasse	Pauillac
Château Haut-Batailley	Pauillac
Château Lynch-Bages	Pauillac
Château Lynch-Moussas	Pauillac
Château Dauzac	Labarde
Château Mouton-Baron-Philippe	Pauillac
Château du Tertre	Arsac
Château Haut-Bages-Libéral	Pauillac
Château Pédesclaux	Pauillac
Château Belgrave	St.-Laurent
Château Camensac	St.-Laurent
Château Cos Labory	St.-Estèphe
Château Clerc-Milon-Mondon	Pauillac
Château Croizet-Bages	Pauillac
Château Cantemerle	Macau

III

BURGUNDY, COMPLICATED KING

A comparison of the wines and wine lands of the Bordelais with those of
Burgundy is a remarkable study in contrasts. The human imagination
could hardly have contrived a set of variables as fascinatingly diverse as
were assembled by nature and the accidents of history.

The best wines of Bordeaux are "wines of the plain," wines grown on
gravel, in vineyards near the coast, close to the tempering influence of
water. The best wines of Burgundy are "wines of the hill," wines grown on
limestone, at the edge of an upland valley between two mountain ranges
almost three hundred miles from the sea. The nearest water is the trickle of
the Saône, twenty or so miles away.

With all these influences pushing it that way, it is not surprising that
red Burgundy is known as a "bigger" wine, a more "manly" wine, than red
Bordeaux, appropriate to the hell-raising dukes who shaped the early history of the province, to the rich, robust foods for which it is famous, to the
earthy peasant-owners who grow the grapes. But if Burgundy has the
earthiness of peasants, the best of it raises this quality to a sublime height.
Burgundy is a northern wine, as the map shows, about 150 miles farther
north than Bordeaux, the most northerly great red wine grown anywhere.
Thus, in a good year nature again gets the best of both worlds: the gradual, gentle ripening made possible by cool nights and temperate mornings,
the full, rich maturity brought out by the hot, inland sun. The great Burgundies combine to an astonishing degree the seemingly contradictory
qualities of body and delicacy.

Burgundy Anyone?

Since Burgundy and Bordeaux are the two most famous and important red wines on earth (although by no means the most plentiful) and since even the rankest of novices is at least vaguely aware that there is some sort of fundamental difference between them, there is probably no question asked more often in connection with the use of wine than: What should I serve with the lamb chops tonight (or the steak or the roast or the veal scallopini)—Burgundy or Bordeaux?

The easiest answer, and the only one that can be offered with a lecture of less than half an hour, is that for most dishes calling for or permitting red wine—beef, veal, lamb, chicken—any good red will do.

But the game of wine is a game of distinctions. Even if you do not absolutely *need* to know the precise difference between red Burgundy and red Bordeaux, it is interesting to know, it is fun to know. And at the higher levels of eating and drinking, where every tiny nuance counts, it is essential that you know.

In commonplace distinctions, as we have just noted, red Bordeaux is known as a light, delicate, "feminine" wine, whereas red Burgundy is considered a fuller-bodied, more robust, more "masculine" wine. But as we have also seen, there are areas of the Haut-Médoc, where the lightest, most delicate of Bordeaux are grown, that are famous for their relatively full-bodied wines. And, as we shall soon see, there are areas of the Côte de Nuits, where the fullest-bodied, most masculine Burgundies are made, that produce wines that are lighter and more delicate than many a true-to-type Bordeaux.

So while it remains a fair generalization that most Burgundies tend to be fuller than most Bordeaux, the prime distinction is not whether a particular wine happens to be heavy or light, but a certain character, a "style," if you wish, to the flavor and bouquet of each. When Forrest Wallace is asked about this problem, he likes to draw an analogy to various kinds of automobiles (if one *dares* to compare a famous wine to an automobile). If you choose to buy a General Motors car rather than a Ford Motor Company car, say, or an American car in preference to a European car, that in itself says nothing about whether the car you pick will be heavy or light (although the average of one group might well be lighter or heavier than the average of another). But if you buy a General Motors car, be it Cadillac or Camaro, there will be—or at least the designers hope there will be—a stamp or style to it that gives it something in common with any other General Motors car, and sets it apart from all the rest.

Writers on wine, especially the earlier ones, have virtually made careers of describing and discussing the contrasting "styles" of these two great categories of wine. Witness the late P. Morton Shand, in his classic *A Book of French Wines,* published in 1928:

Bordeaux, which was first belauded by Ausonius, has been called
"austere" and again "un gentilhomme par excellence, le vin d'un cor-
rection impeccable." Maurice des Ombiaux defines it as a wine of perfect scansion and rhythm, evocative of the polished verses of Racine
or La Fontaine. To compare the magnificent harmony of a fine Bordeaux to a flight of alexandrines is to pay it a doubtful compliment—
outside of France at least—for the genius of no great wine is less emphatic, declamatory or monotonous. Grandeur it has, and in high degree, but I find the "scansion" of Bordeaux, if scansion there must be,
ranges from the Horatian to the Miltonic, from the rippling lyrics of
Herrick to the sway and surge of Swinburne in the infinite variety of
its scope; the rhythm of its incarnadine burden, the lilt of splendid
majesty, never the din of rant drowning the creaking of the buskins.

For those who are wondering, buskins are the shoes worn by the
chorus in a Greek drama. Thus we have a vision of the purity, the loft-
iness, the stateliness, of Classic Greek to add to a scansion that ranges
from the Horatian to the Miltonic, and all with such restraint that you can
even hear the shoes creak.

On Burgundy, Mr. Shand tells us: "Burgundy throughout a dinner is
like trumpets throughout a sonata."

He goes on:

The wine of Burgundy may justly be termed the symbol of the glory
that is France, the clear and resolute flame of the French genius, the
milk which, as Erasmus says, has nourished the noblest of her sons; a
wine polished and suave as the French language; generous, brave and
pithy as the temper of her people, subtle as their grace and courtly as
their fine irony. "Le coq gaulois est un coq que boit du vin." [Freely,
"The rooster which is the symbol of France is a rooster that drinks
wine."]

It would be folly to argue with Erasmus or Shand, either one. *Vive la
France!* But this still leaves some question about what to have with the
lamb chops.

To deal with this issue it is necessary to move from poetry to chemistry. The best way to understand the essential, persisting difference between
Burgundy and Bordeaux is to look at the grapes from which they are
made. The "informing," that is, characterizing, vine of Bordeaux is the
Cabernet Sauvignon, which has been growing and adapting itself to the
conditions of the Bordelais for centuries. As we noted in the previous
chapter, the Cabernet has a tendency to run strong to tannin—tannic acid
—the same acid that gives a puckery, astringent flavor to tea, and is also
used to tan hides. When you drink a wine that is strong in tannin, you can
feel a slight roughness at the back of your teeth with the tip of your
tongue.

Tannin, as noted, acts as a preservative, giving a wine long life, and also taking a long time to mature, as the harsh, astringent acid is gradually transformed to perfumelike esters. But even when mature, a good Bordeaux has enough tannin remaining to give it a clean, aloof, austere quality.

By contrast, the Pinot Noir, the great grape of Burgundy, is relatively short on tannin, but has a tendency to run heavy to glycerine. The lesser dose of tannin means that big, rugged-seeming Burgundy actually has a shorter life span than delicate, gentle Bordeaux, and by the same token is "ready" sooner. A lesser Burgundy will be mature and ready to drink two years after the harvest; a fine one in five. But the same Burgundy may start to go over the hill in fifteen years, whereas a fine Bordeaux might not reach its peak for fifteen years, but can live as long as eighty.

To return to Shand: "Burgundy has great genius. It does wonders within its period. It does all except to keep up in the race. It is shortlived."

(For a wine to go "over the hill" does not mean that it spoils or turns to vinegar, although that can happen, too. When it passes its prime, it begins to seem tired, even though it is still "sound"—that is, unspoiled. It loses the full power of its flavor and bouquet, and its color begins to fade as well.)

But within its life span, the high glycerine content of red Burgundy gives it a fullness, a roundness, a sweetness, when there is no sugar, a kind of warm, earthy simplicity. Thus, even the most delicate of Burgundies are still Burgundies: sweeter, simpler, rounder, more straightforward, somehow more "generous" than their Bordeaux counterparts. When Burgundy has a fault, it is an excess of this chief virtue: an earthy, rooty quality.

The bouquet—"nose"—of a fine Burgundy can be almost overpowering and remind one of woodsy, simple, tangible, edible things: violets, raspberries, truffles, beeswax. By contrast, the bouquet of a great Bordeaux, more a "perfume" than a "nose," reminds one not of bosky dells or the hell-raising dukes of old Burgundy, but of poetry . . . classic poetry.

So it is not surprising that red Burgundy will in general be paired with richer, more robust foods than red Bordeaux: If Bordeaux goes best with lamb, veal, ham, liver, or sweetbreads, Burgundy is particularly suited to the red meats: beef and game, particularly if they are sauced with a good, rich sauce; and with stews, the kind that are made with onions, mushrooms, garlic, and red wine (often red Burgundy wine). But again it is essential to remember that there is wide overlap. For duck or chicken, Burgundy and Bordeaux are largely interchangeable, even to a purist, although, as we shall see later, the sauce can tilt the balance to one or the other. And even in cases where one wine might ideally be drunk, the other can normally be substituted with ease, depending on the available supply and your own personal preference.

A Glass of Nibelung

The first beginnings of the great vineyards of Burgundy, like those of Bordeaux, are lost in the mists of prehistory. The first recorded evidence of wine in that general area dates from about 600 B.C. When the Greek mariners who founded the settlement that was to become Marseilles first stepped ashore, they were greeted by the natives with a goblet of wine.

So someone had been busy.

By the time that Caesar invaded Gaul, the vineyards to the north, in what is now Burgundy proper, were known and cultivated. But the name of Burgundy, both the province and the wine, dates from several centuries later. Some time around the beginning of the Christian era, a Scandinavian tribe called the Burgundii migrated from the island of Burgundarholm (now called Bornholm) off what is now Denmark to the valley of the Vistula in what is Poland today. But the Burgundii were not able to defend themselves against the Gepidae, another Nordic tribe that got there first, so they migrated westward to the valley of what is called the Main River in modern-day Germany, where they formed a powerful kingdom.

Under King Gundicar the Burgundii became involved in hostilities with the Romans and the Huns. This was a poor choice of enemies, since the Romans and the Huns ganged up on them and in 437 destroyed their kingdom. The massacre of the Burgundian royal family by the Huns is told in the *Nibelungenlied*. (The name "Nibelungen" is thought by some scholars to mean Burgundian, although it is a little hard to conceive of anyone settling down to a meal accompanied by a nice glass of Nibelung.)

In 443 the surviving Burgundii/Nibelungen were transferred by the Romans to the Savoy, on the southwestern slopes of the Alps. In the latter half of the fifth century A.D., as the influence of the Romans declined, that of the vigorous Burgundians expanded, and gradually they extended their control to areas to the north and west of Savoy, including the already famous vineyard region on the west bank of the Saône River. In time the Kingdom of Burgundy became the Duchy of Burgundy, a part of France. When Philip the Bold of Burgundy married Margaret of Flanders in 1369, the territory she brought as dowry extended his domain to include all the lands north of Paris. (Curiously, just as the marriage in 1152 of Eleanor of Aquitaine to Henry of Anjou resulted in a taste for Claret—Bordeaux —in England which persists to this day, so the joining by marriage two hundred years later of Burgundy and Flanders created a preference for Burgundy wines in modern-day Belgium which still endures. There is a saying in Europe that nowhere does a fine Burgundy mature so well as in the cellar of a Belgian wine merchant. But of course this may in part be because the Belgian merchant, with his historic trading relationships, knows where to get good Burgundy in the first place.)

With the marriage of Philip to Margaret, the Burgundian dukes now controlled the major part of France and felt they should be the kings of France. They joined with the British, who still held Bordeaux, in fighting for the crown of France during the Hundred Years War. Joan of Arc finally turned the tide against them in the Battle of Orléans.

The names of such stout figures as John the Fearless, Philip the Good, and Charles the Bold could as well describe the wines as the dukes of Burgundy. Their power was finally broken by crafty Louis XI in 1477, and with the French Revolution even the province of Burgundy disappeared as a unit of government. But the memory lingers on in song, story, and the names of some very great wines.

THE SINS OF HYPHENATION

In Bordeaux, with its large, relatively reliable supply of wine, and its disciplined, rational set of institutions, the business aspects of a decision about what to have with the lamb chops do not need to get in your way (except for the confusion created by classification itself) as you select your wine on the basis of physical characteristics. In dealing with the Burgundies, by contrast, unless you are considering a bottle that is a known and tested entry in your own cellar, or are working with a cellar-master or merchant of distinguished qualification and unimpeachable repute (and even here there can be slippage), you can hardly consider a wine without considering the hazards involved in getting your hands on some of it. In fact, in making up your mind about whether or not to have Burgundy for a particular occasion, very often the decisive issue, regardless of natural affinities or personal preference, is whether you can have enough faith in a given label to have any reasonable assurance that it represents what it says it does.

Notwithstanding the limitless supply of Burgundy-type wines from California and New York on any dealer's shelf, and the number of wines of no particular distinction actually grown or alleged to have grown within the district of Burgundy, true Burgundy, great Burgundy, is a rare commodity. Over-all, Burgundy produces only about one-third the volume of wine of Bordeaux. The fine and great Burgundies account for only a tiny proportion of this. Moreover, Burgundy, with its inland, northerly location, is a risky wine. If the grapes survive the frosts of spring, the risk of drought in summer and unseasonable autumn rains, there is always the chance of hail, which can wipe out an entire crop in ten minutes. All summer long the thunderheads hover behind the vineyard slope, while the peasants pray. From the finest vineyards of Burgundy the growers feel lucky if they get three good years in ten. This still further reduces the supply of first-rate merchandise, increases the price, and renders more irresistible the temptation to cheat.

The temptation and opportunity to cheat are in turn compounded by the institutions of wine that exist—or rather do not exist—in Burgundy. Here the contrast with Bordeaux could hardly be more complete. Not only is the organized wine trade of Bordeaux of much larger volume and longer duration than that of Burgundy, but as we noted in the previous chapter, in Bordeaux, tucked away in a corner of France, relatively distant from the political mainstream of the country, wine and its concerns have tended to influence the course of other events. In Burgundy it is the other way around. Located on the main north-south corridor of travel and invasion from central France to the Mediterranean, situated within reach of both Paris and, in the thirteenth and fourteenth centuries, the seat of the popes at Avignon, the drinking of its great wines has long been a favorite activity of kings and princes of the church, but the process of making and selling them has since the time of the Caesars been overshadowed and at times distorted by larger events.

From the standpoint of the modern drinker of wine, the decisive event in Burgundy was, of course, the French Revolution. In the centuries before the Revolution a high proportion of the best vineyards gradually came into the hands of the church, either because they were started by the monks in order to assure a supply of sacramental wine or because they had been bequeathed to the great abbeys by noblemen seeking to improve their chances of getting into heaven. In terms of improving the technique of making and handling wine, this was a good thing. The monks, less concerned than their secular neighbors with markets and profits or the passage of time in this transitory life, could give the wine the time and care it needed to achieve its rich potential.

The contribution of the medieval church to the *art* of wine making was enormous. But events then proceeded to shatter the *institutions* of wine. With the coming of the Revolution, the church lands, including the wine lands, were confiscated by the state and auctioned off to the people as *biens nationals,* national goods. Then with the operation of the French inheritance laws, under which a man's holdings are divided equally among his heirs, the ownership of the vineyards was fragmented among a large number of individual owners. For example, in the 125-acre Clos de Vougeot (*clos* means literally "wall," "enclosure," and therefore, "vineyard") there are at present twenty-seven individual owners, some owning no more than a few rows of grapes. In Bordeaux the vineyards were divided, too. But the influence of the growers and merchants was enough to see that they were soon reassembled.

The results of this situation in Burgundy are obvious and widely known. The owners of individual plots in a given vineyard vary in competence, technique, and sometimes just luck. One man prunes one way, another another. One fertilizes one way, another another. One harvests at precisely the right moment. Another guesses wrong. And what happens in the cellar is anybody's guess. Until relatively recently it was rare for a Burgundy grower to bottle his own wines; some of them merely sold the ripe grapes direct to shippers, who pressed them and made the wine. There are châteaux in Burgundy as there are in Bordeaux. But in Burgundy these are merely big stone houses, with no necessary operating connection with the wines grown around them. It has been said that Bordeaux is a viticultural feudality, whereas Burgundy is a viticultural democracy. Feudal Bordeaux may be, but it is also businesslike. Burgundy is less a democracy of wine than an anarchy.

In a vacuum like this the locus of power has followed the lines of commerce to the middleman, the shipper or *négociant*. In Bordeaux, as we pointed out, the name of a shipper on a label is relatively unimportant; the name of the château (vineyard) is everything. In Burgundy the name of a good or great vineyard means little unless the name of a reliable shipper certifies that it is authentic.*

The list of the shippers of Burgundy is endless. Here (in alphabetical order) are a few of the best known and most reliable:

Bouchard Père et Fils	Louis Jadot
Bouchard Aîné	Louis Latour
J. Calvet et Cie	J. Moreau et Fils
Joseph Drouhin	J. Morin
J. Faiveley	J. H. Remy

But even an honest label, certified by a good shipper, may be misleading. The appellation contrôlée laws do not prevent this; they might even be considered "appellations uncontrôlée. The great vineyard of Chambertin is a case in point. A thousand or more years ago the monks of the Abbey of Bèze near the little town of Gevrey planted a vineyard on the slopes of the Côte de Nuits which came to be called the Vineyard of Bèze or Clos de Bèze. Either because they were lucky or because they had superior Guidance, the monks of Bèze planted on a spot capable of producing magnificent wine. Some time later an enterprising peasant named Bertin came along, cleared the land next to the Clos de Bèze, and planted a vineyard of his

---

* In recent years there has been a trend in Burgundy to follow Bordeaux in adopting the institution of château bottling. If any of the following language appears on a Burgundy label, there is a presumption, at least, that the wine is genuine:

Mis en bouteilles par le propriétaire	Mis au domaine
Mis de la propriété	Mise du domaine
Mis à la propriété	Mis en bouteilles au domaine

In Burgundy they cannot ordinarily say "Mis en bouteilles au château" as they do in Bordeaux, because rarely does one individual own an entire vineyard. If the label says, "Mis en bouteilles dans mes caves," that means "Bottled in my cellar," and is meaningless, since all wine is bottled in a cellar. If it says, "Mis en bouteilles au Château Such-and-such," be careful. Shippers will sometimes rent office space in a château, bottle wine that comes from anywhere down in the cellar, and then state on the label the correct but meaningless fact that the wine was bottled in that cellar.

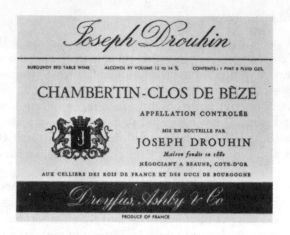

own. This vineyard turned out to be of nearly equal quality to the Clos de Bèze, and came to be known as Bertin's Field, or Champ de Bertin, and later simply Chambertin.

Perhaps because of the secular, enterprising nature of Bertin and his successors, the wines of Chambertin came in time to be better known than those of the original vineyard. So not only did six neighboring vineyards of somewhat lesser quality hyphenate the name Chambertin to their own, the Clos de Bèze itself, by now in secular hands, felt compelled to hyphenate the name Chambertin also, and the law allowed them all to do it. So now the buyer of these wines was confronted not only with a choice between Le Chambertin and Chambertin-Clos de Bèze, but also Latricières-Chambertin, Mazoyères-Chambertin, Charmes-Chambertin, Mazis-Chambertin, Ruchottes-Chambertin, Griotte-Chambertin, and Chapelle-Chambertin. This is not so bad, however, since all the lesser seven are very good wines, although none is as good as the original two.

But then the town fathers of little Gevrey nearby, not wanting to be left out of the good fortune, hyphenated the name of the great vineyard to the name of their town: Gevrey-Chambertin. This means that any wine of the entire village, including some eminently indifferent ones, can legally go to market under that name. Now the relatively inexperienced buyer does have a problem. In buying a bottle labeled Gevrey-Chambertin for perhaps six dollars, he may be under the impression that he is getting anything from a true Chambertin worth twenty dollars or more to a Charmes-Chambertin worth twelve dollars. And the quality even of the Gevrey-Chambertin can vary enormously, depending on the vineyard, the grower, the shipper, and the year.

This arrangement in the naming of Burgundy wines would be complicated enough if it were systematic. But it is anything but that. Some of the near neighbors of other great vineyards share their names through hyphenation; many, including some of the best, do not. The names of other villages have been hyphenated to that of their best vineyard; not all are.

The jurisdictions of the various wine villages *tend* to follow the natural boundaries of the vineyard clusters in which wines of a particular character occur, but jurisdiction over some clusters, and even some individual vineyards, is divided between more than one village.

The contrast between the business institutions of Bordeaux and those of Burgundy is nowhere more clearly dramatized than in methods of setting prices. In Bordeaux, as we noted, prices are set daily, on the basis of open, competitive bids on an orderly, established market, which in turn is supported by (and supports) the institutions of classification and the château. In Burgundy the basic price structure for each vintage is established by an auction, held once a year in November, at a curious institution called the Hospices de Beaune. The Hospices is a charity hospital, founded in 1433 by Nicolas Rolin, the tax collector of Louis XI. It controls more than forty parcels of vineyard land in the Côte de Beaune (*côte* means "slope"), one of the two outstanding regions of Burgundy. The parcels, including some in the best vineyards of that region, have been donated to the Hospices over the past five centuries, and the income from the wine supports its charitable activities.

There is obviously a greater continuity and quality to the management given by the Hospices to its considerable holdings than there is likely to be to the management given by any single peasant owner, chosen at random, to his few rows of grapes. So the wines of the Hospices not only as a rule sell at a premium over wines from the other parcels of the same vineyard, they have become more or less bench marks of value for most of the wines of Burgundy. The bids at the annual auction tend to establish the general price level for the whole district in a particular year, with prices of all other wines set—and changed—not in open daily auctions, but informally, within the trade, still further confirming the controlling position of the shipper.

All these commercial variables and imponderables raise problems for the buyer of wine that are all but insurmountable. He must distinguish the

name of a great vineyard from those of its hyphenated hangers-on (although some of them, like Chambertin-Clos de Bèze, are not hangers-on at all but as good as the original—in fact, Clos de Bèze *was* the original) and in turn distinguish these from that of a hyphenated township nearby. Then he needs to know the reputation of the shipper to check the fairness of the price and the reliability of whatever the label says; and it does not hurt to know the name of the importer and wholesaler, which also usually appear on the label, to double-check the reputation of the shipper.

Since no one can possibly know all this, it should be clear that drinking Burgundy, like growing it, is a tricky business. But because there are rewards in both cases, people go on doing it. However, a lover of Burgundies, even more than a lover of Bordeaux, has strong incentive to keep his own cellar, so that the effort required for prudent buying can be justified by volume purchases, and there can be a systematic accumulation of experience and records to improve your batting average in choosing the wines.

THE VINEYARDS OF THE DUCHY

Now the wines themselves: Bordeaux is a relatively unified, orderly district, and a geographically compact one. Burgundy is none of these. Its boundaries were set not by the growing range of one particular grape, nor by the trading area of a particular shipping center, but largely by the political boundaries of the old duchy. It can be said that it is really three districts, or even four. The most northerly vineyards, in the region of Chablis, have the location and characteristics of the northern third of the Wine Zone, where the lightest, almost delicate of white wines are grown. The most southerly regions, Mâcon and Beaujolais, one hundred or more miles to the south, begin to be transitional in climate and characteristics to the southern third. In between, in the twin regions of the Côte de Nuits and the Côte de Beaune, are grown some of the greatest reds and whites of the mid-zone. But although these last two regions adjoin each other, and their wines are related, the differences between them are more pronounced than the most extreme differences, let us say, between the wines of the Haut-Médoc and those of St.-Émilion of Bordeaux.

From these five widely separated regions of Burgundy come seven categories of wine (in contrast to the four from Bordeaux) that are popular enough, produced in enough volume, and widely enough available to win a place on our Spectrum of Possibility.

There are four white wines from:

> Chablis
> Meursault
> Montrachet
> Pouilly-Fuissé

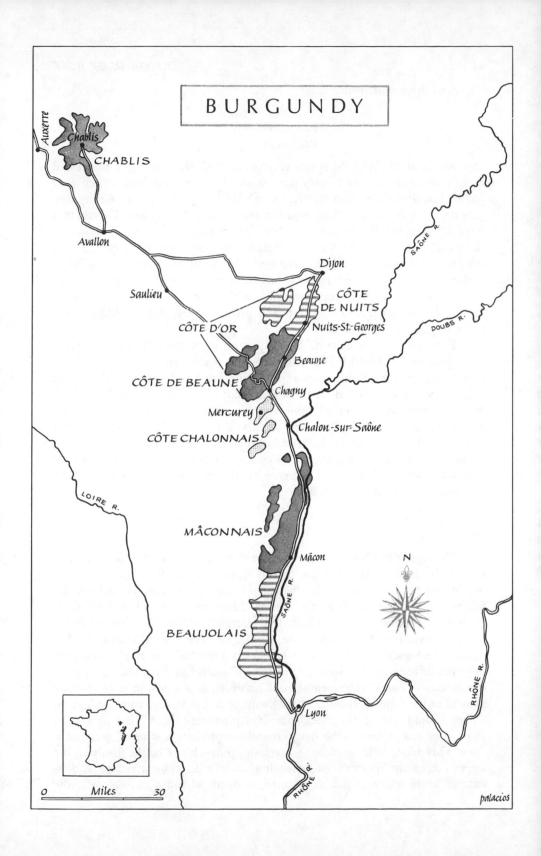

BURGUNDY

Auxerre

Chablis

CHABLIS

Avallon

Saulieu

Dijon

CÔTE DE NUITS

Nuits-St.-Georges

CÔTE D'OR

Beaune

CÔTE DE BEAUNE

Chagny

Mercurey

Chalon-sur-Saône

CÔTE CHALONNAIS

SAÔNE R.

DOUBS R.

LOIRE R.

MÂCONNAIS

Mâcon

N

BEAUJOLAIS

SAÔNE R.

Lyon

RHÔNE R.

RHÔNE R.

0   Miles   30

palacios

And three reds from:

> The Côte de Nuits
> Pommard
> Beaujolais

But even this brief list is not very orderly. Chablis from the north and Beaujolais from the south carry the names of the *regions* from which they come. Pouilly-Fuissé from the region of Mâcon, just north of Beaujolais, gets its name from two villages within the region, Pouilly and Fuissé, that have hyphenated themselves together. Pommard, Meursault, and Montrachet all come from the Côte de Beaune, the more southerly of the twin regions of the mid-zone. Pommard and Meursault are named for *villages* within the region. Montrachet was originally the name of a great *vineyard*, which was then hyphenated not only to the names of several adjoining vineyards, but to the names of *two* nearby villages; Puligny-Montrachet and Chassagne-Montrachet.

The region of the Côte de Nuits, just north of the Côte de Beaune, is analogous to the Haut-Médoc of Bordeaux in that it produces in a relatively small area an astonishing proportion of the great red wines of the world (all of the truly great red wine, in fact, that is produced outside of Bordeaux) along with a considerable number of very fine ones. It is quite proper to go into a wine store and ask for a Côte de Nuits (they are also called Northern Burgundies), but as in the case of the wines of the Haut-Médoc, the bottle you buy is more likely to carry the name of a village or individual vineyard within the region, and you will need experience or guidance to know it for what it is.

CHABLIS

The region of Chablis does not even share a watershed with the rest of Burgundy. It is located on the banks of the Yonne River, which flows northward to the Seine, while the rest of the *vignoble* is located on the Saône, which flows south to the Rhône. Moreover, the soil of Chablis is chalky (the same band of chalk that forms the famous white cliffs of Dover) in contrast to the limestone pebbles or decomposed granite farther south. Geologically, flint sometimes occurs imbedded in chalk, and perhaps for this reason the clean, dry taste of Chablis has for a long time been described as "flinty." The weather of Chablis is, in a word, terrible. As one grower of the Côte de Beaune to the south once put it, referring to Chablis, "They should tear up the vines and plant pine trees there." But in a good year—one out of three—the risky conditions produce a wine of great delicacy. This, along with its clean, flinty taste, puts white Chablis firmly at the upper end of our Spectrum of Possibility, among the lightest and most delicate of white wines. It is a good wine to drink with fish or seafoods, the

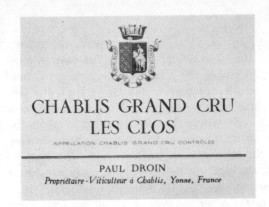

lightest and most delicate of dishes, and is the classic accompaniment to raw oysters.

The best wines of Chablis are grown in a semicircle of hills facing, as might be expected, to the south, where the grapes can bask in the sun, sheltered from the cold northern winds. These are the best vineyards, the Grands Crus, or Great Growths:

Blanchot	Vaudésir
Les Clos	Bougros
Grenouilles	La Moutonne
Valmur	Les Preuses

And here are some of the next best but very fine vineyards, the Premiers Crus, or First Growths:

Beauroy	Mélinots	Vaîllons
Côte de Léchet	Monts de Milieu	Vaucoupin
Fourchaume	Montée de Tonnerre	Vaulorent
Les Fourneaux	Montmains	Vosgros and Vogiras

The vineyards of Chablis, like those of the rest of Burgundy, are heavily subdivided among a number of owners. This far north, subdivision is a form of insurance. If hail or frost wipes out the crop on a man's holdings in one vineyard, his holdings in others will hopefully not be touched. But this means that a vineyard name on a Chablis label has no more meaning here than elsewhere in Burgundy unless it is backed by the name of a reputable shipper, or indicates estate-bottling by a reliable grower.

THE CÔTE DE NUITS

Even leaving aside purely commercial deception, there seems to be an evil demon in the naming of wines. The Côte de Nuits and its neighbor to the south, the Côte de Beaune, are actually subdivisions of a chain of hills known as the Côte d'Or, the Slope of Gold. The Slope of Gold (both sections together) is a limestone ridge about thirty-five miles long, facing slightly to the south of east, where, of course, it catches the sun's first light. The Côte d'Or is actually the eastern-most range of foothills of the Massif Central, the great mountain range of south-central France. Particularly on the northern of the two slopes, the Côte de Nuits, the very best vineyards occupy what might be called the "elbow" of the mountain, the slight angle where the tilt of the slope meets the flat of the plain. Here a wine of the hill comes very close to being a wine of the plain—nature getting the best of both worlds again. The best vineyards of all, with their faint tilt, pick up the rays of the early sun just a bit sooner than the ones below, and are slightly better drained. The vineyards just below or to one side or the other are very good but not truly great. The wines on the flat of the plain a few hundred feet away are little more than *ordinaires*. The average width of the entire vineyard strip of the Côte d'Or is only about six hundred feet, and the difference in altitude between its upper and lower edges is no more than fifty feet. (Not surprisingly, in Burgundy the name for vineyard is *climat,* showing that Burgundians know very well just how crucial is exposure to the growing of fine wines.)

The red wines of the Côte de Nuits are what people mean when they refer simply to "Burgundy"—a big, "booty," full-bodied, earthy red wine (although, as we have already indicated, there are exceptions to this generalization too).

Because of the luxuriant profusion of hyphenated names in the Côte de Nuits, and the lack of system in the way the hyphens are applied, there is no easy, shorthand way for remembering the names of its vineyards and villages. However, Burgundians have a saying to cover this problem, as Frenchmen do for all problems. They say *"Respectez les crus":* Pay attention to the names of the vineyards themselves, and don't be distracted by hyphenated glitter. The guideposts of northern Burgundy are the names of its very great vineyards. On these hang all the law—and much of the profit.

The best wines of the Côte de Nuits occur in a series of eight clusters, running north and south along the slope.* Of these eight, six are preeminent. In each of these six clusters is one vineyard (or in one case a section of a vineyard) which stands out above the rest. Any attempt to master the wine names of the Côte de Nuits begins with the names of these six famous vineyards. Here they are, in generally accepted order of merit:

> Romanée-Conti
> Chambertin (and Chambertin-Clos de Bèze)
> Musigny
> Clos de Vougeot
> Bonnes Mares
> Grands-Échézeaux

* A map of the Côte de Nuits appears on page 79.

These six great vineyards are analogous in a very rough sort of way to the four immortals of the Haut-Médoc. The vineyard of Romanée-Conti is comparable only to the great Château Lafite itself, and since it consists of only 4½ acres, compared to 150 acres for Lafite, the wines of Romanée-Conti are that much more rare.

Now here, north to south, are the names of the seven communes in which these six famous vineyard clusters are located:

Vineyard	Commune
Chambertin	Gevrey-Chambertin
Bonnes Mares	Chambolle-Musigny and Morey-St.-Denis
Musigny	Chambolle-Musigny
Clos de Vougeot	Vougeot
Grands-Échézeaux	Flagey-Échézeaux
Romanée-Conti	Vosne-Romanée

Just to the north and south of the six best-known clusters are the two lesser clusters, near the commune of Fixin to the north and Nuits-St.-Georges to the south. (The town of Nuits—*nuit* means "night"—gave the Côte de Nuits its name.)

These nine communes of the Côte de Nuits are analogous to the four best-known communes of the Haut-Médoc of Bordeaux as points of origin for the finest wines. In the matter of labeling, however, there is a difference. In Bordeaux the individual châteaux (vineyards) do not carry their own appellations contrôlées, the presumption being that in Bordeaux the châteaux name alone is guarantee enough. So the appellation appearing on the label of a château-bottling from Bordeaux will be that of the *commune* of origin; this can help the inexperienced buyer to identify the source and character of the wine. In most of Burgundy by contrast *individual vineyards* do in fact have their own separate appellations contrôlées. So the finer wines will not necessarily carry the commune of origin on the label, and the beginner may be denied even this little extra guidance.

There are several dozen other vineyards of exceptional merit, and hundreds more that can be better than average, in the eight principal wine

Côte de Beaune

N

CÔTE DE NUITS

Pernand-
Vergelesses

CORTON-CHARLEMAGNE

Aloxe-Corton

Savigny-
les-Beaune

Beaune

Pommard

Volnay

Meursault

Puligny-Montrachet

MONTRACHET

Chassagne-
Montrachet

Chagny

Santenay

▲ Outstanding Vineyards

O   Miles   4

palacios

clusters of the Côte de Nuits. We shall say more about them later. But this is enough for purposes of constructing our Spectrum of Possibility.

THE CÔTE DE BEAUNE: POMMARD, MEURSAULT, MONTRACHET

South of Nuits-St.-Georges, the ridge line of the Côte d'Or breaks and the vineyards peter out. A short distance farther down, the ridge begins again, with a hill called Corton, and so do the vineyards. This is the beginning of the Côte de Beaune, the more southerly of the two regions of the Côte d'Or. But here the character of the slope changes, and with it the character of the wines: the exposure is more southerly and the hills gentler, softer. In place of the awesome nobility of the great, full reds of the north we now find generally softer, rounder, lighter reds, along with unique, fascinating, and noble whites.

The Côte de Beaune is unlike any other region of either Burgundy or Bordeaux in the variety it offers, not only of fine wines but of *important* wines in commercial terms. No other region of either of the two major districts offers more than one wine of sufficient quality that is sold in adequate volume to rate a place on our Spectrum of Possibility. The Côte de Beaune offers three, along with three others no person who wants to be well informed about wines can afford to ignore. In all the world of wines, no other area offers this combination of superior quality, fascinating diversity, and volume production.

The key to the variety of the wines of the Côte de Beaune is the fact that this is a transitional region. At its northern end are grown the great reds of Corton. At its southern end are grown the great whites of Montrachet. In between are grown five lesser wines—three reds, two whites—which illustrate, step by step, the evolution from conditions which make possible great reds to those which produce great whites.

The red wines of Corton, at the northern end of the Côte de Beaune, are rich and full, the only wines of the Beaune slope comparable to the great, full reds of the Côte de Nuits, with which they are usually classed. As you move southward, the reds grow progressively lighter. Up to a point this is not a bad thing. The soft, delightful red wines from in between are very popular, very plentiful, very profitable. Finally they become too light to command a really good price, but are still much too fine and delicate to be sold off merely as common reds. Now we have a situation where there is incentive for experimentation. Some time in the last two thousand years someone found that the land that produces too-light reds will make white wines of unique fullness and fascination.*

Here are the six principal wines of the Côte de Beaune, north to south, with entries on the Spectrum of Possibility capitalized:

Wine	Character	Quality
Corton	Full red	Great
	Full white	Great
Beaune	Medium red	Good
POMMARD	Medium red	Fine
Volnay	Light red	Finer
MEURSAULT	Full white	Very fine
MONTRACHET	Very full white	Very great

* The line between conditions suited for growing red wines and those appropriate for growing whites can be very fine indeed. On the hill of Corton in the north of the Côte de Beaune, the great full reds are grown across one part of the slope; great whites are grown on a strip of soil just above it. The greatest whites are grown in Montrachet, farther south. But just south of Montrachet, soil conditions abruptly turn favorable to reds again. In between, in a number of vineyards known for fine reds, good whites are also grown.

Corton. The wines of Corton are grown at an average altitude of about 900 feet above sea level; the other fine wines farther south on the Côte de Beaune at an average of about 750 feet. It is probably this added altitude, compensating for their more southerly location, that makes it possible to grow red wines here that are comparable in fullness to those of the Côte de Nuits to the north. Jurisdiction over the vineyards of the Corton cluster is divided between no fewer than three little communes, of which the most important is Aloxe-Corton. A list of superior vineyards is given below. The Cortons, red and white, are not separately named in the Spectrum of Possibility only because the supply is not large. A full red Corton, like the full reds of the Côte de Nuits to the north, would go best with beef or game or a stew with a rich, full sauce.

Here are some of the best vineyards of Corton:

Red Wines	*Red and White Wines*
Le Corton	Charlemagne
Les Bressandes	
Le Clos du Roi	
Les Renardes	

The great white wine from the Charlemagne vineyard is called Corton-Charlemagne. Tradition has it that the Emperor Charles himself planted that vineyard (although no one can prove it).

Beaune. The charming medieval town of Beaune is the main shipping point for all of Burgundy, has given its name to the entire southern section of the Côte d'Or, and stores in its *caves* (that is, cellars) many of the greatest wines of the province, but the bulk of the red wines grown there are not especially distinguished. The ridge line at Beaune is broken by a series of shallow ravines, which do not offer precisely the correct angle of exposure to the early sun, and perhaps allow too much wind to reach the grapes. The wines of Beaune are plentiful, however, and good, and a few of the best vineyards are very fine. One of the best vineyards, Le Clos des Mouches, also produces a soft, full white. (The *village* wines of Beaune should not be confused with the lesser *regional* wines which carry the name *Côte de Beaune* and can come from any of the villages of the Beaune slope.)

Here are some of the best vineyards of Beaune:

Les Fèves	Les Bressandes
Les Grèves	Le Clos des Mouches
Les Marconnets	

The famous Hospices de Beaune is located at Beaune. Its wines go to market under the name of the Hospices itself along with the name of the original donor of the parcel in question and the name of its commune of origin (see Appendix, page 312). Here are some of the better-known wines of the Hospices de Beaune:

RED WINES

Commune	Parcel
Beaune	Brunet
Beaune	Dames Hospitalières
Beaune	Guigone de Salins
Beaune	Nicolas Rolin
Pommard	Billardet
Pommard	Dames de la Charité
Aloxe-Corton	Charlotte Dumay
Aloxe-Corton	Dr. Peste
Volnay	Blondeau

WHITE WINES

Meursault-Charmes	de Bahèzre de Lanlay
Meursault-Charmes	Albert Grivault
Meursault-Genevrières	Baudot

Pommard. South of Beaune, without a break in the vineyards, is the commune of Pommard. Like the wines of Beaune, those of Pommard are lighter, softer reds, typical of the Beaune slope. But the best vineyards of Pommard lie at the mouth of a little ravine that makes a deep indentation into the ridge, but does not pierce it. This box-canyon effect apparently provides better protection from the wind than the fluted slopes above Beaune. As a result, these soft gentle reds, rarely great, are *very* good— even the ones of the village grade. Lacking the distinction and subtlety, along with the fullness, of the great reds to the north, they are actually more pleasing to the untrained palate. Thus the village wines of Pommard are perhaps the best known and most popular of all red Burgundies. Three times as much Pommard is shipped to the United States, for example, as any other red wine of the Côte d'Or. But herein lies the problem. Because of its popularity, Pommard is among the most forged and tampered-with wines in the world. A very high proportion of the communal grade Pommard that makes its way to the United States is Pommard in name only. Thus the name of a good shipper—or merchant or restaurateur, if you

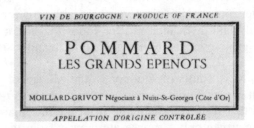

VIN DE BOURGOGNE - PRODUCE OF FRANCE

POMMARD
LES GRANDS EPENOTS

MOILLARD-GRIVOT Négociant à Nuits-St-Georges (Côte d'Or)

APPELLATION D'ORIGINE CONTRÔLÉE

know him well—is your only assurance, and by no means an iron-clad one.

The finest vineyards of Pommard are listed below. The name of one of these on a label gives better assurance of quality and authenticity, particularly if followed by the name of a good shipper (although the price may be more than double that of a communal Pommard):

Les Épenots	Les Petits-Épenots
Les Rugiens-Bas	Les Rugiens-Hauts
La Platière	Clos de la Commaraine
Les Pézerolles	

Volnay. Just south of Pommard, again without a break in the vineyards, is Volnay, which in terms of general characteristics can be discussed in the same breath as Pommard. The best wines of Volnay are grown against a slightly concave hill face which perhaps offers better wind protection but also a slightly lower average temperature than the indentation of Pommard. A Volnay is usually a finer wine than Pommard, somewhat more delicate, a bit more expensive. Volnay is also less plentiful. But being harder to find and more expensive, Volnay is in less demand than Pommard, and therefore more likely to be reliable. So the added cost is in part an insurance policy.

Here are some of the best vineyards of Volnay:

Les Caillerets	Santenots
Les Champans	Clos des Ducs
Les Fremiers	En Chevret

In terms of matching, the lighter reds of the Beaune slope—Beaune, Pommard, Volnay—are in a situation quite analogous to that of the St.-Émilions of Bordeaux. As we have noted, the St.-Émilions are fuller than a "typical" Bordeaux, not as full as most Burgundies. By the same token, Beaune reds are lighter, on average, than those of the Côte de Nuits, but are still not "light wines" by the standards of Bordeaux. (If we had a category called "Medium-bodied Reds," both St.-Émilion and the Beaune reds would probably fall into it.)

Thus it is correct to drink the Beaune reds with the same foods—beef, game, rich stews—with which you would have drunk one of the great reds of the Côte de Nuits had you been able to afford it. But given a choice, you could take a Beaune red for foods that are a shade lighter in flavor—winged game over the four-legged kind, blander stews, beef served without a rich sauce.

Meursault. Next south of Volnay is the village of Meursault. The name Meursault means "mouse-jump," and one of the oft-told tales of the wine country is that it derived its name from the fact that the white wines of Meursault are grown only a mouse-jump away from the reds of Volnay.

A charming story, but a doubtful one, perhaps the conclusion of some wine writer who drove by in a car. The wines of Meursault that grow only a mouse-jump away from those of Volnay are by and large red wines, and go to market under the name Volnay, as they properly should, since conditions are comparable. All the best *white* wines of Meursault are grown in another cluster, on the slopes of the next hill south, across the Meursault River (which few mice have ever been known to jump).

The best white wines of Meursault (like the white wines of Corton to the north) are grown not on the slopes that face conventionally east, but on steeper slopes that face more to the south. The steepness tends perhaps to create a greater fullness in the wine, abetted, no doubt, by the southward-facing position, with its more direct exposure to the midday sun.

The Meursault whites, like those of Montrachet, its greater neighbor to the south, are totally different in character from the wines of Chablis, seventy-five miles to the west and north: fuller in body, broader in range, but still bone-dry, without the heaviness, the seeming sweetness, of even the better white Graves of Bordeaux. As between the two, Meursault is usually softer than Montrachet and not as big. Meursault in a sense is a prefatory township, where conditions for producing truly great wine have not quite come into focus. But if Meursault is a preface, it is a delightful and rewarding preface. It is also an honest preface, relatively honest anyway; it is profitable to tamper with Meursault, and it is done. But it is vastly more profitable to tamper with great Montrachet next door, and more frequently done.

Listed below are some of the better vineyards of Meursault:

Santenots	Les Charmes
Clos des Perrières	La Goutte d'Or
Les Perrières	Sous-Blagny
Les Genevrières (Dessus & Dessous)	

Montrachet. The southernmost of the fine vineyards of the Meursault cluster spill over into the jurisdiction of the village of Puligny, which has naturally taken unto itself the name of its great vineyard, Montrachet. The Montrachet cluster itself is located against the eastward face of the next hill south of the Meursault cluster. Here we do find a counterpart of the classic *climat* of the Côte d'Or: vineyards nestling in the "elbow" of the mountain, with a slightly concave hill face providing exceptional protection from the wind. And here we find the greatest *dry* white wine on earth, perhaps the only truly great one.

The genius of most of the best white wines is their delicacy; yet the secret of real greatness in any wine, red or white, is sufficient amplitude, range, force, to make a statement of a certain vigor, and to provide room for significant complexity of flavor. Thus, Chablis, which is delicate, lacks fullness, while white Graves, which is full, lacks delicacy. Montrachet, which has both, is once again a contradiction in terms, nature getting the best of both worlds—and achieving a transcendent result because she does.

Listed below, in generally accepted order of quality, are the great and near-great vineyards of Puligny-Montrachet:

Montrachet (in part)	Blagny-Blanc
Le Bâtard-Montrachet (in part)	Champ-Canet
Le Chevalier-Montrachet	Pucelles
Bienvenue-Bâtard	Les Chalumeaux
Les Combettes	

The white wines of the Beaune slope—white Corton, Meursault, Montrachet—being relatively full-bodied, would not ordinarily be served with so light a dish as oysters, but with something fuller: chicken or veal, unsauced or in a relatively light sauce; or fish or seafood in a rich, creamy white sauce.

Most of the acreage of the truly great vineyards of Montrachet lies within the commune of Puligny, but enough lies across the line in neighboring Chassagne to give it a hyphenated claim to fame, which it willingly exercises. Aside from its segments of the two best vineyards of all, Le Montrachet and Bâtard-Montrachet, along with the vineyard of Criots which has hyphenated itself to Bâtard-Montrachet—a not uncommon double hyphenation—the remaining vineyards of Chassagne are not part of the Montrachet cluster at all, but grow on the flat face of the next hill down. And as it happens, the best wines of this cluster are reds, not whites. These are nice minor red wines, very pleasant, and not notable or expensive enough to be tampered with. But because of their commune of origin, these minor reds carry with them to market the name and some of the glory of the greatest white wine in the world, an anomaly all too typical of the world of wines.

Here are the wines of Chassagne-Montrachet, red and white:

White Wines	Red Wines
Montrachet (in part)	Le Clos St.-Jean
Le Bâtard-Montrachet (in part)	Clos de la Boudriotte
Les Ruchottes	Les Boudriottes
Morgeot	La Maltroie or La Maltroye
Cailleret	
Criots-Bâtard-Montrachet	

Below Chassagne, the slope tapers off, with a little village called Santenay, the last wine town of the Côte d'Or. It produces minor red wines in the same cluster that produces the reds of Chassagne.

SOUTHERN BURGUNDY:
POUILLY-FUISSÉ, BEAUJOLAIS

A few miles south of the Slope of Gold is a region called the Côte Chalonnaise after the city of Chalon on the Saône nearby. Here are grown light reds, similar in character but not in quality to those of Pommard and Volnay, along with fullish but not distinguished whites.

Pouilly-Fuissé. Perhaps ten miles south of the Côte Chalonnaise, at the southern end of the region of Mâcon, named for the adjoining city, is grown the good and extremely popular white wine, Pouilly-Fuissé, which gets its name from the villages of Pouilly and Fuissé, which have hyphenated themselves together.

The slopes of Pouilly and Fuissé face generally north of east. A few miles farther north this exposure might at best produce *ordinaires*. Down here there is enough warmth to mature the grapes, but not enough to produce good reds. So the skins are removed after the crush, and the result is the green-gold, dry, and delightful Pouilly-Fuissé, a wine midway in body between the very delicate Chablis and the fuller Meursault and Montrachet—but not as fine as the best of the others.

Three other villages that share the slope with Pouilly and Fuissé have the right to send their wines to market as Pouilly-Fuissé. In addition, two other nearby villages have adopted the name Pouilly: Pouilly-Loché and Pouilly-Vinzelles. The vineyard slope is less gradual in these last two, the average quality of the wine not as high. But considering the great demand for wine under the label of Pouilly-Fuissé, and the tampering that is therefore profitable, a bottle of one of its less-known neighbors, if you can find one, might easily present better value.

Like the white wines of the Beaune slope, Pouilly-Fuissé and its neighbors would ordinarily be drunk with fish, chicken, or veal. But this is a simpler wine, calling for a dish of simpler preparation: fish that is baked or served in a light sauce, broiled chicken in a light sauce, veal that is served very plain.*

Beaujolais. The white wines of Pouilly-Fuissé are grown at the southern end of the region of Mâcon, while the best of the reds of Beaujolais are grown in the northern end of the region of that name, so the two are near neighbors. But the slopes of Beaujolais face generally to the south of east, in contrast to the northeasterly exposure of Pouilly-Fuissé, so the more sunlit exposure makes it possible to produce red wines. But there is another important difference. The soil of Pouilly-Fuissé is composed of the same chalky limestone as most of the rest of Burgundy. In Beaujolais next door the soil is made up of decomposed granite and clay. As we have noted, the great grape of the Côte d'Or is called Pinot Noir. Another grape, Gamay, is a more plentiful producer, but in the Côte d'Or produces horrible wine. On the granite soil of Beaujolais, however, the situation is reversed. Presumably because the granite absorbs water less well than limestone and reflects light better, here the despised Gamay produces a simple, vigorous wine of unique freshness and charm, while the Pinot Noir makes wine of no particular distinction.

Red Beaujolais is a popular wine in every sense of the word. A simple, direct wine, in diametric contrast to the subtlety and complexity of the great reds of the Côte d'Or; a plentiful wine, sold at a price within the reach of most pocketbooks; a reliable wine, at least meteorologically, its vineyards being located far enough south to escape the risky weather farther north; from here on south the vintage years do not matter as much. In another sense it is not so reliable, of course. Since the demand is very great the incentive to tamper is great, too. Far more wine goes to market under the label Beaujolais than could ever be grown in the region of that name.

Beaujolais is a rather full wine, speaking in terms of body alone. But it has a fruity freshness, in total contrast to the great reds to the north. The noble reds of northern Burgundy are best drunk at room temperature, so as to release every nuance of flavor and bouquet, and are so big a drinker tends to sip them. Fruity, sprightly, thirst-quenching Beaujolais is best served chilled, like beer or cider, and like beer or cider is a wine you want to gulp, not sip.

It could be said that the wines of Beaujolais are what a person who had never tasted wine might expect from wine, and no doubt that is why they are so very popular with beginning wine drinkers. But their popularity

---

* In the midsummer of 1971 there was big news in the area of Pouilly and Fuissé. After a wait of twenty-four years—they applied in 1947—seven other wine towns of the area had been granted the right to an appellation of their own. They will henceforth go to market as St.-Véran. Curiously, none of the seven towns itself is called St.-Véran, although one of them is called St.-Vérand, with a "d." However, there is another St.-Vérand, with a "d," down in the Beaujolais country, and so to avoid giving a commercial advantage to a neighbor, the seven towns insisted that their appellation be St.-Véran, without the "d." St.-Véran is a kind of a petit Pouilly-Fuissé, and since it sells for about half the price, it should represent excellent value, at least until the American market discovers it fully.

goes beyond novices. For simple, forthright dishes such as bouillabaisse, various other stews, calf's liver, chicken liver, kidneys, or the famous bean stew cassoulet, simple, forthright Beaujolais is perfect.

An old rule for ordering wine in any unfamiliar or uncertain situation is "When in doubt, Beaujolais." If you don't know the establishment or the wine list, you can assume the Beaujolais will not be too bad, both because it is such a popular wine the management cannot afford to serve too awful a bottle, and because the supply turns over so fast it is unlikely to be spoiled, even by clumsy handling. Many people of excellent palate, when they have been to a cocktail party and have ruined their taste buds with martinis, will order Beaujolais when they go to dinner—at this point they could hardly appreciate anything more.

There are eight important villages in the region of Beaujolais. Their names on a bottle tend to be an indication of superior wine. Here they are:

Juliénas	Chénas
St.-Amour	Fleurie
Moulin-à-Vent	Morgon
Chiroubles	Brouilly

Below Beaujolais the Saône River joins the great river Rhône, and on this geographic pretext the wine district of the Rhône begins. We shall survey the wines of the Rhône in the next chapter.

Here is the Spectrum of Possibility as it has developed for Burgundy:

	Basic Spectrum	*Secondary Listings*
Light and Delicate White	CHABLIS POUILLY-FUISSÉ	—
Fuller-bodied White	MEURSAULT MONTRACHET	White Corton
Light-bodied Red	—	—
Fuller-bodied Red	POMMARD BEAUJOLAIS CÔTE DE NUITS*	Volnay Côte de Beaune Red Corton

* Oversimplification: Not all red wines of the Côte de Nuits are full-bodied.

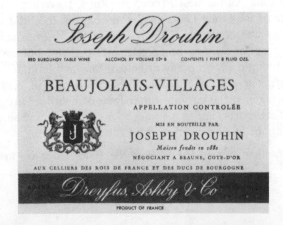

478 THE GAME OF WINE

And here is the combined Spectrum for Burgundy and Bordeaux. This shows that the two districts together provide a good range along most of the Spectrum:

	Basic Spectrum	Secondary Listings
Light and Delicate White	CHABLIS POUILLY-FUISSÉ	—
Fuller-bodied White	MEURSAULT MONTRACHET	White Corton White Graves
Light-bodied Red	HAUT-MÉDOC* RED GRAVES	(Bas-) Médoc
Fuller-bodied Red	ST.-ÉMILION POMMARD BEAUJOLAIS CÔTE DE NUITS*	Volnay Côte de Beaune Pomerol Red Corton

THE MIRACLE OF THE CÔTE DE NUITS

Before we can leave the great *vignoble* of Burgundy, we must, as we did in Bordeaux, return to its most famous region and take a closer look at the treasures there. In the Haut-Médoc we studied the role of the gravelly terrain and the distance from the river, along with the proportion of pebbles and sand in the soil, for clues to the quality and character of the wine. As for the Côte d'Or, of which the Côte de Nuits is the northern section, we have already seen that the character and quality of the wines are determined by the location of each vineyard relative to a chain of rounded, brush-covered hills that rises three to six hundred feet above the plain of the Saône River. In the Côte de Nuits, four little hills are the ones that count. We shall call them in the military manner Hill A, Hill B, Hill C, and Hill D.

Let us now take a tour, north to south, along the slopes of the Côte de Nuits.

Fixin. Not far south of Dijon, the seat of the old dukes of Burgundy and the source today of the best French mustard, traveling along Highway 74, "The Route of the Great Growths," you come to the little wine town of Fixin. (Route 74 was obviously built to service the vineyards. It goes close enough to the greatest ones to be convenient to them, but not so high up the slope that it would chew up any priceless vineyard land.)

Fixin is situated a bit over three miles north of Hill A. Its vineyards are not located against the curving outer face of a hill as are many of the very greatest Burgundies, but in a small pocket or indentation in the slope, much in the manner of Pommard in the Côte de Beaune.

* Oversimplification: Not all red wines of the Haut-Médoc are light-bodied, not all from the Côte de Nuits are full-bodied.

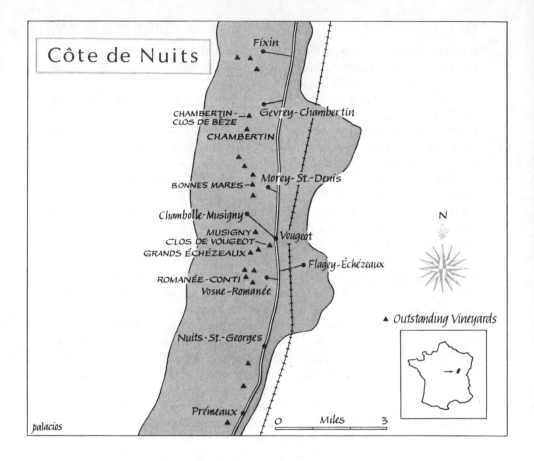

Côte de Nuits

Fixin

CHAMBERTIN- Gevrey-Chambertin
CLOS DE BÈZE
CHAMBERTIN

Morey-St.-Denis
BONNES MARES-

Chambolle-Musigny
MUSIGNY
CLOS DE VOUGEOT Vougeot
GRANDS ÉCHÉZEAUX
Flagey-Échézeaux
ROMANÉE-CONTI
Vosne-Romanée

Nuits-St.-Georges

N

Prémeaux
0   Miles   3

▲ Outstanding Vineyards

palacios

Like the wines of Arcins in the Haut-Médoc, or of Meursault in the Côte de Beaune, the wines of Fixin are introductory wines. They are not great, but they contain a hint of greatness coming. They are true Burgundies and true Northern Burgundies, with a big powerful bouquet, full body, and dark, rich color. Because they have in the past been overlooked for their more famous neighbors, the wines of Fixin are usually better bargains. Here are the two you are likely to see in the United States:

Clos de la Perrière
Clos du Chapitre

The Clos de la Perrière, the best vineyard of the commune, ranks twenty-first in quality among all the vineyards of the Côte de Nuits. This is respectable, but not so eminent that it was considered profitable to hyphenate the vineyard name to the village name. Thus, Fixin is the only commune of the eight principal wine towns of the Côte de Nuits that does not share its name with that of one of its vineyards.

The Chambertin Cluster. About a mile south of Fixin, at the mouth of a ravine (where the wind would be too strong and the wines not good), is

the little town of Gevrey, which has hyphenated unto itself the name of the
great vineyard of Chambertin, located a few hundred yards farther south,
up against the face of Hill A.

In touring the Haut-Médoc, which is noted for the delicacy of its wines,
the first of the immortals you reach is Margaux, the most delicate of all. In
touring the Côte de Nuits, which is famous for its full-bodied wines, the first
great vineyard that appears is Chambertin, the fullest-bodied of them all.
Chambertin was the favorite wine of Napoleon, provided to him even on
his Russian campaign. Of Chambertin, Alexis Lichine writes, "Burgundians talk of its robe, or deep, rich color, and of its balance and fullness,
all its various taste characteristics blending to make a majestic unity. Its
tremendous nose—bouquet is too delicate a word—makes it a veritable
Cyrano. When you have drunk Chambertin you remember it."

The nature of the slope suggests a reason for the supreme full-
bodiedness of Chambertin. Hill A is a square-shouldered hill on its eastern
side, slightly convex, and steeper-faced than its neighbors. This conforma-
tion, similar to that of great, full white Montrachet to the south, not only
gives Chambertin maximum exposure to the early sun and reflects heat in
and down upon the vineyard, but provides the fullest possible protection
from the winds off the mountains to the west, a sort of air pocket in which
the grapes can "bake." The rugged, robust wines of the Rhône to the south
enjoy similar conditions, and one of them, a very full one, comes from the
Côte Rôtie, "the roasted slope." But the cooler general climate of northern
Burgundy gives Chambertin a delicacy, a nobility, in addition to its body,
that few if any of the Rhônes can match.

Here are the great and fine wines of Chambertin that you are likely to
encounter in the market. They all share the powerful bouquet, intensity of
character, and rich color of this manliest of northern Burgundies.

Le Chambertin	Griotte-Chambertin
Chambertin-Clos de Bèze	Chapelle-Chambertin
Latricières-Chambertin	Clos St.-Jacques
Mazis-Chambertin	Véroilles
Mazoyères-Chambertin	Ruchottes-Chambertin
Charmes-Chambertin	

The Bonnes Mares Cluster. Next down the road from the Chambertin cluster is the little town of Morey that has hyphenated itself not with its first vineyard, the Clos de Tart, but with its fifth, Clos St.-Denis. Perhaps the town fathers were reluctant to identify themselves too closely with a Tart. Morey-St.-Denis is located at the mouth of the ravine that separates Hill A from Hill B, and not surprisingly the wines to the north of the town, grown on the southern shoulder of Hill A, are similar in character to the neighboring Chambertins, while those to the south of town, on the northern slope of Hill B, share the character of the far softer, more delicate wines typical of that slope. The wines in the middle, squarely in the mouth of the ravine, are far less distinguished. Too much wind again.

The most famous vineyard of Hill B is Bonnes Mares, located, as the map shows, across the foot of the hill. The northern five acres of Bonnes Mares are in the township of Morey-St.-Denis. Indeed, the best vineyard of Morey, the Clos de Tart, could almost be considered a northern extension of Bonnes Mares. The shoulders of Hill B are rounder than those of Hill A; its face more curved, its top less broad. One can theorize that with the greater ventilation here the wines have less opportunity to "roast" than those of Chambertin. In any case, the wines of Bonnes Mares and its neighbors are far softer and more delicate, among the most "feminine" of the Northern Burgundies.

Here are some of the best vineyards claimed by Morey-St.-Denis:

Clos de Tart	Clos de la Roche
Clos des Lambrays	Clos St.-Denis
Bonnes Mares (in part)	

The Musigny Cluster. The ravine between Hill B and Hill C is much deeper than that between Hills A and B, and not surprisingly there is a wide area of second- and third-class vineyards at the mouth of it, along with the village of Chambolle, which has hyphenated its name to the great vineyard immediately to its south, Musigny. Musigny is located, as we would expect, on the eastern slope of Hill C. But with nature's infinite variety, Hill C is neither flat nor round, it is kidney-shaped. It is easy to theorize that the winds blowing through the ravine to the north of the hill would create an undesirable turbulence in the "pocket" that lies just north and west of Musigny, and indeed the wines grown in that pocket are third-class. With Hill B as long and slim as it is, we might assume that the vines on its southeast face would be even better ventilated than those of Bonnes Mares, and that the wines would be even more delicate, distinguished, and "feminine." They are. Here are the best known of them:

Les Musigny
Les Bonnes Mares (in major part)
Les Amoureuses

There is not a clean break between Hills C and D, but a kind of double ravine, with a steep-sided hillock between, creating almost the effect of an amphitheater, curving southward from Musigny, a little over two miles across. In Bordeaux, when you come to the town of Pauillac, you have reached the grand crescendo of the Haut-Médoc. So in the Côte de Nuits, when you come to the vineyard of Musigny at the northern edge of this ragged little amphitheater, you have reached the culmination, the majestic climax, of the Côte de Nuits. Spread out before you in just a few hundred yards of poor-looking soil are three of the four greatest wines of Burgundy, including the greatest of them all.

The Vineyard of Vougeot. The whole amphitheater affords relatively good protection from the wind, but minor variations in exposure make major differences in the wines. Just a few feet downhill from delicate Musigny and slightly south, literally across the road and over a big stone wall, is the Clos de Vougeot. As the wine books will tell you again and again, for many years it has been a tradition among regiments of the French Army passing the gate of the Clos de Vougeot to stop and salute the greatness of this wine.

Vougeot is farther around the shoulder of the mountain than Musigny and we may assume less exposed to the breezes that blow between Hills B and C. It is also farther down in the flat, less well drained. Not surprisingly, Vougeot is again a full and sturdy wine, not as big as Chambertin, much bigger than Musigny. The best Vougeot has traditionally come from the northwest corner of the vineyard, close against the border of Musigny, where the land begins to rise, improving the drainage, and the hill affords the best protection. Centuries ago the wine from this section was reserved by the abbot of the Monastery of Vougeot for gifts to kings and to princes of the church.

Here are the owners of parcels of Vougeot whose wines are likely to be found in the United States:

J. Morin	G. Grivot	P. Missey
Madame Noëllat	Louis Gros	J. Faiveley
Champy Père & Fils		

The Two Échézeaux. Just uphill from the lower portion of Vougeot—again, just over the wall and across the road—are the two vineyards of Échézeaux: Grands Échézeaux and Échézeaux. The vines of Échézeaux are more exposed than those of Vougeot to such breezes as find their way through the first of the two slight ravines that break the wall of the amphitheater. Perhaps for this reason, they are somewhat lighter than those of Vougeot, though not as light as those of better drained and ventilated Musigny. Because the name Échézeaux is nearly unpronounceable to foreigners, and because its wines have tended to be overshadowed in the market by its three immortal neighbors, they represent relatively good value and there is less temptation on the part of shippers to tamper with them.

The Romanée Cluster. Perhaps a quarter mile south of Vougeot and Échézeaux, the vineyards come under the protection not only of the rounded shoulder of Hill D but of the hillock that lies between Hills C and D. Here is found the vineyard of Romanée-Conti, the very greatest of red Burgundies, the most expensive red wine on earth, contending only with Château Lafite of the Haut-Médoc for the title of the greatest red wine in the world. The only Burgundies in the same class with Romanée-Conti and its near neighbors are Chambertin, the Vougeot that grows up near the back wall, and Musigny.

In terms of body, the wines of Romanée are in between—more delicate than those of Vougeot and Échézeaux, fuller than those of Musigny. They have once again that curious quality found only in the greatest wines, combining in high degree the seemingly opposite qualities of body and delicacy. Shand once called them "the mingling of velvet and satin in a bottle." (Interestingly, Romanée-Conti and Lafite of the Médoc have roughly the same degree of body, to the extent that this quality is directly comparable. The two greatest reds are neither the lightest nor the fullest of their particular regions, but each is big enough to make a good, firm statement.)

Here are the best-known wines of the Romanée cluster:

Romanée-Conti	La Grande Rue
La Romanée	Les Beaux-Monts or
La Tâche	Beaumonts
Les Gaudichots	Les Suchots
Le Richebourg	Clos des Réas
La Romanée-St.-Vivant	Aux Réas
Les Malconsorts	

Just south of Romanée, the face of Hill D bears considerable resemblance to the faces of Hills A and B, where great wine occurs. But the wine grown here is decidedly secondary, and the reason is obvious. South of Hill D is the Meuzin River and a sharp break in the little range of barrier hills. The wind blowing between the steep walls of the valley gives far too much ventilation to the vines nearby.

The Hill of Nights. South of the Meuzin and the town of Nuits-St.-Georges is another hill, a rather broad, sprawling one. Since *nuits* means "night," we shall call this the Hill of Night. Some fairly good vineyards are found along its face, including the vineyard of St.-Georges, which has been hyphenated to the name of the town. The best wines are found in two indentations, out of the wind. Because these wines are not as famous and sought after as the immortals from the six clusters to the north, they represent good value, and are produced in considerable supply. Jurisdiction over the wines of the Hill of Night are divided between Nuits-St.-Georges itself, and the town of Prémeaux to the south. But because the wine of Prémeaux are so similar, they, too go to market as Nuits-St.-Georges. Below the Hill of Night, the little range of hills ends in broken, rolling slopes, and the miracle of the Côte de Nuits has ended.

Here are some of the best vineyards of the cluster:

Nuits-St.-Georges	*Nuits-St.-Georges-Prémeaux*
Les St.-Georges	Clos de la Maréchale
Les Boudots	Les Didiers-St.-Georges
Les Cailles	Clos des Forêts-St.-Georges
Les Porrets and Clos des Porrets	Les Corvées
Les Pruliers	Clos Arlots
Les Vaucrains	Les Perdrix

In describing the wines of the Côte de Nuits it is hard to escape a musical analogy. There is a sort of symphonic progression, a series of movements, rhythmic enough to gather force, irregular enough to sustain interest. Here is the way it goes:

INTRODUCTION — *Fixin*
Thunderous *CHAMBERTIN*

TRANSITIONAL — *Bonnes Mares*
Delicate *MUSIGNY*
Magnificent *VOUGEOT*

TRANSITIONAL — *Échézeaux*
Sublime *ROMANÉE*

CONCLUSION — *Nuits-St.-Georges*

And now we can arrive at some sort of conclusion as to the relative fullness of Burgundy versus Bordeaux. If you set up a scale of fullness, with great, "manly" Chambertin scored at 100, and light, "feminine" Margaux scored at 25, here, roughly, is the way the others rate (with the two greatest of all, Lafite and Romanée, side by side at the golden mean).

	Bordeaux (HAUT-MÉDOC)		*Burgundy* (CÔTE DE NUITS)	
			Chambertin	100
Very Full				
			Vougeot	85
	St.-Estèphe	60	Échézeaux	60
Medium Full	LAFITE	50	ROMANÉE	50
	Mouton	45		
	Latour	40	Bonnes Mares	40
			Musigny	35
Light				
	Margaux	25		

And here is a listing, in approximate order of quality, of the sixty best red vineyards of the entire Côte d'Or (Côte de Nuits and Côte de Beaune together) and the eleven best white ones. This list is reasonably analogous to the classification of 1855 of the Haut-Médoc, although it is an unofficial one, based on comparisons over the years by the wine expert Alexis Lichine.*

RED WINES

Rank	*Vineyard*	*Commune*
1.	La Romanée-Conti	Vosne-Romanée
2.	Chambertin-Clos de Bèze and Chambertin	Gevrey-Chambertin
3.	La Tâche	Vosne-Romanée
4.	Le Richebourg	Vosne-Romanée
5.	Musigny	Chambolle-Musigny
6.	Clos de Vougeot	Vougeot

* *Alexis Lichine's New Encyclopedia of Wines*, rev. ed. (New York: Alfred A. Knopf, 1974), p. 197.

Rank	Vineyard	Commune
7.	Les Bonnes Mares	Chambolle-Musigny
8.	Grands-Échézeaux	Flagey-Échézeaux
9.	La Romanée-Saint-Vivant	Vosne-Romanée
10.	Corton-Clos du Roi	Aloxe-Corton
11.	Les Saint-Georges	Nuits-Saint-Georges
12.	Latricières-Chambertin	Gevrey-Chambertin
13.	Le Corton	Aloxe-Corton
14.	Les Bressandes	Aloxe-Corton
15.	Cuvée Nicolas Rolin	Beaune (Hospices de Beaune)
16.	La Grande Rue	Vosne-Romanée
17.	Les Renardes	Aloxe-Corton
18.	Cuvée Dr. Peste	Aloxe-Corton (Hospices de Beaune)
19.	Clos des Porrets-Saint-Georges	Nuits-Saint-Georges
20.	Mazis-Chambertin	Gevrey-Chambertin
21.	Les Amoureuses	Chambolle-Musigny
22.	Clos de Tart	Morey-Saint-Denis
23.	Les Pruliers	Nuits-Saint-Georges
24.	Les Cailles	Nuits-Saint-Georges
25.	Les Caillerets	Volnay
26.	Clos de la Perrière	Fixin
27.	Clos Saint-Jacques	Gevrey-Chambertin
28.	Les Varoilles	Gevrey-Chambertin
29.	Les Échézeaux	Flagey-Échézeaux
30.	Les Beaux-Monts (also Beaumonts)	Vosne-Romanée
31.	Les Malconsorts	Vosne-Romanée
32.	Clos de la Roche	Morey-Saint-Denis
33.	Les Fremiers	Volnay
34.	Les Champans	Volnay
35.	Les Suchots	Vosne-Romanée
36.	Clos des Réas	Vosne-Romanée
37.	Chapelle-Chambertin	Gevrey-Chambertin
38.	Charmes-Chambertin	Gevrey-Chambertin
39.	Griotte-Chambertin	Gevrey-Chambertin
40.	Clos du Chapitre	Fixin
41.	Clos des Lambrays	Morey-Saint-Denis
42.	Les Rugiens	Pommard
43.	Les Épenots	Pommard
44.	Les Jarollières	Pommard
45.	Clos de la Maréchale	Nuits-Prémeaux
46.	Didiers-Saint-Georges	Nuits-Prémeaux
47.	Clos des Corvées	Nuits-Prémeaux
48.	Les Vaucrains	Nuits-Saint-Georges

Rank	Vineyard	Commune
49.	Les Santenots	Meursault
50.	Les Fèves	Beaune
51.	Les Grèves	Beaune
52.	Clos des Mouches	Beaune
53.	Clos de la Boudriotte	Chassagne-Montrachet
54.	Clos Saint-Jean	Chassagne-Montrachet
55.	Clos Morgeot	Chassagne-Montrachet
56.	Clos de la Commaraine	Pommard
57.	Les Angles	Volnay
58.	Le Clos Blanc	Pommard
59.	Les Pézerolles	Pommard
60.	Clos Saint-Denis	Morey-Saint-Denis

WHITE WINES

Rank	Vineyard	Commune
1.	Le Montrachet	Chassagne and Puligny-Montrachet
2.	ChevalierMontrachet	Puligny-Montrachet
3.	Clos des Perrières	Meursault
4.	Bâtard-Montrachet	Chassagne and Puligny-Montrachet
5.	Corton-Charlemagne	Aloxe-Corton
6.	Les Perrières	Meursault
7.	Les Ruchottes	Chassagne-Montrachet
8.	Musigny Blanc	Chambolle-Musigny
9.	Les Charmes	Meursault
10.	Les Combettes	Puligny-Montrachet
11.	Clos Blanc de Vougeot	Vougeot

THE OTHER WINES OF EUROPE

✻

The rest of Europe can now be disposed of with almost startling speed, at least so far as it concerns the Spectrum of Possibility of wines that are drunk with food. There are other districts—notably the Loire—where there is almost infinite variation among the wines, year to year, region to region, vineyard to vineyard. But the wines you see in an American wine store or look at on an American wine card can be summed up under a very few headings. There are districts—most particularly Germany—where with diligent pedantry the classifications and sub-subclassifications extend quite literally to the time and precise method by which the grapes were picked. But these distinctions apply mostly to the sweet German dessert wines, not the drier ones that are drunk with food. There are plenty of obscure and confusing wine names—not least in Italy—and there is cheating and abuse, fraud and near fraud everywhere. But nowhere else is there the pressure created by commercial demand combined with the breakdown of commercial institutions that produces the luxuriant flowering of deception of Burgundy.

The essential point to be remembered about the rest of Europe is this: There are as a general rule no truly great *dinner* wines outside of Burgundy and Bordeaux. In Germany the best of the sweet dessert wines are considered very great indeed, the only ones comparable to the great Sauternes of Bordeaux. But the German dinner wines, the wines drunk with food, are fine, not great. The fact that these other wines are less than great is no reason to turn up your nose at them, however; quite the contrary. Great wines like great men are often more appropriately admired at a distance than enjoyed in everyday association. At the price level of daily drinking, a Pouilly-Fumé from the Loire, a Châteauneuf-du-Pape from the Rhône, a well-aged Barolo or Chianti, is often to be preferred to a Chablis or Pommard of uncertain parentage or a Claret from some unheard-of château. In the years since World War II, as demand for wine has grown and the better-known wines have become more and more inflated in price and unreliable, the relative value of these outlying wines has increased. And even though there is no such thing, commercially speaking, as a truly undiscovered wine, there are many wines in the outlying areas which deserve more recognition than they currently get in the American market. Anyone who wants to look for them, whether on the ground, in the books, or in a wine shop, has a good chance of making his own "discoveries," with the savings and satisfaction these will bring.

As to which districts remain to be covered, a quick look around any good wine store will tell you: There are the river valleys of the Loire and Rhône in France, the Rhine Basin and its tributaries, and there is Italy. We shall start with the rest of France.

THE LOIRE

The Loire is the longest river in France, running six hundred miles from its headwaters in the mountains of the Massif Central near Burgundy to where it flows into the Atlantic at St.-Nazaire. Red and white wines are grown, but this far north the whites are obviously the better ones. In such a far-flung district, whose only unifying feature is the name of a river, it should be clear that the character of the wines will vary. The white wines grown far upstream and far downstream are generally light and dry; those grown in the middle fuller and richer. The district is best known for the wines grown in between, in the beautiful and famous château country known as "the smile of France."

There seems to be a law of inverse relationships in the world of wines. In the areas where the very greatest wines are grown the vista is often uninspiring and sometimes bleak; world-famous "châteaux" may actually be no more than big, raw farmhouses. By contrast, the scenery of the mid-Loire is world-famous, its vast châteaux are legendary, its cuisine magnificent, the language spoken the purest in France, and some of the vineyard sites spectacular. But the wines do not quite make it.

The difficulty is that the mid-Loire is transitional. In the Côte de Beaune of Burgundy, as we have seen, transitional conditions produce some remarkable and interesting wines. But the transition of the mid-Loire, between the upper third of the Wine Zone and the mid-zone, is not as fortunate. Its white wines do not develop quite the delicacy, and sometimes not the dryness, of the whites farther north, while its reds do not fulfill themselves to nearly the extent of the great reds farther south.

The most important wine of the mid-Loire is fullish, sweetish white

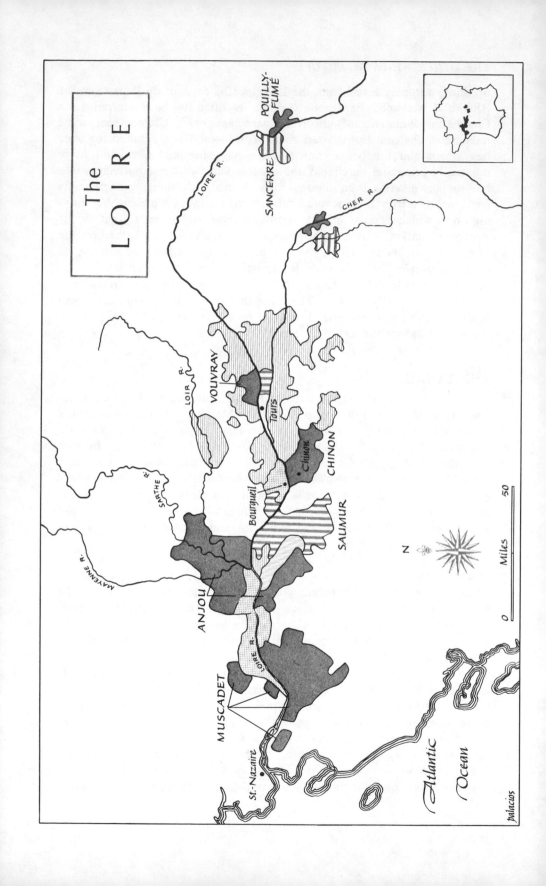

The LOIRE

POUILLY-FUMÉ

SANCERRE

LOIRE R.

CHER R.

VOUVRAY

Tours

Chinon

CHINON

Bourgueil

SARTHE

LOIR R.

SAUMUR

MAYENNE R.

ANJOU

LOIRE R.

MUSCADET

St.-Nazaire

N

0   Miles   50

Atlantic

Ocean

palacios

Vouvray. Not far downstream from Vouvray is produced the rosé wine of Anjou, the second-best rosé in France (the best being Tavel grown on the Rhône). Far upstream, close to Burgundy, are produced the dry white wines of Pouilly-Fumé (no relation to Pouilly-Fuissé of Burgundy, which it nonetheless resembles) and Sancerre, which have gained tremendously in popularity in recent years. Far downstream, near the mouth of the river, is grown the light, extremely dry Muscadet, which has also recently gained a considerable following. Not included on our Spectrum, but good and interesting, are the red wines of Bourgueil and Chinon, along with a number of minor whites.

Vouvray

The vineyards of Vouvray in the mid-Loire perch dramatically on a hillside four hundred feet above the river near Tours. They face directly south, and this, along with the temperate climate here, accounts for the fullness of body and tendency toward sweetness of the wines. Since Vouvray can be variable in sweetness, extreme caution has to be exercised in buying different years under the same label. If you like a bottle of a given vintage, it is not a bad idea to go back and buy more of that same vintage while you can.

A great proportion of Vouvray is made into sparkling wine, the Frenchman's lower-priced substitute for Champagne. Downstream from Vouvray are grown the white wines of Saumur, a little sweeter, a little fuller, also very commonly made into sparkling wine.

The fullish white wines of the mid-Loire go well with many chicken dishes, especially those with a white sauce. They are also good with sweetbreads, with the lighter sorts of curries, and with the Spanish rice and chicken dishes paella or *arroz con pollo*.

Anjou Rosé

In the past, white wines have been grown in Anjou, to the west and north of Vouvray on the Loir River, a tributary of the Loire (but spelled without the "e"). These were even sweeter and fuller than those of Vouvray and Saumur, and known primarily as dessert wines, using the same Noble Rot employed to make Sauternes. But with postwar demand for sweet wines dropping, the growers of Anjou, particularly those with second-class vineyards, had to experiment. There were efforts to make a drier wine, with some success. But the real opportunity has been to supply the booming demand for *rosé*, and this Anjou has done in volume.

Pouilly-Fumé, Sancerre

The chalky soil of these two regions which face each other across the upper reaches of the Loire is very similar to that of Burgundy nearby. So it is not surprising that the wines they produce should be very similar to the white wines of Burgundy—bigger than a Chablis, with less fullness and range than a Meursault or Montrachet. The name Pouilly-Fumé naturally reminds people of Pouilly-Fuissé, and there is a marked similarity between the two wines.

Neither Pouilly-Fumé nor Sancerre reaches the supreme heights of some of their white Burgundian neighbors, and the map suggests why. Pouilly-Fumé has a somewhat southern exposure, but it does not face as directly south as Chablis. Sancerre, across the river, has an easterly exposure, but the slopes of Pouilly opposite cut off the earliest morning light, shortening the growing day; it seems reasonable also to assume that the wind blowing up the narrow valley would not permit the pockets of still air that result in the supreme development of a Meursault or a Montrachet.

Of the two wines, Sancerre is, not surprisingly, the lighter and drier. Either wine is good with seafoods, or almost any rather light luncheon dish calling for white wine, a substitute for Chablis or Pouilly-Fuissé. Additionally, Sancerre is so clean and dry it makes a good appetizer wine, drunk in place of cocktails.

A bottle of Pouilly-Fumé or Sancerre costs somewhat more than the average bottled merely labeled Chablis or Pouilly-Fuissé, but here too the difference in cost is an insurance policy. A bottle of either wine is much more likely to represent good value.

Muscadet

The lower Loire, very close to the Atlantic Ocean, with fog and mist shortening its growing days, manages to produce only one wine of more than local notice, Muscadet, and grown in these conditions it is a very light, very dry, very simple, innocent white wine, without as much character as a Pouilly-Fumé or Sancerre upriver. In the days before appellation contrôlée, Muscadet was quite openly blended with Chablis in order to stretch the supply of that more famous wine. Today, like Pouilly-Fumé and Sancerre, it is more and more often used as a low-priced substitute for Chablis—very good with seafood, especially shellfish.

Here, then, are the major contributions of the Loire:

	Basic Spectrum	Secondary Listings
Light and Delicate White	MUSCADET	
	SANCERRE	—
	POUILLY-FUMÉ	
Fuller-bodied White	VOUVRAY*	Saumur*
Rosé	ANJOU	—
Light-bodied Red	—	Bourgueil
		Chinon

THE RHÔNE

As the Loire occupies a position transitional between the upper and mid-sections of the Wine Zone, so the Rhône occupies one transitional between the mid-zone and the lower third. As the Loire produces reds along with its whites, so the Rhône produces whites along with reds. But just as the more northerly Loire is known primarily for its whites, so on the more southerly Rhône it is the reds that count. A good honest red from the Rhône is almost invariably superior to a minor growth or a wine of questionable origin from Burgundy or Bordeaux. To the rule "When in doubt, Beaujolais" could be added ". . . or a Rhône."

In scenic terms the law of inverse relationships applies here, too. On the upper Rhône, even the most minor vineyard may be found clinging to an incredibly steep, terraced hillside high over the river. This far south, the skies above are clear, the sun is hot, the wind is relentless, the hillsides parched and baking. So, not surprisingly, the adjectives used to describe the wines that result are almost always "big," "rich," "warm," "generous," "full-bodied."

The big, full reds of the Rhône go well with big, full dishes, with heavy or spicy sauces, the finer ones with *boeuf bourguignon,* for example, or game, especially venison, the plainer ones with veal knuckles, steak-and-kidney pie, or again the Spanish paella or *arroz con pollo.* You will also find yourself using them when you would have preferred a big Burgundy, but cannot find one or cannot afford one.

Vintage years do not count for much on the Rhône. The climate does not vary greatly, and a rainy autumn is not in the cards. Even where there are accidents of weather, the hand of man, which has been at it in this lo-

* Also sparkling.

cality since at least 600 B.C., is very skillful at making corrections. In the best regions of Burgundy to the north, a very great wine results from the miracle performed by nature with a single, remarkable grape variety, the Pinot Noir. Down here, where the results of nature operating on her own leave more to be desired, a fine-but-not-great wine is quite literally manufactured by human skill, learned over the centuries, at blending as many as a dozen varieties together.

The *vignoble* of the Rhône provides us with five entries on our Spectrum of Possibility. On the sheer slopes of the upper Rhône are two red wines—Côte Rôtie and Hermitage—very full-bodied, near great in quality, whose characteristics echo those of the great Burgundies to the north (and whose prices have been more within reason). Sixty miles downstream, near the city of Avignon, the red wines of Châteauneuf-du-Pape are grown. These are not as full or fine as the wines of the upper Rhône, but they are medium-priced, very good, and extremely popular. All along the Rhône Valley between, on lesser slopes, are grown lighter, softer reds of modest price carrying the appellation Côtes du Rhône. Finally, across the river from Châteauneuf is grown the rosé of Tavel, the finest rosé of France, considered by many connoisseurs to be the only really interesting rosé there is.

CÔTE RÔTIE, HERMITAGE

Just south of where the river Saône of Burgundy joins the Rhône, on southeast-facing slopes so steep that from the road below they look like nothing more than a series of stone walls, is the Côte Rôtie. Translated literally, this means "roasted slope," giving some idea of conditions. This excellent, full-bodied red is hard to find, but when it can be found it is worth it.

Forty miles downstream, on southward-facing slopes along a westward-flowing tributary of the Rhône, is the spectacular Hill of Hermitage. The southerly exposure gives if anything more sun than the eastward-facing vineyards of the Côte Rôtie, and the red wines grown here are even fuller-bodied. They are also easier to find in American wine stores. Both red Hermitage and Côte Rôtie need a long time to mature, and can be harsh if drunk too soon.

White wines as well as reds are grown at Hermitage. Here again the hand of man counts for more than any mysteries of exposure. Where white wines are desired, white grapes instead of red are planted. White Hermitage is one of the fullest truly dry white wines made, and one of the longest-lived.

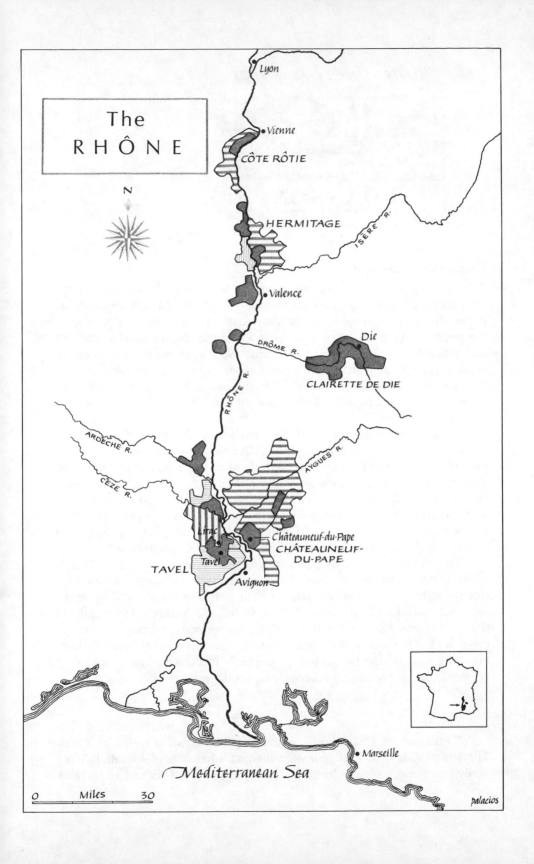

The
RHÔNE

N

Lyon

Vienne

CÔTE RÔTIE

HERMITAGE

ISÈRE R.

Valence

Die

DRÔME R.

CLAIRETTE DE DIE

RHÔNE R.

ARDÈCHE R.

AYGUES R.

CÈZE R.

Lirac

Châteauneuf-du-Pape

CHÂTEAUNEUF-
DU-PAPE

TAVEL

Tavel

Avignon

Marseille

Mediterranean Sea

0   Miles   30

palacios

Châteauneuf-du-Pape

In the past dozen years the good red wine of Châteauneuf-du-Pape has become the best known on the Rhône. The name means "the new castle of the Pope," and comes from the fourteenth century, during the exile of the popes in Avignon, when they built a summer palace outside the city and planted a vineyard there. Any wine with a religious title seems to enjoy a greater popularity than a similar one without it, perhaps because this adds a naughty note of sacrilege to the carnal business of sopping up the wine. But the popularity of Châteauneuf is not based merely on its title. It is very good wine.

Unlike the other wines of the Rhône, and those of Burgundy, Châteauneuf is not grown on slopes, but like the St.-Émilions of Bordeaux, on a plateau—a bleak, stony tableland of the coarsest sort of gravel mixed with boulders. The composition of the soil provides the necessary drainage; the elevated position provides better ventilation than on the surrounding lowlands. It seems reasonable to assume that the popes built their summer palace here in order to gain relief from the heat. (Popes and grapes apparently have similar requirements in the summertime.)

The hand of man is as much in evidence here as anywhere. This is where literally a dozen varieties of grape are carefully blended to produce just the right combination of qualities. The resulting wine is a deep crimson, full-bodied and "generous." It is softer and matures more quickly than red Hermitage or Côte Rôtie. (This earlier maturity may in part account for the popularity of the wine, since it results in a lower price. A slow-maturing wine ties up the grower or shipper's investment longer, and runs up more costs for storage, breakage, and spoilage.)

Tavel Rosé

To the west of Châteauneuf, across the Rhône, is the region of Tavel. The situation here is even grimmer than at Châteauneuf—small hills of sandy limestone, walled in by cliffs, baking in the sun. It is easy to imagine that any red or white wine grown here would be rough and harsh—but at the same time would have more character than one from the fertile flatlands nearby. So the experimentation began. It was eventually found that the combination of four grape varieties, of which the chief one is called Grenache, would make a most acceptable rosé. With this manipulation, the harsh growing conditions become an advantage. The skins of the sun-burned grapes impart character to the wine, but are not left in the vat long enough to make it rough or harsh. The blending keeps the sugar content low enough to produce a wine that is bone-dry. A good Tavel costs more than other rosés, and it should. Rosé is said to go well with everything (although in any given situation there is usually a better choice). Rosé is also an excellent picnic wine. It is excellent also for luncheons and casseroles. A neighbor of Tavel is the commune of Lirac, whose rosés, harder to find, offer good value.

Côtes du Rhône

The valley of the Rhône is full of vineyards that because of some quirk of exposure do not quite make it into the class deserving a regional appellation like Hermitage or Châteauneuf, but produce good and reliable wines for daily drinking, far superior to *ordinaires,* or even to wines deserving the lowest or district appellation, Rhône. These are sold under the appellation Côtes du Rhône, "slopes of the Rhône." A Côte du Rhône is a pleasant and soft wine, sound and good, without the body of its more aristocratic neighbors.

	Basic Spectrum	*Secondary Listings*
Fuller-bodied White	—	White Hermitage
Rosé	TAVEL	Lirac
Fuller-bodied Red	CÔTES DU RHÔNE CHÂTEAUNEUF-DU-PAPE RED HERMITAGE CÔTE RÔTIE	—

THE RHINE

The long-time dominance of things French in the wine world has a self-perpetuating quality. For one thing, there are the labels. Anyone who becomes competent in reading wine labels from one district of France can do at least a fairly adequate job of reading a label from any other district (except Alsace, which we shall discuss in a moment). So if he fails to satisfy his needs among the white Burgundies, let us say, his inclination will be to see what he can do among the wines of the Loire; to order intelligently a German or California or Italian wine involves not only a different language but a different mode of thought. There is also the influence of food. Even the customary name of elegant food, *haute cuisine,* is French, and as one's taste develops for good French food, his taste in wine tends to follow. This tendency in turn is abetted by nationalism. The memories of the Franco-Prussian War of 1870 and the two World Wars are still fresh enough in the minds of those who prepare the wine lists of French restaurants that the offering of German wines usually begins and ends with a Liebfraumilch and a Moselblümchen. As we shall see, that is often not saying much, and does not tend to encourage repeat business.

For all these reasons many people who have developed a fairly advanced competence in handling French wines are slow to acquire an understanding of the German ones, and therefore avoid them. This is not a sin. But they are missing something because the Rhine River with its tributaries is the one remaining major source of fine white wine in Europe. (We have already indicated that what we are talking about here is the dry dinner wines and not the sweet, luscious dessert wines, with which the Rhine is also plentifully supplied.)

The position of the Rhine Basin on the map shows what in general to expect. The vineyards on its upper reaches are the most northerly in Europe, producing white wines of astonishing lightness and delicacy. Those a bit farther south produce whites that are fuller in body but still very delicate and fine. (Red wines are made in Germany, but as we pointed out in Chapter II, nobody much drinks them but Germans.) The unique feature of the German white wines, however, is not their lightness and delicacy, but a curious fruity, flowery bouquet or tang. This quality results from the grape varieties from which the wine is made, and gives any wine of the Rhine Basin more in common with any other wine of the Rhine Basin than with any other wine (except possibly one grown from Rhine-type grapes in Chile or California). The three principal varieties of grape used to make Rhine or Rhine-type wines are:

Riesling—the best wine, with few exceptions, is made from this grape, the lightest, most delicate of the three.

Traminer or *Gewürtztraminer*—the second grape in terms of quality, producing a spicier, fuller wine than the Riesling.

Sylvaner—much ordinary wine of soft, sweetish character, is made from the Sylvaner.

More often than not, if the wine is of any quality, the name of the grape variety used is noted on the label.

The delicacy and flowery bouquet of these wines make them very popular with the ladies. Their lightness in alcohol makes them an ideal luncheon wine; you can drink them in the middle of the day and still hope to get some work done when you get back to the office. If you have them with your dinner, you use them as you would any other light- or medium-

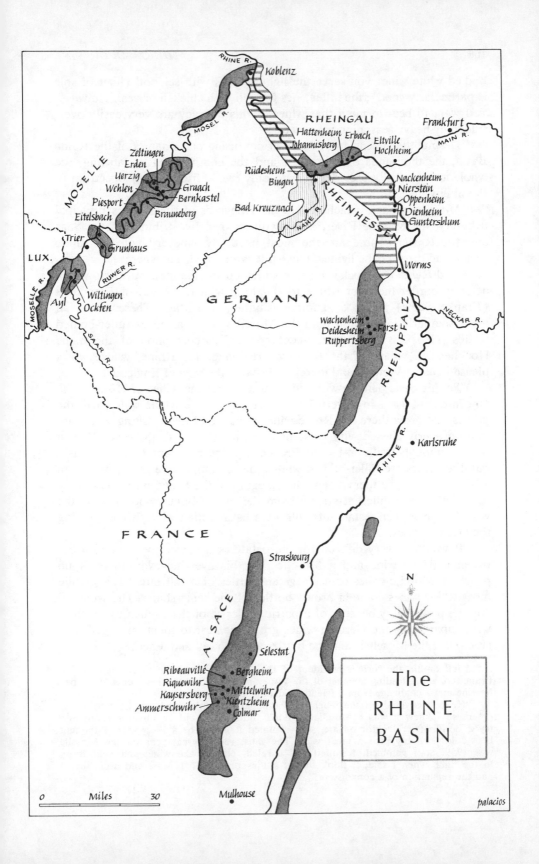

RHINE R.

Koblenz

MOSEL R.

RHEINGAU

Frankfurt

Hattenheim   Erbach
Johannisberg   Eltville
                    Hochheim   MAIN R.

Zeltingen
Erden
Uerzig   Rüdesheim
Wehlen   Graach   Bingen   Nackenheim
Piesport   Bernkastel   Nierstein
Eitelsbach   Brauneberg   Bad Kreuznach   Oppenheim
                                                            Dienheim
                                                            Guntersblum

MOSELLE   Grunhaus

Trier

LUX.   Worms

MOSELLE R.   RUWER R.

        Wiltingen   G E R M A N Y
Ayl   Ockfen
                                            Wachenheim
                                            Deidesheim   Forst
        SAAR R.   Ruppertsberg

                                                            RHEINPFALZ

                                                NECKAR R.

                                    RHINE R.   Karlsruhe

F R A N C E

                    Strasbourg

                                                    N

A L S A C E

            Sélestat

Ribeauvillé   Bergheim
Riquewihr
Kaysersberg   Mittelwihr
Ammerschwihr   Kientzheim
               Colmar   The
                                        RHINE
                                        BASIN

0   Miles   30

                Mulhouse   palacios

bodied white wine: you serve the lightest ones with seafood (fillet of sole is particularly good); the fuller ones go well with chicken or veal. However, you want to bear in mind that wines of this delicacy are very easily over-ridden by heavy seasonings or sauces.

Despite the dozens and dozens of confusing place names of the Rhine Basin, the thousands of vineyards, and the complexities of labeling, the whole area basically provides us with only two entries for our Spectrum of Possibility:

Moselle, a name which covers the vineyards of the Rhine's principal tributary, the Moselle River, along with its own two tributaries, the Saar and the Ruwer. These are the most northerly vineyards of the Rhine Basin, and produce the lightest fine white wines made anywhere;

And *Rhine* (or Hock), a name which covers the major districts which actually border the river Rhine itself, along with the wines of Franconia (Frankenweins) grown on another tributary, the Main. These wines, all more southerly in location than the Moselles, are classed as fuller-bodied whites. (Hock is a nineteenth-century English corruption of the name Hochheim, a village of the Rheingau region of the Rhine, whose wines pleased Queen Victoria and therefore became the rage of England.)

To this basic pair we will add a third name: the wines of *Alsace.* The vineyards of Alsace in eastern France are part of the Rhine watershed, the grapes that grow there are Rhine-wine grapes, and the resulting wines are more properly classed with those of Germany than with the other French ones (although tradition-bound Frenchmen are reluctant to admit this). Alsatian wines are fuller-bodied whites, more comparable to a Rhine than a Moselle. We give them a separate category in the Spectrum because they are labeled by a different system from the other Rhines, and because the wine lists in French restaurants will often list Alsatian wines while ignoring the German ones.

It would be very difficult for the palate of a novice to distinguish be-tween a Rhine wine and a Moselle. For his eye, however, there is no problem. Moselle wines come in green bottles of a tall fluted type, while most Rhine wines come in brown bottles of the same shape. The wines of Alsace, presumably because of a patriotic desire of the French to set their wines apart from the German wines grown nearest to them, are bottled in green, like the Moselles, and the bottles are also tall and fluted.*

* Jeff Smith, the former president of the French Club, an eating group in San Francisco, and a leading member of the Wine and Food Society there, once described how he met a challenge from a friend to identify a German wine:

"He had covered up the label with a napkin, but the neck of the bottle was green, so I knew it was a Moselle. I didn't think he would be obvious enough to try a Bernkasteler Doktor on me, so I assumed it would be a Piesporter. I thought he would probably pick a great year. The most recent great year on the Moselle was 1959. So I gambled. I sniffed and gargled, chewed the wine, and held it up to the light. Then I said, 'I think this is a Piesporter '59.' It was, and after that I had the reputation of a connoisseur."

Moselle

The wines of the Moselle and its two tributaries, the Saar and the Ruwer, are so similar in character that they are nearly always lumped together, and the district designation on the label of any of the three is Moselle-Saar-Ruwer. The best vineyards of the Moselle itself skip from side to side across the winding river, depending on which shore faces south to catch every available ray of sun.

If there is a scenic exception to our rule of inverse relationships, it is the Rhine country. The steep-sided shores of the winding Moselle, the orderly grandeur of the great river Rhine, the charming slopes and villages of Alsace, are some of the most beautiful vineyard country anywhere, while some of the wines grown along it are incontestably great. However, as we have already noted, the *dry dinner* wines which are the principal subject of this discussion are, like the whites of the Loire and the reds of the Rhône, fine and useful but not truly great.

The wines of the Saar River are slightly more "steely" in flavor than the Moselles, those of the Ruwer perhaps a little lighter and drier, if that is possible. All the best wines without exception are made from the Riesling grape, so the fact does not need to be noted on the label.

Here are the best wine towns of the three rivers:

Moselle	*Saar*	*Ruwer*
Piesport	Wiltingen	Maximin Grünhaus
Bernkastel	Sanzem	Eitelsbach
Graach	Oberemmel	
Wehlen	Ayl	
Zeltingen	Ockfen	
Brauneberg		
Erden		
Uerzig		

The name of the vineyard on a Moselle label is usually combined with the name of the town where it is located. Here are some of the best ones from Bernkastel, Piesport, Wehlen, Wiltingen, and Ockfen:

Bernkasteler Doktor
Piesporter Goldtröpfchen ("gold drops")
Wehlener Sonnenuhr
Wiltinger Scharzhofberg
Ockfener Bockstein

German wine shippers, not necessarily more scrupulous than their French counterparts, capitalize on the fame abroad of the Moselle wines with one called Moselblümchen. This is a "shipper's wine," a blend of the products of secondary vineyards. The name, translated, is "little flower of the Moselle," charming, meaningless, and often overpriced. From a reliable shipper, however, Moselblümchen is a pleasant accompaniment to a simple meal.

The Rhines

As the map shows, the three districts that lie on the main stem of the river Rhine are, north to south, the Rheingau, the Rheinhessen, and the Rheinpfalz. The wine lands of Alsace in France are located south of the German Rheinpfalz.

The *Rheingau* produces more famous wine than any other area of Germany and ranks with the Haut-Médoc of Bordeaux and the Côte de Nuits of Burgundy as one of the great wine regions of the world (for its dessert wines). This once again is a case of nature getting the best of several worlds. The vineyards are located, as the map shows, on the southward-facing foothills of the Taunus Mountains, along a twenty-mile stretch where the river Rhine runs east to west. The southern exposure catches maximum sunlight; the surface of the river reflects even more sun onto the grapes. The curve of the slope and the ridge behind protect the grapes from cold winds from the north; at the same time the elevated position and location along the river give superb ventilation. Here suddenly in the chilly north is a blooming garden. The wines of the Rheingau are fuller than the Moselles, with a kind of classic, stately elegance.

Here are the most famous wine-producing villages of the Rheingau:

Rauenthal   Hochheim
Erbach   Eltville
Hattenheim   Kiedrich
Winkel   Hallgarten
Johannisberg   Geisenheim
Rüdesheim

As on the Moselle, the names of the vineyards are usually linked on the label with the name of a village. However, some vineyards of the Rheingau are so famous their names stand alone. These include:

Schloss Johannisberg	Schloss Eltz
Schloss Vollrads	Schloss Reinhartshausen
Steinberg	

(*Schloss* means "castle"—that is, "château.")

Of these, the most famous of all is Schloss Johannisberg, a name to rank with Lafite, Romanée-Conti, and Yquem among the legendary vineyards of the world.

The *Rheinhessen,* next south across the river from the Rheingau, produces far more wine than the Rheingau. The best of it is just a little softer and sweeter, less classic than the Rheingau wines. The best wines are grown in the ten villages of the "Rhine Front," on the west bank of the river facing east (and this far north an eastward exposure is not ideal).

Here are the names of the villages of the Rhine Front:

Nierstein	Bodenheim
Nackenheim	Laubenheim
Oppenheim	Guntersblum
Bingen	Alsheim
Dienheim	Worms

(Of the 155 villages of the Rheinhessen, 120 have names that end in *-heim,* which gives a kind of Hans Christian Andersen quality to the whole operation.)

In the other wine villages of the Rheinhessen, in the fertile, rolling country to the west and south of the Rhine Front, a great deal of ordinary wine is made, including Liebfraumilch, a shipper's wine, the Rhine-wine counterpart of Moselblümchen. Liebfraumilch was originally the wine produced in two vineyards belonging to the Liebfrauenkirche, "The Church of Our Lady," in Worms. The wine, a typical, soft, sweetish wine of the

Rheinhessen, became immensely popular, helped along by the story that the name Liebfraumilch means "Milk of the Blessed Virgin," although in fact it means "Milk of the Church of Our Lady." The name Liebfraumilch was gradually adopted by other villages and vineyards and finally came to be simply a generic term for any blend of wine from the Rheinhessen. A Liebfraumilch from a reliable shipper is, like a Moselblümchen, acceptable. Some shippers, however, might price at $3.75 retail a wine which in Germany would cost no more than $.50 a bottle. But there are many, many instances when a Liebfraumilch from a known shipper would be a far better gamble than some pretentious unknown. Here are some of the better, more reliable "brands" of Liebfraumilch:

Blue Nun	Madonna
Hans Christoff	The Madrigal Wines
Glockenspiel	Meister Krone

Another generic-named wine of the Rheinhessen, in the same class as Liebfraumilch, is Niersteiner Domtal. Domtal (meaning "cathedral-valley") was originally the name of a popular vineyard of the village of Nierstein. It was gradually adopted by its neighbors and now, like Liebfraumilch, means merely a blend of ordinary wines from the Rheinhessen.

Still farther south along the river is the *Rheinpfalz,* which produces even more wine than the Rheinhessen. The best vineyards are located about fifteen miles back from the river, on the eastward-facing lower slopes of the Haardt Mountains, while great quantities of common wine are produced on the fertile plain between the mountains and the river. Protected by the mountains this far south, and at this distance from the water, the summer temperatures here are warm and the wines are even sweeter and more luscious than those to the north. Thus the Rheinpfalz is particularly noted for its sweet dessert wines, the best of which bring astronomical prices.

In all the 35,000 acres of vineyards of the Rheinpfalz, four villages are outstanding. These are, north to south:

> Wachenheim
> Forst
> Deidesheim
> Ruppertsberg

Ranked not too far behind those are four others:

> Bad Dürkheim
> Kallstadt
> Leistadt
> Königsbach

The most famous vineyards of the Rheinpfalz, from Forst, Deidesheim, and Ruppertsberg, are:

Forster Jesuitengarten Deidesheimer Kieselberg
Forster Kirchenstück   Ruppertsberger Hoheburg
Deidesheimer Leinhöhle

To the east of the Rhine, on its tributary the Main, on steep south-ward-looking slopes in the region of *Franconia,* are produced the so-called Frankenweins. The most immediately obvious feature of these wines is the fact that they come not in the fluted bottles of the Moselles and the Rhines, but in dumpy little medieval-type flagons called *Bocksbeutel,* delicately so named because of their resemblance to the scrotum of a billy goat. With the well-ventilated southern exposure of their hillside vineyards, these wines are full, "hard," dry, and well regarded. The best known of the Frankenweins are the Steinweins from the city of Würzburg.

Alsace

The vineyards of Alsace are located in the eastward-facing lower slopes of the Vosges Mountains, which are in effect a southern extension of the Haardt Mountains of the German Rheinpfalz. Like the vineyards of the Rheinpfalz they are located back from the river, and the wines of Alsace are very similar to those of the Rheinpfalz, full-bodied, tending toward sweetness. The best wines occur in the center of the district, in seven villages along a twenty-mile stretch of foothills between Sélestat on the north and Colmar on the south. These are, north to south:

Bergheim
Ribeauvillé
Riquewihr
Mittelwihr
Kaysersberg
Kientzheim
Ammerschwihr

The best wines of all are produced in Ribeauvillé and Riquewihr. Riquewihr is a fairy-tale place, surpassed only by St.-Émilion of Bordeaux as the loveliest wine town of France. A town of almost equal beauty is Kaysersberg nearby, birthplace of Albert Schweitzer.

If the wine lands of Alsace are among the most beautiful in the world, they are also some of the most troubled. After the Franco-Prussian War, while they were in the hands of the Germans, production of fine wines was discontinued, and the vineyards were turned over to making ordinary wines to blend for Liebfraumilch. In both World Wars the lands were heavily fought over and some of the villages nearly destroyed, but they have been rebuilt. Because of the total disruption of both the traditions and institutions of wine making, no adequate classification of the vineyards of Alsace exists, and the appellation contrôlée laws apply loosely at best.

Because of this situation, the primary description of the wines on an Alsatian label is the name of the grape from which it was made—chiefly Riesling, Traminer or Gewürtztraminer, and Sylvaner, although there is now a trend toward identifying the village where the grapes were grown. Under these conditions, the shippers of Alsace, no more scrupulous here than elsewhere, have wide opportunities for abuse. Second-rate blends of Alsatian wines are sold so cheaply that they undercut the better ones. As time passes, the quality and prices of the better Alsatian wines should rise. Currently, if you are willing to take the trouble to find a good one, they represent good value for the money.

These are some of the better-regarded shippers of Alsace:

> Hügel
> Willm
> Dopf & Irion
> Château de Mittelwihr

Here, then, is the Spectrum of Possibility as it has developed for the Rhine Basin:

	Basic Spectrum	*Secondary Listings*
Light and Delicate White (Dry)	MOSELLE	—
Fuller-bodied White (Dry)	RHINE ALSACE	Frankenweins
(Sweet Dessert Wines)*	MOSELLE RHINE ALSACE	—

* Not a part of the basic Spectrum, but essential in any listing of wines of the Rhine Basin.

The Drama of the Vintage

In terms of fundamentals, that is all that it is necessary to know about the awesome-appearing subject of German and Alsatian wines. The principal remaining barrier is the problem of knowing whether the wine you are getting is sweet or dry.

Like the wines of the Loire, the wines of the Rhine can vary widely both in sweetness and quality, depending not only on whether the summer was hot or cool but also on the amount of sunshine the grapes received in the last few days or even hours before they were harvested. If after a reasonably warm autumn they are picked at the regular time, say late September or early October, they will produce a regular dry dinner wine. If they are picked a few days or a week later, after more sugar has had a chance to form and some of the moisture has left the grapes, they will produce a moderately sweet wine. If they are picked very, very late, after the Noble Rot (the very same mold that works in Anjou and Sauternes) has had a chance to attack the grapes and draw away most of the moisture, they will be very sweet indeed. This assumes, of course, that it does not rain. If it rains, the grapes will swell up with moisture again, the resulting wine will be thin, and the grower will have lost his gamble. As in Burgundy, the tension at harvest time is enormous, as some growers pick early and take an assured if modest profit, while others go for broke and wait day by day, watching the sky, and either make a killing or produce a thin bad wine that scarcely covers costs.*

The tension of this annual drama is not fully reflected on the label of the bottle, but the results are. If the label says nothing about the time of picking, you can assume the grapes were picked at the regular time, and the resulting wine will be a regular dry white dinner wine. If the grower has picked some of his grapes later than the others (this is almost inevitable, since labor is short and the harvest takes a long time), the word *Spätlese,* "late-picked," will appear on the label. This as a rule is a sweeter wine, but still not so sweet you could not serve it with dinner.

If the weather has been singularly good, the grower may send his workers out to pick only selected bunches that seem especially ripe. The wine from these will be known as *Auslese,* "selected bunches." If it is a very, very good year, the grower may go to some extra trouble and tell his people to select not merely bunches but individual grapes. The wine from this picking is called *Beerenauslese,* "selected grapes." If the weather has been still better yet, promising to be one of the great years of the century, and the grower is a super-perfectionist, a real nut, he will go whole hog and tell his people to go out and select only the most withered, raisinous,

---

* A well-known curse in the German wine country is "May you inherit a vineyard." This reflects both the back-breaking labor of tilling the steep slopes and the risk and tension of harvest time.

mildewed grapes. This is called *Trockenbeerenauslese,* "selected dry berries," and is obviously the sweetest, most luscious wine of all.

The last three categories, *Auslese, Beerenauslese,* and *Trockenbeerenauslese* are *never* dinner wines. They should be drunk either alone after the meal or with dessert. *Spätlese* is interchangeable, if you don't mind a somewhat sweet wine with your dinner. The normal choice for a dinner wine, however, is a "normal" wine, one picked at the regular time.

As if these refinements were not enough, there is one more. If a grower feels that a wine from one of the above categories is particularly outstanding, he gives it the added designation *Kabinett.* As originally used this meant that this was a wine so good that he was setting it aside for his own personal stock—in his "cabinet"—and if he was willing to let you have any, it was because he knew you well and liked you. The relationship is more impersonal now, but the description *Kabinett,* when honestly used, still means the best wine there is of a given category of a given vineyard of a given year.

A German Label

The descriptions of time and method of picking are used on the labels of both the German and the Alsatian wines. Aside from this, the principles governing the labeling of a German wine are generally the same as those governing the labeling of most of the French ones. (In fact, there is more similarity between the labeling methods of Germany and the rest of France than there is between either of them and a label from Alsace.)

1. *Vintage year.* In this northerly location the vintage year is of the utmost importance. This is often indicated on a small separate label on the neck of the bottle.

2. *Geographic location.* As in most of France, a German label gives the name of the region within which the wine is grown, usually the name of

RHEINGAU

1964er

Steinberger

Riesling Spätlese

Faß Nr. 317/216   Alc. 9.8% by Vol.

SPÄTLESE

Verwaltung der Staatsweingüter Eltville

Eigener Kellerabzug und Korkbrand

the village within the region and, for a wine of any quality, the name of the vineyard.

3. *Grower.* As in Burgundy, the ownership of most of the fine vineyards is highly fragmented. (Here, as in Chablis, this provides insurance in case of frost or hail.) As in Burgundy, some growers are well known and reliable; others unknown or unreliable.

4. *Bottling.* As in Bordeaux there is the institution of château bottling, along with the branding of corks to assure that the wine in the bottle when it is opened is the same wine that was put into it by the grower. Any of the following language appearing on a German label indicates estate bottling:

> *Original Abfüllung, Original Abzug* (original bottling by the owner of
> the vineyard)
> *Kellerabfüllung, Kellerabzug* (cellar bottling)
> *Schlossabzug* (château bottling)

The word *Korkbrand* also appears on an estate-bottled wine, indicating that the owner's seal and the vineyard name have been branded into the cork.

5. *Grapes.* As already noted, in Germany as in Alsace, the name of the grape used is usually noted on the label of all but the cheapest of wines. Riesling for the best; Gewürztraminer, spicier and fuller wine; Sylvaner grape, a soft, sweetish *ordinaire*. The exception is the Moselle. Since all wine of any quality from the Moselle is made from the Riesling grape, it does not need to be noted on the bottle.

6. *Sugaring.* As in Burgundy, in a poor year sugar will be added to the grapes before they are fermented to make sure they develop the alcoholic strength necessary for the wine to keep. (But this does not necessarily make the wine sweeter.) A sugared wine may have a strong aftertaste that a natural wine will not have. In a reverse sort of way, the winegrowers of the Rhine are more candid than those of Burgundy, and tell you on the label if sugar has *not* been added. The language on the label for a natural, unsugared wine is *Natur, Naturrein, Naturwein, Ungerzuckert* (unsugared), or *Unverbessert* (unimproved). As in most of France, wine grown by small holders in small vineyards in the German part of the Rhine can sometimes be as fine as or finer than that grown in the large ones. But for a beginner, until he learns the ground, it is safer to stick to estate-bottled wines from the larger vineyards.

For wines in a modest price range, the wines from the better shippers are the best bet for the beginner, unless his wine merchant or wine steward is not only honest but competent in this field. Here are some of the better shippers of German wines to watch for:

Sichel	Langenbach
Dienhard	Julius Kayser
Valckenberg	

ITALY

As the Rhine Basin is the major European source of white wines outside of France, so Italy is the prime supplier of reds, along with some pleasant and useful whites, and promises to become a more important one as time passes. In fact, as an emerging, evolving situation, Italy is in many respects a much more interesting source of wine than its better-established neighbors.

Vines grow everywhere in Italy, from the foothills of the Alps to the tip of the "boot" and on the island of Sicily. In the time since Algeria has ceased to be counted as part of Metropolitan France, Italy has ranked first in volume among all wine-producing countries. Italy and France together account for about half the total wine production of the world.

Italy is also a major exporter of wine, with a significant portion of those exports going to the United States. This is what earns the wines of Italy their place in a book like this. Like Mount Everest, your local Italian restaurant is there, and when you stop by for a meal the chances are that you will either find no other wine on the list (except for the inevitable New York State entries) or the other wines will be relatively overpriced and uninteresting. By the same token, if you are eating at home, be it linguini with clam sauce, white, char-broiled chicken, or *boeuf bourgignon,* market economics and current trends in Italian wine making suggest that the wine of choice may well be Italian.

To understand the situation of Italian wine today, it is necessary to know something about the last three thousand years of Italian history.

Wine making had its origins in the eastern Mediterranean, and was known in Italy before Roman times. There is one tradition that the ancient Etruscans, who gave their name to what is now Tuscany, taught the Romans how to make wine. Experts argue about that, but in any case the Etruscans were rather haphazard wine makers. It was the Greeks, who had established settlements in southern Italy and Sicily at about the time of the founding of Rome (753 B.C.), who passed on to the Romans their own high skill at making wine.

By A.D. 420 some of the wines of Italy were famous. As Rome expanded, its legions carried the art of wine making to the farthest reaches of the known world. Most of the vineyard districts of Europe that are famous today were first planted in Roman times.

At the height of the Roman Empire Italy had become the center of wine for the ancient world. It had its own "great growths," much like the France of today; the better wines were carefully aged before they were drunk; vintage years were known and discussed by connoisseurs.

After the fall of the Roman Empire and the closing off of trade, wine making like the other arts declined in Italy as in the rest of Europe. With the Renaissance, the arts revived, and vineyards began to prosper again near the major centers of commerce. Particularly around Florence (Tus-

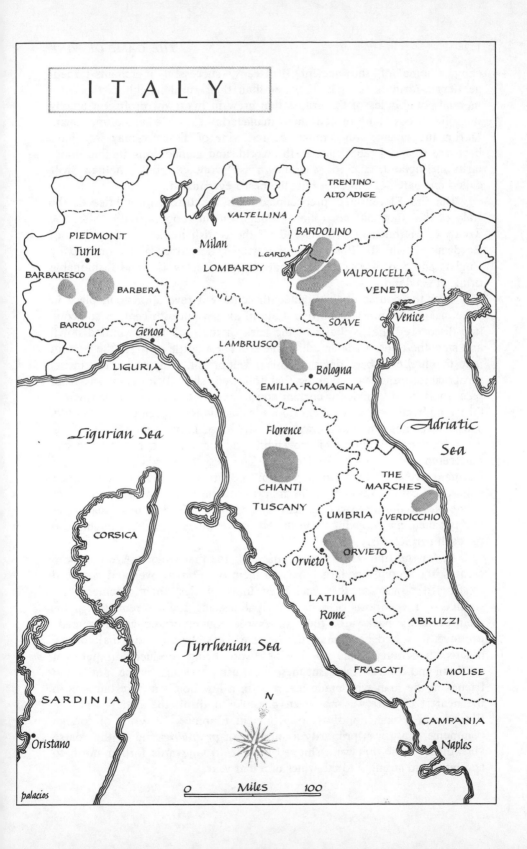

ITALY

PIEDMONT
Turin

BARBARESCO

BARBERA

BAROLO

Genoa

LIGURIA

Milan

LOMBARDY

VALTELLINA

TRENTINO-
ALTO ADIGE

BARDOLINO

L.GARDA

VALPOLICELLA

VENETO

SOAVE

Venice

LAMBRUSCO

Bologna

EMILIA-ROMAGNA

Ligurian Sea

Florence

CHIANTI

TUSCANY

Adriatic
Sea

THE
MARCHES

UMBRIA

VERDICCHIO

CORSICA

Orvieto

ORVIETO

LATIUM
Rome

ABRUZZI

Tyrrhenian Sea

FRASCATI

MOLISE

N

SARDINIA

CAMPANIA

Oristano

Naples

palacios

0   Miles   100

cany), home of the ancient Etruscans, successful merchants-turned-gentlemen-farmers recognized better than their rural neighbors the commercial possibilities of the grapes that grew in luxuriant profusion among the olive trees, and turned their managerial skills to exploiting them. During the seventeenth century the red wine of Tuscany may well have been the best red table wine in the world, and gained considerable popularity in England, where it was known as "Florence red." Jonathan Swift called one batch of Florence red "the best I ever tasted."

But the Florentines, preoccupied with the turbulent politics of the Italy of that day, did not follow through on their opportunity. After the Treaty of Methuen in 1703 closed off the British market to the wines of Bordeaux, it was the Port wines of Portugal, developed and promoted by English and Scottish merchants, that became the favorite and fashionable drink of England.

Over the course of the eighteenth century a revolution took place in wine making for most of Europe. Late in the seventeenth century someone had discovered that a chunk of the bark of the cork tree, whittled down and smoothed out, made an admirable seal for a bottle or flask, the best, in fact, that had ever been devised. This development, plus the improvements in agriculture and wine making that followed, shifted the emphasis from pale, short-lived "wines for current consumption" to strong, subtle, incredibly long-lived wines with enormous capacity for developing in bottle. This was the beginning of the wine industry as we know it today.

The wine revolution of the eighteenth century was followed in the nineteenth century by a Golden Age. The best vineyards of France and Germany were bringing to perfection the art of producing truly great wines, and came to dominate the markets of the world. A select group of connoisseurs, the first since ancient Rome, could afford to buy great wines and put them away, giving them the twenty or thirty years they might need to reach perfection.

As for the Italians, in whose vineyards the first Golden Age had been created, the second one largely passed them by. Fought over and occupied by foreign powers as they had been for centuries, their commerce restricted by the imposts of petty principalities, the Italians remained poor, their economy backward, their wines the rough, crude, casually made products they had been since the Middle Ages. In the latter half of the nineteenth century some good wines were being produced in parts of northern and central Italy. But these were usually drunk by the family and friends of the man who made them, or in a few hotels and restaurants in the nearest city. It was not even possible to drink the better wines of Florence in Rome, nor those of Rome in Florence. In terms of foreign commerce, Italy was primarily a supplier of *ordinaires* and of the coarse "blending wines" that were shipped in bulk to vineyards farther north to add body and strength to the wines of a bad year.

This situation continued largely unchanged until after World War II. In the early postwar years Italy joined the European Common Market, which reduced the barriers to trade between the Western European nations. But the price of entry for Italy was a raising of standards to meet those of her partners in the Market. This at first caused some upheaval. The meticulous Germans demanded that Italian wines be as chemically pure as their own, and the Italians resented this, feeling that their wines were being robbed of their historic individuality. But they conformed, and today Germany is one of Italy's best customers.

The price of full membership in the Market was also a new wine law. The Italians passed one in 1963, more strict in some ways than the French one. It provides for a Denominazione di Origine Controllata, equivalent to the French appellations contrôlées, controlled place names, along with precise specifications as to what grapes should go into a given wine and how they should be handled.

Meanwhile, despite frequent changes of government, Italy remained reasonably stable and prosperous, with a rising middle class that wanted its share of the better things, including wine. And over the 1960s and into the 1970s, as the middle class of other countries came more and more to appreciate good wine and was willing to pay steadily higher prices for it, there has been a growing overseas market for Italy's increasingly good wines (with the foreign prejudice against them gradually fading away).

In terms of the character of its wine, all of Italy, unlike all of Gaul, can be divided into four parts.

There is *the Northwest,* chiefly the Piedmont and Lombardy, where the warm climate is transitional, like the Rhône, between the mid-zone of wine and the southern third. The big, full red wines grown here are similar in character to those of the Rhône.

There is *the Northeast,* chiefly the Veneto and Emilia-Romagna, along with the Marches on the coast farther south. The climate here is cooler, influenced by breezes off the Alps and the Adriatic. The wines are typically mid-zone wines: light red, dry, relatively delicate whites.

There is *West-Central Italy,* Tuscany, Latium (near Rome), Umbria. It is warm here, but with the coastal exposure not as warm as in the Piedmont farther north. The red wines of Tuscany are fuller than those of the Northeast, not as full as those of the Northwest. The white wines of Umbria and Latium are full-bodied and somewhat rough.

And there is *the South,* including Sicily, firmly in the southern third of the Wine Zone, producing in enormous volume rough, coarse *ordinaires,* along with the "blending wines" that go north to France by the tank-truck load. There are also being produced in increasing quantity good but simple *vins du pays,* country wines, both red and white.

From these four areas come literally thousands of wines of every kind and quality. Those that concern the American buyer fall under one of

three headings: those wines that *commonly appear* on the wine lists of
Italian restaurants in the United States, those that *sometimes appear* on
such a list, and those of more than usual interest that *almost never appear*.

The wines that commonly appear are obviously primary entries on the
Spectrum of Possibility. There are six: three reds, Chianti, Valpolicella,
and Bardolino; and three whites, Soave, Verdicchio, and Orvieto.

The ones that sometimes appear are the secondary entries. It is hard
to make a definitive list, since relative positions change. The list would
include, among the reds, Barolo, Barbaresco, Barbera and Lambrusco; for
the whites, Frascati and Lacrima Christi.

Those wines that almost never appear on a wine list in this country
and may be difficult or impossible to find in wine shops are the ones to
sample when you visit Italy, and to search out and treasure in your cellar
when you find the opportunity. We shall describe a few of them on the
pages that follow.

Wine names are as confusing in Italy as they are anywhere, since a
given name may, without any particular system, represent a region, a
village, a grape, a grape name joined to a village name, a shipper, or a
pure fantasy name. In addition, the look-alikes are staggering: Rufina and
Ruffino; Valpolicella, Valpantena, Valtellina; Barolo, Brolio, Bolla, Barbera, Barbaresco, Bardolino.

But the names you actually must know are few and can be memorized
quickly. Beyond that it is up to you how many of the nuances you want to
master. In Italy as elsewhere the learning process will be greatly enhanced
if you are buying not at random for tonight's dinner, but carefully and systematically for your own collection.

TUSCANY: CHIANTI

It is appropriate that Tuscany, seat of the ancient Etruscans, cradle of
the Renaissance, home of Florence red, should be the source of Chianti,
the best-known wine of Italy today—and at its best a very good wine. According to tradition, Chianti was "invented" in the mid-nineteenth century
by Barone Bettino Ricasoli, a member of an ancient Florentine family, at
the family castle called Brolio, in the Chianti hills south of Florence. What
is more likely is that Ricasoli drew together and systematized practices that
had been known in Tuscan wine making for a long time. In any case, in
part because of the quality of the wine that resulted, in part because the
straw-covered *fiasco,* or flask, captured the public imagination as a symbol
of the romance of Italy, and in part because the large estates of Tuscany
provided a plentiful supply of wine along with the resources to promote it,
Chianti achieved world fame. (Ironically, there is a movement now afoot
to abolish the *fiasco* because at present Italian wage rates the cost of putting the straw around the flask has become too great.)

As might have been expected, once there was a large commercial demand for "Chianti," wine of that label gushed forth in a flood, most of it of very doubtful quality. So the growers of authentic Chianti formed a *consorzio,* or association, which in 1932 persuaded the Italian government to define a *classico,* or classic zone, where real Chianti had originated. A classic Chianti bears on its neck a seal showing a gold cockerel on a black background.

But the Italian government, subject to other pressures also, granted to several adjoining regions the right to use the Chianti name, but not the *classico* designation. Here are the names of six other Chianti regions, along with their neck-label designations:

Region	*Neck Label*
Chianti Montalbano Pistoiese	Towers of Montalbano
Chianti Rufina	Putto (cherub)
Chianti Colli Fiorentini (Florentine Hills)	Putto (cherub)
Chianti Colli Senesi (Sienna Hills)	Romulus, Remus, and the she-wolf
Chianti Colli Aretini (Arezzo Hills)	Chimera (mythical monster)
Chianti Coline Pisane (Pisa Hills)	Centaur

It is well known that the Chianti to be found on the American market is of two grades: the cheaper grade, sold in the past in straw-covered *fiaschi,* intended to be drunk almost as soon as it is bottled (and losing quality if held too long); and the more expensive Chiantis, ordinarily

Ettorucci's Restaurant

CHAMPAGNE and SPARKLING WINE

	Bottle	½ Bot.
MUMM'S BRUT, N/V	15.50	9.00
GANCIA LACRIMA CHRISTI	9.50	
GANCIA ASTI SPUMANTE	9.50	5.00
TAYLOR BRUT, N. Y. State	7.75	4.50
TAYLOR SPARKLING BURGUNDY	7.75	4.50
TAYLOR PINK CHAMPAGNE	7.75	4.50

ITALIAN RED WINE

VILLA ANTINORI (Estate-bottled Chianti)	6.50	3.50
Rich and elegant.		
RUFFINO CHIANTI	6.50	3.50
Full-bodied and dry.		
BOLLA BARDOLINO	6.00	3.25
Elegant and soft.		
BOLLA VALPOLICELLA	6.00	3.25
Polished and fruity.		
VERDICCHIO RED	6.00	3.25
Fresh and lively.		
BARBERA, Guido Giri	6.50	
A rich, robust Piedmont Classic.		
LAMBRUSCO	6.00	
Light, refreshing, and lively.		

FRENCH RED WINE

BEAUJOLAIS VILLAGE ST.-VINCENT, Chanson ..	7.00	3.75
Light, fruity, and well rounded.		
CHÂTEAUNEUF-DU-PAPE ST.-VINCENT, Chanson	9.25	5.25
Robust and flavorful; from the Rhône district.		
CHÂTEAU LA GARDE	9.25	5.25
Fine dry Claret; versatile and flavorful.		
POMMARD, Chanson	15.00	
Richest of Burgundies, a full bouquet.		

The wine list of Ettorucci's Restaurant in Stamford, Connecticut, illustrates clearly the economics of Italian wine. A fine estate-bottled Chianti sells for less than half the price of a Pommard of no particular credential, and for substantially less than a Châteauneuf-du-Pape or obscure Bordeaux. The best Italian white on the list, the Bianco of the house of Antinori, is priced $3.50 below the Pouilly-Fuissé, $2.50 less than the Chablis, and goes for the same price as a regional Liebfraumilch. The sparkling Asti Spumante or Lacrima

ROSÉ WINES

	Bottle	½ Bot.
LANCER'S VIN ROSÉ (Portugal)	6.50	3.50
The best-known Portuguese wine.		
NECTAROSÉ (Anjou)	5.50	3.00
Medium dry and soft.		
MATEUS ROSÉ	6.00	3.25
Light and fruity, a soft bouquet.		

ITALIAN WHITE WINE

	Bottle	½ Bot.
BIANCO, Antinori, Fish Bottle	6.50	3.50
Light and fruity, medium dry wine in a unique fish-shaped bottle.		
BOLLA SOAVE	6.00	3.25
Dry and crisp.		
VERDICCHIO	6.00	3.25
Refreshing, crisp, and light.		

FRENCH WHITE WINE

	Bottle	½ Bot.
CHABLIS ST.-VINCENT, Chanson	9.00	4.75
The favorite white Burgundy; dry, flinty, with a tangy freshness.		
POUILLY-FUISSÉ ST.-VINCENT, Chanson	10.00	5.50
Very dry, with a delicate bouquet.		

GERMAN WINE

	Bottle	½ Bot.
HANS CHRISTOF LIEBFRAUMILCH, Deinhard . . .	6.50	4.00
Superior grade of Germany's most popular Rhine wine; soft, well balanced.		

AMERICAN WINE
TAYLOR NEW YORK STATE

	Bottle	½ Bot.
BURGUNDY	3.50	2.00
A fruity rich red wine with a delightful balance of taste and bouquet.		
ROSÉ	3.50	2.00
A light crisp wine with a flowery bouquet.		
SAUTERNE	3.50	2.00
A luscious, full white with a charming taste and bouquet.		

Christi sells for $6.00 less than a nonvintage French Champagne. At the time of publication the management of Ettorucci's was planning to replace its New York State wines with some from California, to add Chianti *riserva* and a Barolo to its selection of reds, and to introduce a moderately priced St.-Véran from France (see footnote, page 76) among the whites. This indicates a growing sophistication on the part of both management and clientele.

found in conventional wine bottles of the Bordeaux shape, which require and reward a certain amount of aging. (An aged Chianti is called a *riserva.*)

Because the name Chianti has been so often used and abused, many of the most important producers stress a proprietary name for their better wines, using Chianti only as a secondary designation. Here is a list of some of the best known proprietary names, and what they stand for:

Brolio Riserva	The best Ricasoli Chianti, aged five years before bottling
Castello di Meleto	Also from the Ricasoli firm
Nipozzano	The best wine from the Frescobaldi firm
Riserva Ducale	The best from Ruffino
Stravecchio Melini	The best from Melini
Villa Antinori	The best from Antinori
Machiavelli	The best from Serristori

The wine of Chianti, like the wines of the Rhône, is a made-up wine, a blend of five different grape varieties. Well aged, it is a full-bodied wine, about the same degree of fullness as a Burgundy.

Another red wine of Tuscany, considered better than any but the very best Chiantis, is Brunello di Montalcino. Brunello is a stronger, fuller wine than Chianti, with a tremendous capacity for aging. Another very good Tuscan red, similar to the Brunello, is Vin Nobile di Montepulciano. Either would be difficult to find in the United States.

There is also a Brolio Bianco (white), marketed by the Ricasoli firm, a fresh and delicate wine that is considered to be one of the best white wines of Italy.

THE PIEDMONT: BAROLO, BARBARESCO, BARBERA

The rolling Piedmont section of Italy, encircled by the Alps, produces what are regarded as the finest red wines of all Italy, along with Asti Spumante, the Italian "Champagne," and a wide variety of spiced and flavored Vermouths. The location of the Piedmont, hard against the French border, doubtless has something to do with the volume, variety, and quality of the wine it produces today. Also important is the fact that during much of the nineteenth century, when the rest of Italy was in turmoil, the Piedmont enjoyed relative stability as part of the Kingdom of Savoy, whose rulers encouraged improvement in the making of wine. In addition, the three cities of Turin, Milan, and Genoa, along with the Italian Riviera, have provided big, rich, and stable markets for the wines produced in the Piedmont area.

The latitude of the Piedmont is the same as that of the Rhône, and the climate is similar, except that the surrounding mountains provide protection from the harsh winds that sweep over the vineyards of the Rhône. The wines of the Piedmont are big and full, like those of the Rhône. The best of these is Barolo, named for its village, which some experts consider the best red wine of Italy. (It is certainly the best Italian red wine generally available in the United States.) Like good Chiantis, Barolos need to age. A Barolo aged four years is entitled to the designation *riserva*. Aged five years it may be called a *riserva speciale*.

Next in ranking to Barolo among the red wines of the Piedmont is Barbaresco, named for a village not far from Barolo, made from the same grape. A Barbaresco is also a big, full wine, but not quite as big and full as Barolo. It also matures more quickly.

The commonest grape of the Piedmont is the Barbera, which produces in considerable volume a wine called by that name that is good, not fine, of about the quality and character of a simple Côtes du Rhône.

Barolo, Barbaresco, and Barbera are not listed as primary entries on the Spectrum of Possibility simply because they are not as commonly found on wine lists in the United States as the Chiantis and one or two others. But anyone who cares about fine wine, at prices more attractive than the great Burgundies and Bordeaux, should not overlook the better Piedmont wines.

Perhaps eighty miles north of Barolo, close against the Alpine foothills, there is produced a wine called Gattinara, after its village. A somewhat lighter, more delicate wine than Barolo, and available only in small quantities, Gattinara is considered by some experts to be even better than Barolo, and thus the finest red wine of all Italy.

LOMBARDY: THE VALTELLINA

In the neighboring province of Lombardy, far to the north, in a valley called the Valtellina, are grown three red wines very similar in character to big, full Barolo, perhaps not quite as fine. Their names are Sassella, Grumello, and Inferno. One of the prncipal growers of the Valtellina chooses the best grapes from each year's harvest and makes a wine which he keeps in reserve for as much as six or seven years before he bottles it. This excellent wine goes to market as Castel Chiuro, and some experts say that *this* is the best red wine of all Italy. Not many people know for sure, though, because the quantity of Castel Chiuro is limited, and in any case there is no classification of 1855 or 1975 to make it official. Perhaps someday there will be.

According to the Italians, their very finest red wines, the Barolos, Gattinaras, Brunellos, and well-aged Chiantis should be drunk with four-legged game—venison, chamois, wild boar. How often you do this will depend in part on how many wild boar you have snuffling around your back yard. For everyday purposes these fine, full wines can be used as you would a Rhône or a Burgundy, with red meat of any sort, and the richer kinds of stews.

THE VENETO: VALPOLICELLA, BARDOLINO, SOAVE

The Veneto in northeast Italy is one of the largest producers of wine in the country and one of the largest exporters, with much of its output going north across the Alps to Germany and Austria. The wine industry of the Veneto is much more systematic and organized than that of the rest of Italy, perhaps because of the businesslike spirit of the Venetians, perhaps because of the influence of the Austrians, who occupied the province during much of the nineteenth century, and perhaps because of the more temperate, less Mediterranean climate, influenced as it is by breezes off the Adriatic and the foothills of the Alps.

Like the climate, the wines are temperate. The two best-known reds, Bardolino and Valpolicella, are light, fresh, clear reds, best drunk cool, like a Beaujolais. They go very well with the lighter meats, veal and chicken, or with summer dishes. Valpolicella is the better of the two.

White Soave, grown nearby, styles itself the Italian Chablis (although the growers of Chablis would have something to say about that). Cyril Ray, a British writer on wine, in his book *The Wines of Italy,* tells of sitting next to a French diplomat at a dinner party in Venice. When a glass of Soave was served, the Frenchman "sniffed it suspiciously, tasted it dubiously," turned to Ray, and said, "You know, they call a lot of things *vino* in Italy that we should never call *vin* in France."

"Politer to him than he was to his hosts," Ray continued, "I forebore to say how much better this admirable, fresh, dry wine was than many a so-called Chablis or Pouilly-Fuissé that I had drunk, not only in English oyster bars but in Paris restaurants that ought to have known better."

Soave is a light and delicate wine, but not as light and delicate as Chablis, and Chablis at its best is more interesting. Like Chablis, Soave is a good "fish wine." One hazard of all three principal wines of the Veneto is that they should all be drunk as young as possible. Too often in the United States they are allowed to get too old, losing their bright freshness and becoming instead rather dull and harsh.

Any of the three wines of the Veneto are likely to be found in the United States under the label of a major shipper such as Bolla or Ruffino.

EMILIA-ROMAGNA: LAMBRUSCO

South of the Veneto, in the Emilia-Romagna, is grown the red wine of Lambrusco, which appears on Italian wine lists in America perhaps 30 per cent of the time. Like Bardolino and Valpolicella, Lambrusco is light and fresh. Unlike them, it is a somewhat carbonated, "prickly" wine, which is considered good offset to the rich, well-seasoned dishes of that region—or to rich, well-seasoned dishes anywhere.

THE MARCHES: VERDICCHIO

Next south along the Adriatic coast is a province called the Marches, a rugged, isolated place whose only wine of distinction is a very popular white called Verdicchio, after its grape. Presumably because of the cool Adriatic breezes here, fresh, relatively light Verdicchio is much more comparable in style to Soave to the north than to the neighboring white wines of central Italy. Like Soave or Chablis, Verdicchio goes very well with fish. The better wines of the area come from a group of villages that call themselves the "Castelli di Jesi," and these words are added to the grape name on the label. A wine called simply Verdicchio is usually not quite as good.

UMBRIA: ORVIETO

Between the Marches to the east and Latium to the west is landlocked Umbria, which produces the white wine called Orvieto. Famous for centuries, Orvieto in the past has usually been *abboccato,* semisweet. Now drier wines are being made in response to current market demand. But a dry Orvieto is a fullish wine, sometimes rather rough. It goes well enough with, let us say, a garlicky clam sauce or a veal dish. But it is tending to be crowded off some wine lists by lighter, fresher Soave and Verdicchio.

LATIUM: FRASCATI

Every major city in Italy has a vineyard region nearby which in the times of poor transportation was doubtless its principal source of wine. For the city of Rome the local source is the Alban Hills, southeast of the city, also called the Castelli Romani, where the Roman aristocracy has kept its summer villas since ancient times. The best-known wine of the Castelli Romani is white Frascati, which can be dry, semisweet, or sweet. Like a dry Orvieto, a dry Frascati is a fullish wine, to be drunk with pasta dishes or the lighter sorts of meat.

CAMPANIA: LACRIMA CHRISTI

Campania, the province where Naples is located, is the Cumae of ancient times, the Greek colony whose occupants may well have taught the Romans how to make good wine. There was a saying in ancient times that no fine wine was made north of Rome. It is a fact in modern times that little if any fine wine is made south of Rome. Part of that shift may reflect trends in taste. Wine making began in places like Egypt and Greece, and the palates of men of those times came to be tuned to the strong, sweet Mediterranean wines that resulted. But in addition, the centers of wealth and civilization in ancient Italy were located from Rome south, and where the most sophisticated demand was, the greatest care would be devoted to the cultivation of the grape.

In any case, the wines grown around the Bay of Naples, once world-famous, are not very notable today. The best-known one, Lacrima Christi, "The Tears of Christ," like Liebfraumilch owes much of its fame to the apparent sacrilege of its name. Lacrima Christi can be red or white, sweet or dry, sparkling or still, fairly good or nondescript. True Lacrima Christi is a white wine, grown on the seaward side of Mount Vesuvius. As a dry wine it is fullish and flowery, with a hint of sweetness, a bit like a white Graves or a German wine. It is considered good to drink in the fish restaurants of Naples, and appears intermittently, in both still and sparkling form, on wine lists in the United States.

Now here is the Spectrum of Possibility for Italy:

Light and Delicate White	SOAVE	—
	VERDICCHIO	
Fuller-bodied White	ORVIETO	Frascati
		Lacrima Christi
Light-bodied Red	BARDOLINO	Lambrusco
	VALPOLICELLA	
Fuller-bodied Red	CHIANTI	Barbera
		Barbaresco
		Barolo

And here is the basic Spectrum for the rest of Europe (leaving out Burgundy and Bordeaux):

Light and Delicate White	MOSELLE — Rhine Basin
	MUSCADET — Loire
	SANCERRE — Loire
	POUILLY-FUMÉ — Loire
	SOAVE — Italy
	VERDICCHIO — Italy
Fuller-bodied White	RHINE WINE
	ALSACE — Rhine Basin
	VOUVRAY — Loire
	ORVIETO — Italy
Rosé	TAVEL — Rhône
	ANJOU — Loire
Light-bodied Red	BARDOLINO — Italy
	VALPOLICELLA — Italy
Fuller-bodied Red	CHIANTI — Italy
	CÔTES DU RHÔNE
	CHÂTEAUNEUF-DU-PAPE — Rhône
	RED HERMITAGE — Rhône
	CÔTE RÔTIE — Rhône

It is clear from this that just as you can get wine from almost any category of the Spectrum without leaving Burgundy and Bordeaux, so you can get wine from any category without ever going there. At times, as we shall see, your purpose will be to find your wine in one of the two great districts. At other times you will be no less resolved to avoid those and find what you need in the hinterlands of wine.

And here now is the Spectrum for all of Europe together, the master key, the Rosetta stone, to the mysteries of the world of wine:

Light and Delicate White	MOSELLE — Rhine Basin
	MUSCADET — Loire
	CHABLIS — Burgundy
	SANCERRE — Loire
	POUILLY-FUISSÉ — Burgundy
	POUILLY-FUMÉ — Loire
	SOAVE — Italy
	VERDICCHIO — Italy
Fuller-bodied White	RHINE — Rhine
	ALSACE — Rhine
	'VOUVRAY — Loire
	MEURSAULT — Burgundy
	MONTRACHET — Burgundy
	ORVIETO — Italy

Rosé

TAVEL — Rhône
ANJOU — Loire

Light-bodied Red

BARDOLINO — Italy
VALPOLICELLA — Italy
HAUT-MÉDOC — Bordeaux*
RED GRAVES — Bordeaux

Fuller-bodied Red

ST.-ÉMILION — Bordeaux
POMMARD — Burgundy
BEAUJOLAIS — Burgundy
CÔTE DE NUITS — Burgundy*
CÔTES DU RHÔNE — Rhône
CHIANTI — Italy
CHÂTEAUNEUF-DU-PAPE — Rhône
RED HERMITAGE — Rhône
CÔTE RÔTIE — Rhône

* Oversimplification: Some wines of the Haut-Médoc are full-bodied; some of the Côte de Nuits are light-bodied. See page 85.

CALIFORNIA: BRAVE NEW WORLD

The last wine district of major concern to us in constructing our Spectrum of Possibility is California. The last but by no means the least in the volume and variety of wine produced and its average level of quality, in the fascinating interplay of geography, meteorology, and history that makes it what it is, and in the problems and opportunities created by its unusual business institutions.

Imported wines, for all the attention they have traditionally received in the wine books, account for only about 15 per cent of the table wine drunk each year in the United States. California, by contrast, ships about 70 per cent, almost three bottles in four, of the wine that is drunk by Americans.

A high proportion of Americans who have excellent palates today, and thoroughly respectable wine cellars, learned their first lessons in wine with the cheaper sorts from California, usually from gallon or half-gallon jugs at parties and cookouts. But until quite recently these same Americans, who had reached the point where they could knowledgeably compare the middle-grade châteaux of Bordeaux or the vineyards and shippers of Burgundy, were at best only semicompetent in buying the best of their own American wines—and for that reason seldom bought them.

In part this was a matter of snobbery. A mere "domestic" wine was okay for beginners, but anything with an imported label was considered to have more class.

That sort of provincialism is now largely gone. As the prices of the better European wines have doubled and trebled under the pressure of escalating demand, as the quality of the California product has improved and Americans have gained competence and confidence in buying wine, it has been natural for them to seek out the California wines on the basis of merit—to the point where the prices of some of the best of those are now beyond a reasonable level.

But a more fundamental problem was, and still is, that the better California wines are hard to buy. In most cities of America it is *much* easier to lay your hands on a Romanée-Conti of a great year, provided you have the money, or a Lafite or a Mouton, than to buy a bottle of the very best that California offers.

Many of the best wines of California are not generally available outside the state, or have to be obtained by special arrangement. More fundamentally, the institutions that govern the marketing of those premium wines that are widely available are still decidedly immature, with the result that the pricing and labeling practices that reflect these institutions are not adequate to transmit to the buyer the information he needs to do a competent job.

But if this situation poses a problem for the buyer of wines, it also provides both opportunity and challenge. Because they do have curious pricing and labeling practices, there are certain to be bargains among the better wines of California. All you have to do is seek them out. And in the seeking is not merely good sport, but an excellent means of developing the palate and judgment that set off a legitimate player of the game from the many would-bes. Moreover, as time passes, as the sophistication of the American palate continues to improve, as the volume of the better California products continues to grow and their business institutions mature, there seems little doubt that California will become a steadily more accessible source of increasingly good wine.

A Double Standard

With an extravagance that might almost seem the result of advance planning by its well-known Chamber of Commerce, the state of California offers within its borders practically the entire range of climatic conditions to be found anywhere in the Wine Zone, and produces the full range of wines. Despite their marvelous diversity, however, the wine lands of California can be divided into two broad categories, and so can the wines. On the one hand are the broad, flat, hot, fertile, often irrigated vineyards of the San Joaquin and Sacramento valleys, located inland, between the Coast Range and the Sierra Nevada, along with the San Bernardino area of southern California. Here, in conditions approximating those of the southern third of the Wine Zone, are grown not only Sherries, Ports, and Brandies but what is called the standard wines of California, cheap, simple, plentiful wines, costing $1.25 to $3.00 a bottle retail, that go to market either as simple red or white wine or under the traditional "ge-

GUILD · VINO DA
TAVOLA RED
CALIFORNIA TABLE WINE

MADE AND BOTTLED BY GUILD WINE CO. LODI, CALIF. ALC. 12½% BY VOL.

neric" names of the best-known European wines: Burgundy, Claret, Chablis, Rhine Wine, Moselle, Chianti. In price and in broad market base these wines are comparable to the *ordinaires,* the workingman's wines of Europe. In average quality they are decidedly superior, some of the best bargains in wine to be found.

The other principal winegrowing area of California is, of course, the famous North Coast Counties near San Francisco Bay, not far from the Pacific Ocean. Here in far more temperate conditions are grown all the better and more expensive table wines. These are the "varietal" wines, so called because they are named not for pieces of European real estate, but for the fine grape varieties that grow there, transplanted to California. The better-known names include Cabernet Sauvignon, the great red wine grape of Bordeaux, Pinot Noir, the grape from which the best red Burgundies are made, Pinot Chardonnay, the grape of the great white Burgundies, Riesling and Traminer of the Rhine, and Grenache from which the rosé of Tavel on the Rhône is made. These varietal wines, the best of which are equal in quality to some of the Classed Growths of Bordeaux, usually range in price from three to ten dollars, with exceptional bottles selling for twenty-five to fifty dollars or more.

A Collision of Cultures

The story of the California wine industry and its curious institutions is in considerable measure the story of a collision between two cultures in a new land: between the fun-loving, wine-loving, backward perhaps, but urbane, Catholic and relaxed culture of southern and central Europe, and the austere, organized, industrious, but somewhat naïve and provincial and above all Protestant—not to say Puritan—culture of northern Europe as transplanted to the United States.

The wine grape of Europe, *Vitis vinifera,* came to North America in 1524 when Cortes, the Spanish conqueror of Mexico, decided that wine making was to become one of the industries of the New World and ordained that for five years the holders of land grants must plant one thousand vines per year for each one hundred Indians living on their land. As was the case of many of the best wine districts of Europe, the wine lands of California had their beginnings through the instrument of the Church, which needed the wine for sacramental purposes. In 1769 Father Junípero Serra planted vines at the new Franciscan mission in San Diego, and the harvest was said to have been the best in the New World thus far. The wine itself did not amount to much—the grape variety used, now called the Mission, was too coarse. But the feasibility of viticulture in California had been established.

The first commercial plantation of wine grapes was made in 1824 by one of the early settlers at the little pueblo of Los Angeles. Six years later Jean-Louis Vignes, a Frenchman from Bordeaux, started a vineyard about where Los Angeles Union Station now stands. By 1833, Vignes's wines and brandies were known throughout the state; by 1840 he was chartering ships to carry his products to Santa Barbara, Monterey, and San Francisco; within a generation, wine making had become the principal industry of the Los Angeles area. Even so, the total production remained small.

Then came the Gold Rush of 1849, and with it a boom in demand for all good things, including wine. And the Gold Rush brought not only wealth but people: wanderers, adventurers, fortune-hunters, drifters from every part of the world. Many of these, like Jean-Louis Vignes, came from areas and often from families with long traditions of growing wine: France, Italy, Germany, Spain, Hungary. So just as the eyes of those Greeks or Phoenicians who first sailed into the estuary of the Gironde four thousand years before had recognized in the Bordelais conditions favorable to the growing of the grape, the practiced eyes of these newcomers to California recognized in the hills and valleys around San Francisco Bay a situation favorable to producing wine. With only one or two exceptions the wineries which dominate wine making in California today were founded by immigrants from other important winegrowing areas of the world.

The most notable among the wine pioneers of the Gold Rush days was of course Colonel (actually Count) Ágoston Haraszthy, an eccentric Hungarian nobleman from a long line of winegrowers. He has been called the Johnny Appleseed of California wines. Haraszthy started a winery in Sonoma County which never really made it into the first rank. But more important, in 1861 he went to Europe and brought back with him 100,000 cuttings of some two hundred varieties·of European grapes, and then was tireless in his efforts to persuade the California growers to plant them. This was really the start of the premium or "varietal" segment of the wine industry of California. (Cold, critical Protestant hindsight suggests that in the best of all possible wine worlds Haraszthy might have been a little less "catholic" in his enthusiasm: that he or someone else might first have conducted experiments to find out which varieties did the best job in which area, so that California wine makers might have become more specialized from the start. But regardless of that, Haraszthy's efforts resulted in a giant step forward in the quality of California wines.)

In 1875 California produced four million gallons of wine. In 1895 it produced fifteen million and was shipping its wines not only in the United States but to Mexico, Central America, and the Far East. By 1900 California wines were winning prizes at international expositions and beginning to compete with European wines on their own ground.

However, no great wine industry was ever built on exports alone. But in terms of developing their own American market, the California wine-growers had a problem. It was well stated by Árpád Haraszthy, son of the famous colonel. "The average American is a whiskey-drinking, water-drinking, coffee-drinking, tea-drinking, and consequently dyspepsia-inviting subject who does not know the use or value of pure light wine taken at the proper time and in moderate quantities. The task before us lies in teaching our people how to drink wine, when to drink it, and how much of it to drink."

Your average American, in short, was a transplant from the austere Protestant cultures of northern Europe, where the vine does not flourish and where wine consequently is not a habit of daily life, at least among the common folk. It was to be three generations, two World Wars, a Prohibition, and a depression later before the task would be in any degree accomplished of teaching Americans "how to drink wine, when to drink it, and how much of it to drink."

As the French Revolution was the determining event in the modern history of the vineyards of Burgundy, and the German occupation of 1870–1919 the same for the vineyards of Alsace, so, of course, the Prohibition of 1919–1933, that misguided triumph of legislated morality, had a decisive influence on the shape of the wine industry of California. Not only were the wineries closed down and their staffs and skills disrupted, but many of the fine vineyards themselves were rooted up. A clause of the Prohibition law permitted wine making at home, for the use of the immediate family. But the high cost and small berries of the fine wine varieties made them not very appealing in the market place, and their delicate skins made them difficult to ship. So the fine vines were pulled up, to be replaced by coarse, high-yielding varieties of grapes, whose thick skins could withstand the rigors of shipment across the United States.

It has been said that the history of wine making in California does not even begin until the Repeal of 1933. That is putting it a little strong. The tradition was still there, and some of the records. Disused or misused vineyards were still there, many of them in the hands of the founding families. A few of the vines were left. (For anyone who lived in San Francisco it had been possible all through Prohibition to drive up to Napa County and buy good wine from a farmer.) But the continuity and momentum were gone. In particular, whatever rudimentary taste for or interest in drinking wine there had been on the part of Americans was gone. So far as its home market was concerned, the California wine industry was starting from dead scratch.

Then whatever little reputation the California vineyards had left was quickly squandered. As soon as the making of wine became legal again, opportunists in search of a quick buck bought up hugh quantities of raisin and table grapes and converted them into cheap, fortified appetizer and dessert wines, the kind of thing favored by Skid Row bums and high school kids on their first binge. As a result the term "domestic wine" became a byword, and the good name of the California wine industry remained under a cloud for almost twenty years.

Then, just when it seemed things couldn't get worse, they did. With the onset of World War II, and the rationing of alcohol supplies, large national distilling companies began buying up wineries for the assured supply of alcohol they could provide. But running a wine business is more complicated than running a whiskey business, as the distillers found out. So, after having fouled things up pretty thoroughly, the whiskey companies sold the wine companies again, accomplishing a further disruption of their continuity of management.

But as so often happens in human affairs, just when things looked blackest, the roots of meaningful progress were quietly being put down.

Being planted in a literal sense were new vines, of the fine grape varieties required to produce superior wines. However, commercial yields do not come from the best varieties for three or four years and are not ready for drinking for another three, so the California industry was going to have to make do for a while with the vines it had.

Also being planted politically and socially were the roots of change in the drinking habits of Americans. When the National Recovery Administration was created in 1933, the wine makers of California joined together to create a self-help society called the California Wine Institute, whose purpose was to educate Americans in the pleasures of drinking wine, particularly California wine. The NRA was declared unconstitutional in 1935, but the Wine Institute, because it filled a need, lived on, and has labored valiantly since, employing all of publicity's mysterious arts to teach Americans "how to drink wine, when to drink it, and how much of it to drink." A generation of wine writers, schooled in the subtleties and complexities of European wine, has grumbled about the simplistic "Now-dearie-just-don't-you-bother-your-little-head" approach of the Wine Institute, and its attitude of defensive chauvinism. But those fancy writers are a bunch of snobs anyway, and the diligent, patient efforts of the California Wine Institute without doubt have played a significant part in the change in American drinking habits that finally came.

The End of the Shipper

The most radical change made by Prohibition in the California wine industry was the elimination of the shippers. Before 1919 there was in California, as in every other important wine district in the world, a degree of specialization of function. Growers grew the grapes and then either made them into wine, which they sold to shippers, or sold the grapes direct to the shippers, who then made the wine. In either case, the shippers picked and chose among the products of the various growers to find wines, at prices they liked, that suited whatever clientele they had developed. It was up to the shipper, not the grower, to see that the wine reached his customers in distant places, and to promote the sale of the wine.

With Prohibition, the shippers, like the growers, had to find other ways to make a living. But while the growers at least kept their land, and many continued to grow grapes for one purpose or another, the shippers could keep nothing. When Repeal came, some of the old shippers tried to re-establish themselves, but the market was too disorganized so they gave up the attempt. That meant that growers had to deal direct with wholesalers if they wanted to sell their wine. But a wholesaler in New York did not want to deal with fifteen different California growers for fifteen different kinds of wine. He wanted one source to sell him fifteen kinds of wine, or whatever. So the grower in order to stay in business had to take over the functions of a shipper. He had to be ready to market a "full line" of wines, which today comes to about twenty-eight different kinds, and to promote them himself.

Thus, far more than in Burgundy or even Alsace, the impact of an accident of history accomplished a radical change in the structure of the California wine industry. In the standard wine segment of the business the result has been dramatic innovation and spectacular success. In the premium wine segment the result so far has been much less satisfactory.

Italian Renaissance

While only hindsight reveals it, it could be argued that the most decisive single event in the post-Prohibition history of California wine, comparable in importance to the trip to Europe in 1861 of the famous Colonel Haraszthy to collect wine cuttings, was the decision in 1933 of two young brothers in Modesto, California, Ernest Gallo, twenty-four, and Julio Gallo, twenty-three, to revive the family wine business there. With their Italian ancestry—their forebears had been winegrowers in the Piedmont section of Italy—combined with their American birth and education, the brothers Gallo formed a kind of bridge between the old southern European love for and understanding of wine, and the aggressive, organized business efficiency of the northern European cultures, as transplanted to the United States.

The Gallo story is primarily a story of marketing: of moving with vigorous innovation into the vacuum left behind by the elimination of the shippers. The fast-buck artists of the immediate post-Repeal period were very sensitive to the drinking requirements of the Skid Row and cheap-drunk sets, and quite successful in meeting them. The more responsible producers, with their traditional European backgrounds, were wittingly or unwittingly oriented to producing wines that appealed to people with palates like their own, and their markets were thereby self-limiting. The Gallos were the first to take dead aim at the preferences, blind spots, and hang-ups of your average American "whiskey-drinking, water-drinking, coffee-drinking, tea-drinking, and consequently dyspepsia-inviting subject." The result is a heart-warming story of Yankee Ingenuity (Italian style) and a triumph of the Great American Free Enterprise Tradition.

The Gallos' marketing research at first amounted to little more than persistent questioning of customers about what they liked, but it underlined in an increasingly organized way what has been known informally for a long time: that novice wine drinkers of whatever nationality prefer somewhat sweet wines to bone-dry ones, white or pink wines to red ones, simple wines to complex ones, light and sprightly wines to full, rich ones, and one- or two-dollar-a-bottle wines to four- or five-dollar ones.

Furthermore, they want the next bottle they buy to be just like the last bottle they had, and never mind the hocus-pocus about the vintage of '64. (Every member of every generation in any culture obviously begins as a novice in wine. But in wine-loving cultures this novitiate rarely lasts beyond puberty. The Gallos were the first to face up fully to the fact that they were dealing with a Nation of Novices.)

Those were the specifications and the Gallo boys set out to meet them.

GALLO

HEARTY BURGUNDY

OF CALIFORNIA

We are often told by knowledgeable people that they are delighted in having discovered a great wine in Hearty Burgundy. Its rich, full-bodied flavor—from extremely fine varietal grapes—will surprise you. Made and bottled at the Gallo Vineyards in Modesto, Ca. Alc. 13.5% by vol.

Julio in the vineyard and the winery, Ernest in the market place, starting with a grape crusher and some casks in a warehouse rented with borrowed money and a small wine cellar on the bank of Dry Creek near Modesto. While other people were cleaning up with fortified appetizer and dessert wines for the cheap-drunk market, the Gallo boys began with the table wines that were their heritage. It was to be seven years before they felt they were producing wine good enough even to put their label on. But when they did enter the market under their own name, in 1940, the wine pleased the customers and generated repeat business.

At just about the time the Gallos were beginning to gain a foothold, the broader forces of history were working in a way that was to have a profound effect on California wine in general and on the Gallos in particular. With United States entry into World War II in 1941, millions of impressionable young Americans went overseas, to be exposed to ancient cultures where wine is a staple of life. After the war, thousands more went over on Fulbright scholarships or junior years abroad, and millions of their elders followed as tourists. As the forties wore on to the fifties, and the fifties to the sixties, more and more people became educated (and educated people are more open to new life styles), more and more people had money, and traveled, and entertained on the expense account. Thus there developed an interest in wine, abetted no doubt by the patient pedagogy of the California Wine Institute, that was first a trickle and then a trend and finally a boom.

Between 1960 and 1972 the total quantity of wine sold in the United States increased from 163 million gallons to 337 million, and the volume of California wine production increased from 129 million to 237 million. Within this total the volume of table and sparkling wines increased fourfold, from nearly 60 million gallons to more than 240 million, while the volume of strong appetizer and dessert wines, the carry-over from the early post-Repeal days, actually declined by almost a third. By 1970 the volume of Gallo wines sold had reached an estimated 75 million annually, or almost two bottles of every five shipped in California, one in every three consumed in the United States. Gallo was thus firmly established as the largest, most innovative, and assuredly most profitable wine maker in the world.

Other wine makers were not slow to follow the Gallo lead, but Gallo got there first and holds the commanding position. (Also, not only is Ernest Gallo a highly talented marketer, but the Gallo brothers have been in continuous, personal control of their company from the start, while their principal competitors have been penalized by the shifting ownership of distant corporations.) Next in size to Gallo is United Vintners, owner of Italian Swiss Colony, Inglenook, Petri, and Lejon (vermouth and brandy), which shipped 47 million gallons in 1970. In third place, at 7.6 million gallons in 1970, barely 10 per cent of Gallo's volume, is the Guild Wine

Company, which also owns the Roma label. Next in line is Franzia, which shipped 7.2 million gallons in 1970. (Most of the larger premium producers from the North Coast Counties, and some of the small ones, too, also produce standard wines, as well as the higher-priced varietals.)

The Standard Wines

The standard wines from these various sources are produced in three classes. First are the traditional generic wines, whose names go back to the earliest days of commercial wine making in California: Burgundy, Claret, Chablis, Rhine Wine, Moselle, Chianti. California also produces what is called Dry Sauterne, without the "s" as in the true French Sauternes. (Apparently those dumb Americans thought "Sauternes" was plural.) A *dry* "Sauterne," or Sauternes, either one, is, of course, a contradiction in terms. Its very existence would confirm in the mind of a loyal Frenchman all he has heard, and would prefer to believe in any case, about *les Americains*. But it sells real good, Americans have grown used to it, so now it is a fixture of the market. A "Sweet Sauterne" is produced also, although this is a moderately sweet table wine, not a dessert wine.

These standard wines, as noted earlier, are the American counterpart of the *vins ordinaires* of Europe. The quality varies, but by and large, with their massive market research, their scientific blending and careful stabilization, they are greatly superior to the rough, raw, bulk products that are drunk every day by millions of French and Italian workingmen, and are exported to the United States to compete in the $1.29-a-bottle class. (A distinction needs to be made, however, between the cheap, coarse, high-volume *ordinaires,* which in the past have been composed all or in part of rough Algerian wines, and the legitimate *vins du pays,* the country wines

of Europe, produced by the people of a particular area for their own consumption. The *vins du pays* obviously hold the prospect of a variety and delightful surprise which would not be expected from the standardized generic wines of California. A high-volume European *ordinaire* would not.)

Be they ever so humble, and by whatever name, the standard wines of California belong on our Spectrum of Possibility because they are so universally available, because they (usually) represent exceptional value at the price, because this is where the average American drinker of wine begins to learn, and because in many situations—a simple, shoreside seafood restaurant, for example, or a friendly neighborhood pub—either you have no alternative or the alternatives are questionable.

But positioning these wines on the Spectrum is at best an approximate matter. A California "Claret" is usually a reasonably light red wine, but a California "Burgundy" can be anything from very light to fairly heavy (and by definition neither one bears resemblance in anything more than name to the authentic Bordeaux or Burgundies of France). As for the white wines, some California producers cheerfully admit that their "Chablis" and "Dry Sauterne" and "Rhine Wine" all come from the same vat, depending on what the market calls for that day. So there is nothing much to be done except arrange these wines on the Spectrum in the order their European names suggest:

Light and Delicate White	CALIFORNIA "MOSELLE"
	CALIFORNIA "CHABLIS"
Fuller-bodied White	CALIFORNIA "RHINE WINE"
	CALIFORNIA "DRY SAUTERNE"
Rosé	CALIFORNIA ROSÉ
Light-bodied Red	CALIFORNIA "CLARET"
Fuller-bodied Red	CALIFORNIA "BURGUNDY"
	CALIFORNIA "CHIANTI"

The prices of the California standard wines vary, as does the quality, although here as elsewhere a higher price does not in every case indicate better value. In general, standard wines from the big producers like Gallo or Petri or Italian Swiss Colony sell in New York for about $1.50 a bottle; those from the "Big Three" among premium producers—Almadén, the Christian Brothers, Paul Masson—in the $2.00 range. Those of the medium-sized premium producers such as Charles Krug or Louis Martini are priced at about $2.25. A California Burgundy from Beaulieu Vineyard, one of the best regarded of the premium producers, would cost around $2.50. A "limited edition" of the same wine from the same producer would cost upward of $4.00.

The best bargains among the standard wines come, of course, in gallon or half-gallon jugs. A California Burgundy which costs $1.49 in an individual bottle (one fifth of a gallon) might cost $2.95 for a half gallon (two and a half bottles) or $5.29 for a full gallon (five bottles). This works out to a price equivalent of $1.19 a bottle or $1.06 a bottle, respectively.

A whole cult has grown up around the jug wines. For a while there was a kind of antisnob snobbery about them. The willingness to serve an "adequate little domestic wine" over a more expensive import indicated that you were a true sophisticate. One lady faculty member of a well-known eastern university even went so far as to serve California jug wines to visiting members of European royalty. Their reactions are not recorded, although they were undoubtedly polite.

Proprietary Wines

The requirements of the market place being what they are, these basic generic names have undergone steady modification for the sake of competitive advantage. After all, if you market a "Burgundy," and your competitor markets a "Burgundy," the unsophisticate is likely to assume they are pretty much the same, and it is not hard to get him to switch. But if, for example, you market a "Hearty Burgundy," then hopefully the customer can be persuaded that that wine is different, and you can pour the advertising dollars on.

The very popular rosé has become Beaurosé, Petite Rosé (literally "small rosé"), Navelle rosé, Rose Brook, Vin Rosé Sec ("dry pink wine"), and not least the hugely successful Gallo "Pink Chablis," another ghastly anomaly in the mind of any proper Frenchman. Among the Rhines we find such romantic titles as Rhine Castle, Rhine Garten, and Rhineskeller.

Beyond the proprietary modifications are the purely made-up names.

These began with the appetizer wines such as Thunderbird, Eden Roc, and Gypsy Rose, then moved into the table wines: Gallo's Paisano, another huge success, was probably the first. It was followed by wines from other producers carrying such names as Baroque, Barberone, Rubion, Barenblut (Bear's Blood), Mountain Nectar, and Emerald Dry. This is brand-naming in its purest form. The wine need have no characteristic except what the producer wants it to have, and if the novice tries Rubion or Barenblut and likes it, the odds are good that he will go back looking for that and no other.

Ripple and Pot

And beyond the strictly proprietary blends is the newest trend of all, the "flavored" wines: red, white, or pink wine, with sugar, fruit flavoring, and sometimes a hint of carbonation added. These appeal mainly to the youngest members of the drinking class, whose palates have been shaped by Coke and raspberry soda. They can be drunk with food, but can also be consumed between meals and in the evening (as can Coke and raspberry soda) which profitably extends the drinking day. It is said that the flavored wines, particularly Gallo Ripple, are especially popular with the younger set while they are smoking marijuana.

Here are the chief entries from the two biggest producers:

Gallo	*Italian Swiss Colony*
Ripple	Swizzle
Spañada	Bali Hai
Boone's Farm Wild Mountain Grape	Swiss-Up
Boone's Farm Strawberry Hill	Annie Green Springs Country
Boone's Farm Apple Wine	Cherry-Berry Frost
	Annie Green Springs Peach Creek
	Annie Green Springs Plum Hollow

A general note is in order here on the blending and flavoring of wines. It should not be assumed that blending is either unique to California or a somehow not-quite-respectable thing to do. Champagne is in eminent degree a blended product, with sugar syrup added, and brandy, too. All Sherries are blended and doctored with brandy; most Ports are both blended and flavored; Vermouths are by definition flavored wines; and some even whisper that in the dark of night caramel is added to the noble brandies of Cognac to make them smooth. Among table wines as such, Châteauneuf-du-Pape, as we have noted, is blended from as many as twelve wines, Chianti from five, and even Queen Bordeaux is not made from a single grape at all, but usually from a blend of three.

So California blended products may be good or they may be bad. But the blending itself is not a wicked sin.

The Premium Wines

While all this blending and flavoring was going on down in standard wine country, back in the North Coast Counties the makers of premium wines were laboring in their own respective vineyards. To understand North Coast wines it is first necessary to know something about the topography and climate of the North Coast.

In the most northerly of the North Coast Counties, Mendocino, and in the northern part of Sonoma County, along the banks of the Russian River, lies a flat, hot, fertile valley, cut off from the tempering influence of the ocean breezes by the Coast Range. Here, in conditions not very different from those of the Sacramento and San Joaquin valleys to the south and east, is a small region that produces generic and lesser varietal wines. The dominant operator is Italian Swiss Colony. Farther downstream on the Russian River, in much cooler country where the river cuts westward through the Coast Range on its way to the sea, is located the Korbel winery, which grows California "Champagne" among the huge stumps of a cut-over redwood forest.

In the southern portion of Sonoma County and in the Napa Valley, just to the east across the Mayacamas Range, conditions are temperate, ventilated by the breezes blowing in through the Golden Gate and across the Bay. The grape varieties that thrive here are the noble ones, red and white, of Burgundy and Bordeaux. Most of California's best wineries are located in the Napa Valley.

Fifty miles to the south and east, farther inland from the coast and less exposed to breezes off the water, is the flat, warm, sunny Livermore Valley, where conditions are similar to those of the Graves and Sauternes regions of Bordeaux. The full-bodied white wines that grow here, both dry and sweet, are, not surprisingly, grown from the grape varieties that are native to Graves and Sauternes.

South and a bit west of the Bay is the Santa Clara Valley. The climate here is somewhat warmer than that of Napa and southern Sonoma County, the quality of the medium-bodied reds and whites not as high, but the vol-

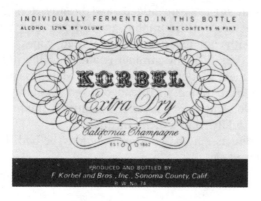

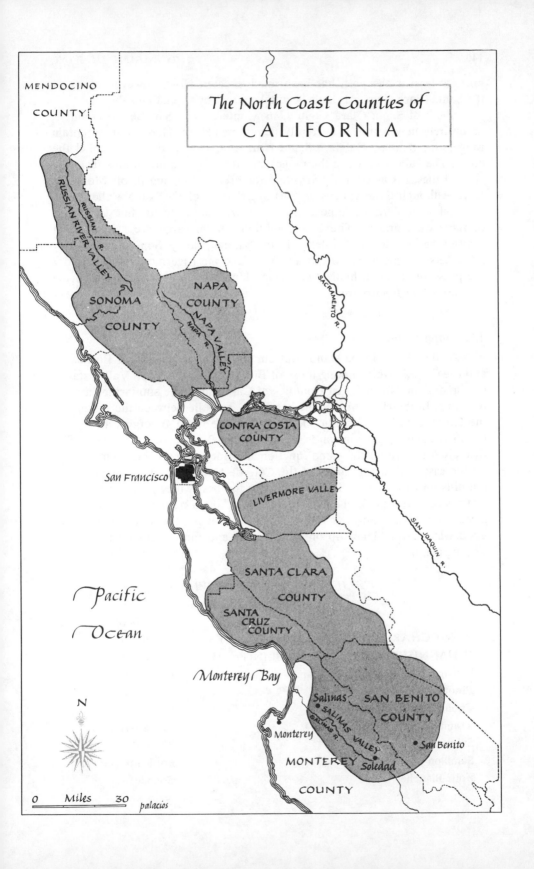

The North Coast Counties of
CALIFORNIA

MENDOCINO
COUNTY

RUSSIAN RIVER VALLEY
RUSSIAN R.

SONOMA
COUNTY

NAPA
COUNTY
NAPA VALLEY
NAPA R.

SACRAMENTO R.

CONTRA COSTA
COUNTY

San Francisco

LIVERMORE VALLEY

SAN JOAQUIN R.

SANTA CLARA
COUNTY

SANTA
CRUZ
COUNTY

Pacific
Ocean

Monterey Bay

Salinas
SALINAS R.
SALINAS VALLEY

SAN BENITO
COUNTY

Monterey

San Benito

MONTEREY
Soledad

COUNTY

N

0   Miles   30   palacios

ume, at least in the past, has been much greater. Now, however, many of the Santa Clara vineyards have been taken over by spreading suburbs.

South of Santa Clara County, in Monterey and San Benito counties, an entirely new region is currently being opened up. Here, four mountain ranges, the Salinas, Gabilan, Santa Cruz, and Diablo ranges, parallel the coast. The valleys between the ranges, sheltered by the mountains from the coastal fogs, act as cool-air corridors for breezes blowing in off Monterey Bay. Although these valleys lie 150 miles south of the Napa Valley, they are slightly cooler, and appear to be very well suited to the finest varieties of table wine grapes. The best conditions in this area are said to exist around the little town of Soledad in the Salinas Valley. Some of the major producers of wine in Santa Clara County and the Livermore Valley, under the pressures of suburbanization, have planted large new vineyards in the Monterey-San Benito area.

The Napa Valley

As the Haut-Médoc stands out among the wine regions of Bordeaux, and the Côte de Nuits among those of Burgundy, so the Napa Valley stands out among the North Coast Counties of California. The similarities are interesting. In the Haut-Médoc the best wine lands lie between the estuary of the Gironde and the Atlantic Ocean, where the water functions as a giant thermostat. For the vineyards of the Napa Valley the waters of San Francisco Bay fulfill the same function. In Burgundy the best wines grow on the eastward-facing slopes of the Côte de Nuits, just at the angle where the hills touch the plain. In Napa County the best wines grow on the eastward-facing west bank of the Napa River, although perhaps because of the more even climate and the wider distribution of pebbly, well-drained soil, good wines grow higher up on the hillsides and farther out on the gently sloping plain.

CALIFORNIA VARIETAL WINES
WHITE WINE

Variety	Origin of Grape
PINOT CHARDONNAY or CHARDONNAY	Burgundy
JOHANNISBERG or WHITE RIESLING	Rhine Basin
Sauvignon Blanc (or Fumé Blanc)	Bordeaux (Graves)
Pinot Blanc	Burgundy
Chenin Blanc (or White Pinot)	Loire
Traminer (or Gewürztraminer)	Rhine Basin
Sylvaner	Rhine Basin
Semillon	Bordeaux (Graves)
Folle Blanche	Cognac

Grey Riesling	France
Emerald Riesling	California hybrid
Green Hungarian	Unknown

RED WINE

CABERNET SAUVIGNON	Bordeaux
PINOT NOIR	Burgundy
ZINFANDEL	Unknown
Gamay Beaujolais	Beaujolais
Barbera	Italy
Ruby Cabernet	California hybrid
Petite Sirah	Rhône

ROSÉ

GRENACHE ROSÉ	Rhône
Gamay Rosé	Beaujolais
Grignolino	Italy

The Noble Varieties

The best red wine of California is made from the Cabernet Sauvignon, the great red wine grape of Bordeaux. The best white wine is made from the Pinot Chardonnay or Chardonnay, the premier white wine grape of Burgundy, from which Chablis, Meursault, and Montrachet are made. But the Cabernet in California (when planted on suitable soil) usually produces a wine that is fuller in body than the typical red Bordeaux, while the white wine produced by the Pinot Chardonnay is lighter than Meursault or Montrachet, fuller than Chablis. So these are emphatically California wines, although they do not deny their origin.

Among the red wines the runner-up in quality to the Cabernet Sauvignon is Pinot Noir, the great red wine grape of Burgundy. In California the Pinot Noir at its best makes a good, somewhat lightish red wine, but not one in the same class with the Cabernet. Among dry white wines the close runner-up in quality to the Pinot Chardonnay is the White Riesling or Johannisberg Riesling, from which all the best wines of the Rhine, Moselle, and Alsace are made. The best rosé of California is made from the Grenache grape, from Tavel on the Rhône, where the best rosé of Europe is made. To this basic list should be added the name of the Zinfandel, a grape of mysterious origin, which produces in considerable volume a simple, good, widely popular red wine.

There are better than a dozen other grape varieties, as the table on pages 140–141 shows, whose names appear on the labels of bottles of California wines, and anyone who wants to study those wines will get to know them. But the six above are enough for purposes of our Spectrum of Possibility. Here, then, is the Spectrum in full for California:

	Standard Wines	Varietal Wines
Light and Delicate White	"MOSELLE" "CHABLIS"	JOHANNISBERG or WHITE RIESLING
Fuller-bodied White	"RHINE WINE" "DRY SAUTERNE"	PINOT CHARDONNAY
Rosé	ROSÉ	GRENACHE ROSÉ
Light-bodied Red	"CLARET"	PINOT NOIR ZINFANDEL
Fuller-bodied Red	"BURGUNDY" "CHIANTI"	CABERNET SAUVIGNON

The range of prices for California wines bearing a given varietal label is extremely wide (reflecting, as we shall note a bit later, some of the labeling problems of the better wines). If a Cabernet Sauvignon from one of the "Big Three" premium producers—Almadén, the Christian Brothers, Paul Masson—sells in New York for $3, one from one of the medium-sized producers—Beaulieu Vineyard, Charles Krug, Inglenook—might go for $4 to $5, one from an elegant newcomer like Mirassou or Robert Mondavi or Chappelet for $6 to $9. A 1969 Napa Valley Cabernet Sauvignon, "Lot C-91," from Heitz Wine Cellars might cost $10, a Heitz 1968 "Martha's Vineyard" Cabernet, $27, a 1948 Beaulieu Vineyard "Private Reserve" from the same grape, $29. (The prices themselves change, of course, but this illustrates relationships.)

All the California varietal wines, with the exception of some of the very finest bottlings, tend to be simpler, less complex than their European counterparts. Part of the explanation may lie in the California soil and climate, but part lies in the fact that California wines are usually more thoroughly filtered than European wines. Americans are not used to finding sediment in the bottom of a wine bottle, and think it means there is something wrong with the wine, so the producers filter them more carefully. This produces a cleaner, more brilliant wine, but takes away some of the possibility of interesting development. However, since novices prefer a simple wine over a complex one anyway, this does not hurt in the market place.

Some of the small, special California producers are now making it a point to produce much less filtered wines that do throw sediment as they age. People who take the trouble to buy these wines accept this—indeed, prefer it.

The Premium Producers

In 1970 premium wines accounted for no more than 10 to 12 per cent of the total volume of California wine produced (but a substantially greater percentage of the dollar volume, since they average two to three times more expensive than standard wines). Premium wine producers fall into three classes: the Big Three, the thirty or so medium producers, and a number of smaller producers. The Big Three and most of the medium producers market a full line. The smaller producers sell a more limited selection.

The Big Three among the premium wine makers—Almadén, Paul Masson, and the Christian Brothers—together produce more wine annually than all the rest of the premium producers put together. Almadén, which produced about 6 million gallons in 1970, and Paul Masson, which produced 4.5 million, have historically been located in the Santa Clara Valley south of San Francisco, but as the suburbs have pressed in on their vineyards, they have become involved in developing new acreage in the Monterey-San Benito region farther south.

The Christian Brothers' Mont La Salle winery is located in the hills overlooking the lower end of the Napa Valley. The winery is owned by the Brothers of the Christian Schools, a Catholic teaching order, and its profits go to the support of the order's schools in the northern California area. The order's wine-making efforts produced about 4 million gallons in 1970. Current opinion ranks the quality of Christian Brothers wines somewhat higher than those of the other two.

Almadén and Paul Masson market their own wines. A few years ago the Christian Brothers did their own, too. However, they ran into problems. David Ogilvie, in his *Confessions of an Advertising Man,* tells how his advertising agency once tried to produce a series of advertisements for the Christian Brothers' wines. The Brother Winemaster liked the work, but

it was sent to the Vatican for approval. The dictum came back that the campaign must be "without impact." Ogilvie resigned the account. Now the Christian Brothers' wines are marketed by Fromm and Sichel, a fallible, finite, human, and indeed commercial distribution company, controlled by Seagram's Whisky. One assumes the Christian Brothers' advertising now has impact.

As noted, the generic wines produced by the Big Three premium producers are usually considered a cut above the average, both in quality and in price, of those of the standard wine producers. Their varietals as a rule do not measure up to the best produced by the medium and small producers (although such comparisons and generalizations are hard to make). Almadén also produces huge quantities of jug wines—Mountain Red, Mountain White, Mountain Rosé—in a premium-jug price class. Opinions differ as to whether they are worth the difference.

Any limited selection among the medium-sized producers of premium wines must necessarily be arbitrary. Following are ten of the best known:

Producer	Location
Beaulieu Vineyard	Napa
Beringer	Napa
Inglenook	Napa
Charles Krug	Napa
Louis Martini	Napa
Robert Mondavi	Napa
Korbel	Upper Sonoma
Wente Brothers	Livermore and San Benito
Weibel	Livermore and Mendocino
Mirassou Vineyards	Santa Clara and Monterey

The primacy of the Napa Valley among California premium wines is clearly shown by this list. Among long-established producers, Beaulieu Vineyard, Louis Martini, and Charles Krug have perhaps the highest repu-

tation. The two newest entries in the group, Robert Mondavi and Mirassou, both representatives of old California wine families, began operations
under their own labels only in the 1960s. Both are now challenging the
best of the old-timers in the quality of their wines. Louis Martini and
Inglenook produce jug wines of exceptional quality for this class. In the
last few years Wente has been able to withdraw somewhat from the full-
line production into which competition had forced it, and to concentrate
on the white wines it is best suited to produce.

Below the medium producers are the smaller, more specialized wineries, producing one or several wines, in volumes that usually run less than
100,000 gallons a year. Some of their wines are excellent. Some are considered overrated. Many are extremely hard to buy outside of California,
both because production is limited and because varying legal barriers and
requirements in the other forty-nine states make it uneconomic for them to
try to market their wines outside the state. Here are the names of some of
the better known among the smaller vineyards:

Vineyard	Location
Chappellet	Napa
Freemark Abbey	Napa
Heitz Wine Cellars	Napa
Mayacamas Vineyards	Napa
Oakville Vineyards	Napa
Schramsberg Vineyards (Champagne)	Napa
Souverain Cellars	Napa
Spring Mountain Vineyards	Napa
Stony Hill Vineyard	Napa
Sterling Vineyards	Napa
Hanzel Winery	Sonoma
Llords and Elwood	Santa Clara
Martin Ray Vineyards	Santa Clara

In the last few years all the California producers except the smallest
ones have become the subject of keen interest on the part of various corporations, who have wanted to acquire them in order to get a piece of the
exciting growth of California wine. The only conspicuous holdouts have
been Gallo, the Christian Brothers (but its distribution, as noted, is controlled by Seagram's), and two medium-sized producers of premium wines,
Louis Martini and Wente Brothers.

The impact of corporate control on major standard-wine producers
like Italian Swiss Colony and Petri may or may not be great, since what
they produce is in effect a mass-produced industrial product anyway. For
those premium producers which have been acquired, the access to practically unlimited corporate capital has undoubtedly helped in the fabu-
lously expensive business of buying and developing new vineyard land (to
the extent that there is any good land that has not already been spoken

for). But here once again is the potential for a conflict between the cultures: Can the normal American corporate concern with steady year-to-year increases in sales and earnings be reconciled with the uncertain business of growing grapes, and the traditional European approach of devoting to each year's vintage the time and love required to produce the best wine possible? Time will have to tell.

To Buy a California Bottle

Anyone who buys a bottle of California wine is operating right at the meeting point, the "interface" between the two cultures. The most immediately obvious point from the standpoint of the American buyer is that a California label is so "foreign." Now, this is a rather odd statement, considering that the California bottle is labeled in his native tongue, while the others are not. But the problem is not so much one of language as of modes and systems of thought. Once you have mastered the "grammar" of labeling for almost any wine district in Europe (Alsace being the only notable exception) you have a long leg up in learning that of almost any other district in Europe, despite regional variations and imperfections. California is a totally different ball game.

A wine label is a medium of communication. If it is an effective medium, it transmits to the potential buyer adequate information in two areas: *identity* and *responsibility:* identity as to the materials used and methods employed (including where and when the grapes were grown); responsibility to indicate whether or not the information on identity is to be trusted, whether or not the methods used were skillfully used, and whether the handling of the wine since has been honest and competent. In buying the better wines of a place like Bordeaux, you come about as close as human institutions can bring you to establishing clear identity and full responsibility. The boundaries of a particular vineyard are officially delimited (and safeguarded by the rules of classification). The general quality of the vineyard is testified not simply by its official classification, but by records, going back several centuries, of the judgment of free and orderly markets; these markets put a value on each year's production based on actual sampling by some of the most sophisticated palates in the world.

There is no need for the buyer to ask what grape or grapes went into the batch or how they were handled. Those matters are traditional, and in any case the appellation contrôlée regulations specify what grapes are permitted, and the claim to identity cannot be made unless the regulations have been complied with.

Thus, if the label says "Lafite '59," it has pretty much said it all. And even if it only says "St.-Julien" or "St.-Émilion" or just "Bordeaux Rouge," it has told you a great deal, subject to verification as to responsibility, usually through the name of a good shipper.

In Burgundy or Germany the basic system is the same, but because the ownership of the vineyards themselves is often fragmented, the name of the shipper assumes greater importance in certifying both identity and responsibility. The Burgundian saying *"Respectez les crus"*—Pay attention to the vineyard name—is a way of saying, "Keep in mind the issue of identity." In Alsace the institutions certifying identity have not yet been fully rebuilt, but here, also, there are shippers, some of them responsible, to step in and at least partially fill the gap. In Italy institutions of wine are not as well developed as in France and Germany. But the large estates of regions like Chianti establish both identity and responsibility; there are shippers and exporters of solid reputation; and the new wine laws are fully in line with those of the rest of Europe.

In California among the standard wines the requirements of identity and responsibility are admirably fulfilled, particularly among the proprietary names. (The "grammar" is different from a European label, but the message is the same.) If you buy a bottle of Gallo Paisano, say, or Hearty Burgundy or Pink Chablis, you have absolutely no idea what the grapes are or when they were grown, but you have no need to know. If Ernest and Julio Gallo say the wine's okay, the wine's okay. Gallo is to *ordinaire* what Rothschild is to Lafite. In each case there has been enormous investment in love and pride and treasure in building that name, and there is a tremendous backup of talent and skill to maintain it. They are not going to throw it all away just to gyp you on one bottle. (Of course, if an outside corporation buys a producer and deliberately prostitutes the name for the sake of quick profit, that is another question. But the same thing can happen to the finest European vineyards. More than once it has.)

To go to the other end of the scale, a wine from one of the little vine-

Paisano

THE NATURAL MELLOW RED WINE

PURE COUNTRY RED TABLE WINE

THIS FINE WINE WAS MADE AND BOTTLED BY THE GALLO VINEYARDS · MODESTO, CALIF. · ALC. 13% BY VOL.

yards of California, if you can find one, creates no great problem of identity or responsibility. This is wine making in the ancient European tradition. The vineyard is a specific, defined piece of ground. The product line is limited to a few wines. The ownership and management are usually the same people, often members of one family, who have worked hard to build whatever name and following they have. Frequently there is personal acquaintance and trust between the owner-managers and customers.

Thus, the problems of buying California wines are centered in the premium products, the varietal wines, of the full-line producers—which, alas, in most of the country are the only fine California wines readily available. The difficulties are twofold: First of all, the institution of varietal labeling simply does not offer precise information in identity; second, the institution of full-line production not only does not clear up the question of identity, it seriously blurs the issue of responsibility as well.

Varietal Labeling

If only one or a few grape varieties produced good wine in all of California, or in all the North Coast Counties, say; or if one grape accounted for all the best red wine of the Napa and lower Sonoma valleys and some other grape produced the best reds of the Santa Clara-San Benito-Monterey area, then very likely the resulting wines would be known in the market as Napa Red or Santa Clara White, just as we today talk about the Red Bordeaux or the White Burgundies or the Moselle-Saar-Ruwer wines. The buyer would not need to know the name of the grape in order to know the character of the wine. And if the Napa Valley had been producing wine for a thousand years—or even for the last hundred or so without disastrous interruption—then almost certainly it would have become a matter of common knowledge that such-and-such a plot, perhaps named for a Spanish general, produced an incomparable red, and such-and-such, named for an Indian princess, produced superb white, and they would now be legendary as Vallejo Red or Tamalpais White, or whatever, just as Lafite or Montrachet are legendary, and again the names of the grapes would not matter.

But California winegrowers are still learning which grapes grow best on a particular patch of soil—and even where there is knowledge it is not general knowledge—the kind that makes a difference in the market. So because usable geographic designations are not available, the California winegrowers have had to adopt grape names instead of place names as the primary designation of their better wines.

However, the problems with varietal labeling as such are quickly apparent. In the first place there are too many varieties. In Bordeaux, for all its myriad geographic classifications, we identified only four major entries on our Spectrum of Possibility. In Burgundy, with its greater diversity, we identified seven. California markets varietal wine of no fewer than thirty varieties. A major producer may carry twelve to fourteen in his line. Even some of the more specialized carry six to nine. For the collector, the hobbyist, this diversity can be a wonderland. For the average drinker of wine it is a hopeless mess.

But the basic difficulty goes deeper: The name of a grape, taken by itself, does not adequately identify a wine. Take the Cabernet Sauvignon as a case in point. The Cabernet by common agreement is the grape variety capable of producing the finest red wine, and indeed the finest wine, that California offers. And when it is planted on soil ideally suited to that variety, it will, other things being equal, produce superb wine. But if the Cabernet is planted on soil better suited to, say, the Folle Blanche or the Grignolio, it might produce indifferent wine. But it is still entitled to go to market under the varietal label. And the level of demand being what it is, any drinkable wine carrying that magic tag sells very readily.

The legislators and regulators, sensitive, obviously, to the desires of California producers, have not helped the buyer very much. Under existing rules a wine may be labeled Cabernet Sauvignon (or Pinot Chardonnay or Johannisberg Riesling) if it contains no less than 51 per cent of those grapes. That means the other grapes can be any old thing (as long as they come from California). So a bottle quite properly and legally labeled Cabernet Sauvignon may be only 51 per cent Cabernet (of whatever quality) or 100 per cent, or any amount between. And the blending may be superbly judicious or totally incompetent; there is no way to be sure.

If a vintage year is given on the label, you get better protection, and it is obviously the counsel of wisdom to spend more money and get this protection. Under the law, wine sold with a vintage label must be not only 95 per cent from the year noted, but 75 per cent from the place noted—Napa Valley, Livermore Valley, Monterey County.

There is no guarantee, of course, that a Napa Cabernet of 1972 will

be anything special. But if they went to this much trouble, the odds are improving in your favor. However, no designation of identity is enough in itself without supporting assurance as to responsibility. And this is where the institution of full-line production falls down.

The Full-line Problem

A "full line" today normally consists of separately labeled table wines made from perhaps a dozen different grape varieties, along with appetizer wines, dessert wines, Champagnes, and brandies (this does not count the generic and proprietary wines which many premium full-line producers also carry). A full-line producer will grow as many grapes as he can on his own land, and will buy the rest of what he needs, either as newly harvested grapes or as wine in bulk. This means the vines he plants on his own land are planted not necessarily with an eye to producing the very best wine a particular spot of land is capable of producing, but to meeting his requirements for a number of grape varieties. It also means—particularly for the larger producers—that his people do not have the time, as the better European wine makers do, to specialize, to focus their time and skill on bringing out the best of a particular location and grape variety. Instead, they must spread themselves very thin trying to do reasonably well with a considerable number of varieties, sometimes in scattered locations. The same is true with the wine making itself. The staff is working not only with various batches of the same variety but also simultaneously with different batches of a number of varieties. So their chances of coming to understand and excel with any one of them, much less all of them, are not great.

As for the grapes or bulk wine the full-line producer buys outside, if he is a very large producer he will buy from a number of sources and there is no way for him to be fully assured of how and where the grapes were grown, or how responsibly and professionally the wine was made. Thus the output of wine of a given variety of a given year from a given producer can be widely variable. It is not unheard-of at a dinner party for two bottles of wine with identical labels—same producer, same grape, same year—to be opened, one of which will be excellent, the other thin and entirely uninteresting.

The California wine laws do require that the label give you some indication of the history of what went into the bottle.

If the label says, *Produced and bottled by* such-and-such, it means that at least 75 per cent of the wine in the bottle was crushed by and fermented at the winery. From a winery of good reputation this is still further insurance, particularly if a vintage year and location are also given.

If it says, *Made and bottled by* . . . , that means that anything from 10 to 75 per cent of the wine was crushed and fermented at the winery, while the rest was merely "finished" (aged, blended bottled) there. From a less-than-first-rate winery, particularly on a wine in the two-dollar range, it can be pretty much a license to steal.

Cellared and bottled by . . . , *Perfected and bottled by* . . . , and just plain *Bottled by* . . . mean that 100 per cent of the wine was brought from somewhere else and finished at the winery.

The difficulty with any of the above is that in no case does it give an indication of where or by whom the grapes from which the wine was made were grown. Moreover, excellent wines from various producers are marketed bearing any of the three legends, and indifferent wines can also be found carrying any of them.

The term *estate-bottled* is also found on California bottles. That means, as in Europe, that the wine was made exclusively from grapes grown on the winery's own adjacent vineyards. Once again, on a good label this can have meaning, but it can also work to the advantage of wineries with huge holdings of not necessarily first-rate land adjacent to the winery, and work to the disadvantage of those that produce grapes in several locations, or do an excellent job of buying grapes or wine in bulk from a fine, responsible producer down the road. Also, some of the finer wineries produce wines that are technically entitled to the estate-bottled designation, but do not bother to put it on because of the red tape involved.

The terms *limited bottling* or *private reserve* will also appear on a label. These have no standing under the law. They can indicate an unusually good wine if they are found on the label of a responsible winery. On another label they can be meaningless. The language *private stock* can mean anything. A numbered label, or a *cask* or *cuvée* number appearing on the label, can mean an exceptional wine if the producer is a responsible one, although here, too, there is no legal definition of what it stands for.

Pricing Policy

The traditional institutions of wine contain a number of safeguards. Château bottling of a fine Bordeaux can insure you against everything but actual thievery, total incompetence, or acts of God. The institution of the shipper can also step in, as notably in Burgundy, in case the institution of the château has broken down. The final check point, the final guide, is the price of the wine itself. As we have suggested before, if you are sitting in a restaurant and at a loss as to what to do, just let your eye travel over to the right-hand column of the wine list, decide what you can afford, and order that. If it is a too-well-known name, it may be somewhat overpriced. If it is a total unknown, it might be quite a bargain (or it might be a dog). But the price that is charged usually mirrors with some degree of accuracy what the wine trade thinks the wine is worth. However, in buying the majority of the California varietals you are denied even this assistance, except in a very rough way. Once again, the culprit is full-line production. If a producer is carrying let us say a dozen varieties of wine, grown at ten different locations over a number of years, thus representing several hundred individual batches, it would be an impossibility for him even to think of trying to put a separate price on each lot, and then to change the price as the wine developed and demand shifted. Usually the best he can do is divide them at the time of bottling between run-of-the-mill and the better wines. Thus, most of the California varietals are sold somewhere in the two-to-five-dollar range. Directly competing price categories normally sell within a few pennies of each other, and the price is adjusted (always upward in recent years) as over-all demand grows and production costs increase.

Aging

Related to the uniform price situation is the problem of aging. In the past many California wine makers have been reluctant to put vintage years on their wines, not simply because it complicates the printing of labels, but because if a particular year develops a poor reputation they can be stuck with slow-moving inventory, while if it has a good reputation it is not feasible under the uniform price system to charge extra. Also, until recently under California law, wines held in storage were taxed every year. The result was that the producers could not afford to hold wines until they had matured, but sold them off as soon as they could. This meant that by the time a particular vintage of a good Cabernet was really ready to drink there was no more of it left on the market.

There has been some recent improvement in the vintaging-aging area. Increasing numbers of producers are putting vintage years on their bottles. Meanwhile, the California tax on inventory has been limited to a single year, and some of the better producers are now holding back a respectable percentage of each year's production to give it a chance to age. However, in California a vintage label is still not simply an indication that the wine hopefully received extra care and was grown in a good year, but of whether or not it is old enough to be drunk at all—and some of the best wines do not reach their peak for ten or fifteen years. If you do not find a vintage year on the label, there is usually a date—'70, '72, '74—blown into the glass in the bottle's base. This reflects the year the bottle was made, and, normally, the year the wine was bottled. Red wines are usually bottled two years after they were made, white wines in one year, rosés in less than a year.

In an effort to differentiate its too-often-undifferentiated products, the California wine industry has long resorted to competitive tastings, held at state fairs and like occasions. The concept is sound enough, but the execution has a tendency to resemble a children's birthday party, where everyone plays and each gets a prize. Public tasting rooms of wineries all over the state are encrusted with ribbons and medals of every sort. But tasting panels are often asked to rate dozens of wines in a single hurried session— an impossible assignment. One story is told of a panel of judges who gave up trying to classify a group of wines by taste, and instead decided to watch the flies buzzing around the hot, stuffy tasting room under the bleachers at a state fair in southern California, and award first place to whichever bottle a fly lit on first. The story may be apocryphal, but it gives an indication.

One of the most interesting and hopeful developments in the recent history of California wines came in 1971 when two young men, Hurst Hannum and Robert Blumberg, published a small book, *The Fine Wines of California*. The two had spent the same junior year abroad at the University of Bordeaux, of all places, and being young and open to new experience they had learned a good deal about the wines of that area. Then, both having decided to attend law school at the University of California at Berkeley, they transferred their researches to the North Coast wines of California. As they traveled from winery to winery tasting, they found that for varietal wines in the roughly two-dollar class the price "bore little if any relationship to what was inside." (In fairness, let it be reiterated that any wine for about two dollars can be a pretty chancy proposition.) For the higher-priced wines, they did find a closer relationship between price and quality. But even here, a wine which according to the credentials on its label should have been superb was not, while wines bearing less imposing insignia might be quite respectable.

The result was their book, providing for the first time to the general public systematic, comparative ratings of the wines of the best-known varietal producers of California. Messrs. Hannum and Blumberg do not pretend that they have the best-tuned palates in the world, nor that their evaluations are the final word. But the results of their efforts demonstrate clearly the variation of quality that occurs within the present system of labeling and marketing, and not only provide a current guide to specific wines but give some clues to who are the better producers over-all.

Hannum and Blumberg rated the California varietals according to a five-point scale:

☆☆☆☆	Excellent
☆☆☆	Very good
☆☆	Good
☆	Average
BA	Below average

Here is a tabulation of their ratings (as updated in 1973) of wines being marketed by twenty-nine of the best-known producers of California.

What the table of ratings demonstrates dramatically is that you cannot walk into a store and buy a bottle bearing any one of these twenty-nine labels with the assurance that the wine it contains will be of a given level of quality (although it shows that your chances are better in some cases than others). Among the Big Three the ratings give a clear-cut edge to Christian Brothers over Almadén and Paul Masson. Among the medium-sized producers the continued strength of Beaulieu Vineyard shows clearly and, to a lesser degree, that of Charles Krug and Louis Martini (although there has not yet been time to determine the impact on B.V. of its new status as a corporate subsidiary). But the biggest news among the medium producers is the strong bid for leadership by Mirassou and Robert Mondavi, newcomers under their own labels, but—significantly—members of old California wine families.

Among the smaller producers the impact of newcomers is even more striking. Freemark, Heitz, Oakville, and Spring Mountain all began operations in the 1960s, Sterling in 1973.

The Hannum and Blumberg ratings have by no means the authority and antiquity of the ratings of the best wines of Bordeaux and Burgundy, nor do they have the durability, since they are ratings of bottles and years, not vineyards. But they provide a start for anyone interested in searching out superior California wines.

Now, what does all this mean in practical terms to the would-be buyer of a bottle of wine? It means, to repeat what we said at the outset, that anyone who wants to get full value for his money and full pleasure from the game of wine will not turn his back on the varietals of California simply because of the problems of buying them, but will let the problems work to his advantage, in providing him with better wine than he might get elsewhere at the price.

The first step, obviously, is to get a general familiarity with what is there. On an evening when you need two bottles of wine you might buy

	☆☆☆☆	☆☆☆	☆☆	☆	BA
THE BIG THREE					
Almadén	—	—	4	13	2
Christian Brothers	—	1	12	9	—
Paul Masson	—	—	6	15	3
THE MEDIUM-SIZED PRODUCERS					
Beaulieu	3	5	14	10	1
Beringer	—	—	9	6	1
Buena Vista	—	3	4	6	5
Krug	1	4	16	9	—
Concannon	—	2	8	10	2
Inglenook	—	3	16	15	2
Korbel	—	—	3	4	2
Martini	1	3	12	11	1
Mirassou	1	13	19	10	3
Mondavi	1	12	9	—	—
San Martin	—	—	5	10	4
Sebastiani	—	4	8	14	4
Weibel	—	—	4	13	2
Wente	—	1	10	12	4
THE SMALLER PRODUCERS					
Chappellet	—	4	1	3	—
Cresta Blanca	—	—	3	9	3
Freemark Abbey	4	5	3	—	—
Heitz	3	7	9	3	—
Llords & Elwood	—	2	3	3	—
Mayacamas	—	3	1	2	—
Oakville	2	2	11	1	—
Souverain	1	5	8	8	2
Spring Mountain	2	2	2	—	—
Sterling	2	4	2	1	—
Ville Fontaine	—	—	2	1	—
Windsor (Sonoma Vineyards)	—	—	6	7	—

one from Europe and one from California—perhaps both representing the same grape—and you and your guests can compare and study the differences. Forrest Wallace has long made it a practice at his dinner table to let his guests compare a moderately priced California product with a fine European one. This not only provides a sure-fire conversation piece, but those (including the host) whose palates are tuned to the European product can concentrate on that, while the novices often discover to their surprise that they much prefer the California wine and concentrate on that. (This saves money, too.)

You can also compare a two-dollar bottle and a four- or five-dollar bottle, both from California, or two different varietals, or the same varietal from two different producers—this is particularly interesting—or two vintages of the same varietal from the same producer. You can compare a premium proprietary with a varietal in the same price class and try to figure out what grapes were used to make the proprietary.

An obviously sound move would be to try out the Hannum and Blumberg recommendations to see whether their palates match yours; if the match is good, find out which of their top choices are available in your market area and put in a supply while they last. You should also be first in line to buy any later editions of their book with ratings of new wines.

But you cannot carry the Hannum and Blumberg ratings with you, and there will be times when you will find yourself in a restaurant where the wine list either gives you the option of buying an interesting California bottle or gives you no alternative. So it is a good idea to develop a general familiarity with the quality of the various producers, bearing in mind that you are likely to get better wine from any of them if there is a vintage year on the label, and still better if it is an estate-bottling. But obviously a wine from a good producer with these added assurances will not be

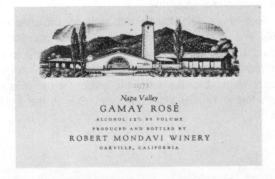

cheap, nor should it be. For all the defects of standard pricing, a wine in the $4.50 class ($9.00 or so eating out) is going to be a better wine, on average, and a more reliable one, than one in the $2.00 class ($4.00 in a restaurant). If you only want to spend the lesser amount, a strong case can be made for buying an above-average generic over an uncertain varietal.

It also makes sense to try, if you can, to find a merchant who really knows about and cares about California wines, and can give you both advice and a good selection. Until recently this was not easy. Perhaps as a hangover from the bad reputation from the thirties and forties, perhaps because of the near-identical, "branded" look of the labels of the full-line producers, perhaps because the screw caps and pasteurized contents of the standard products make these wines very hard to spoil, in the average wine shop California wines were not treated with the respect accorded their European counterparts—some still are not. Too often they were kept on the shelf standing up, so the cork dried out and the wine went bad, while the European wines were cradled reverently in racks on their sides.

Nowadays your chances are better. As the demand for the premium California wines has grown and the marketing efforts supporting them increased, as the price per bottle has risen, they have gained in shelf space and respectability in the eyes of the trade.

Even so, genuine knowledge and understanding are still hard to find, and you may find it to your advantage to educate your merchant: ask him to special-order a particular California bottling for you; persuade him to compare the wines himself. If a good customer and a man whose judgment he respects shows an interest in a particular category of merchandise, the merchant will suddenly discover that he is more interested, now, and will begin to learn. Herd instinct is a powerful thing in wines. If one man says with seeming authority that something is good, everybody else will begin assuming it is, too.

Obviously a trip to California will give you opportunity not only to visit the vineyards themselves and taste their wines (most producers offer free tastings at the winery) but to try out the wines that are not ordinarily available outside California. If you like some of these, you can try to get on the mailing list of the winery, or special-order a case or two. With some of the smallest wineries, this can be hard—sometimes impossible. But there is no harm in trying.

And here, also, more even than in the case of the best wines of Bordeaux and Burgundy, you find yourself almost forced to accumulate a "cellar" in one form or another—perhaps only a bin in the back room of your merchant. Then you will be able to snap up the balance of a particular case when you like a sample bottle, or put in a supply of an outstanding year while it is still available, and give it the aging required to reach its peak.

Tomorrow and Tomorrow

Beyond these current buying problems the question is: Where is all this leading?

Several years ago the Bank of America predicted that California wine makers would have no trouble selling all the table wine they could produce at least until 1980; and when things are going well, people do not have much incentive to change. More recently there has been clear evidence that the rush to get into the wine business has produced serious overcapacity in California both in vineyards and in wine-making facilities. Experts predict that in an effort to counteract this situation the California industry is likely to put great stress on raising the quality and consumer acceptability of its product. Already some of the better California producers are reducing their lines. One major new entry into the field, Monterey Vineyard, is beginning to identify the specific vineyard (only they call it a ranch) where a particular wine is grown.

It is interesting to note that neither Mirassou nor Robert Mondavi, the two new stars among the medium-sized producers, markets a full line. Robert Mondavi sells table wines only, Mirassou table and sparkling wines. Moreover, Mondavi began his operation by growing no grapes of his own, but rather buying them all from other producers. Mirassou has long been a major supplier of premium wines in bulk to other wineries, has only in the last few years begun to market under its own label, and obviously has the pick of its bulk production in selecting its brand-named wines.

Among the smaller producers the lines are even more limited. Furthermore, at least three of the small producers—Heitz, Spring Mountain, and Llords and Elwood—also got their start not as growers but as buyers of grapes or "finishers" of other people's wines, picking and choosing from what was available in the market place.

All five of these successful operations have thus provided in effect the "missing link" in the California wine industry, a service equivalent to that provided by a shipper, whose function is not primarily to grow and harvest grapes but to pick and choose among available materials, and then to blend them skillfully and age them carefully to meet the requirements of a particular market. (Revealingly, J. M. Elwood, founder of Llords and Elwood, spent twenty highly successful years as a retailer of wines and spirits, so his primary loyalty has been to people who buy and drink wine, rather than to parcels of real estate and the vines that grow there.)

The quick arrival of all five enterprises testifies to the receptivity of the market to the service they provide—and in the long run what a market demands is what its wine industry, or any other industry, supplies.

This leaves one final question, a question that captures the imagination of anyone who thinks very long about California wines: Will California one day produce truly great wines, immortal, incomparable growths on a par with Château Lafite or Romanée-Conti? Somewhere, on some neglected hillside, is there a unique exposure, a certain mix of pebbles and soil, that has the potential to accomplish one of nature's miracles, to burst forth in some astounding combination of fullness and fineness and bouquet?

Only time can tell, but current evidence suggests that the destiny of the California vineyards (barring some new accident of history) will not be to burst forth one day in a blaze of sudden glory, but to go on doing better and better what they are doing now: producing in great abundance, with considerable year-to-year reliability, wines in the good-to-very-fine class, the red ones being the best, with emphasis not so much on a single grape and a few supreme locations as on a small group of well-adapted varieties that can be blended gracefully to suit the market's taste. The best

THE SPECTRUM OF POSSIBILITY

Category of Wine	Bordeaux and Burgundy
Light and Delicate White	CHABLIS (Burgundy) POUILLY-FUISSÉ (Burgundy)
Fuller-bodied White	MEURSAULT (Burgundy) MONTRACHET (Burgundy)
Rosé	—
Light-bodied Red	HAUT-MÉDOC* (Bordeaux) RED GRAVES (Bordeaux)
Fuller-bodied Red	ST.-ÉMILION (Bordeaux) POMMARD (Burgundy) BEAUJOLAIS (Burgundy) CÔTE DE NUITS* (Burgundy)

* Oversimplification: Some wines of the Haut-Médoc are full-bodied; some wines of the Côte de Nuits are light-bodied.

analogy that comes to mind is the well-blended wines of the Rhône, particularly Châteauneuf-du-Pape. The proprietary blends that California is now producing could well be precursors of such a trend.

But for the moment all of this is moot. California is capable of producing far finer wines, on a consistent basis, than she does now, and of making the best ones easier for ordinary people to buy and enjoy. Until these more immediate and achievable goals are reached, immortality can wait.

Shown below, at long last, is the full Spectrum of Possibility, in all its diversity and majesty.

With this master list in hand and in mind, in the next section of the book we turn to the delightful matter of putting it to work in matching foods and wines.

The Rest of Europe	*California*
MOSELLE (Rhine)	JOHANNISBERG or
MUSCADET (Loire)	WHITE RIESLING
SANCERRE (Loire)	"MOSELLE"
POUILLY-FUMÉ (Loire)	"CHABLIS"
SOAVE (Italy)	
VERDICCHIO (Italy)	
RHINE (Rhine)	PINOT CHARDONNAY
ALSACE (Rhine)	"RHINE WINE"
VOUVRAY (Loire)	"DRY SAUTERNE"
ORVIETO (Italy)	
TAVEL (Rhône)	GRENACHE ROSÉ
ANJOU (Loire)	ROSÉ
BARDOLINO (Italy)	"CLARET"
VALPOLICELLA (Italy)	PINOT NOIR
	ZINFANDEL
CHIANTI (Italy)	CABERNET SAUVIGNON
CÔTES DU RHÔNE (Rhône)	"BURGUNDY"
CHÂTEAUNEUF-DU-PAPE	"CHIANTI"
(Rhône)	
RED HERMITAGE (Rhône)	
CÔTE RÔTIE (Rhône)	

NOTES: 1. Classifying California standard wines by character is at best an approximate matter, since the character of a "Chablis" or a "Rhine" or a "Burgundy" will vary from one producer to another. See page 135.

2. See Appendix, page 291, for summary of Spectrum, with page references to the description of each wine.

Food and Wine

❧ VI

THE CATEGORIES OF AFFINITY

❧

In the actual business of pairing a certain food with a given wine, as in most other areas of human life and commerce, there are two extreme and opposite goals that may be sought. One is to be absolutely right. The other is not to be absolutely wrong. The novice will be so paralyzed by the wish to find the absolutely right wine to go with a given dish, and by the illusion that a final answer exists somewhere, carved on a tablet of stone and waiting to be discovered, that he misses the fun of the game and fails to take advantage of the resources available. A connoisseur, by contrast, will in some circumstances lavish time, treasure, and thought on the most esoteric and ridiculous perfectionism, even though he knows perfectly well the goal he seeks is unattainable. In other situations, either because of limitations on the available choices or because he doesn't happen to give a damn, he will unconcernedly accept and enjoy the roughest of matches, in the confident knowledge they are not absolutely wrong.

What is absolutely wrong in matching foods and wines is not something that would have caused Marie Antoinette or Amy Vanderbilt to arch her eyebrows, but any combination that tastes bad in the mouth. Essentially, there are two: Any *dry* wine, drunk with a *sweet* dessert, tends to taste sour. Any *red* wine, drunk with fish, usually tastes bitter.

As for the first thou-shalt-not: As we have noted in earlier chapters, wine, being made from the grape, has acid in it like any fruit product. If you attempt to drink any dry wine—red, white, or pink—with a sweet dessert such as pudding, custard, or ice cream, the sweetness of the dish will highlight the acid of the wine on your palate, and the result will be decidedly unpleasant. So if you are drinking wine with your main dish—

and it will normally be dry—it is wise to finish it or set it aside before you take the first spoonful of sweet dessert. (If you want to be absolutely correct, the dinner wineglasses should be removed from the table before the dessert is served.) Or, if you want to go on drinking the dry wine, have cheese and/or fruit—apples, peaches, pears—in place of a sweet dessert. Cheese is the perfect accompaniment to almost any wine. In fact, if you are going to open a bottle of very great, very old wine, it is probably better to sip it with cheese after a meal than any other way. Fruit has enough acid in it to balance the acid of the wine, so the combination works. But there is this caution: The tart delicacy of fruit will bring out the quality of a wine, good or bad, so unless you are having a fairly good wine, it is better to stick to cheese.

On the other hand, if you are determined to have a sweet dessert and wish to drink wine with it, then obviously you order a dessert wine—a luscious, rich Sauternes or one of the sweet German wines. Here the sugar in the wine cancels its own acid, and the sweet wine and sweet dessert work very well together.

The second thou-shalt-not in matching, that red wine usually tastes bitter if it is drunk with fish, is cousin to the first. As we have noted, red wine gets its red color from the skin of the grape. But part of the red color is tannin—tannic acid. Tannic acid reacts with the halogens, primarily iodine, of which fish is a rich source, to produce a bitter, oily taste repugnant to almost everyone. (Rosé has a slight amount of tannin in it, but it is so slight that it does not create this problem.)

As with every rule of wine, however, there are exceptions. In those areas of the world where fish has historically been a staple food, but no good white wine has been available, the local housewives have learned over time to create fish dishes which taste good accompanied by red wine. What they do, essentially, is override the halogens with other flavors. There are two principal ways of doing this, the wine method and the tomato-spice method.

In the St.-Émilion region of Bordeaux, for example, which is famous for its fullish red wines, the lamprey is an eel that is plentiful in the Gironde River there. Lampreys are traditionally cooked in the local red St.-Émilion, served in a sauce made up of it, and eaten along with a glass of same. But by the time the dish is served, the halogen reaction has long since taken place, the resulting flavor has been dissipated by the cooking and blanketed by other seasonings.

Lampreys are in somewhat short supply in the United States. But here is a recipe for braising bass in red wine, taken from the New York *Times,* that illustrates the method. A total of three bottles of red wine is used to cook a 3½-pound fish, along with onions and anchovy paste, and the red wine "fumet" which makes up part of the cooking liquid is itself made from boiling fish bones and heads in red wine.

BRAISED BASS IN RED WINE

6½ tablespoons butter
1 tablespoon chopped
  parsley
1 2½- to 3½-pound sea
  bass or striped bass,
  cleaned but with head and
  tail left on
  Salt and freshly ground
  black pepper
2 cups diced carrots
2 medium-size onions, diced

1 rib celery, halved
1 bay leaf
2 sprigs parsley
1 sprig fresh thyme or
  ¼ teaspoon dried
1 recipe red wine fumet
  (below)
2 bottles red Graves wine
2 tablespoons flour
1 teaspoon anchovy paste

1. Preheat oven to 350 degrees.

2. Mix two tablespoons of the butter with the parsley and spread over the cavity of the fish. With a sharp knife, notch the skin on the back of the fish, making three or four shallow incisions on each side.

3. Season fish inside and out with salt and pepper to taste.

4. Melt three tablespoons of the remaining butter and sauté the carrots and onions until the onions are translucent.

5. Butter the rack of a fish poacher and cover it with the sautéed carrots and onions. Place the fish on top of the vegetables. Fit rack into the poacher.

6. Tie together the celery, bay leaf, parsley sprigs, and thyme. If dried thyme is used, sprinkle it along the celery rib. Add the bundle to the fish poacher.

7. Put aside one-quarter cup of the fumet and then pour in equal quantities of the fish fumet and red wine until the liquid rises about two-thirds of the way up the fish.

8. Bring to a boil on top of the stove, cover and bake 20 to 30 minutes or until fish flakes easily. The fish should be basted with cooking liquid at least three times during the baking.

9. Drain the fish on the rack and transfer to a heatproof serving platter to keep warm while the sauce is being made.

10. Strain the cooking liquid (discard the vegetables), and measure three cups into a shallow saucepan. (See note.) Boil vigorously to reduce the quantity to about two cups. Blend together the remaining butter, the flour, and the anchovy paste and whisk into the sauce a little at a time while cooking gently until the desired consistency is reached.

11. Brush the fish with some of the remaining cooking liquid and glaze under a preheated broiler. Serve the sauce either spooned over the fish or separately.

YIELD: Six to eight servings.

NOTE: Any excess cooking liquid should be reserved after straining and can be frozen for future use in making sauce.

RED WINE FUMET

2 *to 3 pounds fish bones and*
   heads, roughly chopped
	⅛ *teaspoon thyme*
	   Salt and freshly ground

1 *large onion, chopped*	*black pepper to taste*
6 *to 8 sprigs parsley*	1 *quart water*
1 *bay leaf*	1 *bottle red Graves wine*

1. Place all the ingredients in a large saucepan, bring to a boil, cover and cook over medium heat for 30 minutes. Skim as necessary.

2. Strain the broth, discard bones and seasonings.

YIELD: About two quarts.

The tomato-spice method of neutralizing the halogen reaction is more widely used than the wine method. All through southern France and Italy fish more often than not is served thoroughly laced with tomatoes (a vegetable containing plenty of acid) and such powerful, assertive seasonings as garlic, saffron, and fennel. The classic bouillabaisse is perhaps the most famous example of this approach.

A fine and delicate white would be lost with a dish so seasoned. A robust white would be in balance, but so would a light red *vin du pays*.

If it is wise, then, not to drink a dry wine with a sweet dish, nor in most circumstances a red wine with a fish dish, it is instructive to stand these two rules on their heads: May a sweet wine be drunk with a dish that is not sweet? Could you have white wine with a juicy red piece of beef?

If a sweet wine were drunk with a definitely acid dish—salad with a vinegar dressing, for example—the delicacy of flavor of the sweet wine would be overridden and destroyed by the harshness of the vinegar (as would the delicacy of a dry wine). But as for drinking a sweet wine with a dish that merely happens to have no sweetness in it, there is no physiological contraction here. Beginners in fact prefer a sweetish wine with almost anything, as we have already noted.

When it comes to drinking a white wine with red meat: In contrast to what the average person believes, red meat—a piece of roast or beefsteak—is actually a relatively bland dish. Not delicate, *bland*. To combine a bland piece of meat with a delicate white wine is by no means a perfect marriage, but there is nothing offensive about it. If you have in your icebox some leftover Chablis, Moselle, or any good white wine, and feel like drinking it with stew or steak or hamburger, by all means go ahead. It will wash the food down well enough, add a little novelty and zest to the meal, and is a lot better than letting good wine spoil.

In Germany, where the best wines are white, they have ways of cooking red meat that are somewhat analogous to the method of cooking lampreys in St.-Émilion. The meat will be cooked very thoroughly in white wine itself, or in a purée of lightly seasoned vegetables, or with various rather aromatic seasonings. With the method of cooking adding a degree of interest to the blandness of the meat, it is served—and enjoyed—with a glass of fragrant German white wine.

Sometimes a German will even order a very fine, semisweet *Auslese* from the Rhine to go with a simply roasted piece of venison or hare. The best explanation of this combination is that it is an acquired taste, although many a visitor to Germany has found it a taste not hard to acquire. And yet even here, the relative sweetness of an *Auslese* and the relative fullness of a Rhine can approach some sort of balance with the flavor of a meat that is neither delicate nor robust.

Balance, that is the key. The reason a very sweet wine is not ordinarily drunk with the main course of a meal, if there are alternatives, and why a delicate white wine will not usually be served with red meat, is a matter of balance. A luscious sweetness will tend to overwhelm almost any dish that is not sweet. By the same token, if you drink a delicate Chablis or one of the slightly more assertive Pouillys with highly flavored meat—barbecued beef with all that charcoal, or gamy venison or wild duck—these flavors would dominate, and you would not get full pleasure from the wine.

Thus, from the rules about what you *should not* do with foods and wines, because it tastes bad, emerges the basic rule of what you *should* try to do, because it tastes so good. The key is balance—dry with dry, sweet with sweet, heavy with heavy, light with light, fine with fine, coarse with coarse. As your mouth rejects the combinations that clash or contrast, so it accepts with increasing pleasure the ones that work gracefully together.

The basic affinities between foods and wines, which reflect this balance in its simplest form, are easy to remember, flexible to apply, and applicable to 80 or 90 per cent of the food-wine matching problems of ordinary living. They are shown on the next page in chart form.

The chart is an oversimplification and, once again, a necessary one. It shows general relationships only, and ignores entirely the influence of sauces and seasonings on the choice of a wine. (There are cases, such as the lampreys of St.-Émilion already noted, when the sauce will count for more in your decision than whatsoever goes under it.)

The chart demonstrates the very broad usefulness of red wines in the light-to-medium range, the more limited usefulness of the wines at the two ends of the scale, the light, delicate whites and the fullest reds, and indicates the sometimes neglected potential of the fuller whites for pairing with such meats as chicken, veal, and heavier poultry. It also reflects the rule that rosé "goes with everything" (if not always ideally) and the parallel rule that cheese is the ideal accompaniment for any wine.

Here is the information on the chart in a little more detail:

Fish, along with shellfish, generally takes a dry, delicate white wine. But a very delicate white for a relatively full-flavored fish like salmon would not be wrong, nor would a medium-bodied white for delicate shellfish such as oysters.

THE CATEGORIES OF AFFINITY

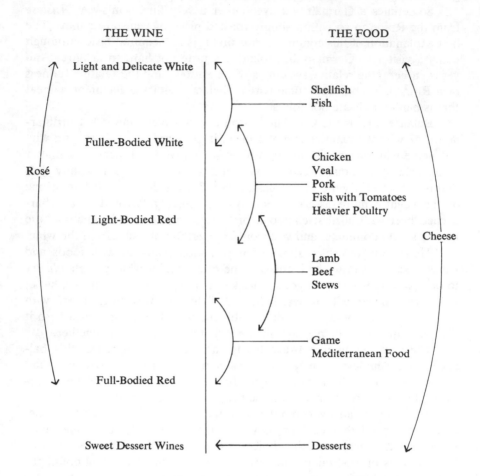

THE WINE   THE FOOD

Light and Delicate White

Shellfish
Fish

Fuller-Bodied White

Rosé

Chicken
Veal
Pork
Fish with Tomatoes
Heavier Poultry

Light-Bodied Red

Cheese

Lamb
Beef
Stews

Game
Mediterranean Food

Full-Bodied Red

Sweet Dessert Wines   Desserts

Chicken in general will take one of the lighter reds or, if you like, one of the fuller whites. Yet in a small, inexpensive restaurant you may have no choice except white Chablis or red Burgundy, one of which might be too light, the other too full. In this case you flip a coin, with the reasonable confidence that the Chablis will not taste much like Chablis, nor the Burgundy like Burgundy.

Veal, like chicken, falls almost dead center in the Spectrum—fuller white, lighter red (although with veal scallopini the sauce is of such paramount importance that it is usually determining).

Pork just does not seem to possess the character to go really well with any wine. The English have made a tradition of Claret with ham, although a really noble Bordeaux would be out of place. Rosé is bland enough to provide a reasonably balanced accompaniment; any lighter red or fuller-bodied white would work about as well. Champagne with ham is a pleasant and traditional solution. Beer can be drunk, too.

What we are trying to say is that it doesn't really matter very much.

Fish with tomatoes, as indicated, takes either a fairly robust white or a light, simple red.

Heavier poultry—turkey, duck, goose—goes a bit better with a red of light-to-medium body than with any white, unless you can get one of the big ones like Haut-Brion Blanc or Hermitage. But an awful lot of Germans eat an awful lot of goose with an awful lot of Rhine wine and from all reports enjoy it; a big Meursault or Montrachet, while not ideal, would not be out of place, either.

Game birds, with their fuller, stronger flavor, usually take a red on the full side.

Lamb is slightly darker in color than veal and fuller in flavor. Bordeaux is the classic accompaniment to lamb, the tannin in the wine serving to cut the fattiness of the meat. But any lighter-bodied red will do.

Beef usually takes a red wine, period. When you have said that, you have nearly said it all. As in the case of veal, unless you are using an exciting sauce, refinements are hard to come by. Ordinary beefsteak or roast calls for a not-too-heavy wine—Pommard or Volnay among the Burgundies, a middle-range Bordeaux, a California Cabernet. Steak or prime roast beef, if you are spending a lot of money for it at an expensive place, should probably have an expensive wine with it, just to be in harmony with the environment. But since the wine at such a place is probably overpriced, you should have no difficulty obtaining something at a suitable markup. If you are having hamburger or an ordinary, American style, meat loaf, Gallo Paisano would do it too much honor. Beer or Coke is strongly indicated here. If you are having barbecued steak, with all that charcoal and smoke, a nice, cheap Chianti, with acid enough to put little sweaters on your teeth, or a good, broad-shouldered Rhône would be just the ticket.

Stews and meat pies: usually the same as beef—almost anything red. A chicken stew, if it is creamy, a preference for white; but *coq au vin,* chicken cooked in red Burgundy, takes a red wine—a Burgundy obviously being the best.

Game—venison, elk, moose, wild boar, bear—a heavy red.

Sweetbreads, brains, tripe: a white on the full side, or for the sweetbreads and tripe, a lighter red.

Liver, kidneys: a medium red.

Italian food: Italian wine, with perhaps a preference for white with the fish or the pasta or if the dish is from northern Italy and thus not saturated with tomatoes.

Chinese food or sukiyaki: tea, sake, Chinese rice wine, or as an imitation of sake, dry Vermouth, drunk slightly heated from tiny cups. Or, if you must have a conventional wine, a fullish white, such as Bordeaux, not too fine.

Picnic sandwiches: a bottle of good rosé, unchilled and shaken about, drunk like Coke from paper cups, or chilled Champagne if you want to live it up, or Gallo Paisano, or Almadén Mountain Red.

The above guidance will serve pretty well for most meals where everyone eats the same thing. But what do you do in a restaurant if half the table is having *filet de sole almandine* and the other half *boeuf bourguignon?* You can avoid this problem by using a pre-emptive strategy. You pick up the wine list and say firmly, "Shall we decide what wine to try tonight?" This usually draws attention away from the menu until the wine is chosen, and then the company is more or less locked in and begins to ask questions about what to order to go with the wine.

However, if you are caught with a split table of four, unless you choose to go the rosé route you can easily order two half bottles—Chablis for the sole, Pommard for the beef. For a table of six, evenly divided, a full bottle of each will not get you into serious trouble, unless you overdid your cocktail hour.

But if the difference is not as extreme as between fish and beef, then you can begin to play. You can try to work out something that will bridge the difference—Pouilly-Fuissé to go with both fish and chicken, let us say, or a Meursault or Montrachet with salmon and veal. Or, reaching, a red Bordeaux with chicken and venison. Everybody will think you are very sophisticated for suggesting such daring solutions.

The knowledge of how far you can go in bridging two dissimilar dishes with a single wine is important not only in healing the rift in a split table but, at the higher levels, in the orchestration and progression of several wines in a single meal.

But we shall get to that later.

VII

THE HUMAN VARIABLE

So much for the basic physiological facts of life in matching foods and wines. But these at best set rough guidelines, the outer limits on what is permissible. They ignore the refinements, the nuances, in which lie much of the fascination of the game of wine. These refinements are of two sorts: There are the increasingly complicated culinary questions, having to do with the influence of sauces and seasonings on your choice, and there are the nonculinary matters, having largely to do with people. We will start with nonculinary factors since even the rankest beginner can benefit at once from a knowledge of these.

A novice will naturally assume that the food for a meal is always chosen first, and then the wine is more or less forced into line to match. For most people, on most occasions, this is so, especially when a skill at wine is just beginning to emerge. But as an interest in wine grows, as a palate develops, more and more often the wine will be selected as the centerpiece, and then the dish chosen to provide an appropriate setting.

And yet in many cases, far more than the beginner could imagine, neither food nor wine is the starting point. Consider, for example, a dinner given by the Wine and Food Society in Chicago a few years back, where ten different vintages of Champagne were served at a single meal, and furthermore, all ten came from a single shipper.

Now granted, Champagne, in some people's view, can go with anything. But why Champagne at all that night, and why *ten,* and why all from the same shipper?

Quite simple. The shipper in question was the guest of honor. They served him his own merchandise to compliment him. So the starting point of that meal was neither a food nor a wine, but a human being, an occasion. (Actually, the guest might *personally* have been more interested in sampling an exceptional California Cabernet Sauvignon than the product he had spent a lifetime tasting. But that was not the purpose for which the company had gathered.)

So the real key to the art of matching is not to memorize a set of pedantic rules or categories but to recognize the extent to which the employment of any rule will be governed and modified by the human variable, the wholly nonculinary considerations that provide the theme, the focus for all but the most rudimentary of meals. The focus of a meal can be anything: an occasion, a situation, an intent. It is Easter that calls for ham and Thanksgiving that demands turkey. This in turn suggests Champagne (if you can afford it) and red Bordeaux respectively. Seduction has been the animating purpose of many a fine meal since time immemorial. Diplomacy, the same game in a different ball park, has been another. Salesmanship, a third variation on the basic theme, has been another.

A primary consideration in the planning of almost any occasion (and this certainly applied to the Champagne dinner in Chicago) is how the host himself feels about it. What you like to do and feel easy doing counts for a great deal, regardless of all the other questions. If, for example, you are a lover of Burgundy wine, the featured wine at meals served in your home is very likely to be Burgundy, no matter who comes to dinner or why. And that makes sense. Your cellar would be better stocked with Burgundies than anything else. And you would discuss Burgundy more fascinatingly (assuming you can discuss anything fascinatingly) than any other wine.

If you have eaten at a particular restaurant for many years, it is almost certain that you have come to know and like and understand and trust certain items on the menu and certain entries on the wine list. The odds are that you will offer your friends a better evening if you order those than if you experiment with the unknown—unless, of course, your purpose in going out was to experiment with the unknown.

A related human consideration is how you happen to feel about the people who are going to eat your food and drink your wine. There are some connoisseurs who, if they really care about a guest, will not hesitate to open one or two hundred dollars' worth of wine, the pride of their cellars, just to show him the fine shades of distinction between the three greatest growths of Bordeaux in the year 1963, let us say, or the incredible staying power and pre-phylloxera magic of a Cos d'Estournel '78. On the other hand, if they *don't* like the people, they may go to some pains to arrange a secret insult: an unpretentious Beaujolais for an occasion that might justify more, or the wine of a year that turned out badly that its owner is trying to unload.

But if regardless of the warmth of the relationship you don't want to spend money that night, you may find it convenient to substitute a very modest bottle, and a charming little lecture on its origins, for a more expensive one with a famous name.

If your guest of honor happens to have a superb palate and you do not, you have a problem of another kind. You might go out and buy, let us say, a Château Latour of a fine year, having learned from reading a book that this is one of the three great châteaux of the Haut-Médoc. You bought the Latour over the Lafite because it was forty dollars compared to fifty dollars. But it cost only forty dollars because in the view of most experts Latour has gone downhill somewhat in recent years and is now, relatively speaking, a dog.

Or you might take a trip across town, to the finest merchant in the area, and, trusting him, buy a Cheval Blanc '49. You have overlooked, of course, the fact that when you get a wine this old home it will take no less than three months to settle, approximately two and a half months past the date of dinner.

Perhaps the best thing to do in this case is to serve the nicest meal you can, within your limits, with a respectable but not overwhelming bottle, and trust that your guest came to dinner because he likes you. Here again, it is you yourself, in important degree, that governs the final design.

Not only the palate of your principal guest but his background may be cranked into the equation. A European of sophisticated palate, visiting in Chicago, might as we suggested be quite intrigued to sample the best wine California offers. A San Franciscan of comparable taste, visiting in New York or Paris, might be flattered beyond words to be served a bottle of the same wine. (San Franciscans are a bit chauvinistic in their loyalty to the local product.) But an American of indifferent palate, served the very same bottle, might be insulted, thinking you were trying to save money on him. Give him a bottle of a horrible import, on the other hand, with a fancy label, and he would be quite content.

When a great wine finds its way to the great palate of a great friend, it is often more by chance than by calculated contrivance. This is in part because these elements, even occurring in isolation, are so rare.

One cold and snowy night in 1957, when Forrest Wallace was entertaining a client at the late, great Chambord Restaurant in New York, the client knew something about wines, so he and his host discussed them. It was not a busy evening, so Victor, the wine steward, joined the conversation and brought out various famous bottles for viewing as they were mentioned.

The client was delighted with all of this. Shortly before the end of the meal, he excused himself, and then when Wallace left, Victor presented Wallace with a carefully wrapped bottle—a token of gratitude from his guest. Wallace thanked the client, but he was catching the night train to Chicago, so he left the wrapping on and did not inspect the bottle. It was only when he got aboard the train that he opened the package and found a bottle of 1906 Romanée-St.-Vivant, considered by many experts to be the greatest Burgundy of the century.

But now the question was how to keep the bottle during the trip. The train bedroom was hot—too hot for a very old wine. But a place by the window would be much too cold. So Wallace obtained an extra blanket from the porter, wrapped the bottle as carefully as a baby, and placed it on the foot of the bed close to the window—but not *too* close. All night long he worried about how the wine was getting along.

In the morning Wallace went from the train to the office and again put the bottle close to the window—but not too close—then that evening carefully drove home with the bottle beside him in the car. For weeks after that he inspected it at intervals, watching the sediment—driven through the wine by the movement of the trip—settle back to the bottom. It took nearly three months for the settling to be complete. (And all the shaking and settling had probably added two to four years to the bottle's age.)

While the bottle was resting in the cellar, Wallace wondered what occasion could *possibly* be great enough for such a bottle. Years passed and still he had found no occasion worthy of the wine. Then one day Henry Van der Voort, the wine importer from San Francisco, passed through town. Van der Voort is a very old friend, a distinguished connoisseur, and his advice helped Wallace build his cellar. Clearly this was the night. But such a bottle should never be opened just for two. In addition to Van der Voort, Wallace invited two other good friends, John Nuveen and Ted Diller of Chicago, both fine judges of wine.

The Romanée '06 was preceded by the Romanée-St.-Vivants of 1945 and 1929, two other great years, so the three could be compared. With the wines Wallace served a beef tenderloin—baked plain so there would be no competition with the wines—cooked by his own hand, followed by a ripe Brie cheese, so the tasting could continue until all the wine was gone.

The tasting and the talking continued until 2 A.M., and the meal is discussed to this day.

It is one thing to wonder what to serve a guest with incomparable palate, and quite another to serve one, however much you love him, with no palate at all. Here we enter again into the realm of physiology. As we noted in the chapter on California wines, comparative tastings over the years have shown that a novice will usually prefer a sweet wine over a dry one, a light wine to a full-bodied one, a simple wine to a complex one, and, therefore, often a good, straightforward California wine to a fine, subtle European one. But, as noted, if you serve your novice friend a California bottle, he may think you are merely saving money on him. Moreover, if you choose a wine solely to please your unschooled guest, you may find the meal a little tiresome yourself.

The best way out is the comparative tasting noted in Chapter V. You offer as fine an imported wine as pleases you, and at the same time a good domestic one. This with rare exceptions makes the wine the center of the conversation, lets the novice discover for himself what he really likes, and allows the host to enjoy the better wine (usually hogging most of it). It also saves money, and for a host who uses the device thoughtfully and conscientiously over time is the best means there is for developing and educating his own palate as well as those of his guests.

The age of your guest is also a factor in selecting a wine. People under the age of twenty-three seem to have a physiological need for sugar, and so an incurable sweet tooth. For a young company, presumably also novices, a moderately sweet wine is indicated.

There is also a tradition, verified by long experience, that as a man grows older his taste shifts from the broad robustness of Burgundy to the elegant subtleties of Bordeaux. But this rule should be applied with caution, since your elderly guest may turn out to care about nothing but Thunderbird, or Bourbon and Coke, or Champagne and dancing girls.

Age can count in another way, too. Where it can be done without offense, the guest of honor can be asked his or her birth year, and the wine can be ordered from that year. This assumes that the available cellar has a sufficient selection, and one of the other guests will not mutter, "1924? That was a *terrible* year."

Sex also counts in the choice of a wine in more than situations of seduction. The experience of centuries has shown that women in general, like young people and beginners, tend to prefer the sweeter, simpler, lighter wines, the white and pink ones, the bubbly ones. But that applies to women *in general*. There can always appear at your table a lady of exceptional discrimination, such as Louise Gault, who edited this book, who may never forgive you if you patronize her palate. (In fact, Miss Gault's knowledge of wine can be a source of frustration when she accepts an invitation to dinner from a man she does not know well. Her companion may prove very charming, but a novice when it comes to wine—although of course he does not think so. So, not wanting to threaten his ego by flaunting her knowledge, Miss Gault is forced to suffer through some insipid bottling, and perhaps a totally uninformed lecture on its origins.)

Bordeaux is also known as more a feminine than a masculine wine. In Europe, Burgundy traditionally is presented to a groom, Bordeaux to the bride. But many women will prefer a clean, uncomplicated California red —or any white wine—to either Burgundy or Bordeaux.

Women in general are also more easily bored with the whole subject of wine than men. So if you are trying to please the little lady, the best thing is often just to order the wine, whatever it is, and let the talk drift to other things.

There is no limit to the possible variations and refinements of these nonculinary influences on the choice of wine. As the level of elegance of a meal rises, as the number of wines offered multiplies (and the list of more obvious themes has been exhausted), you may decide to give the meal a geographic theme. You might taste your way up the rungs of quality of Bordeaux or northward through the vineyards of Burgundy, or south along the Rhône (and here teaching intertwines with geography), with the food native to the region chosen to go along.

There is no limit, but this is enough to give the feel. Now we must turn to the even more complex question of the influence of sauces and seasonings on the pairing of foods and wines.

❧ VIII

CHERCHEZ LA SAUCE

When we consider the influence of sauces and seasonings on the matching process, we have turned our backs entirely on the goal of merely trying to avoid what is absolutely wrong, and are attempting to move as far as human effort will carry us toward doing what is, if not absolutely right, then at least appropriate, elegant, and delightful. We are no longer satisfied merely to arrange an approximate *balance* between a dish and its accompanying wine. Increasingly, we are looking for a high degree of *synergy* between them.

Synergy is a presently overused word which means that the whole must equal more than the sum of its parts: two and two must total not less than five, and hopefully much more. It is a word that had its beginnings in theology ("the doctrine that the human will cooperates with the Holy Ghost in the work of regeneration") and chemistry ("the joint action of agents, as drugs, which when taken together increase each other's effectiveness"). It has had an active career in business—whether or not a corporate merger is synergistic is of the essence—and in the realm of *haute cuisine* it is no less vital. Whenever possible, a food and a wine should work together to create a combination that is far more exciting than either of its elements taken alone.

It is because of the search for synergy that it is good policy, other things being equal, to match a wine from a given region with a dish from that region. You are gambling that over the centuries the natives have come to season this dish so that no wine from any other place could work as well.

You can look for synergy between a food and a wine whether the dish in question be sauced or plain. The synergy of a simple loaf of bread, an ordinary jug of wine, a book of poems of indeterminate merit, and a pretty girl sitting under a tree has long been noted.

It is not too great an oversimplification to say that a given food can be served in only one of three ways:

- unsauced—that is, fried, roasted, broiled, boiled, and so on, adorned with nothing more than melted butter, its own juice, or a simple gravy.
- with a strong, assertive sauce, whose tomatoes, oil, garlic, and herbs speak in unmistakable tones of the Mediterranean, or whose curry from the Indies will set your throat on fire.
- or with a relatively subtle, interesting sauce, reflecting in varying measure the arts of *haute cuisine*.

A piece of meat, fish, or chicken, served without significant adornment, is not in itself very interesting. A piece of flesh, nothing more. It will almost invariably work better with a simpler wine and often a lighter wine than the same dish interestingly sauced. A little more guidance will be needed if you are to know the precise difference between the wine you would ideally serve with clams as opposed to oysters, let us say, or turkey as opposed to chicken, but not much more. And, as we have seen, even if you did not know, you would not get into any particular trouble.

To go to the other end of the scale, if a dish, any dish, is served with a strong, assertive, Mediterranean sauce, it obviously takes a stronger, more assertive, more Mediterranean wine than otherwise. But picking out robust, assertive wines is not a much more complicated job than picking out simple, unassertive ones. As for curries, if your curry is a hot one, the best you can do is beer to quench the burning in your gullet.

So it is in the mid-zone of sauces, as in the mid-zone of wines, where the action is. Our work is cut out for us in determining the proper wines to go with dishes carrying sauces of varying body, subtlety, and distinction.

No one knows what was the first sauce or when it was employed, but there are clues. In Roman times there was a sauce called garum, so ancient even then, and so universal, that no one thought to write its recipe down. In its simplest form garum was apparently made from the juices obtained by pressing or squeezing raw fish, with perhaps honey, vinegar, and water added.

This ancient Roman sauce bears a marked resemblance to a sauce called *nuoc-mam* that is used in Vietnam to this day. *Nuoc-mam* is also made from the juice pressed from raw fish, with lime or lemon juice added, and is apparently very ancient also.

The revealing fact is that neither sauce requires cooking, so both might have come into being among very primitive people. All that would have been required were flat stones for pressing the fish and hollowed-out logs or gourds for storing the sauce. Raymond Oliver, the well-known Paris restaurateur and writer on gastronomy, believes that these two ancient sauces are at root one sauce, perhaps the oldest sauce of all. He suggests that they may derive from paleolithic times, before the invention of fire, when early man was looking for something to relieve the blandness of his diet of raw meat, raw fish, raw vegetables. The strips of anchovy used today to help give interest to ground raw beefsteak—steak *tartare*—may be related to this primordial practice, as could be the adding of lemon juice or hot sauce to raw oysters, and the Japanese *sashimi*, strips of raw fish dipped in a mixture of soy sauce and hot mustard. In fact, soy sauce itself, used to add savor to food, may stem indirectly from the same practice.

These ancient sauces of flavored fish juice may thus be the ancestors of the whole great class of sauces which are known today as "accompanying sauces." An accompanying sauce is one whose preparation and ingredients have little or no connection with the preparation of the dish with which it is served. Included in this category today is everything from the chocolate sauce that adorns an ice cream sundae to the oil and vinegar (*vinaigrette*) dressing on a salad. The chiefest among the accompanying sauces are mayonnaise, made of oil and egg yolks, and its heated cousin, hollandaise, perhaps the most famous sauce of all. Derived from mayonnaise are *sauce rémoulade,* made by adding pickles, capers, and herbs; *sauce tartare* (tartar sauce), made with hard-boiled egg yolks, along with mustard, pickles, capers, and herbs; and *sauce aïoli,* a strong garlic-flavored mayonnaise. Derived from hollandaise is *sauce béarnaise,* a hollandaise flavored with wine vinegar, shallots, and tarragon.

Other accompanying sauces include the butter sauces, which are really only flavored butters: shrimp butter, anchovy butter, garlic butter, *beurre maître d'hôtel* (parsley butter), *beurre marchand de vins* (literally "wine merchant's butter"), flavored with shallots and red wine. Then there is tomato sauce, primarily puréed tomatoes, and its derivative, cocktail sauce —tomato sauce spiced up with horseradish and Tabasco. There are also the famous English mint sauce, mustard sauce, horseradish sauce, and so on, and so on.*

The accompanying sauces are ancient, many of them; they are interesting; and from the standpoint of making ordinary life tolerable, they are very nearly essential. But in terms of the wine you choose for dinner, they

* For the purist, a distinction needs to be made between an accompanying sauce and a "condiment." A condiment is an aromatic or spicy substance that can be added to the food even after it is served. A true sauce is usually served as part of the dish. Substances like salt, pepper, sugar, paprika, ginger, vinegar, lemon juice, onions, garlic, and your grandmother's favorite watermelon pickles are condiments, along with Worcestershire "sauce" and A.1. "sauce." Prepared mustard or horseradish are condiments, but sauces in the true sense can also be made that are flavored with mustard or horseradish. Tomato catsup is a condiment. Tomato sauce is a sauce.

don't make a lot of difference. We have already noted that oil and vinegar, *vinaigrette,* will kill a wine. Mayonnaise and its cousin, hollandaise, and their derivatives, along with the butter sauces, with rare exceptions leave a dish pretty much where they found it so far as the choice of wine is concerned. The tomato sauces, with their strong, assertive flavor and their acid, we have already covered. They call for a strong, assertive, full-bodied red wine. (However, the fact that a sauce may have a trace of tomato in it, or mustard, or vinegar, or even curry, does not automatically rule out the possibility of good wine. The range of combinations and variations approaches infinity. Many sauces with traces of one or several of these elements are nonetheless fine and elegant and call for a fine and elegant wine.)

With the discovery of fire, man at some point learned the benefits of cooking his meat, and doubtless soon after, at the cost of a few burned fingers, learned the tastiness of the juices that dripped from the roast, which could be caught in a bowl of clay or stone. The modern practice of "deglazing," dissolving the hardened juices at the bottom of a roast pan with water or wine, is a latter-day derivation of this ancient practice.

But it was only when cooking pots came into use, first of clay and then of bronze and then of iron, starting about 7000 B.C., that the sauces with which we are primarily concerned here became possible. Meat could now be boiled—perhaps several kinds of meat—with a bird or two and even some fish thrown in, along with vegetables and herbs and seasonings. Some hungry person at some point found that the broth in which this mess had cooked tasted good—the line between a soup and a stew and a sauce is not at all clear; in modern times, at least one famous seafood soup or stew, bouillabaisse, is regarded by some experts as being neither of these, but a sauce, the fluid element counting for more in a culinary sense than the solids from which it is derived. Later someone found that if this broth that is created in the stewpot is boiled for a while, it thickens and becomes more rich and flavorsome. Someone else discovered that the addition of stone-ground grain—flour to us—and fat made the concoction still thicker as well as smoother and more manageable for eating with the fingers.

The process of marination—preserving meat by soaking it in salt or vinegar or wine—is very ancient also. The obvious next step for the thrifty and experimental-minded housewife would be to attempt to add flavor to the meat when it is cooked by boiling it in its own marinade. (Our modern word "sauce" derives from the Gascon word *salsa,* which derives in turn from the Latin word for salt. The same Gascon word *salsa* also meant marinade.) Many modern-day sweet-sour dishes, be they Oriental or European, may well be derived from the need to offset the salt and/or vinegar of a marinade.

No matter how complex and sophisticated the sauces of this family have become, if you examine their ingredients you see in them traces of their beginnings in the bubbling kettles of the late Stone Age. The basic elements are very simple and very old: the meat, bones, and by-products of animals, birds, or fish, along with those commonest, most "garden variety" of vegetables—onions, carrots, perhaps celery—and the most available of herbs: a bay leaf (the laurel of ancient times), parsley, and thyme. Then flour and oil or fat are added, and perhaps some wine, or the vinegar made from wine, or blood if the meat is fresh-killed (waste not, want not).

Boeuf bourguignon and every other beef stew; *coq au vin,* the Burgundian fricassee of chicken; *pot-au-feu* and its cousin, the New England boiled dinner; along with jugged hare (rabbit stew, really); Irish stew; and dozens more are all members of this same ancient tribe, the fluid in which the meat and vegetables have simmered comprising the "sauce" for our purposes. For most of these stews, being essentially country cooking, the wine of choice can be a simple one, a *vin du pays* (literally a "wine of the country"). But if these are country cooking, some of them are also classics. A fine wine is not out of order with *coq au vin,* and for something like jugged hare (or goose or pheasant), the flavor of the meat itself, combined with a method of cooking and seasoning worked out lovingly over the centuries, calls for a wine as fine as you could afford to buy.

The ancient culinary art of the stewpot achieved perhaps the pinnacle of its development on November 29, 1898, when a Senator Couteaux, who contributed a regular political column to the Paris newspaper *Le Temps,* on that day published instead a recipe for *lièvre à la royale,* an elegant form of jugged hare. The senator had spent a week in Poitou hunting for just the right kind of hare. When he got the one he wanted, he instantly took the train to Paris, sent out invitations to dinner the following night to a group of friends, then hurried off to consult his friend Spüller, who ran a well-known Paris restaurant, to arrange for the cooking of the hare. The preparation took seven hours, from noon until seven o'clock, and by six o'clock, according to the senator, the exquisite aroma had penetrated the doors of Spüller's restaurant, floated down the street and out into the boulevard, where they drew an excited crowd of passers-by. Here is the recipe of Senator Couteaux, as translated by Elizabeth David, the noted writer on French food:

Ingredients

You require a male hare, with red fur, killed if possible in mountainous country; of fine French descent (characterized by the light nervous elegance of head and limbs), weighing from 5 to 6 pounds, that is to say older than a leveret but still adolescent. The important thing is that the hare should have been cleanly killed and so not have lost a drop of blood.

The fat to cook it: 2 or 3 tablespoons of goose fat, ¼ lb of fat bacon rashers; ¼ lb of bacon in one piece.

Liquid: 6 oz of good red wine vinegar. Two bottles of Mâcon or Médoc, whichever you please, but in any case not less than 2 years old.

Utensils: A *daubière,* or oblong stewing pan, of well-tinned copper, 8 inches high, 15 inches long, 8 inches wide, and possessed of a hermetically closing cover; a small bowl in which to preserve the blood of the hare, and later to stir it when it comes to incorporating it in the sauce; a double-handled vegetable chopper; a large shallow serving dish; a sieve; a small wooden pestle.

Preliminary Preparations

Skin and clean the hare. Keep aside the heart, the liver, and the lungs. Keep aside also and with great care the blood. (It is traditional to add 2 or 3 small glasses of fine old cognac to the blood; but this is not indispensable; M. Couteaux finally decided against this addition.)

In the usual way prepare a medium-sized carrot, cut into four; 4 medium onions each stuck with a clove; 20 cloves of garlic; 40 cloves of shallot; a bouquet garni, composed of a bay leaf, a sprig of thyme, and some pieces of parsley.

Get ready some charcoal, in *large pieces,* which you will presently be needing, *burning fast.*

First Operation (*from half-past twelve until four o'clock*) *

At 12:30 coat the bottom and sides of the stew pan with the goose fat; then at the bottom of the pan arrange a bed of rashers of bacon.

Cut off the head and neck of the hare, leaving only the back and the legs. Then place the hare at full length on the bed of bacon, on its back. Cover it with another layer of bacon. Now all your bacon rashers are used up.

Now add the carrot; the onions; the 20 cloves of garlic; the 40 cloves of shallot†; the bouquet garni.

Pour over the hare:

(i) the 6 oz of red wine vinegar, and

(ii) a bottle and a half of 2-year-old Mâcon (or Médoc).

Season with pepper and salt in reasonable quantity.

At one o'clock. The *daubière* being thus arranged, put on the lid and set the fire going (either a gas stove or an ordinary range). On the top of the lid place 3 or 4 large pieces of charcoal in an incandescent state, *well alight and glowing.*

Regulate your heat so that the hare may cook for 3 hours, over a gentle and regular fire, continuously.

---

* These times are given for a dinner to be served at seven o'clock.

† In spite of the enormous quantity of garlic and shallots which enter into the composition of *lièvre à la royale,* the remarkable fact is that to a certain extent the two ingredients cancel each other out, so that the uninitiated would hardly suspect their presence.

Second Operation (to be carried out during the first cooking of the hare)

First chop exceedingly finely the four following ingredients, chopping each one separately:

(i) ¼ lb of bacon,
(ii) the heart, liver, and lungs of the hare,
(iii) 10 cloves of garlic,
(iv) 20 cloves of shallot.

The chopping of the garlic and the shallots must be so fine that each of them attains as nearly as possible a molecular state.

This is one of the first conditions of success of this marvelous dish, in which the multiple and diverse perfumes and aromas melt into a whole so harmonious that neither one dominates, nor discloses its particular origin, and so arouse some preconceived prejudice, however regrettable.

The bacon, the insides of the hare, the garlic, and shallots being chopped very fine, and separately, blend them all together thoroughly, so as to obtain an absolutely perfect mixture. Keep this mixture aside.

Third Operation (from four o'clock until a quarter to seven)

At four o'clock. Remove the stew pan from the fire. Take the hare out very delicately; put it on a dish. Then remove all the debris of the bacon, carrot, onions, garlic, shallot, which may be clinging to it; return these debris to the pan.

The sauce. Now take a large deep dish and a sieve. Empty the contents of the pan into the sieve, which you have placed over the dish; with a small wooden pestle pound the contents of the sieve, extracting all the juice, which forms a *coulis* in the dish.

Mixing the coulis and the hachis (the chopped mixture). Now comes the moment to make use of the mixture which was the subject of the second operation. Incorporate this into the *coulis.*

Heat the half bottle of wine left over from the first operation. Pour this hot wine into the mixture of *coulis* and *hachis* and stir the whole well together.

At half-past four. Return to the stew pan:

(i) the mixture of *coulis* and *hachis,*
(ii) the hare, together with any of the bones which may have become detached during the cooking.

Return the pan to the stove, with the same *gentle and regular fire* underneath and on the top, for another 1½ hours' cooking.

At six o'clock. As the excess of fat, issuing from the necessary quantity of bacon, will prevent you from judging the state of the sauce, you must now proceed to operate a *first removal of the fat.* Your work will not actually be completed until the sauce has become sufficiently amalgamated to attain a consistence approximating to that of a purée of potatoes; not quite, however, for if you tried to make it too thick, you would end by so reducing it that there would not be sufficient to moisten the flesh (by nature dry) of the hare.

Your hare having therefore had the fat removed, can continue to cook, *still on a very slow fire,* until the moment comes for you to add the blood which you have reserved with the utmost care as has already been instructed.

Fourth Operation (*quarter of an hour before serving*)

At quarter to seven. The amalgamation of the sauce proceeding successfully, a fourth and last operation will finally and rapidly bring it to completion.

Addition of the blood to the hare. With the addition of the blood, not only will you hasten the amalgamation of the sauce but also give it a fine brown color; the darker it is the more appetizing. This addition of the blood should not be made more than 30 minutes before serving; it must also be preceded by a *second removal of the fat.*

Therefore, effectively remove the fat; after which, without losing a minute, turn to the operation of adding the blood.

(i) Whip the blood with a fork, until, if any of it has become curdled, it is smooth again. (Note: The optional addition of the brandy mentioned at the beginning helps to prevent the curdling of the blood.)

(ii) Pour the blood into the sauce, taking care to stir the contents of the pan from top to bottom and from right to left, so that the blood will penetrate into every corner of the pan.

Now taste; add pepper and salt *if necessary.* A little later (45 minutes at a maximum) get ready to serve.

Arrangements for serving

At seven o'clock. Remove from the pan your hare, whose volume by this time has naturally somewhat shrunk.

At any rate, in the center of the serving dish, place all that still has the consistency of meat, the bones, entirely denuded, and now useless, being thrown away, and now finally around this hare *en compote* pour the admirable sauce which has been so carefully created.

Needless to say (concludes the senator) that to use a knife to serve the hare would be a sacrilege. A spoon alone is amply sufficient.

As time passed there evolved an important subdivision of the sauces that have descended from the stewpot—those that are emerged from the stockpot—and some of these at their peak surpassed in elegance and complexity even the *lièvre à la royale* of Senator Couteaux.

The thrifty housewives of neolithic times were faced, like a modern housewife, with the problem of leftovers. And what would be left over from a soup or a stew would be not only scraps of meat and bits of vegetable but a remnant of the broth or juice in which the mess had cooked. So in starting a stew for the next night, it would seem natural and economical to begin with the remnants of the stew from last night. Or in serving the leftovers of the roast from some other night it was discovered that they would taste better if moistened and flavored by the liquid element remaining from some recent stew. Thus it came about that the broth from a chicken might adorn the flesh of a fish, the broth from a calf the flesh of a chicken, and so on.

In time it was found that various combinations were not merely economical when they were left over but tasty when they were not.

As more time passed and cooking became more subtle, complicated, and organized, it was no longer sufficient to hope that there would be available, at a given moment, just the right leftover to create a tasty concoction. So it became the practice in large, organized kitchens, to cook up what we now call stock, essentially the equivalent of the ancient stewpot— meat, bones, vegetables, herbs—except that its purpose now was not to create a dish or a meal, but simply to provide the broth from which a sauce, the adornment of the dish, could then be created.

As the art of cuisine developed in the great palaces and châteaux of the seventeenth and eighteenth centuries, with their large staffs devoted to no purpose other than cooking for large and presumably discriminating gatherings, the creation of a stock, and then a sauce from that stock, became a major production.

The preparation of a classic brown sauce in one of these great kitchens might take as much as three days. First, a mass of bones and meat scraps would be browned in an oven. Then they would be boiled in water for several hours with vegetables and seasonings. The resulting fluid, called a stock, would be strained and cooled and then mixed with a roux (flour and butter blended together) to produce a basic brown sauce. To the brown sauce base would then be added water and more vegetables and seasonings, and the combination would again be boiled and skimmed and strained and strained and skimmed and boiled for several more hours, and then cooled. The result would then be *sauce espagnole,* a "foundation sauce" or "mother sauce," which could be either used as is or mixed with still other ingredients to form the final sauce for a particular dish.

In *La Cuisine Classique,* by Urbain Dubois and Émile Bernard, published in 1856, is a recipe for brown sauce which includes not only ham, knuckle of veal, sides of beef, and poultry, but saddle of hare, partridge carcasses, Champagne, white wine, meat gravies, and finally, clear stock or soup.

Today in fine cooking there are literally hundreds of sauces descended directly or by way of the stockpot from the stewpots of the Iron Age. There is a common joke in France that England has one sauce (mint sauce) and 260 religions, whereas France has one religion and 260 sauces. For France, at least, the figures are understated. There are something like 275 officially accepted recipes for fillet of sole alone. But despite their great number, all stewpot/stockpot sauces can be divided into two major categories: white sauces and brown ones.

A brown sauce today is not quite the eighteenth-century production. At its simplest it is merely a brown roux (it has been browned in a pan) mixed with a brown beef stock. A white sauce is made with a white roux (it has not been browned) mixed with either milk and/or cream or a light stock. Technically, white sauces come in two basic forms, two "mother sauces" analogous to *espagnole*. These are *sauce béchamel,* made with milk and cream, and *sauce velouté,* made with light stock. But in fact a cream-based *béchamel* will often have stock added also, and a *velouté* made with stock will then be enriched with cream, so this is often more a distinction than a difference.

As to when a brown sauce will be used, and when a white: At the lighter end of the scale of foods—fish and seafoods—a white sauce will be used more often than otherwise. At the heavy end of the scale—red meat and game—a brown sauce will be used more often. In between—poultry and veal—the two are interchangeable.

Here is the pattern expressed graphically:

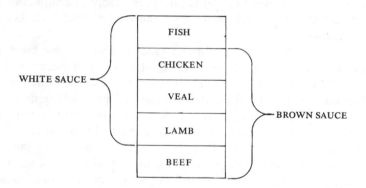

In a very general, oversimplified way it can be said that a brown sauce usually calls for a red wine to accompany: the richer and fuller the sauce, the fuller the wine. By the same token, a white sauce ordinarily takes a white wine (although in many cases a red is by no means ruled out): the richer and creamier the sauce, the fuller the wine to go along. In either case, brown or white, the more interesting, complex, and sophisticated the sauce, the more interesting, complex, and sophisticated should be the wine. A very important exception to this quality rule needs to be noted, however. If you are sampling some incomparable vintage, one of the great wines of the world, you will want to go a little easy on the elegance of the food to accompany. (Witness the Forrest Wallace dinner for Henry Van der Voort.) Since everybody wants to concentrate on the wine, you serve a good dish but not a spectacular one. By the same token, if you are serving an exquisitively fine, unusual dish, or a great old favorite such as duck *à l'orange,* everybody wants to concentrate on the dish, so you will serve a good wine but not a great one. We shall call this variation of emphasis the See-Saw Principle.

Another general point is important to note here: At the light end of the scale, many of the foods, such as oysters or crab meat, are so delicate, and others, such as swordfish and tuna, so bland, that they really cannot support a fine and interesting sauce, and thus do not call for a fine and interesting wine. (In the view of Raymond Oliver, the restaurateur, one of the very few "serious" shellfish sauces is the lobster-based *américaine.*)

At the other end of the scale, red meat and game, the flavor of the meat itself is at once full enough and bland enough so that, again with only one or two exceptions, it will not support a really interesting sauce, and therefore will not justify a really fine red wine. So here again we find ourselves working largely in the mid-zone. It is the in-between foods—fish that are big enough to be cut into fillets (small fish are clumsy to sauce), chicken, and veal, that are neither too delicate, too coarse, or too bland— that can be married to an infinite and fascinating variety of good sauces, and thus offer the greatest challenge in matching foods and wines.

One additional offspring of the stockpot needs to be noted. This is the aspic. The knowledge of most Americans of aspics is limited to the tomato aspic quivering on a lettuce leaf that is found from time to time in cafeterias and other institutional eating places. To see an aspic as nothing more than that is to do it grave injustice. Aspic essentially is jellied stock. Nowadays the jelling is caused deliberately by the adding of gelatin. In the old days the jelling occurred naturally in a cool climate because stock or broth contained a good supply of the protein substance collagen, resulting from the long boiling of animal tissues.

Aspics can be either dark or light, depending on how they are made. They are used to embellish an almost limitless number of cold meat dishes —fish, chicken, pheasant, tongue. The use of aspic by itself does not particularly ennoble a dish. But the aspic used as a vehicle for other garnishes and flavorings can produce some very elegant dishes indeed.

Here, now, are some common variations on basic brown sauce:

Sauce Bordelaise	red wine (ideally Bordeaux) and beef marrow added.
Sauce Bourguignonne	red wine (ideally Burgundy) and bacon, mushrooms, and onions added. The sauce for *boeuf bourguignon* and *coq au vin.*
Sauce à l'Orange or *Bigarade*	orange flavoring and orange peel added. The sauce for duck *à l'orange.*
Sauce Poivrade	wine or marinade added, highly seasoned with pepper. A sauce from the Middle Ages.
Sauce Venaison	*Sauce poivrade* with red currant jelly and whipping cream added.

Sauce Diable	pepper added.
Sauce Piquante	pickles and capers added.
Sauce Robert	onions, wine, and mustard added. Another sauce from the Middle Ages.
Sauce d'Uxelles	mushroom sauce.
Sauce Chasseur	mushroom sauce with tomatoes, garlic, and herbs.
Sauce Madère or au Porto	Madeira or Port wine added.
Sauce à l'Italienne	ham, mushrooms, and herbs added.

Here are some of the better-known variations on basic white sauce:

Sauce Suprême	cream added.
Sauce Mornay	cheese added.
Sauce Aurore	tomato added.
Sauce à l'Estragon	tarragon added.
Sauce au Currie	light curry flavoring.
Sauce Soubise	onion added.
Sauce aux Câpres	capers added.
Sauce à la Moutarde	mustard added.
Sauce aux Anchois	anchovies added.
Sauce Poulette	meat or fish flavoring, cream and egg yolks added.
Sauce Normande	cream, egg yolks, and butter added.

Those are only a few of the many, many sauces that can be made from the basic brown and white sauces, and for most people it will be difficult to remember even a list that long. But even if you could remember a much longer list, it would still not solve all the problems involved in matching wines with variously sauced foods. A beef stew made with a *sauce bourguignonne* is called *boeuf bourguignon,* and if you know what goes into a *sauce bourguignonne,* you will be able to decide what wine goes well with *boeuf bourguignon.* But a chicken fricassee or stew made with the same *sauce bourguignonne* (although this time, obviously, with a chicken base) is not called *coq bourguignon,* as logically it should be (a foolish consistency is not the hobgoblin of the Gallic mind), but *coq au vin.* And unless you just happen to *know* the sauce in *coq au vin,* the name gives you no help at all in picking out the wine.

By the same token, roast chicken served with a Port wine sauce is called, logically enough, *poulet au Porto.* But sliced tenderloin of beef (tournedos) served in a sauce based on Madeira wine would not automatically be called *tournedos au Madère.* If there are also shallots and mushrooms in the sauce, the dish is called *tournedos chasseur* (*chasseur* means "hunter"—this is a hunter's sauce, or so the chef liked to think). If before the *sauce madère* is added, you top the tournedos with an artichoke bottom filled with *sauce béarnaise* and truffles, you have *tournedos Henri VI,* in honor of that great king. If to the *sauce Madère* you add chopped truffles directly, you have *tournedos périgueux,* reflecting the

Perigord area of France where the best truffles are found. If your truffles
are *sliced* instead of chopped, you have *tournedos périgourdine,* a fine distinction indeed. If you top the tournedos with a slice of fois gras, chopped
goose liver, and then add truffles and *sauce Madère,* you have *tournedos
Rossini,* which is about as high up in this particular kind of eating as you
can get.

If you are eating at home, you don't care what the name of the dish is,
because you know what went into it. If you eat out a lot, you will gradually
come to know what is meant by such designations as *dieppoise, Nantua,
bonne femme* (good woman), *grand-mère* (grandmother), *ancienne* (old-
time), *moderne, favorite, cardinal, Richelieu, Renaissance, Romanov,
royale, régence, parisienne, banquière, financière, princesse, duchesse,
sultane, orientale, morocaine, persane, portugaise, tyrolienne, Walewska,*
and *Vladimir.* But if you don't know, it is no shame to ask, and asking will
put the waiter on his toes and gain his respect for the fact that you had the
guts and *savoir-faire* to do so.

Of course, even when you know what the name of a dish is supposed
to mean, you can go astray. Gilbert Cross, one of the authors of this book,
was once on vacation in Aruba, the Dutch-owned island off the coast of
Venezuela. In a small restaurant he ordered *sole meunière*—and expected
to be served what the name indicates, a fish fillet dipped in flour, fried simply in butter, and served with lemon juice and parsley. But the cooking of
Aruba has been influenced both by the South American mainland, only
fifteen miles away, and by the spices of Indonesia, which the Dutch held
for so long. That particular *sole meunière* had a spicy pungency that would
have caused the great chef Carême to rotate in his grave.

Against this background, let us now move quickly back through our
Categories of Affinity to see what are the variations in wine called for by
individual foods, and by different sauces, seaonings, and methods of
preparation:

SHELLFISH

We already know that any fish takes a relatively dry, delicate white
wine. Shellfish—oysters, clams, mussels, scallops—being perhaps the most
delicate sea life available, in general take the lightest, most delicate wine
around. The most common ways of serving shellfish are raw on the half
shell, steamed with melted butter, fried, baked, or broiled with tartar
sauce, or included in stews, chowders, or bisques, either whole, minced, or
puréed. Barring some unusual embellishment, none of these methods of
serving has significant influence on the choice of wine.

Oysters. With any shellfish or seafood served as an appetizer no wine
is usually served unless the next course is a fish course, in which case a wine
is served that can be drunk with both. With oysters on the half shell (and

clams, too) it is necessary to be careful, as we have pointed out. Too much tomato, horseradish, and Tabasco in the cocktail sauce will kill your palate for a wine. Most people who are drinking wine with raw shellfish will merely squeeze a little lemon juice on them.

Chablis is the classic wine, described in numberless books as the perfect wine to drink with raw oysters; Champagne is mentioned, too. This may in part be because in the old days of poor transportation Chablis and Champagne were the areas closest to Paris producing really clean, dry white wines, and it was in Paris that the rules were made. Yet even the experts do not agree that Chablis and Champagne are the only wines to serve with raw oysters. The late, very great George Saintsbury preferred dry Sherry. Pouilly-Fuissé or Fumé obviously would also go well, as would Sancerre. Muscadet has the required lightness, but is a little innocent. In any case, it would not be wise to serve the very best Chablis; it is too early in the meal for such a fine wine. The lightest German wines are light enough and, chosen carefully, dry enough. But their characteristic flowery tang does not quite fit the delicate simplicity of oysters.

The next most common way of serving oysters is oysters Rockefeller —with minced bacon and puréed spinach. This dish is greatly more flavorsome than oysters on the half shell. With it you could serve any of the above, including a German wine, or some of the medium grades of the fine white Burgundies—Corton, Meursault, Montrachet. Here again, a great wine is not in order, both because the quality of the dish does not justify it and because you want to wait for that until later in the meal.

The next oyster dish that comes to mind is scalloped oysters, with a thin, milk-based sauce (a simple *béchamel*). This is usually served as a side dish to some other entree, without a wine of its own. Like most stews and casseroles, scalloped oysters is a fairly bland dish. If you do serve it as a main dish, for lunch, say, it calls for a simple wine. Muscadet or a Swiss wine would be ideal. With oyster stew, by the same token, a simple white wine would not be wrong, but neither would a beer.

Clams. The next most common shellfish in this country is clams. Clams are not as delicate as oysters, but this is a fine distinction. For clams on the half shell, if you are having a wine, you might decide to take a Pouilly over a Chablis, just a shade fuller, and to spend twenty-five or fifty cents less for the bottle, but this is laboring the point. Fried clams or oysters, either one, is serving them very plain indeed. If this calls for a wine at all, again it is unpretentious Muscadet, or a lower-priced Chablis, or a California "Chablis." Steamed clams with drawn butter, when prepared at the shore with fresh, tiny local clams, have a charmingly sweet, uncomplicated flavor. Beer again is not out of order, or California "Chablis," or a simple Muscadet, or a decent Moselblümchen.

Mussels. Mussels (*moules* in French) are largely unfamiliar to Americans who do not frequent French restaurants, very familiar to those who do. They are known in France as "the poor man's oyster," because their flavor is somewhat robust and astringent compared to oysters or clams. Mussels are seldom served raw because cooking makes them more digestible. The commonest ways of serving them are steamed and then chilled with a *rémoulade* or *ravigote* sauce (mayonnaise derivatives), or *moules marinière,* steamed and then served hot in a sauce made of its own broth, white wine, and garlic—the French equivalent of American steamed clams. For any of these preparations, just a good white wine, not too heavy, not too light, not too costly: Vouvray, for example.

Scallops. The only other generally available shellfish is scallops. This is an extremely light dish, especially the tiny scallops from Peconic Bay near Long Island, but somewhat sweeter than oysters or clams. If you were serving broiled or fried scallops as the main feature at lunch, you would serve the very lightest thing around, Muscadet or Moselle. As a fish course at dinner what you had for soup and the next course would govern the decision and you might for that reason move up the scale of fullness a bit to Chablis.

As an appetizer, the scallop occurs most often as *coquille St.-Jacques,* with mushrooms and a rich, Sherry-laced cream sauce, calling obviously for one of the heavier white Burgundies, but not a great one, or a good white Graves or a big Hermitage Blanc.

SEAFOODS

We now come to the second broad class of crustacea, lumped together as "seafoods" in order to distinguish them from shellfish on the one hand and "finny" fish on the other. A more precisely descriptive title might be "shellfish that walk around." This group includes lobsters, crabs, shrimp, crayfish, prawns. They are separated from the shellfish by perhaps ten million years of evolution along with certain fundamentally different cooking and eating practices.

Like the shellfish, the seafoods are often served as appetizers, the difference being that they are not usually served raw, except by the Japanese, but are steamed or boiled and then served chilled with a cocktail sauce (and the admonition about too strong a sauce applies here, too, of course; lemon is better). Seafoods are not likely to be wasted on chowder, by the same token are less likely than oysters or clams to appear in a stew, and are much more likely to turn up as a main course or fish course in the main body of a meal. Seafoods may be served in their own shells, hot with melted butter, or cold with mayonnaise. The meat may also be removed from the shells and served hot, sautéed in butter or sauced, or cold in a salad, again with mayonnaise.

The shellfish that walk around are in general somewhat fuller and softer in flavor than the ones that stay put on the ocean floor. Thus, while

it is anything but a major point, they tend in general to take a fuller, softer
wine than their stay-put cousins: white Graves, a Vouvray, or a German
or Alsatian wine, in place of light, clean Muscadet or Chablis. They also
are more suited to serving with interesting sauces, so the sauce will more
often be a factor in choosing the wine.

Another minor note, but an interesting one: There is a definite spectrum of flavor within the seafood class, from lobster to crab to shrimp,
running from mildly sweet to dry. The nineteenth-century custom, unthink-
able today, of serving a very sweet white wine with the fish course started
in France with the idea that a sweet wine complimented the sweetish
taste of lobster. But even today a less than utterly dry German or German-
type wine with lobster or soft-shelled crabs is not out of the question.

As mussels are "the poor man's oyster," so there is a caste system
among the seafoods. A cheaper version of lobster is lobster tails, actually a
crawfish; a substitute for the fine, expensive Maryland or Pacific Coast
crabs is Alaska king crab; a humbler alternative to regular or small-sized
shrimp are the larger-sized prawns. In each case the lower-priced substitute is coarser in texture, less delicate in flavor, calling for the same wine;
but again you hesitate to spend as much money on it.

The commonest ways of saucing crab or lobster are "Norfolk," which
means sautéed in melted butter, and "à la Newburg," which means in a
sherried, perhaps even brandied spiced cream sauce. This latter demands
an interesting more than a distinguished wine, an unusual white Châteauneuf-du-Pape or a fairly good white Graves.

Another crab and/or lobster dish suited to displaying a good wine is
thermidor, mentioned in the Introduction, whose seasonings include tarragon and shallots, in a cheese-and-cream-based sauce. Here an assertive
wine can also be a very good, if not a fine one. An unusual white Beaune
or Mercurey would be appropriate, although a Meursault or white Graves
or German *Auslese* would be more available.

The heavier, more Mediterranean sauces—Marengo, *provençale,* Fra
Diavolo—would detract from any but a simple wine, whether served with
seafoods or with other dishes. In the first two cases, a good Sancerre or
Pouilly-Fumé would be about as high on the scale as you would want to
go; in the last case, one of the few good white Chiantis or an Orvieto.
With any of these, an inexpensive California nonvarietal would do as well.

A discussion of seafoods raises the question of what are the limits of
the seafood category. A frog is not a fish and tastes something like
chicken, although frogs' legs are generally listed in the seafood section of
the menu. Considering the garlic with which it is usually laced: serve a
lesser white Burgundy. By the same token, French snails—*escargots*—are
usually from the land and not the sea, but at least have shells, and are
prepared in butter and garlic like frogs' legs. They would call for a Sancerre

or perhaps even a simple red Burgundy (permissible since there is no iodine in snails, even though they come in a shell).

This brings us to squid, conch, sea urchin, sea anemone, and eel. To the extent that any of these are served Italian style the tomato rule applies. You want an assertive wine, palatable, but not exceptional. Greeks serve squid temptingly, stuffed with little vermicelli. Here a Greek wine (but not the resin-laced Retsina) or a white California or Italian wine would do well.

FISH

From seafood we move on to the domain of the "finny" fish, and here, as noted, we reach the take-off point into the world of *haute cuisine*. In preparing fillet of sole, let us say, the care that may be employed and the wine that might be justified are limited only by your time, your budget, and your imagination.

Unlike oysters and clams, finny fish are never eaten raw (except by the Japanese), and do not as a rule occur as appetizers, except salted, pickled, or smoked or in the sort of restaurant that lists "seafood cocktail" on the menu and then gives you cold, leftover salmon in a spiced-up tomato sauce. There is not much advice to be offered in this latter case except to change restaurants. Salted, pickled, or smoked fish do not have much to offer to a wine, nor vice versa. Finny fish do not usually occur in soup except in the various French fish soups, most notably bouillabaisse, which are substantial enough to double as main courses. The province of the finny fish is thus almost exclusively the main body of the meal.

Fish may be pan-fried, sautéed, boiled, steamed, poached, baked, braised, served cold in aspic, or ground up and made into little dumpling-like cakes, croquettes, soufflés, or mousses. Unless an interesting sauce is used, none of the above methods has much influence on the wine.

In terms of cooking and saucing, all finny fish fall into four categories. First, there are what might be called *humble fish*. These are so unpretentious, like catfish, or so oily, like mackerel, that they do not justify much of a sauce, a very simple cream or egg sauce at the most. If you had a wine with them at all, it would be because you wanted to drink some wine that night, not because there was any hope of synergy, and it would be the simplest, humblest white wine to be found.

One notch above the humble fish are what we will call *big fish*— salmon, swordfish, tuna, and such. With their coarse texture and bland flavor, in general, there is not much you can do with big fish. Fried cod, tuna casserole, or swordfish steak would take no better wine than a modest Chablis, Muscadet, or simple domestic white. Most of the time, salmon deserves the same treatment. However, a good salmon (young, and preferably caught heading upriver to the spawning grounds) can be an exception.

Cold salmon may be served smoked as an hors d'oeuvre, in which case a sturdy white Burgundy or even a fine Sherry would go well. *Saumon à la Russe,* served with a good (not store-bought) mayonnaise, has a slight sweetness which is complemented by a good white Graves: Haut-Brion Blanc, Château Carbonnieux. A *saumon glacé au Bourgogne blanc* is served in an aspic containing a fine white Burgundy, sometimes even Corton-Charlemagne, and needs a fine white Burgundy to go with it: Montrachet, Meursault, or Corton-Charlemagne itself. Another variant is made with red Burgundy (remember the lampreys of St.-Émilion) and calls for red wine, preferably Burgundy, to accompany.

The next level above the big fish is *pan fish.* These are fish which have a more delicate texture and a finer flavor than either of the first two groups but are just not big enough physically to do much with except·toss in a pan with a little butter and serve up with lemon or tartar sauce. This group includes such fish as brook trout, sand dabs, and smelt, which were not endowed by nature with the capacity to grow very large, and others, like flounder, brill, and turbot, which sometimes will be caught too small to cook any other way. In either case, fish so simply cooked take a simple wine, a lesser Chablis or Mâcon Blanc.

The fourth category, the main one for our purposes, is *fillet fish.* These are the ones of fine enough texture and delicate enough flavor to deserve being cut into fillets (a fish steak is cut across the grain; a fillet with the grain) and enough size to permit it. The fillets are usually poached or sautéed and served with a sauce ranging from rather simple to very elegant.

The queen of the fillet fish is sole, of course, and its look-alikes or cook-alikes the world around. The classic, traditional English Channel (or Dover) sole does not occur in the Western Hemisphere, but every region has fish that meet the specifications—fine texture, delicate flavor, reasonable size—and is sold in the fish stores as sole. Pompano, for example, and flounder, while a bit more robust in flavor than sole and its equivalents, lend themselves very well to the same sauces.

Here are just a very few, in escalating order of elegance, of the better-known ones out of the 275 methods of saucing and serving fish fillets, along with the characteristics of the sauces, and the wines with which they could be served:

Filet de Sole Bonne Femme. The sauce (a *velouté*) is made with white wine, lemon juice, and the thickened juices of the fish left after cooking. Calls for a Muscadet or Pouilly-Fuissé.

Filet de Sole Marguery. Made with white wine, shrimp, mushrooms, thickened with butter. A dry white Graves or Muscadet.

Filet de Sole Mornay. A heavy white *béchamel,* half cream, half cheese. Pouilly-Fumé, Pouilly-Fuissé.

Filet de Sole Véronique. Poached in white wine, the sauce resulting from adding hollandaise, egg yolk, whipped cream, and small white grapes either fresh or canned. A Meursault or white Haut-Brion.

Filet de Sole Normande. Velouté containing eggs, cream, and fish stock, garnished with mussels and oysters. A good white Burgundy: Bâtard-Montrachet, Corton-Charlemagne.

In real French cooking there is a fifth category of fish. These are the fish that are used to make *quenelles.* Quenelles are little dumplings or croquettes made of ground fish (they can also be made with ground veal or chicken) which are poached and served with a fine sauce. Their origin lies in French country cooking. French cooks near the sea have salt-water fish to turn to. Those near rivers and lakes have fish from those sources. But every landlocked farming area has its ponds, natural or artificial, which at once conserve water and provide a place to grow fish. One of the most plentiful of these fish is pike, which has very good flesh but is difficult to eat because of its peculiar bone structure. Rather than waste the pike, however, the thrifty French farm wife grinds it in a stone mortar and then forces it through a sieve (the result is called forcemeat). The forcemeat is then made into quenelles and poached. (Cod, halibut, and haddock can be used in place of pike for making quenelles.) Quenelles can be served with the same sauces as sole, or sometimes will appear as *quenelles à la lyonnaise,* in a casserole with a cream sauce, olives, truffles, and mushrooms. A medium white Burgundy is appropriate for this.

CHICKEN

With chicken we take another giant step into the world of *la haute cuisine,* since red wines as well as white can now be used, multiplying both options and challenges.

It should be noted that neither fish nor veal nor chicken is necessarily expensive or rare, none by itself is particularly distinguished. But each is, above all things, amenable, and because it is you can do things with it. Some of the finest dishes of the French cuisine are made with chicken, and nearly all the principles of fine cooking and saucing are demonstrated here.

Chicken may be fried, sautéed, roasted, broiled or barbecued, fricasseed or stewed, poached or boiled. However you do it, it calls for light red wine, as we have already seen, with a full white permitted, unless something additional is done. If you sauté the chicken *herbes de Provence,*—a Mediterranean treatment with herbs (basil, thyme, etc.), garlic, egg yolk, and butter sauce—or broil it *à la diable* (sauced with a mustard-flavored sauce), you tend toward a simple rosé rather than a red. If the chicken is roasted *à la Normande* (basted with cream), our basic sauce rule applies. But gently. You are on the border line. You could still serve a light red wine, but with the cream you should perhaps move over to a fullish white —a white Burgundy. If you serve sautéed chicken breasts—light meat—in one of a variety of light cream sauces, you are over the line. Here you would prefer a fullish white to the red. Sautéed breasts in a brown sauce, on the other hand, tilts you back toward preference for a red. Roast chicken *au Porto,* sliced, flambéed in brandy, and served in a sauce of Port wine, cream, and mushrooms, raises a question. The red Port would suggest a red wine; the cream calls for white. The cream wins. A white wine is called for, and for a dish so elegant, an elegant white—a very good white Burgundy or a château-bottled Graves. Fricassee of chicken, in a simple, creamy sauce, calls for a white wine—a simple one. The classic Burgundian fricassee or stew, *coq au vin,* done in red wine, with onions, mushrooms, and bacon, calls for a full red wine, humble or great, according to your pocketbook. Although it is usually thought of as a red-wine dish, *coq au vin* not surprisingly has plenty of regional variants; in the Jura region it is made and drunk with a semisweet yellow wine (Vin de Paille), in Alsace with a Riesling, and in Anjou with a rosé. There is no problem with any of these—you drink whatever wine you used to create the dish.

Simple American fried chicken will take to a modest California white, although you can have a better one if you feel like it. Chicken Kiev, on the other hand, elegant boned breasts of chicken stuffed with herbs and foi gras before frying, demands something pretty good and quite dry— perhaps a Bâtard-Montrachet. A wine this good would also not be wasted on chicken breasts Jeannette, cold chicken encased in chicken aspic and truffles.

A plain roasted or stuffed bird might be well served with a village-grade Beaujolais or regional Médoc. The same would be true with a Cornish game hen or a squab.

TURKEY

Of all the common domestic fowl, the turkey gets the lowest marks in fine food circles. The barnyard variety, at least, is too bland and frequently too dry, once baked or roasted, to inspire the culinary imagination. But the turkey is a bird of occasion and celebration. For this purpose, Champagne, perhaps. In everyday use, a medium-grade St.-Émilion or other Bordeaux would cover the situation.

DUCK

Plain roast duck, as we know, calls for red wine, or a full-bodied, spicy, perhaps sweetish white, a German or Alsatian Traminer or a

Graves. If the duck is roasted with sausage and apple stuffing, a German or Alsatian treatment, you would be more likely to go the German or Alsatian route. The famous duck *à l'orange* or *bigarade,* in an orange-flavored brown sauce, is a fine dish calling for a fine wine. Orange suggests white wine, brown sauce favors red; you can go either way. In any case, it is a fine sauce, the dish is a delicacy, so you want a good wine. But remember the See-Saw Principle. The sauce is such an old friend to so many people that it is usually the duck and the sauce you want to concentrate on, so you don't want too good a wine. A good but not great Médoc will do. Roast duckling Montmorency is a similar dish, with black cherries in place of the orange slices. A Frenchman might take a medium-full red here—a Beaune or a red Loire. The sweetness of the sauce precludes too dry a choice. A fullish white wine could also be used: Vouvray, Saumur, Graves. Roast duck with turnips is a far humbler dish, calling for a humbler wine, such as a Sylvaner or Beaujolais. Roast duck with cabbage, red or white, makes for a decidedly Germanic choice.

GOOSE

Goose calls for either a fuller red than duck or a sweeter white. The goose is a very fat bird, so we want a wine with enough character to deal with the fatty taste. A Côtes du Rhône, more full than fine, is good when the stuffing is to include meat (such as liver or sausage). With a vegetable stuffing—wild rice, chestnuts, and the like—a Rhine *Auslese,* a Gewürztraminer, or even the rare genuine dry Sauternes, Château "Y."

GAME

There are very few exceptions to the rule of red wine with game. Nearly everything wild that runs or flies is eaten with red wine, and since the English and French have been eating game with fine wine for a longer time than the Americans, it is wise to follow their rule that a light red be drunk with unhung game, a full one with aged game. The wines are usually Bordeaux and Burgundy, and usually the finer grades of both categories. For a reasonably fresh batch of game birds—grouse or quail, for instance —a fine second-growth Médoc such as Léoville-Poyferré or Brane-Cantenac would be superb. For a fine aged roast rack of venison, a grand old Chambertin would be perfect. However, if you happen to have shot a six-point buck, and cannot see your way to the required number of cases of fine Burgundy to go through several hundred pounds of meat, you could experiment wth substitutes: the big, assertive Rhônes like Hermitage and Côte Rôtie, or even one of the Spanish red Riojas.

The classic dish jugged hare, as we have already pointed out, will take a very great red if you can afford it, with a preference for Burgundy; otherwise a lesser one.

The exceptions to the above are almost all Germanic, as noted. In Germany, some of the oldest, darkest, ripest game, particularly wild boar and venison, is served accompanied by a fine, fairly sweet white wine— Rhine or even delicate Moselle.

Otherwise, the only times you would be inclined to use a dry white wine with game is with a few species of American waterfowl, like teal or widgeon. Even here, a really dry white, like a Chablis, probably would not do. Possibly a dry Riesling (German, Alsatian, California, or even Austrian) or a German Frankenwein.

VEAL

Veal in the United States is one of the less sought-after meats. In France and Italy it is one of the most popular. Italians like it better than beef (and that means a good place to find superior veal in the United States is in a butcher shop that caters to Italians). The taste for veal in France and Italy, like the taste for quenelles made of pike, originally reflected the nature of the farm economy (although today, of course, the economy has to some extent responded to the demand patterns created by the taste). Grazing land is not as plentiful in France and Italy as in places like the Steppes of Russia, for example, the Pampas of the Argentine, or the wide open spaces of the western United States. In Italy and much of France, most calves not needed for milk or breeding are butchered while only twelve to sixteen weeks old, before they are weaned. This reserves the short supply of pasture land for producing milk, butter, and cheese, and at the same time means that the calves are sold for the premium price milk-fed veal will bring. In places with more grassland the same calves might have been raised to maturity for beef, or at least put out to grass for enough time to add substantial poundage before they are sold. But grass-fed veal, which you find in most butcher shops in the United States, is not nearly as delicate and tender as the milk-fed kind. This fact, plus the lack of inclination on the part of American cooks to make the fine and varied sauces that go so well with veal, plus the plentiful alternatives, account for its lesser popularity in this country.

Throughout all of veal cookery, whether we are talking about a roast stuffed shoulder or a simple ragout, the choice of a red wine or a white one will be primarily up to the host. Only a too-big red or a too-delicate white would be considered wrong. Veal parmigiana and other tomato-sauced and spiced southern veal dishes are obviously best with a red (a California or Italian Barbera, a Zinfandel). A Chianti would not be bad. Similar wines are suited to veal chops provençale (*côtes de veau à la provençale*), garnished with tomatoes stuffed with mushrooms and covered with grated cheese. A Tavel rosé, from the land of that recipe's birth, would also be appropriate.

The unique cut of veal of course is the escalope, or scallopini, an oval piece of meat, three or four ounces in weight, usually taken off the round or rib. These "scallops" are the basis of some of the most elegant dishes in several cuisines: from schnitzel (Austrian) to scallopini (Italian). The best-known escalope dish is veal scallopini Marsala, which appears in slightly differing versions in Italian, French, and even Spanish cooking. As we noted a few pages back with lobster Newburg, a well-spiced sauce laced with a fortified wine will dominate most delicate table wines. Since Marsala (the same is true of the Madeira and Malaga sometimes used) is a white wine, a white is indicated, a soft, full, fairly alcoholic one: Vouvray, Orvieto, or one of the medium-dry Rioja whites of Spain.

For the rest of veal cookery, there are few preparations that call for a special selection of wines: most schnitzels take a Riesling or Sylvaner (or a Hungarian white). Osso buco (knuckle of veal) looks hearty enough to get red wine, but very often the sauce, particularly in the French version, *jarret de veau,* has a large quantity of white wine in with the tomatoes, so here we may choose a forceful Italian white—Orvieto, Brolio Bianco—or rosé. A veal ragout, with a thick, dark sauce, would go well with a red Beaujolais.

PORK

There is little to add here to what we said in a previous chapter. Pork is a no-wines-land, neither assertive nor delicate, somewhat analogous to tuna in the realm of fish. You cannot do much for it with either sauce or wine, nor can it return the favor, or the flavor. If you wish to serve wine with pork, a spicy, fullish white Traminer, a red Côtes du Rhône, not too elegant, is about the limit, and beer will do as well. For ham, which is smoked salt pork, a not-too-heavy red—Beaujolais, Médoc—is acceptable. For a ham slice in a cream and Madeira sauce, a fullish dry white will do. Champagne, with the bubbles, has been traditionally considered to work well with salty ham. With spareribs, wine would almost be an intrusion, whether the cuts are prepared simply or with barbecue sauce.

A large sector of French cuisine called *charcuterie* is built around the fancy preparation of pork. It includes sausages, pâtés, terrines (pâté baked in a troughlike pan lined with bacon or salt-pork strips, and stuffed with truffles), and galantines (an aspiclike preparation of pork and other meats). The latter two dishes are the absolute summit of pork cookery, but even at their best—as hors d'oeuvres or part of a cold lunch on a hot day —they are not improved by really good wine. A soft, fairly dry white, an ordinary Moselle or Alsatian, would be acceptable. Dry Champagne would do.

Most of the world's sausages are made of pork, and sausages also tend to beg the question of wine. Italian hot sausages in a red sauce will take something simple in red: Italian, a California generic. French regional sausages such as *saucissons lyonnaise,* which tend to be dark, sometimes almost black, call for a lively young red: Beaujolais or its northern neighbor, Mercurey, or a Loire red. German sausages, knackwurst, bauerwurst, and so on, seem designed for beer, or a lesser white.

Choucroute is French for sauerkraut and like the German and American versions, is almost always served with pork, either *wurst* or pig's knuckle. Beer or the common Alsatian Sylvaner wine is usually drunk with *choucroute,* but sometimes the cabbage itself is cooked in good white wine, even Champagne. Here, once again, you drink with it what went into it.

One other good bistro-style French dish is cassoulet, a casserole of pork and pork sausage, white beans, and poultry, usually goose legs. Sometimes mutton and duck are also added. Although the dish originates in the Languedoc region, tradition asks for a Loire red, Chinon or Bourgueil, to go with it. Certainly a simple red from some other district—almost any other district—would not be wrong.

LAMB

In France, as with other countries bordering on the Mediterranean, throughout history wool has usually been a fairly small part of the business of sheep-raising. (The climate does not call for wool clothing.) As a result, just as in the case of veal, growers long ago realized the advantages of early slaughter; the meat is better, the grazing land protected. Thus lamb as a dish became popular millenniums ago, on what would today be called a cost-efficiency basis. In England, by contrast, the demand for woolens to keep out the cold and damp made investment in large herds profitable. During the early eighteenth century it was literally a capital crime to slaughter a lamb in some areas of England, and the dispossession of small freeholders for the sake of large sheep "ranches" swelled both the English criminal classes and the thirteen colonies. Sheep were thus rarely slaughtered in Britain until they were extremely "muttony." Hence the traditional English taste for mutton.

In wine terms, with lamb we have reached something of a watershed. This is not "red meat" in the sense that beef is, but it is decidedly pink, and the wine of choice is nearly always red. A young lamb takes a light red wine—medium Bordeaux; the tannin of the Bordeaux seems to go especially well with the fat of the lamb. A more mature lamb takes a heavier red. Mutton takes a full red. With lamb we have reached a watershed of sauces, too. Lamb is too assertive for the more delicate white sauces, not assertive enough for the full brown ones. So it is usually served plain. But this is one case where "served plain" does not necessarily call for a simple wine. Plain roast leg of lamb creates its own interesting "sauce" through the browned juices on its surface, and thus may be accompanied by a fine red Bordeaux. If the lamb has been marinated in red wine before it was roasted, however, the fuller flavor resulting calls for Burgundy, as does rack or crown of lamb, which is really nothing more than lamb chops roasted before they are cut apart. In the case of a "baron" of lamb, the hindquarters, with both legs sticking up, the look of the dish reminds you of Henry VIII, so you might serve a big Burgundy, not because of the flavor, but because of the picture in your mind. Shish kebab would tolerate an off-beat and outspoken red—a Yugoslavian Cabernet or a simple Chilean "Burgundy." Lamb stew, humbler cuts, when done humbly in a rather creamy sauce, call for a simple red, Beaujolais or Bordeaux, a rosé, or a full white Beaujolais or Mâcon Blanc.

BEEF

With most of the calves butchered young for veal, it should be obvious that on a thrifty French farm the primary source of mature beef will be a cow that has retired from dairy duty or herd bull that has been replaced after long and presumably enthusiastic service. Fine cuts, when there are any, make their way to the Paris market for the higher prices they bring there. Thus the cuts of beef that are featured in the kind of traditional French cooking that is close to the soil are tough cuts, and the recipes— the long-cooking variety, stewing, braising, boiling—are true and lineal descendants of the stewpots of the ancient past. *Boeuf bourguignon* and *coq au vin* have been the final resting place for many an old friend from the barnyard. *Boeuf à la mode* is not, as some might think, beef with ice cream, but a French version of the humble pot roast.

Boeuf bourguignon, Burgundian beef stew with onions, mushrooms, and potatoes, calls for a full, young red wine in and with the dish, a Burgundy strongly indicated, with Beaujolais, Côtes du Rhône, St.-Émilion also acceptable. *Boeuf à la mode* is a little better, calling for a good, full-bodied red, Burgundy, Hermitage, Côte Rôtie, or Châteauneuf. *Pot-au-feu,* the Gallic equivalent of the New England boiled dinner, calls for a nice simple red, not too heavy—Beaujolais, Bordeaux, a lesser Chianti. If the beef has been braised in beer, as in *carbonades à la flamande,* it calls, of course, for beer to drink with it. If the dish contains tomatoes, as in *boeuf à la catalane,* we need a strong, young red wine, such as a Loire red.

With American and English beef recipes, the same sort of thing. Light red Burgundy goes well with steak-and-kidney pie; sauerbraten, an Austrian or North Italian red or a Rhône. New England boiled dinner, a simple California red; the same with hamburger. For Swiss steak, a California Zinfandel or Pinot Noir. A good Beaujolais or Côtes du Rhône would be fine with a real paprika-laden goulash. Corned beef, hash, and meat loaf, a glass of red straight from a low-priced jug from California. With the Jewish corned beef called pastrami, beer is the thing.

French country recipes for beef are good. Well made, some are classics. But they are not ideally suited to the taste of Americans who like fine steaks and roasts and can afford them. One reason for the popularity of good steaks and roasts in the United States has been that the meat itself is so much more flavorsome than plain, unsauced chicken, fish, and veal. Unless she overcooked the beef, Mom has been assured that for relatively little trouble she would get compliments or at least satisfied sighs. But, as noted, the advantage of good beef is also its limitation. The flavor of beef, while not itself truly interesting, overrules a high proportion of the more interesting, delicate sauces. When steaks and roasts are sauced at all, it is usually with a simple butter sauce or a *sauce bordelaise,* calling for good, rather young red wines with a certain amount of body—Rhône, St.-Émilion, Beaujolais *villages.*

Some of the simple sauces most commonly used for steaks, with their modest influence on the choice of wine, include the following:

Sauce bordelaise—shallots, stock, and Bordeaux wine—a preference for Bordeaux red.

Sauce moutarde—powdered Dijon mustard with brown stock—a light Burgundy.

Sauce Madère—noted earlier, Madeira wine reduced with meat juices, herbs—a good Médoc.

Sauce bourguignonne—Burgundy wine, stock, shallots, herbs, pepper —takes a medium Burgundy: Beaune or Pommard.

These sauces go well with a prime cut of meat, and set off the delicate flavor of beefsteak without overpowering it as do some of the bottled sauces. For lesser pieces of steak, the round and the chuck, a French kitchen might use a more assertive flavor, as in steak *au poivre* (impregnated with peppercorns) or *biftek andalouse* (garlic, tomatoes, and onions). With either of these, Beaujolais of the better sort, as young as you can get it.

But this state of things leaves us a bit at a loss in knowing what to do for a very festive occasion where beef is preferred, but there is a desire to spend a lot of money, do things up fancy, or both. French cuisine, with its flexibility and resource, has responded to this need with the handful of elegant recipes noted earlier for cooking tournedos, sautéed, sliced tenderloin of beef. For practical purposes, tournedos are extra select filet mignon, the tenderest and most expensive cut of beef there is. As indicated, the Madeira sauce with which they are often served goes well with a good Médoc: the austerity of the Médoc serving as a kind of counterpoint to the richness of the sauce. *Tournedos chasseur* (Madeira, herbs, shallots, mushrooms) would take a second- or third-growth Bordeaux: Châteaux Montrose or Palmer would do well. *Tournedos Henri IV* (topped with an artichoke heart filled with béarnaise sauce and truffles, finished with Madeira sauce) is worth the best from Bordeaux, providing a chance to use your '59 Margaux or Lafite '52 that is at its peak (assuming you have one).

The ultimate, most famous method of preparing tournedos, *tournedos Rossini* (a layer of fois gras, topped with truffle slices, Madeira sauce), is an occasion for the best available: a '37 Haut-Brion or '18 Mouton.

If a sliced beef tenderloin in one of several elegant variations of Madeira sauce provides a superb occasion for showing off a fine Bordeaux, the unsliced tenderloin, simply roasted, creating its own sauce like a leg of lamb, provides a magnificently simple background for a fine Burgundy, as it did for the Romanée-St.-Vivant '06 of Forrest Wallace. The fullness and soft smoothness of a great Chambertin or Romanée-Conti almost sings alongside a standing roast tenderloin slow-cooked to rareness.

To come back to earth, however, if you feel like preparing one of these luxurious dishes and cannot afford to serve one of these extravagant wines, you serve the wine you can afford and let the food, not the wine, become the focus of the meal.

SPECIALTY MEATS

With the specialty meats—liver, sweetbreads, kidneys—there is not too much more to say. Sauces rarely elevate them above their rather humble status. But there are a few exceptions. The Swiss have a way of quickly sautéeing thin slices of calves liver in butter and serving them in a sauce of shallots and red wine that would more than justify a fine red Bordeaux. Sweetbreads (*ris de veau*) can be cooked *à la maréchale,* with cream, lemon juice, and herbs, and would certainly support a good white Graves or white Burgundy. Kidneys (*rognons*) *en casserole,* cooked in butter with a mustard and parsley sauce, go very happily with a decent light red from the Beaune slope or a Bordeaux.

EGGS

Most of the eggs eaten in this country are eaten at breakfast, where wine is rarely called for (although there are such things as a Champagne breakfast). For other meals, a simple plate of scrambled, poached, fried, or boiled eggs does not seem the right occasion for any wine or even beer. But omelets, and several kinds of sauced, poached egg dishes, served at an elegant brunch or luncheon or a midnight supper, while they do not demand wine, are much the better for it. Your first inclination might be to go for a light white wine with all egg dishes. Certainly cheese and herb-filled omelets, eggs Benedict (with hollandaise sauce, and ham or bacon), and eggs Florentine (with white cheese sauce and spinach) would get a modest white, such as a California Riesling. With *oeufs à la bourguignonne,* a light red Burgundy, such as a Mâcon, goes in the glass as well as in the dish.

There are some *great* egg dishes, such as the soufflés of France and the truffle-egg-and-cheese extravaganzas of northern Italy. With all of these, following the See-Saw Principle, the wine should be less grandiose than the *chef d'oeuvre*. A light regional red or a good, modest white would be suitable. As with pork, you just want something pleasant to drink with the dish, rather than any synergistic complement to it.

The influence of sauces and seasonings and methods of preparation on the choice of wines, like the influence of the Human Variable, is a subject not easy to exhaust. But this certainly is enough to give the feel. Beyond this point the best teacher is experience, in the process of matching and blending fine foods and great wines. And that is the subject of the next two chapters.

HOW TO SERVE A MASTERPIECE: THE WINES

❦

Anyone who has paid reasonable attention thus far is now equipped to march into any fine restaurant in Europe or America and with considerable assurance order one of the great or near-great wines of the world, matching it off with a dish of appropriate flavor and elegance. But if you go, let us say, to Père Bis or Grand Véfour, order a Chambertin '55, and drink it with a superb jugged hare or *tournedos périgueux,* the waiter may give you the fish eye, and when he gets to the kitchen mutter *"touriste,"* and wonder why you have forgotten to wear your tennis shoes.

The reason is that you obviously got it all out of a book. A truly great wine and an incomparable dish, however deftly matched, are not ordinarily enjoyed in isolation, but rather as crowning elements of a harmoniously orchestrated whole. Until you can organize and appreciate a meal worthy of great wines and fine dishes, you will remain a gastronomic parvenue, and the waiter will know it.

But to learn to put together a Great Meal, much less enjoy one regularly, raises problems of a thoroughly practical nature. As noted in the Introduction, the price of a training session at any great restaurant could easily run three hundred dollars or more for a party of six, leaving aside the cost of getting the people to Paris or New York. But the fact is that a basically equivalent meal could be served in your home, made with materials readily available, using recipes to be found in any decent cookbook, at a cost somewhere between ten and fifteen dollars a person, twenty and thirty dollars a couple—less than that if you are careful—no more than the price of an ordinary evening out. This is not to say the product of your kitchen will equal the greatest creations of Paris. But the economics of serving great wine at home are decisively in your favor, and with a little care the food you serve will be more than adequate to the occasion.

It is the purpose of this chapter and the one following to show you how to plan and serve a Great Meal in the security and economy of your own kitchen.

A note is in order here, however. Not many readers of this book are likely to sit down to a Great Meal on a regular basis. Our lives are not organized that way. The chief benefit of gaining an understanding of how a Great Meal is put together, aside from the thrill of making an occasional ascent to the very summit, is the pleasure this understanding can give, and the grace it can lend, to the humbler occasions. It is not necessary to have four wines with your dinner, nor even two, nor to prepare some elaborate entree from the classic cuisine, in order to create an occasion of harmony, elegance, and charm.

A Great Meal in any case is not necessarily an elaborate or expensive one. A magnificently tender piece of beef or an incomparable lobster dish might itself cost more per head than one of the menus that follow and still not achieve true greatness in the culinary sense. As in the case of most elegant things, one of the prime virtues of a Great Meal is its simplicity. It is a carefully ordered *progression* of foods, ordinarily not less than four courses, with a harmoniously orchestrated accompaniment of wines; the same number, four, is appropriate, although a very fine meal if not a great one could offer as few as two, and if you add a couple of small courses, it is easy to include six wines or more.*

A Great Meal conventionally assumes hors d'oeuvres of some sort, followed by soup, then a fish course (although current practice is to serve soup *or* fish, not both), next red meat or poultry, along with potatoes and a green vegetable, and finally dessert, which often is no more than fruit and cheese. Accompanying this will be a light white appetizer wine, another fuller, better white wine with the fish, and two reds with the meat course. The second (and better) of the two reds carries over into the fruit and cheese, if that is what you are having. With a sweet dessert there is the option of serving a sweet dessert wine, followed, if you wish, by Port, and then brandy with the coffee. (Go easy on these final options, however. Especially the first few times around, you should be careful about getting yourself and your friends too stuffed or potted.)

The economics of such a repast for a party of six, prepared at home, are about as follows:

Hors d'oeuvres	$ 2.50
Fish with white wine sauce	5.00

---

* The humble home kitchen is not likely to include the necessary glassware, not to mention china, for a spread of this dimension. But you can always ask the other participants to bring extras, or for a modest price your local caterer or rent-all agency will provide very nicely.

Tournedos of beef with a red wine sauce	9.50
Truffles	6.00
Liver pâté in bulk	5.00
2 boxes frozen peas *française*	.75
Potatoes	1.00
Butter	.50
Fruit	2.00
Cheese	2.00
Coffee	.75
Total Food	$35.00
Apéritif wine	$ 4.50
1 bottle good white wine	6.00
1 bottle good red wine	10.00
1 bottle excellent red wine	25.00
Cognac brandy	2.50
Total wines and liquor	$48.00
Tax	4.80
Grand total for meal	$87.80

That comes to just under $15 a head, $30 a couple if three couples share. However, with moderate restraint a very elegant meal could be served for half that money, and even if you wanted to shoot the works and serve much more elegant foods and costly wines, it would not be necessary to push this budget much past $20 a head. If you ordered the same meal à la carte in a fine restaurant, the budget would run something like this:

	Each Person	Total
Hors d'oeuvres	$ 1.75	$ 10.50
Fish	6.50	39.00
Meat and vegetables	9.95	59.70
Dessert	1.50	9.00
Coffee	.75	4.50
Total Food	$20.45	$122.70
Apéritif wine		$ 7.25
White wine		8.25
First red		12.75
Second red		40.00
Brandy		15.00
Total wine and liquor		$ 83.25
Total for meal		$205.95
Tax		14.42
Plus 20 per cent tip		44.00
		$264.37

That comes to $44.06 a head, close to $90 a couple, and a *really* fine meal at a *really* great restaurant would cost much more. Luxury, then, begins emphatically at home.

Since wine, great wine, is to be the focus of this event, the first step is to choose the wine. Let us look again at the Spectrum of Possibility:

> Light and delicate white
> Fuller-bodied white
> Rosé
> Light-bodied red
> Fuller-bodied red

We can eliminate from consideration the lighter-bodied whites and rosé, since as we have noted truly great wine does not occur in these categories. We will add to the list the natural (unfortified) dessert wines of Bordeaux and the Rhine Basin, since the best of these are incontestably among the greatest wines on earth.

Among the fuller-bodied dry white wines the first choice is inevitable: Montrachet and Montrachet alone, at a price anywhere from $16 to $36, depending on the grower, the shipper, and the year. There are alternatives, of course: one of the runner-up vineyards, Bâtard-Montrachet, Chevalier-Montrachet, a fine Meursault, an Haut-Brion Blanc or other good white Graves.

The choice for a sweet dessert wine is no less obvious, at least to the somewhat francophile authors of this book: Château d'Yquem of Sauternes, at $25 to $50 for a recent good year, more for a classic vintage. Alternatives would include the neighboring châteaux of Sauternes or a fine Rhine or Moselle *Beerenauslese* at about $18 to $40. (The ultimate *Trockenbeerenauslese* at up to $90 a bottle should stand alone, with no food.)

Now the reds. As in the case of the whites, while great wines do occur among the lighter-bodied reds, the very greatest wines do not. Also, in ac-

tual menu planning if you try to focus a meal around too delicate a red, you have problems because it is difficult to find anything to precede it that will not upstage it. (This can create a real problem if you are attempting to build a meal around very great, very old red wine that is still sound but has begun to fade. Any younger red you precede it with runs the risk of up-staging and overwhelming the fading masterpiece. In the next chapter we shall suggest a rather unusual solution to this problem.)

The classic sources of the greatest reds are, of course, the Haut-Médoc of Bordeaux and the Côte de Nuits of Burgundy. We will arbitrarily pick one wine from each. For our great Burgundy we will pick Chambertin, because it exemplifies in highest degree the "manliness" of great Burgundy. A '29 might still be wonderful, of course, if you could get one. The price would be well over $100. A more recent year would cost in the $20 to $40 range. But you could as easily pick a Romanée-Conti or Clos de Vougeot at the top level, a Richebourg or Corton just below them.

As for our great Bordeaux, a rereading of Chapter II will quickly bring the names Lafite, Mouton, Latour to mind, the best growths of Pauillac in the Haut-Médoc. From the other areas of Bordeaux, Haut-Brion, Ausone, Cheval Blanc, Petrus, and their neighbors are not to be ig-nored. For our first choice we will take a Lafite, because it is beyond ar-gument the greatest of all. Recent good years would run you $25 to $50, and you can go as much beyond that as you want.

Thus our four ideal choices, in three categories:

Fuller-bodied white	Le Montrachet
Fuller-bodied red	
Burgundy	Chambertin
Bordeaux	Château Lafite
Sweet white dessert wine	Château d'Yquem

Obviously this is the top of the top, the theoretical absolute to which everyone should aspire once in his lifetime, oftener if possible. But at any given moment your cellar may not contain these, your merchant carry them, or your wallet afford them. There is no reason you cannot get very nearly the same experience for much less than the same money. The lesser but still fine châteaux of Bordeaux, the runner-up vineyards of Burgundy, the leading vineyards of the outlying districts, the better varietals of California, would all provide alternatives that are more than suited to the creation of an elegant and charming meal.

A less obvious reason than economics or availability for bearing in mind the lesser wines is that, as we pointed out in Chapter VII, once you have chosen a very great wine you don't simply rush out the week before the dinner and buy it. The trip home from the store would drive the sedi-ment, thrown off by the tannin and other elements as the wine matured, all through the bottle. It would not be undrinkable, but with sediment clouding its clear beauty and feeling rough on the tongue, it would not be adequate to the occasion.

A great red wine, anything more than perhaps five years old, requires *at least* three weeks of resting, and preferably several months, in a dark, cool, quiet place before you serve it. A great white will not throw a sediment of any significance unless it is very, very old (which means a risky wine, unless it is a Sauternes of a very good year). But it is bound to taste the worse for recent agitation. Thus you are virtually forced into starting your own "cellar" and stocking it not so much with particular bottles as with an inventory against delightful contingencies. If you do not have a cellar and the necessary bottles in it, then you must either decant the wine before you move it, so that the sedimentation will be removed, or settle for a younger wine. (Decanting means pouring the wine carefully from its original bottle into another container, leaving the sediment, the "lees," behind.) Decanting right in the wine store is not physically impossible, but, alas, it is illegal. If a friend of yours has an office nearby, you might carry the bottle, with infinite care, up to his office, decant it there, and carry it home. But be careful of these modern, high-speed elevators. They can stir up the sedimentation as thoroughly as an automobile in stop-and-go traffic. (You *could* consider decanting in the car while it is parked, although it might be awkward to decide what to say if a policeman showed up while the process was about halfway finished.)

If you are under necessity to use a younger wine as centerpiece, then it is best to get a lesser wine of a great year, or a great vineyard of an off year. The greatest wines take the longest to mature, and thus have the most time to throw sediment. Lesser wines are ready sooner, before the sediment accumulates. It is both more pleasing and less a sinful waste to drink a lesser wine that is ready than a great one before its prime.

It is important to understand that compromise here is not tragedy. In the first few experimental attempts at these elegant levels of living it is perhaps just as well to start small. Then it will not be as catastrophic if you overcook the roast. As your skill and confidence grow, so can your collection of bottles to provide the focus of future great experiences.

When a meal is to be built around a fine *red* wine (and that is the way it is most often done), it is necessary to pick a lesser, lighter red to go before. There are so many possibilities here that the decision is often more difficult than the choice of the principal wine, where money and availability are the chief concerns. As a general rule of thumb, any wine from a less-good year of a particular vineyard will be lighter and less fine than a wine from a good or great year from the same vineyard. You don't need a vintage chart. Comparative prices will make it very clear which is great and which is not. Similarly, a wine from a lower-classed vineyard of a particular commune will tend to be lighter, on average, than a wine from a higher-classed vineyard of the same commune (although of course the wine from the lesser vineyard in an absolutely superb year may well be better and fuller than the wine from the great vineyard in a horrible year— but the price will usually show it).

If you precede a wine from one commune of a region with a lesser wine from another commune of that same region, you could run into a problem if the lesser wine comes from a commune that normally produces very full wines and the better one comes from a commune that traditionally produces light ones. We have attempted to sort out this question in the table on page 85 that shows the relative fullness of the wines of the Haut-Médoc and the Côte de Nuits.

In this matter of arranging the supporting wines there are so many possibilities that you need some means of putting limits on them. We noted in Chapter VII, "The Human Variable," that a really fine meal needs a theme of some sort around which its elements can be arranged. A great Bordeaux red could form the centerpiece of a Bordeaux dinner, a great Burgundy of a Burgundy dinner, with all foods and supporting wines drawn, where possible, from the same geographic area. Whatever the theme, the wines in such a meal can serve a comparative and therefore an educational function. In a Bordeaux meal a full-bodied Lafite from Pauillac could be prefaced by a more delicate wine from Margaux, and the distinctions mastered. In a Burgundy meal a great, masculine Chambertin or a magnificent, rounded Romanée could be prefaced by the feminine Musigny or Bonnes Mares, or one of the lighter reds of southern Burgundy.

If one meal has a regional theme, you could give the next one a comparative or eclectic or ecumenical theme, expanding your knowledge thereby. We have already suggested the plan of prefacing a fine French wine with a good one from California, so that your guests can learn the difference, and which they really prefer. If you are serving a dinner with a Bordeaux or Burgundy theme, you do not violate the theme; in a sense you complement and dramatize it, by interjecting a California comparison. Of

BONNES-MARES

APPELLATION CONTROLÉE

Domaine Comte Georges de VOGÜÉ

CHAMBOLLE - MUSIGNY (CÔTE-D'OR)

PRODUCE OF FRANCE 1961 Mis en bouteilles au domaine

equal or greater teaching value is a comparison between Burgundy and Bordeaux themselves. A really full-bodied Burgundy can be prefaced by almost any fine Bordeaux. A full-bodied Pauillac (Bordeaux) could be prefaced by a light-bodied Burgundy. (The table on page 85 will also help in making this comparison.)

Another approach is to compare years. This can be done in two ways: the same wine of different years, different wines of the same year. In the first case, you might want to follow a Bordeaux of a lesser year such as 1968 with a good year like '62, '64, or '67 of the same vineyard. Or you might try an exercise in connoisseurship, and sample a second-growth Médoc like Brane-Cantenac of '67 before a Mouton of '67 and see who among the company can identify one or both.

The only limit is set by your own curiosity and imagination, and even if you make a mistake, you will have learned something.

Now we assume the four great centerpiece wines are chosen and bought. In the next chapter we shall select food and lesser wines to go along with each, and examine the method of orchestrating and harmonizing all the various elements into balanced and unified masterworks of the culinary art.

꧁ X

HOW TO SERVE A MASTERPIECE: FOOD AND WINE

꧁

Before we consider the foods that go into a Great Meal, a note is in order about where to go for guidance in preparing them. For most readers of this book the best sources are probably *Mastering the Art of French Cooking*, by Julia Child and Simone Beck, in two volumes, *Gourmet's Basic French Cookbook*, by Louis Diat, or its counterpart in paperback, *French Cooking for Americans*, or Craig Claiborne's *The New York Times Cookbook* or *New York Times Menu Cookbook*. But if these are not available, there is an enormous number of other French cookbooks available, both in hard cover and paperback, and most offer recipes that can be adapted to these purposes. (However, certain of the newer cookbooks are in fact better suited to looking beautiful on your coffee table or adding to the collection in your library than to functioning successfully in the kitchen. Either the recipes in them have not been fully tested, or they contain errors in printing. So with a source of unknown reliability it is well to check out the recipes beforehand to be sure you are not including a pound of shallots where you should be using a pinch.)

If even these resources are not available, the old familiar standbys, *The Joy of Cooking*, by Marion Rombauer, and *The Boston Cooking School Cookbook*, by Fannie Farmer, will get you through, especially if you have a rich and innovative imagination. Or, to move in the other direction, you can turn to those two great classics of the French cuisine, *The Escoffier Cookbook*, by the great French chef of that name, and the encyclopedic *Larousse Gastronomique*. With either of these latter two, however, you may find yourself doing an inordinate amount of cross-referencing, since the recipe for a given dish will refer you to another part of the book for some essential operation, and to still another for instructions on making the required sauce. (One solution here is to use the office Xerox to copy all the relevant pages, and then cut-and-paste the necessary segments into a complete recipe.)

When you consider the foods that are acceptable in composing a Great Meal, it is almost shocking to see how little room there is for most of Mother's home-cooked favorites or the more spectacular American eating-out delicacies. What is called for in a Great Meal is muted, restrained simplicity, with all elements blending gracefully into a balanced, harmonious whole. Most of the home favorites and conventional delicacies are just too bland or spicy or sharp or strong or acid or rich.

The notion of simplicity and restraint in the preparation of food comes and goes in the history of eating in much the same way that it does in the history of music. A poet of ancient Greece once wrote verses complaining about the excessive use of spices and other strong seasonings by the cooks of his day. In Roman times neither the average citizen nor the established aristocracy partook of the extravagant orgies of eating and drinking the writers of the time recorded. This was largely the province of the newly rich (who had made their money in such interesting lines of work as smuggling and prostitution). The daily fare of the typical Roman, even in the greatest days of the Empire, was not very different from the ordinary country cooking of the early days of the Republic. It was simple enough, but it was also decidedly plain, without the fineness, the elegance, that we are looking for.

With the onset of the Middle Ages whatever art there was to cooking and eating in Europe was lost, and the old traditions survived only in a few parts of Italy. With the Renaissance, cooking awakened like the other arts, to be transplanted from Italy to France in 1533 when Catherine de Médicis married the Duc d'Orléans, who later became Henry II of France, and brought her Italian kitchen staff with her to her new home. This was the foundation stone of modern French cookery. But the cooking of the Renaissance was marked more by luxury and opulence than simplicity and restraint. Finally, with the Enlightenment of the seventeenth and eighteenth centuries and the turning back to concepts of Classical times, there emerged the Great Meal as we know it today. But such a repast is a far cry from most of the traditional cooking of the United States, which is descended from the plain, hearty peasant and bourgeois foods of Europe of the seventeenth, eighteenth, and nineteenth centuries, brought here by successive waves of immigrants.

No better-established American institution is threatened by the ground rules of the Great Meal than the martini. A Great Meal in the grand tradition begins, as noted earlier, not with cocktails, but with a glass of light, dry delicate white wine, perhaps served with a few hors d'oeuvres. The reason for this is that strong drink and strong flavors tend to anesthetize and corrupt the palate for the joys that follow, whereas a light white wine will gently cleanse and prepare it for all that is to come.

But this change of routine can come as a severe shock to the tired business type who from four-thirty on looks forward with mounting anticipation to the moment the first slug of gin hits his stomach, and the cares of the day begin to fade. It does no good to tell your snarling guest that with four or-five more wines and a brandy to come he'll be sloshed enough before the night is through. With a reflex as well conditioned as that of one of Dr. Pavlov's dogs, he wants his belt in the belly and he wants it *now.* Let's not be stuffy. If your guests want a martini before the meal, let them have one. If a guest at a fine meal at Forrest Wallace's house asked for Bourbon and Coke, Wallace would certainly be offended and would try to talk him out of it. But a martini or scotch, when indicated, will do no harm to the palate that will not be more than made up by its contribution to morale. Furthermore, a few squares of cheese and/or sour dough French bread, munched between cocktails and the start of dinner, will largely repair the damage to the palate.

When Forrest Wallace inquires of his guests what they want to drink before a meal, if one of them knows wine he will often ask, "Are we having wine tonight?" If Wallace replies that he is offering an exceptional bottle, the guest will say, "In that case, I'll start with wine."

At dinners of the Wine and Food Society or the Chevaliers de Tastevin (the wine fraternity of Burgundy), Chablis or Pouilly-Fuissé or Fumé are most commonly served as an appetizer wine, perhaps half the time. The next most common appetizer is Champagne. This is a brut, not a so-called dry, but a *really* dry one. A less expensive but very good preface is Sancerre from the Loire Valley. Muscadet from the mouth of the Loire would be a good appetizer for a non-Great Meal but it is too slight, too thin, for a great one. You should not serve any cheap wine as an appetizer. It downgrades the occasion. If you are not prepared to spend upward of

$4.50 a bottle for an apéritif wine, cocktails would probably be better, although not too many if the meal is to be enjoyed.

Dry Sherry is a good appetizer, but here again, only if it is really dry; it should be very light in color, of the type called Fino, very, very dry. Much so-called dry Sherry is not that at all. You would very seldom serve a German wine—too much bouquet, too much sweetness here, also. You would not serve a Chablis Grand Cru. Too early in the meal for so much fineness. You would not consider any rich, full-bodied white—Meursault, Montrachet, Hermitage Blanc, or white Graves.

When Forrest Wallace entertains at home, he ordinarily serves cocktails or apéritif in the kitchen, so that the chef (Wallace himself) remains in the party, and those who are not helping at least appreciate what is going on. Eating hot appetizers with a fork while standing up in a kitchen is not easy for guest or chef, however. For this situation, a tray of light hors d'oeuvres is probably better. Cold guacamole, with raw vegetable bits and hot corn chips to dip it with, is a favorite. If you know some guests are starving, the aforementioned squares of cheese and bread, or crackers, are a happy addition. However, a few icy shrimp, roasted nuts, and any of the rather elegant small salted snack crackers available in tins are quite enough before any really good meal. (If you are at the house of Forrest Wallace and are *really* lucky, he has just returned from a business trip to the eastern Mediterranean and has brought with him a tin of fresh Iranian caviar.)

As indicated earlier, many people tend to serve *either* soup *or* fish to start the meal and usually skip the soup in favor of fish, with its much greater potential for interesting wine combinations (and again, with the thought that you don't want to overstuff the company). But it is a free country. If you want to have soup as well as fish, or in place of fish, go ahead.

If you decide to go the soup route, you can either make it yourself or buy one of the excellent canned soups on the market. Either way, we are not talking about old-fashioned vegetable soup or clam chowder, but something with elegance: jellied Madrilene, an excellent consommé, vichyssoise, a seafood bisque, or cucumber, lettuce, watercress, or turtle soup. If you are at the stage of using canned soups, you had better stick to the most elegant one you can find. However, if you choose to do it yourself, almost any good cookbook will offer recipes for superbly balanced versions of everyday standards such as vegetable, beef, and even bean soup—all of which can be great if prepared with loving care. However you do it, for six people you will need about a quart of soup.

If you do have soup, there is no obligation to have wine with it. But if you choose to have wine with the soup, you have a problem. Soup, like cheese or bread, is fine to clear the palate for what comes afterward. But while you are actually eating hot, steaming, aromatic soup, it does not make a very happy combination with a glass of cool, fragrant, delicate wine. Nor does chilled soup. Neither combination tastes bad; it just lacks interest.

Thus, where wine is desired to go with soup, Sherry is often used. Sherry is emphatic enough to hold its own in almost any situation. So in cases where you are already having Sherry as an appetizer, you can simply run the appetizer Sherry on into the soup course. (You might well have chosen Sherry as the appetizer wine on this account.) If you are serving turtle soup, Sherry is almost mandatory in any case, in part because this is tradition, in part because the tradition stems from the fact that turtle soup is ordinarily seasoned with Sherry. (A splash of Sherry helps the flavor of many soups, and gives you a pretext for serving Sherry with them. Go easy, though. The flavor of Sherry is so emphatic you may find you have merely created Sherry soup.)

If you are having white wine as apéritif and your soup is made of seafood, you can run the apéritif wine on into the soup course. While this is not an ideal combination it is acceptable. If there is no fish course after a seafood soup, this is a good place to show off another white, somewhat better and fuller than the one served as apéritif. The guests continue to drink the apéritif white during the first third or so of the soup, then the second white is poured. Ordinarily, you leave both glasses on the table so they can compare one wine with the other.

If there is to be a fish course after a seafood soup, you would probably save the second white until after the fish is served, but the procedure would otherwise be the same—leaving both glasses on the table for comparison.

The debate about what you drink with soup is a good illustration of the debates and discussions that accompany the planning of almost any phase of the Great Meal. But why make life so complicated? You will have enough to worry about the first few times around. At the start it is much simpler just to skip the soup.

As for the fish course: let's not reach for far-out foods. Save the octopus Fra Diavolo for some other occasion. Let us settle for one of the conventional seafoods, shrimp, crab, lobster, served plainly with lemon or butter, but please, no tomato sauce or Tabasco. Or you could serve the scallop dish *coquille St.-Jacques,* in a cream sauce with mushrooms. Or you could serve the fillets of a respectable and preferably local (so it will be as fresh as possible) fish, in a fine but simple sauce: *sole Véronique, filets Bercy aux champignons* (poached in white wine and mushrooms), *filets à la Bretonne* (poached in white wine and julienne vegetables), *filets gratins, à la parisienne* (poached with a cream and egg yolk sauce), fish quenelles, a salmon mousse, hot or cold.

If you are going to serve fish fillets in a sauce, you will most assuredly poach them, and it would be wise if you practiced the art of poaching and

saucing on the family a few times before you try it on company. This
brings up a very central point in the preparation of these repasts. Their
success will depend in very great measure on your acquiring a small
number of rudimentary skills: poaching, sautéeing, roasting, saucing—
above all saucing—and making these processes come out approximately
on schedule. These are the Eternal Verities of *la haute cuisine*. If you have
poached one fish successfully and confidently, you've poached 'em all, or
close to it. And here once again you have not merely learned how to turn
out a fancy meal for a special occasion, you will have greatly increased
your capacity to improvise and innovate and just have fun for the simpler
times.

We have already covered the general idea of wine to go with the fish
course. It will go up a notch in body and quality from the appetizer/soup
wine, unless you had Sherry with either. In the latter case, considering the
fullness of flavor of the Sherry, you would go up still another notch in the
body of the wine with the fish.

Now we come to the main dish. Since we are thinking here only of the
Great Meal in its standard format, reaching its climax with a bottle of
great red wine, we will at this point pick only the dishes to go with our two
great reds. A little later on we will consider a menu to set off the great
Montrachet, along with one to foreshadow a splendid Yquem. Remembering the Categories of Affinity, it is clear that lamb or veal would most
often be served with Bordeaux, duck or game with Burgundy, beef with
either one, depending on how prepared.

We indicated in Chapter VIII "Cherchez la Sauce," that the general
rule of matching is the finer the wine, the finer the food, or vice versa. But
we also set forth the See-Saw Principle: For an immortal, incomparable
wine you go easy on the food so as not to upstage the wine. For a spectacular or much loved dish you ease off a bit on the wine for the same reason.
(Or, as already noted, if you can't afford a truly great wine, or can't find
one, you shoot the works on the dish instead, since the principal investment here is more time and love than money.)

To set off a great Bordeaux, you might serve one of these:

> Roast leg of lamb
> Roast rack of lamb
> Noisette of lamb
> Veal roast

For a great red Burgundy:

> Beef tournedos, either plain or with a sauce
>   such as *marchand de vins* or one of the
>   elegant variations of *sauce Madère*
> Beef Wellington
> Baron of lamb
> *Coq au vin*

N° 000142

Chambertin Clos de Bèze 1962

APPELLATION CONTROLEE

Ce vin, sélectionné en 1971 par les Jurés-Gourmets de la

Confrérie des Chevaliers du Tastevin

a été élevé dans les caves de

Jh. Faiveley

NÉGOCIANT A NUITS-ST-GEORGES (COTE-D'OR)

But precisely how you plan it depends on how you feel about it. There is no absolute.

For purposes of the menus we are building here, we shall select, entirely arbitrarily, plain roast leg of lamb for the Lafite, *tournedos périgueux* for the Chambertin. Why these? Because Forrest Wallace likes them, is familiar with them, and feels confident in handling them—the Human Variable again.

The main dish, as noted, should be accompanied by vegetables and potatoes. The stress is on the verb: *accompanied*. The vegetables play an accompaniment, and a very muted accompaniment, to the entree and the wine. In a fine meal, whether you are concentrating on the wine or the entree or on the combination, you certainly do not want to be distracted by vegetables that are rich or filling or strong in flavor. You would not have beets or brussels sprouts or cabbage, and certainly not rutabagas or parsnips. Green peas, plain or *française* (with lettuce and little onions), would be acceptable, or creamed carrots or cauliflower or artichoke bottoms or braised celery.

As for potatoes, you would not have yams or sweet potatoes. You could have small (half inch) round potatoes, baked in the oven in clarified butter, parsleyed potatoes, or potatoes Anna. Or instead of potatoes you could substitute the French flageolet beans.

If you are planning your meal with friends, the next subject to be proposed will almost assuredly be salad. When Forrest Wallace was active in the planning of the dinners of the Chicago chapter of the Chevaliers de Tastevin, this issue was fussed over time and again. It is part of the conventional wisdom in America that a salad is necessary to contribute roughage to a meal. But salad disturbs the palate, not only the acid of the vinegar in the dressing but the milder acids in raw green and yellow vegetables.

For one of the meals we are assembling, there is in general no cause to serve a salad unless it is with a very heavy entree whose heaviness needs

cutting down, such as beef tournedos in a Madeira sauce. Or you can wind
up a meal with salad in place of the dessert or fruit and cheese. In this
case, the salad serves the same function as the fruit and cheese, cleaning
the palate before you leave the table, topping off the stomach.

If you do serve a salad, we are not talking about a fruit or caesar
salad, nor a mixed salad with tomatoes and string beans, nor one dressed
with mayonnaise or bleu cheese or Thousand Island dressing. We are talking only about the simplest, most bland sort of salad: endive or lettuce
with oil and lemon (*not* vinegar), or sliced avocados and grapefruit
wedges on lettuce, also with oil and lemon. Or you might make a salad of
cold sticks of apple, pear, carrots, or celery root.

With the main dish your friends are also going to expect bread. Bread
is rarely served at a Great Meal, but if your big martini drinkers are also
big bread men, by all means, let 'em eat bread. In that case, hard French
rolls are probably the best, or San Francisco sour dough bread, buttered
and warmed in the oven.

There is also a general prohibition against water at a Great Meal. This
stems not only from the French love of wine but from the fact that in earlier times the water was dangerous in those parts. Some of the gourmet
societies have been known to keep a pitcher of water sitting at the head
table with goldfish swimming around in it, indicating what, in the opinion
of the membership, water should be used for.

There is no salt and pepper on the table at a Great Meal, either. That
would be an insult to the chef.

Now back to procedure: When the main dish is served, the first red
wine is served immediately afterward (make sure that the white-wine
glasses are removed first so there will be no conflict on the palate between
the two). Then, when your guests are about halfway through the main
dish, you bring on the second red. In the case of the meals we are arranging here, you will leave the first red there for comparison. How you time
the second one depends in part on what you plan for dessert. As indicated,
you can either go the fruit and cheese route or serve a regular sweet dessert. Almost all real devotees of wine prefer fruit and cheese because it
gives an opportunity to continue to enjoy the better of the two reds. In that
case, the second red will be served later in the main course, since you want
it to last longer. If you are serving a very great, very old wine, a Mouton
1918, let us say, or a Lafite '29, the very best way to drink it is after the
meal in this way. You don't want heavy food with a great old wine. You
want to concentrate on the wine. But you don't want to drink it alone. You
want something to clear the palate between sips, to force you to take
longer, so you can see how the wine changes in the glass from the moment
you poured it to the last sip.

As for cheese, you don't want a yellow, sharp apple-pie cheese. You
want dessert cheeses: Brie, Camembert, port salut.

Generally, you offer a choice of two or three cheeses.

As for the fruit, a mild apple is acceptable so long as it is not hard or greenish. A pear is a little better; a nice, ripe hard pear. Big green or purple grapes are fine—just the kind you would *not* use for making wine. You would not serve Thompson seedless—too thin and acidy. The eastern eating grapes—Concord, scuppernong, and several others—may also clash with good wine: too sweet. You pass around a big tray with pears, apples, walnuts, whatever, on it and let people take what they want. A similar, smaller tray is passed with the cheese.

When all the red wine is gone, you can then, if you choose, serve a sweet dessert wine—Sauternes or a German one—with what remains of the fruit and cheese, although this is not obligatory. We will go into more detail on the serving of dessert wine later.

If instead of fruit and cheese you decide on a sweet dessert, you have another set of decisions to make. You are not going to serve Mother's best apple pie (or any other pie) or a banana fritter or a piece of melon. You have a choice between something fancy, rich, and complicated: baked Alaska, cherries jubilee, crepes suzette, peach melba, or something smooth in the pudding or custard line. What you serve depends basically on what went before and whether to have wine with it, and whether it is to be followed by a sweet liqueur.

There are few times Forrest Wallace would serve crepes suzette at the end of a fine meal. Normally for him it is a main course, a rich but light main course. But if you had it for dessert and wanted wine with it, you would, of course, serve Sauternes or a sweet Rhine or Moselle. Cherries jubilee and baked Alaska are easier to prepare. With either of them you probably should serve either Champagne or nothing. These are showy desserts, with extravagant flavors. They suggest a not-too-dry Champagne.

If you are less inclined to stuff your people or to give them a circus spectacular, a simple custard-type dish is better, and in fact more sophisticated. There is the floating island, a very light custard, almost the consistency of heavy cream, with whipped cream or beat-up egg white on top. You may put this under the broiler for a few minutes if you like. Almost any really good cookbook includes this and it is simple to make. Other possibilities in this line are flan (Spanish caramel custard), Bavarian cream, *créme brûlée,* and zabaglione, an Italian concoction, consisting primarily of egg yolks and Marsala wine. Zabaglione is the source of the idea for a French dessert sauce, *sauce sabayon,* which is made about the same way as zabaglione.

One night some years back Forrest Wallace was having dinner with some friends at the old Châteaubriand Restaurant in New York. The place had a large plate-glass window between the kitchen and the dining room so the guests might watch a magnificent kitchen in operation. Wallace noticed there was trouble in the kitchen. The staff was beating and beating at something in a bowl but didn't seem to be able to get it finished.

Wallace became curious and went out to the kitchen. He found they

were trying to make a *sauce sabayon*. One man would beat it, and when he got tired would hand it to another man to beat. One of the men was left-handed, the other was right. Wallace pointed out to them that they were alternately beating and unbeating the *sabayon*. They traded the left-hander for a second right-hander, and at last were able to complete the sauce.

With either floating island or zabaglione, the wine of choice, if you want one, would be Sauternes or a German dessert wine. Marsala from Sicily would be acceptable, too.

The coffee served at a meal such as this would be *espresso* or *filtre*. After the coffee has been served there is the option of offering each guest a glass of Port as well.

This is not the movie set scene, with the women going to the drawing room. Everyone sits around the table finishing his coffee and enjoying his Port. The Port should be one of the high-grade ruby or tawny Ports, with the bottle passed clockwise around the table. You should perhaps not serve an American Port for this occasion, nor is a truly great Port indicated. Something in the four-to-eight-dollar range would be about right.

After the Port is finished and everybody has moved to the living room, you can bring out the brandy. There are three arguments for this: (1) It avoids a sweet liqueur whose heavy sugar content is too much after dessert and dessert wine, (2) it is a nice custom, and (3) it seals the stomach, so to speak, after a big meal, relaxing the muscles and aiding digestion.

Here, now, are the menus we have developed for these two fine meals. First, the one to go with a Lafite:

Sancerre or Pouilly-Fumé	Hors d'oeuvres
Chablis	Fillet of sole aspic or cracked crab*

* If you prefer soup instead of fish, or in addition to the fish, you can follow the hors d'oeuvres with clear turtle soup accompanied by very dry Sherry. If the soup is to be in addition to the fish course, the Chablis with the fish should be replaced with Meursault or a hyphenated Montrachet, the better to follow the Sherry.

Third Growth Bordeaux such as Château Kirwan	Roast leg of lamb
	Peas *française*
Château Lafite	Flageolet beans
Château d'Yquem	Fruit and cheese
Cognac (or Armagnac)	Coffee

As for our great Chambertin:

Champagne brut	Hors d'oeuvres
Meursault or any smaller white Burgundy	*Coquilles St.-Jacques**
Bonnes Mares or Échézeaux	*Tournedos périgueux*
Chambertin	Braised celery
	Artichoke bottoms
Medium dry Champagne	Floating island or flan or Bavarian cream
Marc de Bourgignonne	Coffee

Now we must create the menu to show off a great white Montrachet. But here we encounter a problem. In a Great Meal as it is conventionally organized, the pinnacle of the occasion, the crowning wine, is always a red wine, not a white. The white wines, in ascending degrees of fullness and fineness, provide a preface to the red ones, or at best the first and lighter movement of a two-part symphony.

There are two ways to approach this situation. One would be to follow the main course, when the Montrachet is served, with fruit and cheese, using this as an opportunity to serve a red wine. The other and less usual solution would be to create a "white wine dinner."

Either exercise could be interesting. A meal featuring only white wines and culminating with Montrachet could begin with light, clean dry Sancerre accompanied by perhaps oysters on the half shell, then move on to fillet of sole in an interesting but not overwhelming sauce, or crab or lobster similarly prepared, accompanied by a Chablis Premier Cru (but not a Grand Cru—still too early). Halfway through the sole a fine, soft Meursault could be served (and at this point the Sancerre glasses should probably be taken away, if only in the interest of tidy housekeeping). Then the plates for the sole could be removed, and a good, plain roast chicken served. (The See-Saw Principle applying here—if the wine is the center of attention, the dish should not compete.) Partway through the chicken, the Chablis glasses could be removed, leaving the Meursault, and then the Montrachet could be served. To complete the white wine theme, this un-usual meal could be finished off with Sauternes or a German dessert wine,

---

* For soup as an alternate or addition, watercress soup, hot or cold, after the hors d'oeuvres, along with Madeira Sercial.

either served alone, or with fruit and cheese, or with an appropriate dessert (see pages 222–223).

Sancerre	Hors d'oeuvres
Chablis Premier Cru	Filet de sole normande
Meursault	Roast chicken
Le Montrachet	Green peas Pan-roasted potatoes
Château d'Yquem	Fruit and cheese
Cognac	Coffee

As for the alternative and more conventional approach, culminating with a red wine and fruit and cheese at the end, we will start by pairing the Montrachet with *filet de sole Véronique* (with fresh or canned grapes in a cream sauce), another favorite of Forrest Wallace. But this presents another difficulty. If the main course is going to be fish, it is somewhat redundant (though not forbidden) to start the meal with a fish dish. So in this case we *will* serve soup, cucumber, lettuce, consommé, or turtle soup, and have Sherry with it. For an appetizer wine you could serve Chablis once again. As for the fruit and cheese, because the main course is so light you would want to have two or three of the bigger cheeses: Camembert, the heavier Bries, or Stilton.

As a prefatory wine for the Montrachet you *could* use Meursault again, but for variety we will instead pick Haut-Brion Blanc.

After all this trouble you should serve a good red wine at the end of the meal. In fact, this is an interesting menu for really showing off an exceptional red wine—different from what most people would do. And this is the solution to a problem mentioned in the previous chapter—how to serve a very great, very old red wine that no longer has the vigor to stand up against a younger red of lesser quality. If you don't have a particular wine on hand, however, any excellent red will do, including any of the more delicate ones. Since Montrachet is a Burgundy, a Musigny or Bonnes Mares would be ideal. If you want to cross over to Bordeaux, a fine, delicate Margaux or one of its satellites.

You don't have to stick to the more delicate reds unless you want to. A huge Chambertin or a robust Mouton or Cos d'Estournel might be too big to follow directly after any white, even Montrachet. But within these broad limits your range is virtually unlimited.

That being said, the menu is quickly composed:

Chablis	Hors d'oeuvres
Fino Sherry	Hot lettuce soup
Haut-Brion Blanc	*Sole Véronique*
Le Montrachet	Peas *française* Parsleyed potatoes

SAUTERNES·APPELLATION CONTRÔLÉE

Château d'Yquem

Lur-Saluces

1959

MIS EN BOUTEILLE AU CHÂTEAU

Musigny	Fruit and cheese
Port or Cognac	Coffee

Now all that remains is to work with the final category: a great sweet dessert wine, say a Château d'Yquem of '67.

It is not possible to build a meal around a dessert wine in the same sense that you would build it around a dinner wine. Asking what kind of meal you would serve to feature an Yquem is about as sensible as asking what kind of main dish you would serve to show off a very fine brand of vanilla ice cream. You serve what you wish. However, you should not serve a great Yquem with a truly great red wine beforehand. That would be like hanging too many Rembrandts in one room. Neither should you serve an Yquem with too plain a meal or wine. That would not do it enough honor. You want a fine but not spectacular meal that moves forward in hushed, civilized tones, as though a little awed by what lies ahead.

Since Yquem is one of the supreme products of Bordeaux, we will arbitrarily plan a Bordeaux dinner. Since we have already featured lamb with the Lafite, beef with the Chambertin, and sole with the Montrachet, for a little variety we will have sweetbreads *en brochette* for this meal. With the sweetbreads, for additional variety, we will have spinach, either *au jus* or *à la crème*. Sweetbreads can take the hardness of spinach. Not many dishes can.

For hors d'oeuvres we will have smoked Dundee salmon, accompanied by Montilla Sherry. For the fish course, oysters Rockefeller accompanied by a good Poully-Fuissé. With our main course we will drink a Château Mouton Baron Philippe, a well-regarded Fifth Growth Bordeaux, followed by Château Pichon-Longueville, a Second Growth.

As in the other cases we face the choice of fruit and cheese, *or* sweet dessert. With a great Sauternes we can also, if we choose, serve it alone, as dessert, accompanied by nothing. If you are going to have a sweet dessert, as noted earlier, you are not going to have baked Alaska, peach melba, or cherries jubilee, since Champagne is more suitable with these. You *could* have one of the custard-type choices, floating island, zabaglione, flan, or Bavarian cream. However, for this event we will serve the Sauternes alone, in splendid solitude, as we reverently partake.

In the case of a mature (ten to twenty years old) great Sauternes, there will be a minimum of sediment in the bottle; but no wine of this stature will benefit from shaking around, so you should have it on hand a week or more before serving. With Yquem, there are no off years (in the bad years, a fair dry wine is bottled under the name Château "Y," pronounced *ygrec*), but a bottle less than six years old has not begun to hit its stride.

An Yquem glass is a very small wineglass, but not as small as a liqueur glass. You don't want a Champagne glass, nor Aunt Mamie's clear or colored cut-glass crystal. You want to be able to see the thick, glycerine-like quality as the wine adheres and runs slowly down the side of the glass.

You don't serve Sauternes as cold as a white dinner wine. If your cellar is fifty-five degrees, you can bring the bottle out and serve it at that temperature. If it is quite an old Yquem (fifteen years or more), uncork it and let it "breathe" for forty-five minutes before you serve it. The bottle should be stood up on the table and passed around like a bottle of Port. It is too sweet for anyone to have very much of it at a time. You can serve as many as ten or twelve people out of one bottle if you are entertaining on that scale. (If you are entertaining on a lesser scale, the Yquem will keep from three to five days in the refrigerator, but you should use it up as soon as you can, since, once opened, it gradually deteriorates.)

You serve the Yquem after the red wine and the main course have been taken away, and allow plenty of time for people to enjoy it before the coffee comes. With the strong taste of the coffee, and its heat on the tongue, you will no longer appreciate the wine to the fullest.

If you want to serve fruit and cheese, bring out the cheese, then the fruit while there is still red wine in the best bottle. When the red is gone, and while some cheese and fruit remain, bring out the Yquem, being sure first to remove the red-wine glasses to avoid conflict. If you have a sweet dessert, the main course and red wine are taken away, the dessert is served, then the Yquem is brought on.

Montilla Sherry	Smoked Dundee salmon
Pouilly-Fuissé	Oysters Rockefeller
Château Mouton Baron Philippe, recent year	Sweetbreads *en brochette*
	Spinach *à la crème*
Chateau Pichon-Longueville, earlier year	Potatoes Anna
Château d'Yquem	—
Cognac	Coffee

That is all we have to offer toward the enjoyment of a Great Meal except, perhaps, an Alka-Seltzer. But to reiterate, not many readers of this book will be willing—or able—to enjoy Great Meals as a regular thing (if the carbohydrates didn't get you, the cholesterol might). But anyone who gains a reasonable understanding of a Great Meal and how it works will never be quite the same again. You have seen a vision of the Promised Land. You have glimpsed the possibilities. There will be no future occasion, however humble, where you will not begin, at least subconsciously, to calculate how you might create a little more interest, a bit more elegance, a more harmonious blending, with a slight adjustment of materials. You will become more concerned than before with the *progression* of food and drink. Then, timidly at first, you will begin to experiment with more than one wine at a meal. Next you might slip in an extra course, or try a dessert wine, or even a Port.

After you have become familiar with the various components, there will be a natural inclination to pull them together into meals that will advance from Good through Better to Absolutely Great. Then, sooner or later, you will hear that the word is going around the neighborhood: "Hey, you know those Joneses, they really know how to live. They even serve *two wines* with dinner."

At this point, you look at the ground, scratch the dirt with your toe, and say, "Aw shucks, 'tain't nothin', really."

That way, along with everything else, you will be admired for your exquisite modesty.

The Protocol of Wine

🌿 XI

THE BATTLE OF THE TASTEVIN

🌿

With our menu picked and cooking, and the wine selected and resting in the cellar, if any, all that remains now is to enjoy what we have wrought. The service of food is not a great mystery to most of us. The service of wine is.

Opening a bottle of wine in your own home among friends, no matter how rare the vintage or how great the meal, does not ordinarily involve quite the social and commercial pressure of doing it when you are eating out, especially at a fancy place. In an expensive restaurant the sommelier (wine steward) may be a master of his craft and a cruel snob, who will sneer at you quietly if you are clumsy; he may be a chiseler, trying to push bad wine at high prices; he may be incompetent, trying to keep you at a disadvantage to hide his own deficiencies. In a fancy restaurant you are likely to be entertaining a client or a prospect on the expense account, or the parents of a fiancée, concerned not simply to enjoy the meal but to handle things right.

The difficulty with restaurant wine buying, furthermore, aside from the usually astronomic markup, is that it is a complex intertwining of business and art. At home, you will usually have closed the deal with the wine merchant a couple of hours before the meal, at a minimum, and if things don't work out you will have no opportunity to discuss it before tomorrow. In a restaurant the making of the deal and the proving of the deal are mingled in a confrontation as immemorial and inscrutable as the trading of a horse or the purchase of a rug.

Let us now consider the problem of ordering and tasting wine at a fine restaurant. If you can get through that, you can manage things on other occasions. We will first observe the progression of events, then see if we can understand them.

However, a note of caution is in order here, also. The procedure that follows illustrates a set of general principles. How the principles are applied will vary enormously with the situation. If you carry on in the manner described below at Joe's Pizza Parlor, or the little French place where the gang goes on Saturday night, you will not only be considered a pretentious idiot, and will be guilty as charged, but you will be wasting your time. As Aristotle put it: It is the mark of an educated man to attempt to give no more accuracy to a subject than the subject itself permits.

The wines at Joe's or the little French place would under no ordinary circumstances justify so much fuss. And even at a much fancier place it is better to underplay the ritual than to overplay it.

But wherever you go, at whatever level, you are attempting to get fair value for your money, and to make an accurate assessment of the product after it reaches the table.

With that caveat, let us begin:

The food has been ordered, subject to final adjustment if the wine requires. The wine steward, silver *tastevin* resplendent on a chain about his neck, approaches, bearing the wine list. The main dish is to be, let us say, beef tournedos, with a béarnaise sauce. You mental shorthand begins. Beef demands red wine, béarnaise sauce suggests a fairly full one, and of reasonable quality, say nine or ten dollars at restaurant prices (the same bottle would cost you four to five dollars in a store). If they had Mirassou or Beaulieu Vineyard, you might play around with a California bottle, but they don't. Nor do they offer anything in this class in a Rhône or other secondary district. Thus it is, as it so often turns out to be, a choice between red Burgundy and red Bordeaux. Which will it be? You happen to like Burgundy, so you concentrate on the Burgundies. The Human Variable again.

The steward sees your eye go to the Burgundies and steps forward respectfully. "Would M'sieur like perhaps the Clos de Vougeot? It is exceptional." Your eye flickers to the right-hand column. Twenty dollars. Gotcha! In a fine restaurant wine stewards work on a percentage of the gross, and this one was trying to up his take. No, M'sieur does not think he will have the Clos de Vougeot tonight. Your eye comes to rest on a Clos du Chapitre from the commune of Fixin in Burgundy. The Clos du Chapitre appeals because you have heard about it, never tried it. But they have two vintages, '66 and '67. Which will it be? Right-hand column again: '66 is thirteen dollars, '67 is ten. Clearly the '66 is better, or so the trade thinks. What the hell, you only live once.

"We will have the Clos du Chapitre '66," you announce to the steward in a tone not permitting debate. "And could you bring it now and open it?"

The steward was just about to suggest that, but you were too fast. Got 'im again. Most red wines at cellar temperature are too cool. They need to *chambrer*—to be brought to room temperature—in order to bring out flavor and bouquet. You also want to have it opened at once in order to let it "breathe." When oxygen first reaches the wine, it restarts on a minuscule scale the fermentation process, further bringing out flavor and bouquet.

The bottle approaches, carried reverently and gently on its side. You see at ten paces that it is Clos du Chapitre, and by the time that it reaches the table that it is the requested '66. Even so, you reach your hand out to-ward the bottle, perhaps touching it, certainly not jostling it, a sort of lay benediction, as you frown ever so slightly. Then you glance coolly at the steward. "Hmm," you hmm, indicating assent, but not automatic or too easy assent.

Impressed, the steward draws the cork, placing it on a small silver server, which he puts on the table near you. Ordinarily he would do this rather offhandedly. Now he is being careful.

You pick up the cork, glance at the little brown mark branded on its side, then squeeze it fairly hard between thumb and forefinger. Then you run your finger up and down the side of the cork. If you come across any little mottlings or seams, you give them a look like a jeweler sizing up a hot ruby. At last you gravely raise the cork to your nose and sniff. Only then, taking your own sweet time, do you nod a second assent.

Now you tear off a piece of bread, chew it carefully (and conspic-uously), and swallow solemnly, as the steward pours an ounce or so of the rich, red Burgundy into your glass. "Hmm," you hmm again, watching closely. You pick up the glass, tilt it slightly, and peer through the edge of the liquid at the white tablecloth. "Not a trace of brown," you say with a kind of special, secret satisfaction. Then you swirl the wine around in the glass as though it were brandy in a snifter. "Look how it hangs," you say to your companion. "Hmm," responds your companion, with not the *slightest* idea of what is going on.

You warm the wine for a moment in your cupped hand, continuing to

Mis en Bouteilles
au Domaine

MÉDAILLE D'OR
1961

FIXIN
CLOS DU CHAPITRE
DOMAINE MARION
APPELLATION FIXIN CONTRÔLÉE

Pierre GELIN
Viticulteur à Fixin et Gevrey-Chambertin (Côte-d'Or)

swirl it gently. Then, putting your nose well into the top of the glass, you breathe in deeply, absently. You lower the glass long enough to allow yourself to breathe out, then take a moderate-size sip with such concentration your companion can almost hear the taste buds blooming. Now, with head held level, teeth closed, lips slightly open, a bit like a chicken swallowing water in a barnyard, you draw some air through the wine, making a rather unmannerly googling noise as you do. Another, larger sip, and after swallowing you remain still and mute for a moment, absent and detached, as though listening to the call of trumpets from some distant hillside.

At last you give a third and final nod to the steward, more friendly now, more relaxed. Good show, my man! You have fulfilled your function. The steward, vastly relieved and convinced now that he is waiting on a real sport, fills the glasses around the table and through the rest of the meal hovers around to serve you further in any way he can.

Now let us see if we can find out what has been going on, in addition to "psyching" the steward:

In evaluating a wine you are looking first for what may be wrong and bad about it, then by ascending stages for what is right and good. What is wrong might be the result of bacterial action, or it might be human hanky-panky in the cellar. What is right, if it is really right, will go on developing and unfolding through the meal.

Naturally, you check first to see that the wine was from the requested vineyard. It was. When you order a wine by vintage year, it is a good idea to keep the vintage in mind, too, because when the actual bottle is brought it could well be from another year. No inventory lasts forever, especially of the best years, but reprinting wine lists is expensive. Only after a number of bins have run out will the management incur the cost of printing up another list. This problem of keeping up to date explains why in many of the best restaurants and clubs the lists are either typed or hand-lettered. (Some, more practically, merely state on the list that they will bring you the best available vintage of whatever wine you choose.)

If you complain to the steward that he brought you a different year from the one you ordered, he *may* have a few bottles of the other year left in the cellar and bring you one. Chances are, however, that you will have to either accept the new one or change wines. Unless the year listed is a very great one, there is not much point in making a fuss, and if you are a little wobbly in the knowledge of vintages, it is best to go no further than a formal notation of variance. *Do not* in any case pull a little vintage chart out of your pocket. That brands you a beginner, and as anyone who knows wines will tell you, a really good wine from a bad year can be better (and often cheaper) than a bad or even average one from a good year.

If the wine ordered is a Burgundy, or indeed any but a château-bottled Bordeaux, whose label is its guarantee, it is a good idea to remember the name of the shipper, too, if it is noted on the list, and it should be. The steward is less likely to switch shippers than vintages on you, but it is at least theoretically possible that while the list will show the name of an excellent and reputable shipper, the actual bottle would be from one of doubtful reputation, or an unknown. And even if the name of the shipper means nothing to you, which will more often than not be the case at the start, the act of verification will help to smoke out hanky-panky if there has been any, and in time this habit will teach you the names of some of the good shippers.

Checking the cork is another test of the authenticity of wine, since whoever bottled it usually brands his name into the side of the cork. The condition of the cork can indicate the condition of the wine as well. If it has turned mealy and soft, or has a major structural flaw (cork, after all, is only the bark of the cork tree), air has likely been getting to the wine. Wine so exposed will eventually turn bad. But note that you did not have to know what you were feeling for. The wine steward has already squeezed the cork himself, and if there is anything wrong, he will start making apologies the moment he sees you do the same.

In a place like the Twenty-one Club in New York, if the wine is to be decanted, the wine steward will draw the cork in the wine pantry. This gives him an opportunity not only to check the cork out carefully but actually to taste the wine before you do and assure himself that it is sound. (When the cork is drawn in the dining room, the steward very often will take the first sip from a wineglass he has brought with him.) Even so, the cork is presented to you so that you can make your own determination. At some not-so-fine restaurants, especially in Europe, a used bottle bearing a great label will be filled with lesser wine, and the authentically branded cork presented to you will be an old one drawn previously from a genuine bottle. Now, squeezing the cork has another purpose, to find out whether the cork presented to you is fresh and moist, or an old, dried-out substitute.

When wine is more than ten years old, and has just been opened, sniffing the cork is especially important. Wine of that age may have to rest several minutes in the glass before its full aroma emerges. At the moment of opening, the smell from the cork will tell you better than the aroma from the glass whether there is anything wrong.

The color of the wine as it is poured, or as seen through the edge of the glass against the white tablecloth, can provide further clues to its condition. If it has a pale, watery look, it will probably turn out to be rather thin and uninteresting—not, certainly, fine or great. If it is murky or cloudy, it may well be sick; even if not sick, no pleasure to drink, and you are entitled to send it back. If it has a bluish or purplish tinge at the point where the wine meets the side of the glass, it is young and full of tannin. When you smell and taste it, you will find it harsh and raw, but if it is a wine of promise, you will find hints of that promise behind the roughness of its youth. If the wine is too young, but is of the year ordered, it will be a little awkward to send it back unless you make some sort of financial arrangement. The assumption is you knew what you were ordering.

When the wine goes "over the hill" (old and tired, losing body and bouquet), it begins to turn a little brown, so brownish color is a danger sign. However, nearly all fairly old wines have a little brown where the wine meets the glass, when looked at against a white tablecloth. Thus a hint of brown is a signal not to send the bottle back but to do a little more checking. It is worth mentioning to the waiter when the bottle is poured, however, to save argument if you later decide to send the bottle back.

The final proof of the wine of course is in the tasting, and in the olfactory (smell) sensations that are a part of that. The bread or cheese you chew first is to clear your palate for the tasting (and to demonstrate to the wine steward that you know the score). Clearing the palate, as we have pointed out, is especially important if you have been smoking, or drinking strong drink, or eating salad with a vinegar dressing. Swirling the wine in your glass helps it to breathe additionally and release its flavor, and the warmth of your cupped hand raises its temperature, serving the same end. The deep breath before you taste may or may not reveal the positive virtues of the wine; it will provide another important indicator if anything is wrong. The purpose of the strange, unmannerly "googling" that follows, drawing air through the wine between clenched teeth, is to carry the flavor and bouquet of the wine back to the areas of your mouth where taste and smell meet.

The chief enemy of wine is *acetobacter,* the bacteria which, given an opportunity, will turn the whole bottle to vinegar. Acetobacter is present in any vineyard, any wine vat, any bottle or barrel, and so is a trace of the acetic acid it produces. But normally during the early stages of fermentation the yeast bacteria are so active that acetobacter has little opportunity to work. After the yeast bacteria have raised the alcohol content of the batch to the point where it kills them (victims of their own success), the wine master, if he is skillful and diligent, will keep the air from the vats and barrels, and the temperature low, so that acetobacter is held at bay. After bottling, the bottle is kept cool, and lying on its side, so the cork will remain moist, swelled up, and thus airtight, and acetobacter still will have no oxygen with which to work, nor warmth to work in.

If a bottle of wine is truly bad, if it stinks or is undrinkable, the management will replace it with a thousand apologies. It is both fortunate and unfortunate that this rarely happens. What usually happens is that the wine is just a *shade* off. There is some acetobacter in any bottle of wine, but this particular bottle has just a trace, a *soupçon* more than that. You can swallow it. It isn't too bad with the food. Many bottles in this condition are not only drunk but enjoyed, especially if people are full of martinis and marinara sauce and don't know any better. But for people who do know wines this faint shading, this slight "offness," is cause for sending the wine back.

In a fine restaurant, if you express any reasonable doubt about a bottle, they will take it back, even if they don't entirely believe you. In a lesser restaurant, where nobody, including the proprietor, knows anything about wine, they will take your complaint as an insult to the integrity and competence of the management, and give you quite a tussle, first telling you you are mistaken, then if you persist, making it clear that you are either a nut or a swindler. It is difficult at first to understand why this is so, because the wholesaler will always give full credit on any bottle returned. Perhaps it is just too much trouble to take a bottle back, or perhaps they feel it is poor public relations for the other customers to see bottles being sent back. But it is certainly no better public relations for the other customers to see two waiters and the owner standing around and yelling at you.

If a battle with the management were your only problem, you would have little to worry about, provided you don't mind becoming a public spectacle. But the difficulty is that so often you yourself are not sure. You hate to expose your uncertainty to your guests, and you hate to start a battle that you don't know you can, or should, win.

The distinction between sound and unsound wine is as difficult to describe as it often is to detect. It *can* be difficult. On the best occasions a sound wine will come at you with a glorious, fruity freshness, or a subtle, pervasive bouquet that is so whole and healthy that it almost sings, "I am sound, I am sound." It is a kind of integrity, sincerity, joy if you will, and you will know it instantly. Everybody has these memories: a Pommard that was soft and round, a Beaujolais that was full of springtime, a Mouton in its full, glorious prime.

Sometimes this happens. Another time your mouth is all set for a well-loved and familiar experience and it doesn't happen. The wine is dulled somehow, unexciting, curiously disappointing. But perhaps it was only that you forgot to clean your palate; you shouldn't have had that second martini; the wine may be too cool; it has not had time to breathe or perhaps this is a different vintage, not quite the glory of the last one you had.

The difficulty of making this determination is illustrated by an experience Forrest Wallace had some years ago at the French Club in San Francisco. Among the wines, the host had provided a magnum of Petrus '47. It was delicious, and before the company knew it, they had reached the bottom of the bottle. Since the entree was not finished, and the cheese was yet to come, the host ordered another bottle. After the wine of the second bottle had been poured, Wallace swished it around in his glass for a full minute before putting it to his nose and then tasting it. The bouquet seemed below that of the first bottle, and when he tasted he was sure there was something wrong. The wine was not bad, but it was nowhere near the

first bottle. Wallace mentioned this to his dinner partner, the wife of his friend Henry Van der Voort, the wine importer. She did not agree and thought it tasted and smelled exactly like the first. Since her husband was across the table, Wallace asked his advice. Van der Voort had already drunk some and at first did not recognize the difference, but when he was asked specifically, he sniffed and tasted again and agreed that there was a difference—just not quite as good.

The next day Wallace had lunch with Van der Voort, and Van der Voort said, "You know, I got to wondering about that second magnum and before we left I asked the maître d' about the presentation of the bottle. He told me that the second bottle had been brought directly from the cellar and so had not stood on the sideboard as long as the first one. The wine had not reached room temperature and suffered as a result."

So the wine was sound, but had not been allowed to *chambrer*. Yet even a company of experts could not say immediately what was wrong. At the outset there was not even prompt agreement that anything was.

A wine that is going bad does not merely fall short of its potential. It speaks with two voices: the original, authentic, healthy one; and somewhere in the middle distance a discordant, uneasy, foreboding note that clutters and shadows the charm and the sunshine. It faults the flavor. It flaws the bouquet. Now you taste it, now you don't. When the wine has gone a bit further off, the discord is such that the best of the original flavor is largely gone. And yet there is wine still there, and the headwaiter in a less-than-first-rate restaurant will swear to you that *there is not a thing wrong with that bottle*.

A good many times when the issue is a close one you forget your doubts and go ahead and approve the wine. But as the meal wears on you keep tasting, with the unhappy suspicion that you are a bad host and a boob. Finally, as the wine breathes and warms and your palate becomes finer-tuned, you are sure. The wine in fact is off. But with only a third of it left in the bottle, if you send it back now they will be convinced you are a fraud. And in any case, it is too late in the meal to enjoy a fresh bottle.

As in many areas of life, there are just some things that can't be helped.

One argument for going back frequently to restaurants you like is that when they get to know you they will realize you are on the level, will value your good will and respect your growing expertise. If you don't know the management and don't know your ground, however, one way to deal with a doubtful wine is simply to order another bottle and another set of glasses and hold an informal wine tasting on the spot. As difficult as it is for the novice to spot wine that is off when it is tasted alone, it is contrastingly easy to detect it when tasted side by side with a sound one. The bloom, the fruit, the beauty, of the good one come plunging through, and the fault of the flawed one now is unmistakable.

With great confidence you turn to the waiter and suggest he deduct the bad wine from the check. There will be no difficulty either, for now even *he* can tell.

You have to be careful, though, in ordering a second bottle. Granted, the one in doubt may be the unhappy exception, and all its brothers in the bin sound and true. But the problem with your bottle may also be an indication that the entire case was held too long or stored near the furnace and has turned. You take a chance no matter what you do. In some cases it may seem prudent to order some entirely different wine—perhaps a simple Beaujolais. Rosé is usually a safe bet, too, in doubtful situations, if not an overly exciting one.

The art of tasting will go on growing and developing as long as you can hoist a glass. The ceremony of tasting, as you become familiar with it, will increasingly be tailored to the occasion. In a nongreat restaurant, for example, having a non-Great Meal with an ordinary if not *ordinaire* bottle of wine, it is not really necessary to taste the wine at all. One quick sniff will tell you whether or not it is sound. If it is, you got what you paid for. Further deliberation is not required. (Such casual speed in making your decision will also make a great impression on your guests.)

For a somewhat better bottle at a somewhat better place, you should assuredly taste as well as sniff. But you hardly need squeeze or examine the cork unless the tasting and smelling tell you there is something wrong.

If you have been drinking hard liquor or eating an oily, strong-flavored appetizer beforehand, chewing bread or cheese before you try the wine is not an affectation unless you make too much of a big deal of it. It is essential to clear the palate. By the same token, googling air through the wine may make your friends wonder about your upbringing—unless you explain what you are doing, which is not a bad idea. But you will find the googling a definite help in getting a sense for the character of even a relatively humble wine.

If the tasting and googling disclose that you have a somewhat acid wine, then you might as well sneak a look against the white of the table-cloth at the point where wine meets glass, to get an idea of the bluish or purplish look of an acid wine. By the same token, if the wine is a fairly old one, you owe it to your education to look for brown at the edge; in the case of a fine Burgundy, to see how the glycerine hangs.

It is not always the host who tastes the wine. If the host knows that one of his guests has a particularly good knowledge of wine, he can ask him to order the wine. The steward then presents the bottle to this man, and awaits his verdict. If you are serving a real connoisseur at home, you pour the first bit of wine in your own glass to get rid of the corkage, then go to the honored guest, pour him some wine, and ask him to pronounce his verdict. But make sure your guest really knows wine. Forrest Wallace recently did this and his guest said the wine was substandard, so Wallace went to the cellar and got another bottle. Toward the end of the meal Wallace decided to try the first bottle again. It was excellent. The guest had not allowed for the fact that, as in the case of the Petrus '47 in San Francisco, the wine had not *chambré* and breathed quite long enough. And a very expensive bottle of wine was wasted.

When at long last you emerge from the question of whether or not your wine is bad (and the whole consideration normally has taken only a few seconds), you now must find words to describe how good it is. And that will be the subject of the chapter that follows.

XII

THE LANGUAGE OF THE GRAPE

There are perhaps a couple of hundred words used by experts to describe the qualities of wine, and their meaning is surprisingly precise. It has been shown over and over that if two fully qualified wine tasters sample a number of wines and record their reactions, their descriptions will be essentially the same. Yet to an outsider the jargon is hopelessly confusing, especially since definitions tend to be circular: If a wine is called "distinguished," for example, it is in part because it possesses "finesse." Yet if you look up finesse you find one of the words used to describe it is "distinction."

This confusion is particularly great in descriptions of the greatest wines. When every great wine you read about has "astonishing breed and class," along with "incredible bouquet," you begin to wonder whether in fact they do not all come from the same vat.

Out of all the words in the vocabulary of wine, a given bottle can be fairly well described in terms of five qualities: character, balance, body, delicacy, and bouquet. Their definitions do in fact tend to be interlocking and self-reflexive. What you are really trying to define is not many qualities but one—greatness—for which there is no other single adequate word.

Character (also called breed, class). If a Scotchman is very Scottish, and a Sicilian is very Sicilian, then you say that each possesses the character of his type; but the fact that they both have a lot of character does not mean that both characters are the same. A wine from Bordeaux should be eminently Bordeaux-like; one from Burgundy should declare its native ground. A wine made from the Riesling grape must offer the distinctive Riesling bouquet; one from the Cabernet, Pinot, Grenache, or Grignolino should, like Laertes, to its own self be true. A wine of the hill announces its origins, as does its neighbor from the plain. When a wine does this, we say it possesses character. Character in a wine may or may not be an indicator of other merits. It might be an *ordinaire;* it might be supremely great. But if it lacks character, then regardless of its other virtues it will tend to be dull and uninteresting.

At the higher levels the words "class" and "breed" are the rough equivalents of character. Nikita Khrushchev had lots of character; John Kennedy had class. So does Romanée-Conti.

Balance. In his famous *Book of the Courtier* the Renaissance diplomat and author Castiglione attempted to define the qualities of a gentleman, much as we are trying to describe the qualities of wine. In one passage he tells of a would-be courtier who loved to dance so much that while he was dancing he took no notice of anything else; some of his clothes might even fall off and he would not stop. In Castiglione's opinion that man might be considered a fine dancer, but could not be considered a proper gentleman because he did not keep things in balance. In the same way, a truly fine wine must have balance: nothing to excess, no marked deficiencies. If it is a light wine, it should be delicate. If it is a full-bodied wine, it should have a corresponding amount of character (used here in a slightly different but not contradictory sense) and flavor. A wine with too much acid is described in France as "wearing its hat on the side of its head," that is, out of balance.

As in the case of character, a wine may possess balance and still not be great, but it cannot be great or even very good without it.

Body. A wine high in alcohol is sometimes described as having body. We are not using the word in that sense (although in fact a wine which is full-bodied in the other sense will often be high in alcohol, too, because the warm weather that produces a full-flavored wine will also produce plenty of sugar, which converts to alcohol).

Body means substance, bigness, fullness. It is the opposite of delicacy. It is also the opposite of watery or thin. A common source of body in a wine is tannin—tannic acid. A wine high in tannin is never low in body. But sometimes a wine that is low in tannin is high in body as a result of the presence of other materials. This we have seen in the case of the great red Burgundies, which owe their body not to tannin, but to the glycerine they contain.

Body is by no means necessarily a virtue. A cheap Chianti has plenty of body but that is about all. If a Moselle or a Riesling or a Chablis has too much body, it lacks fruit and charm, and thus is out of balance and out of character. By contrast, a great Montrachet must have plenty of body, not to mention the great red Burgundies. We have pointed out earlier that the very greatest wines—Lafite, Romanée—seem to possess a substantial amount of body. Aristotle summed it up: "To be beautiful, a living creature, and every whole made up of parts, must not only present a certain order in its arrangement of parts, but also be of a certain magnitude."

Delicacy (also finesse, distinction). These three are separate but overlapping words. As noted, delicacy is to some extent the opposite of body. It is noteworthy that the most delicate of the great Burgundies and Bordeaux—Bonnes Mares, Musigny, Margaux—while they are famous, much-loved, costly, and sought after, are not the greatest of all. On the other hand, the greatest wines in the greatest years will have ample body— balanced by amazing delicacy.

Finesse is related to delicacy. It is also related to breed or class, that is, character at a high level. Finesse is defined as "the quality that renders a wine out of the ordinary." Now the language is indeed beginning to turn in upon itself.

When a wine possesses both finesse (that is, delicacy and breed) and balance, then it is considered to have distinction. And here we come very close to saying a wine is great because it has greatness. Yet if you have ever tasted a wine with finesse and distinction, you know it, even if you cannot clearly define the words.

Bouquet. It can be said without argument that no wine will be really great without bouquet, and none that could be considered fine or even very good can lack it. (As noted earlier, our sense of smell actually provides much of what we consider the "taste" of a wine.) Young wines may have aroma or odor or perfume; bouquet is distinct from these. It comes mainly from esters developed by the gradual oxidation of various elements in wine, including particularly the tannin. Wines coming from northern vineyards, as in the case of Burgundy, almost invariably have more bouquet than others, as do wines from grapes that have matured slowly in a temperate climate, as in Bordeaux. Before a wine has aged long enough to transmute its tannin to bouquet, it will often be raw and rough, and thus lack finesse and balance; but even so its potential will show through. A wine with plenty of tannin will, as noted, have plenty of body and character as well. Tannin also tends to preserve a wine and keep it from spoiling, as does alcohol. Thus a wine high in tannin, but not too high, and in alcohol, will have both the potential for developing to greatness and a life span long enough to permit this to occur. This is what happens in a vintage year.

Breed, body, balance, delicacy, and bouquet: these five. No one of them can be missing if the wine is to be great, but in their presence is infinite variety and delight.

The Business of Wine

XIII

WINES AND WALL STREET

As noted at the start of this book, much of the fascination—the sometimes maddening fascination—of the game of wine lies in the fact that the serene intellectual process of pairing off wines with appropriate foods so often intertwines with and interacts upon the practical business of going out and taking title to a bottle of the stuff.

To return to the example we offered in the Introduction:

Is there leg of lamb on the menu tonight? Then obviously we must enjoy its classic accompaniment, red Bordeaux. But look at the wine list. The vineyards are not first-rate and the bottles appear overpriced. Then what else looks good? *Filet de sole Véronique.* Haut-Brion Blanc is perfect with that, of course. But it is not on this list (and if it were they would charge too much for it). What about Montrachet? They have one, but it is suspiciously hyphenated and of uncertain sponsorship. The Chablis? Too light for that sauce, and in any case, Chablis would also be risky in a place like this. Well, then, what wine? Pouilly-Fumé. Pouilly-Fumé from de Ladoucette. You can count on de Ladoucette.

Would *sole Véronique* go with the Fumé? It could, but it is not an inspired solution. Then how about crab meat, sautéed in butter? Perfection. A simple wine of medium body, a simple dish that is medium-full.

The difference between the mental operations required for selecting *in principle* the correct wine to have with your dinner and those required for acquiring it *in fact* is the difference between theory and practice, between concept and execution, between formulating a policy and actually carrying it out. A doctor making a diagnosis as such is merely looking for an answer. If the patient then dies, well, that's show biz. At least he had the satisfaction of knowing he figured out what was wrong. A woodsman on unfamiliar terrain, by contrast, must get himself from there to here. Even if he sees incomparably beautiful scenery along the way, or thinks up a modification to the theory of relativity, it would be small compensation if he never found his way out of the woods.

It is possible, theoretically, at least, to know all there is to know about fine foods and how to match them. Few if any really important new dishes are developed in a given year, and the characteristics of a general category of wine change little if at all. Thus you are, in effect, working with a finite body of knowledge. By contrast, the body of knowledge in the business end of wine is infinite and ever-changing. No one could ever know it all, and even to keep abreast of major developments is a full-time job. Not only is each vintage in each vineyard different, but the evolution of each barrel and each bottle is different, too. The management of a vineyard may change, or the management of a shipper or an importer or a cellar or a store; even if the people remain the same, their performance can vary— they may start drinking more than they sell.

Thus, what Peter Drucker has said about business decisions in general applies with particular force to a decision about a bottle of wine: "It is not the 'facts that decide'; people have to choose between imperfect alternatives on the basis of uncertain knowledge and fragmentary understanding."

In their essence, the practical problems of buying wines have much in common with the problems of buying common stocks. In each case the range of choice is enormous, the fluctuation in value continuous, and the names of the individual items reveal little if anything to the inexperienced eye about the character of the merchandise. In both cases there are fools too easily parted with their money and scoundrels and incompetents who would lead them astray: A successful buying strategy takes account of all three groups.

In the wine trade as in the securities market merchandise tends to be either undervalued or overvalued in a kind of tidal ebb and flow of public estimation. A bottle of wine is normally overvalued if it comes from a vineyard with a great name or a region of great popularity or a vintage of great reputation. All the people not in position to think for themselves flock to buy, and bid against each other. A bottle is usually undervalued if its vineyard or vintage is out of style; if a vineyard which was mismanaged is now being well managed but the word has not got around yet; if by some fluke of weather a particular vineyard turned out excellent wine in a generally terrible year; if a wine that is young and harsh has unrecognized potential for maturing in a blaze of glory; if the output of a particular region is so erratic in quality or low in quantity that there has been no advantage in promoting its commercial reputation, despite an occasional magnificent crop.

Thus the art, in buying wines as in buying stocks, is to bet against the crowd, to swim against the tides of popular opinion, searching out what Wall Street calls "neglected value."

There are differences, of course. In wines, if you locate a treasure, nobody needs to know about it but you, and you collect your reward each time you open a bottle, happily savor its merits, and reflect on your superior abilities in searching it out. Or you serve it without comment to a little group of friends, and when someone says, "My God, this is *good!*" you smirk and say, "It's just a little château I discovered on the Loire last year."

In stocks, by contrast, it is not enough to have been right about the intrinsic merits of a company. Before you can liquidate your holding and take your just reward, the "general market" must come to recognize that you were right and reflect this in the price of the stock. As the saying goes, "If you're right too soon, it's the same as being wrong."

The wine market like the stock market has been in basic uptrend since World War II, and for largely the same reasons—spreading affluence and education, more people wanting to be in on the action. The results in each case have been an inflated scale of values and a changed set of rules and priorities—very painful to traditionalists who liked things the way they were, keenly challenging to anyone intent on getting value for his money, and playing skillfully a complex and difficult game.

Although in both the wine trade and the stock market the variety of merchandise available is almost infinite, in each case there are two categories posing the chief buying problems and against which your strategy must be directed. The two categories can be called the Blue Chips and the Popular Names.

In stocks the Blue Chips are, of course, the shares of the great, established companies, with vast resources, enormous depth of management, and records of stable dividends and profitable operation going back many years. In wines the Blue Chips are the products of the very greatest vineyards of all, the immortals of Burgundy and Bordeaux whose records of excellence go back more centuries than the records of many corporations go back in decades.

In stocks the Popular Names are the creatures of investment fashion. At one moment the market is in love with computers, let us say, then copiers, then conglomerates, then computer-leasing, then oceanography or

CHÂTEAU AUSONE
Sᵗ ÉMILION
÷ 1917 ÷
EDOUARD DUBOIS-CHALLON
Propriétaire

MIS EN BOUTEILLE AU CHÂTEAU

pollution control or whatever. Any stock carrying one of those magic tags is likely to go like gangbusters, as long as the name is hot, regardless of the merit of the enterprise in question. In wines the Popular Names are usually wines that are moderate in price, appealing in taste, produced in enough volume and with easily-enough-remembered points of origin to become more or less staple items of merchandise, carried on the tips of tongues of people who otherwise know very little about the subject.

The rising demand for wines over the past twenty years has inflated the price of almost anything drinkable (and some that is really not), but in particular it has inflated the prices of the Blue Chips and the Popular Names. A millionaire puts in a wine cellar because all his friends have one. He doesn't know anything, so when they ask him what he wants, he waves his hand and says, "Get the best." So, in effect, they "paper the walls" with masterpieces, regardless of cost. With enough of this kind of buying pressure the prices of the Blue Chips go through the roof.

Or Big Daddy takes his dolly out on the town. To prove he is a big spender and a sport, he asks for wine, and when they ask him what he wants, he says, "Bring some Chablis," because he had some once and it tasted good and he remembers the name. As more of this occurs the odds become smaller and smaller that he will get real Chablis, and greater and greater that he will be criminally overcharged.

Not all of us are millionaires or sugar daddies, but each in his way, and most of our friends, have contributed to this gravitation of demand to-ward Blue Chips and Popular Names. This means their prices are necessarily the most inflated, their quality necessarily the most in doubt, and the bargains are certain to lie somewhere else.

There is a useful analogy here to the restaurant field, and what might be called the "Craig Claiborne effect." Mr. Claiborne, for a number of years the restaurant reviewer for the New York *Times,* would have been the first to admit that it could be a serious mistake, particularly on a Saturday night, to go to a restaurant to which he had awarded four stars (the highest rating) in his *New York Times Restaurant Guide.* The delay in being seated, even if you had a reservation, might be an hour. The table, failing a large emolument to the maître d', might be next to the kitchen door, jawbone to jawbone with two other tables. The food might not reach you for still another hour, and meanwhile they are all too ready to keep pushing drinks at you, so that by the time the food comes you are too sousled to know the difference. The food may be cold, the service colder, and for this you pay eighty-five dollars, *plus* a tip and a bribe for the maître d', for a party of two.

This is not to say Mr. Claiborne's rating was "wrong." The kitchen was no doubt as good as he said. But the "delivery system" that carried the product from the kitchen to you broke down under pressure of a demand the rating itself had helped create.

In terms of human pleasure you would have received better value, dollar for dollar, if you had gone to a three-star or a two-star or even a no-star restaurant. But to do that you would have had to know the town, you would have had to be adventurous. And if you had had a visiting fireman or client in tow, they might have thought there was something wrong with you or cheap about you if you failed to take them to a restaurant with a famous name, to be gyped, trampled, and insulted. So the four-star glut goes on.

On the following pages we shall examine various strategies for coping with the buying problems posed by Blue Chips and Popular Names. But value is a function of price, so a note is needed first on that. For our purposes there are five general price categories among wines:

First are what might be called the *ordinaires,* domestic or imported, costing, in New York, anything from 99 cents to perhaps $2.50 retail (that is, in a liquor store). Not all wines in this class are bad. Occasionally you will make a charming little discovery among the imports from Italy or Sicily or Yugoslavia or Chile. As we have noted the producers of California wines make some thoroughly adequate if simple wines in this class, and often these are preferable to more pretentious wines at higher prices. But at one or two dollars a bottle you rarely get more than you pay for.

Then there are what we shall call *commercial wines,* costing some-

where between $2.50 and $4.50 a bottle. The bulk of popular demand for wine in the United States is in this class, and not surprisingly millions of bottles of wine appear on the market each year to satisfy that demand. Even more than the *ordinaires* the commercial wines are a mixed bag. There are the Popular Names aforementioned, in varying degrees of authenticity; there are pretentious fakes; there are time-tested favorites; there are undiscovered bargains. But what must be borne in mind is that much of the wine in this class is intended to sell in strictly price competition to a generally undiscriminating market.

Next up are what we shall call *good wines* (showing where our prejudice lies). These run from about $4.50 to perhaps $8.00. It is sad to have to pay a price like that to get a wine that merely qualifies for the description "good," and some wine in this class deserves much better than that. But in general nowadays if you go out to a wine shop to buy a bottle of wine for dinner and want a reasonable chance of an interesting experience, it is a good idea to spend something in the $4.50 to $8.00 range.

The next category we will call the *fine wines,* whose prices run from $8.00 to perhaps $15 in a store. These are wines for an occasion, wines that create their own occasion, or wines for the man whose palate has outgrown the levels below and whose purse can stand the strain. You are not guaranteed against disappointment here or anywhere else. But from this point on the drinking will hopefully be an adventure, and the skillful matching of the wine with food increasingly an art.

And then of course there are the indisputably *great wines,* from about $15.00 up, and if you wish the *very great* ones, from $30.00, which few readers of this book will drink regularly, but which all should try once in a while, and dream about.

These price levels have approximately doubled, sad to say, over ten years (although there has been some decline recently). Long-term they can be expected to continue to rise, although at perhaps a less rapid rate. But while the prices themselves will change, the levels of drinking they represent, reflecting levels of taste, will remain the same, as will the buying problems related to them.

The question of prices of wines sold in a restaurant is much more difficult than prices in a store, since restaurant markups can range from almost nothing to 300 per cent or more, and often one restaurant will take different markups on different wines: heavy markups on the cheap ones because they can get away with it, little if anything on the expensive ones because they hardly sell as it is.

A further difficulty is the fact that some restaurants will be in position to buy wine earlier and therefore cheaper than most liquor stores, and will mark up from a lower base. For purposes of this discussion we assume arbitrarily that wines in the *ordinaire, commercial,* and *good* categories will cost you 100 per cent more in a restaurant than in a store, those in the *fine* category will cost 50 per cent more, and those in the *great* and *very great* categories will cost around 30 per cent more.

	Store Price	*Restaurant Price*
Ordinaire	$ 2.00	$ 4.00
Commercial	3.50	7.00
Good	6.00	12.00
Fine	10.00	15.00
Great	15.00 up	20.00 up
Very great	30.00 up	37.00 up

On the pages that follow, unless otherwise noted, prices indicated are for wines sold over-the-counter, in a store, with the New York price accepted as a norm.

A Blue Chip Strategy

In dealing with wines in the Blue Chip class you have three choices: You can pay the price, you can play the market, or you can trade down. Most people on most occasions necessarily trade down.

Paying the price. For some lovers of wine the joy of drinking a Lafite '59 is so great that if it costs $125.00 ($165.00 in a restaurant), or even more, they will pay it. But not everyone is in a position to pay $125.00 or indeed $12.50 each time he wants wine with his dinner. This means as we have already suggested that the man of average means who wants to drink superior wines has strong incentive to drink them at home, where they cost less (and where there are substantial savings on the food and liquor as well).

Playing the market. It is possible to save a certain amount of money in buying very good wines, and lesser ones, too, by doing what a layman calls "playing the market," and what Wall Street calls "trading"—taking shrewd advantage of market flukes and temporary situations. This applies particularly to buying for home use, but some of the tricks are useful eating out, too.

Different wine merchants have different ways of setting prices; some will charge for a given wine what the current market will bear. Others, more conservatively, will take a standard markup on their original cost plus carrying charges. Still others will mark up from replacement cost, what it would cost them to replace that bottle today.

Thus, at any one time there may be quite a range of prices in the same city for the same wine, and it can pay to shop around and find these differentials. (This shopping around for simultaneous price differentials forms the basis of what Wall Street calls arbitrage.)

If you wish, as we noted in Chapter II, you can go beyond mere bargain hunting and become a full-fledged speculator in wines. Like your merchant, you, too, can take a "position" in wine futures on the Bordeaux market, exactly as you would take a position in wheat or hog bellies on the Chicago Commodity Exchange. If you hear that the wine harvest is excellent this year, promising the "vintage of the century," you make arrangements, perhaps with a syndicate of five to ten friends, to purchase a few cases each while the wine is still bubbling in the vat. (But be careful. Don't get caught, as too many people have, with the wine off-loaded and sitting at dockside, perhaps freezing or spoiling, while you rush around to find an importer who will clear it through customs for you. Make the deal with the importer in advance.)

The vintage of the century may prove disappointing, of course. The farmers who harvested early in a great year may indeed have produced great wine. The ones who harvested later may have been caught by the rain. But in any case, you have the wine, and if it is not great it is probably very good, for significantly less money than you would have had to pay after it had been bottled, shipped, stored, and placed on your merchant's shelf.

There is another buying tactic, what Wall Street would call a cyclical strategy, that reflects in purest form the effort to bet against the crowd. This is the practice of buying the lesser-classed vineyards in the great years and the great vineyards in the lesser years. (Roughly analogous to going to a Craig Claiborne four-star restaurant on a Monday evening in a blizzard, when you can have the place to yourself, but heading for an out-of-the-way no-star restaurant on a lovely Saturday evening in September.) The assumption is that even in a poor year a very great vineyard usually produces good wine, but the crowd will undervalue it in its mechanic obsession with the greatest vintages. By the same token, in the very greatest years lesser vineyards may produce wines every bit as good as the greatest ones. (A great vineyard is so positioned as to produce superior wines even when the weather may not be ideal. When the weather *is* ideal, other people can do as well or nearly so.) But the crowd does not care about intrinsic merit. They are looking for, and paying for, a Blue Chip name.

A variant of this approach, if you are a *very* good client of a *very* good merchant, is to listen to the market gossip and find out which are the vineyards that luckily produced good or even great wine in an utterly unspeakable year, and order a few cases of that. Wall Street calls these special situations. Here, again, the intrinsic merit of the wine counts for less with the crowd than the magic number of a glamour year.

Finally, you can look for what Wall Street calls turn-around situations, vineyards that have previously been mismanaged, and are now improved, but have not yet been recognized as such by the general market. Château Beychevelle in Bordeaux has been known for years among sophisticates as a turn-around situation, although the price of a Beychevelle by now pretty well reflects its value.

As the ripples of growing demand fan out from the greatest wine districts to the secondary ones, and the secondary areas respond with better wine, whole regions and even whole countries—Chile, Spain, Australia—can come to qualify, in effect, as turn-around situations.

These are all good games to play, particularly if you are keeping a cellar. But this is a lot of work, and is still only of limited usefulness in a restaurant where the worst financial damage is done. And we are still talking mainly about wines in the $15.00 to $30.00 plus class ($20.00 to $40.00 eating out). In today's market, if on any steady sort of basis you want to drink superior wine, you have no realistic choice but to "trade down," to move from the Blue Chip class of drinking to what could be called the Pale Blue Chips.

Trading down. Wall Street faces this precise situation. Let us say a labor union names a group of its officials to serve as trustees of an employee pension fund. These horny-handed sons of toil know little about stocks; the rank and file knows less. But the union trustees know that if they buy an unknown stock and it goes up, nobody will notice. They were just doing their job. But if the stock goes down, they will be accused of speculating with union funds, and in the next union election would lose their jobs. On the other hand, if they buy a royal Blue Chip and it goes down, nobody can say anything. They can tell the members, "We bought the best." But over a period of years this tended to bid up the price of the classic Blue Chips to a point where they no longer represented good value in relation to future earnings growth capability. So the more sophisticated and knowledgeable investor traded down. He turned his attention to the Pale Blue Chips, companies without quite the prestige and "seasoning" of the greatest ones, but excellent companies, less in demand, representing better value in terms of future earnings growth potential per dollar invested—which happens to be the real name of the game.

In wines the Pale Blue Chips are the lesser but still very fine vineyards that surround the greatest ones, along with the finest vineyards of the secondary regions. In Bordeaux, as we noted earlier in the book, there are sixty vineyards listed in the great classification of 1855, out of more than

five thousand vineyards in the whole Bordeaux district. All these sixty classed growths are considered "great wines" in the terms of the classification. But in a good or great year when a First Growth might sell for upward of $30.00 a bottle, wine of lesser classification might sell anywhere from $8.00 to $20.00 a bottle. In a lesser year the prices might be half that for *very* good wine.

The story is the same for the other regions of Bordeaux, for Burgundy, and to a lesser extent for the Rhône or California. The difficulty, of course, with trading down is the lack of certainty. A Lafite is a Lafite is a Lafite, and may cost you $45.00, but you can be sure. If you want a good wine of the same year for $15.00, there will be dozens of candidates for your purchase, and unless you are an expert, or get good advice—or do your homework well—you will have a hard time telling which is which and what it is worth.

Buying the Popular Names

Unlike the Blue Chips, there is no definitive list of Popular Names in wine. There are fads in the wine market as there are in the stock market. As we have seen, over the centuries an expression of enthusiasm about a wine by a reigning monarch has been enough to make its fortune. In 1660 Louis XIV tasted some wine from Mâcon, found it good, and that wine immediately became a favorite of the court. Queen Victoria did the same for the wines of Hochheim on the Rhine, to the extent that "Hock" became synonymous in England with Rhine wine. Henry IV of France was alleged to have a half-dozen "favorite" wines, one, it is said, for each mistress, and each of these endorsements is used to this day to promote the wine in question.

A disturbingly religious name—the Milk of the Blessed Virgin, the Tears of Christ, even the New Castle of the Pope—will do great things for a wine. The only names of wines that many people know are the broad, generic ones—Burgundy, Claret, Rhine wine—which taken by themselves mean almost nothing, but which because of the volume of demand appear on millions of bottles every year.

But the Popular Names that have lasted, some for well over a thousand years, are the ones with a more legitimate basis for popularity: a charmingly appealing flavor of the wine itself, a large enough supply to build a reputation on, a name not too difficult to remember. Among white wines the most popular name of all is Chablis, which to many people has come to be synonymous with light white wine as such. Among red wines the most popular names with merit to back them up are Beaujolais and Pommard in Burgundy, Médoc from Bordeaux, and of course Italian Chianti.

Just as you have three choices in dealing with wines in the Blue Chip

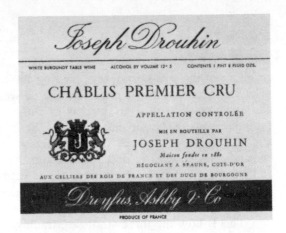

class, so you have three in attempting to get good value among the Popular Names. You can trade up, you can trade over, or you can trade out.

With demand for wine growing as it has over the past fifteen or twenty years, and with the supply of genuine merchandise bearing these names fixed by geographic limits, it should be clear that little if any Chablis or Pommard or Médoc or Beaujolais of superior quality is likely to be available in the $2.50 to $4.50 price range where the bulk of the demand lies. At the same time it should be no less clear that someone is going to try whenever possible to meet the demand in that price class with bottles carrying those very popular labels. So each year more wine is sold under those names than is legitimately produced in those areas. This means that if you are determined to have a Chablis or Pommard or Beaujolais or Chianti that is worth the price, your best bet is to *trade up* from the mini-mum-priced offerings into a range where you have at least a reasonable possibility of getting not only authenticity but quality (and where, inciden-tally, there can be "landmarks" on the label such as vineyards, villages, and shippers' names to give you guidance).

But a trading-up strategy is easier to carry out at home than eating out. The better wines among the Popular Names are usually missing from the average restaurant wine list; where they can be found, the price often runs upward of $10.00. When someone eating out wants a decent wine in a moderate price range, the chances are he will, consciously or uncon-

sciously, either *trade over*—that is, find a wine that is the lesser-known neighbor of the well-known one, offering similar characteristics and greater reliability at a reasonable price—or else he will *trade out:* abandon entirely the great, traditional wine districts of Burgundy and Bordeaux and look for value among the secondary areas. These two trends, trading over and trading out, have been the dominant action of the wine market for easily twenty years, at least in dollar terms, and the mental processes they represent, the juggling and substitution, the adjustment and calculation, are the essential ones involved in choosing and buying most wine for everyday drinking.

This is how the three strategies, trading up, trading over, and trading out, apply to the best of the Popular Names:

Chablis. Chablis may well be the most famous wine name in the world. But of course the vast majority of those who think they are drinking Chablis are drinking a Chablis-type (so called) wine from·California or Australia or Chile or New York.

The real wine of Chablis comes in four grades: the Great Growths (Grand Crus); the First Growths (Premier Crus); regular Chablis, the village appellation; and Petit Chablis (small Chablis), the name given to the lesser, outlying vineyards.

The bulk of the authentic Chablis coming into the United States is either Premier Cru or regular village Chablis. Petit Chablis has had difficulty competing in price with the Chablis-type wines from other countries, and a considerable proportion of those vineyards are going out of production.

Authentic Chablis can be found in the United States from around $4.00 a bottle. But at that, the minimum price, the risks are considerable. Trading up to a Regular Chablis for at least $4.50, or to a Premier Cru, $4.50 to $5.00, or to a Grand Cru, $5.00 to $6.50, gives progressively greater assurance, particularly when a good shipper is involved.

As for trading over, perhaps the closest thing to a look-alike for Chablis, if you can find one, would be a still (nonsparkling) Champagne. The growing conditions in the two areas are remarkably similar. In addition, "still Champagne" on your table is rare enough to make a fine conversation piece.

But in recent history the most common trade-over for Chablis has been Pouilly-Fuissé in southern Burgundy, one hundred miles to the south. Pouilly-Fuissé is a different wine, fuller, less fine, but still a white Burgundy and interchangeable for most uses. But because Pouilly-Fuissé has stood in so often for Chablis, it has become a Popular Name itself, overpriced and tending to be tampered with. However, there is even a trade-over for a trade-over. As noted in Chapter III, Fuissé is merely the largest of the three villages that hyphenate themselves with Pouilly, the other two being Vinzelles and Loché. And there is the new entry in the area, St.-Véran (see footnote, page 76), from about $3.00.

But Pouilly-Vinzelles, Pouilly-Loché, and St.-Véran are not available everywhere. So unless you want to trade over and down considerably to a simple white from Mâcon nearby, your attention will normally swing north and west to the basin of the great Loire River: to Pouilly-Fumé far upstream, and Sancerre, its trade-over across the river, or to Muscadet, far downstream. (Muscadet is an excellent example of the effects on the outlying regions of the trading-out process. Fifteen years ago, Muscadet, grown near the sea where the weather is often overcast or foggy, was too light in alcohol to "travel" well, so it was rarely seen in the United States. But thanks to modern methods of vinification, plus the incentive of financial return, Muscadet now travels very nicely.)

If it is not possible to trade out to the Loire to find a reasonable substitute for Chablis, the logical next place to look might be California, either a Chablis-type blend, or one of the better, varietal wines, a Pinot Chardonnay. As we have noted, a California Chablis-type wine resembles authentic French Chablis only in name, but it is white and it is light and it is dry, and usually represents reasonable value at the price. Particularly in shoreside seafood restaurants, whose wine lists are often as simple as their food is delicious, the California Chablis-type wines are the best and sometimes the only choice.

If you reach this point and do not find an acceptable substitute for Chablis, the chances are in real life that you would not keep looking. Your mind might flicker off to the red wines, looking for an entree to match, or the fuller whites, or you might examine the menu again, looking for an interesting dish on which to make another stab at matching.

But if you are still determined to have a light white wine, perhaps because everybody has already ordered fish, there are still a few options. Aside from California, there are always the Italian whites (although unless you are in an Italian restaurant you are not likely to have much of a selection among Italian whites, and if you *are* in an Italian restaurant you probably would not have considered anything else). Light, dry Soave, as noted in Chapter IV, calls itself the Italian Chablis. There is also Verdicchio.

Failing this, you can use the menu as an excuse to penetrate the mysteries of the German and Alsatian wines (although once again, in a French

restaurant the selections of Germans is likely to be skimpy, while in a German restaurant you would be unlikely to have thought of anything else). Yugoslavia also produces a decidedly acceptable little white from the Riesling, the premium grape of Germany and Alsace; so does Chile; and so, most certainly, does California.

But if by this point you have not found a white wine you want, the odds are very strong you will either give up the idea of drinking wine that evening or move on to something else entirely.

Beaujolais. Fresh and sprightly red Beaujolais outsells any other French wine in the United States. Unlike Chablis, Beaujolais has not been widely imitated, so its lesser wines do not have to compete against cut-rate namesakes, and are available everywhere.

Beaujolais comes in three levels of quality. There is regular Beaujolais or Beaujolais Supérieur (there is no significant difference between the wine of those two appellations). Above them is Beaujolais-Villages, which comes from one of about three dozen villages which are entitled to this higher appellation. At the top is Beaujolais which is entitled to carry the name of one of the eight best villages of all: Moulin-à-Vent, Juliénas, Morgon, Chénas, Fleurie, St.-Amour, Côte de Brouilly, and Chiroubles. These village names will sometimes appear on a label without the designation Beaujolais, so it is important to remember them.

The price of a regional Beaujolais, the lowest appellation, usually runs from about $2.70 to perhaps $3.30; that of a Beaujolais-Villages costs perhaps $.50 more; while a wine from one of the nine best villages normally runs in the $4.00 to $5.00 range. However, if a wine from any of the three levels bears the name of a shipper like Jadot or Louis Latour, or the name of an exceptional vineyard and a good year, the cost may run a dollar or so more, and be well worth it.

There is no close look-alike nor even a very plausible trade-out for Beaujolais, which helps explain the lack of imitation. Beaujolais is Beaujolais, and if you want the charming experience that comes from drinking Beaujolais on a particular night, the best thing to do is pay the price and get a good one, or else take your chances at the cheaper levels. California produces wine from the Gamay grape that is used in Beaujolais, and it is similar, but not being grown on granitic soil it lacks the special verve of the real article. For some purposes a light fresh rosé from Tavel on the Rhône could substitute, or the runner-up rosé from Anjou on the Loire.

But if you do not find a Beaujolais you want, you are not ordinarily going to press the point. You will just look for another good red wine, which might be, according to your taste, a Pommard of Burgundy, a Rhône, or a Médoc from Bordeaux.

Pommard. Pommard comes, of course, from a village of that name in the Côte de Beaune, north of Beaujolais. It is a delightful wine but perhaps not as fine as the level of demand would suggest. Wine experts sometimes puzzle about the consistently strong demand. Part of the reason may be the relatively large volume of wine produced in that village, permitting the demand to continue to be filled once it had been created. Part may be the fact that some important shippers have substantial holdings in Pommard, and thus strong motive for keeping its name before the public.

Pommard has historically been one of the most abused wine names in the world. Before appellation contrôlée put some limits on the cheating, one writer estimated that the amount of Pommard sold throughout the world each week was more than the commune could actually produce in ten years.

Today in Pommard as in Chablis the danger is less a question of actual fraud and more a matter of getting an eminently unimpressive wine for a decidedly impressive price. Sugaring is widely used in Pommard to increase both the body and the strength of the wine. Overused—in the hands of some shippers—the result is a coarser, less interesting wine.

No genuine Pommard is cheap. Prices begin at around $9.00. A bottle with the added assurance of a vineyard name on the label will cost $10.00 to $12.00, or more, depending on the grower and the shipper.

Failing to find a Pommard you want, you have a number of interesting alternatives. The prime trade-over is Volnay, the village next south from Pommard. Volnay is lighter and more delicate than Pommard, and its quality is actually somewhat higher, but the wines are very similar. Because the supply of Volnay is limited, commercial demand has not reached the overwhelming proportions, at least in the United States, of that for Pommard. The price is not cheap, but there is less chance that it will be tampered with, and the wine is excellent.

If you cannot find a Volnay, or don't want to pay for it, then you might trade over and somewhat down to a wine bearing the label of one of the nearby villages, or to a still more modest Côte de Beaune. Or you could go a dozen miles south to the region of Mercurey. Mercurey is not as good a wine as Pommard, but it is a similar light, pleasant wine of southern Burgundy. (In the days before appellation contrôlée, Mercurey was shipped north to stretch the supply of Pommard and Volnay.)

Beyond this point, you are not likely to find a really close look-alike for Pommard, and your attention will probably go south to the Rhône or west to the Bordelais. There is no "right" way to go. But if a man has been looking at Beaujolais and Pommard, one suspects he has a bias toward Burgundies in general, so the probability is that his eye will move to the big, full reds of the Rhône, which have become a natural trade-out for big, full Burgundies.

The trading-out process from Burgundy to the Rhône has been going on so long, in fact, that the buying pressure on Châteauneuf-du-Pape has reached a point where these wines cannot always be trusted. Here, again, a certain amount of trading up among the Châteauneufs is indicated. Or you

can trade down to their more modest neighbor, Côtes du Rhône. Or, available resources permitting, you can trade up to the famous red of Hermitage, or the much rarer wine of the Côte Rôtie.

Most people, failing to find what they want on the Rhône, would then look to the full, cheap reds of Provence, or turn their eyes to a red Bordeaux. But there is a certain amount of logic in trading over to the vastly popular Italian Chianti, if you can get a good one, or to Barolo or Barbaresco. As we noted in Chapter IV, if you want a Chianti of any reliability, you usually have to trade up from the typical straw-covered *fiasco* to a bottle of the "Bordeaux shape," hopefully with the yellow cockerel seal on its neck of a Classico, and a name like Brolio or Serristori or Antinori.

Médoc. As we pointed out in Chapter II, the very popular name of Médoc is not a "Popular Name" in quite the sense we are using it here. While you might speak of a "Médoc" in discussing the category of wine you want to drink on a particular occasion, when it comes to the actual purchase you do not usually look for a bottle bearing that name, because the truly high-quality Médocs, the Médocs people are talking about when they say they want to drink a Médoc, come from the Haut-Médoc, where the better wines generally go to market under the higher appellation of a village or a vineyard (château). So to get a true "Médoc," that is, a wine of the Haut-Médoc, one automatically trades up to one of the village wines—Margaux, Pauillac, St.-Estèphe—or to one of the classed vineyards of the region (if you can remember their names).

As to finding substitutes for Médoc, here again, Bordeaux is different. In particular contrast to those of Burgundy, there is such a family quality to all the wines of the Bordeaux district that they are all to a considerable extent interchangeable. It is possible to trade over from the Médoc to one of the better vineyards of the (Bas-) Médoc to the north, to Graves to the south, to St.-Émilion and Pomerol to the west, and to the secondary areas in between. A St.-Émilion is by no means identical to a Médoc, but the contrast is not nearly as great as that, let us say, between a Chambertin of Burgundy and a Beaujolais.

So it is hardly necessary to trade out from Bordeaux, unless the wine list is very limited indeed. If you choose to trade out, in addition to the pleasant but undistinguished wines such as Bergerac (home of the legendary Cyrano) from the hinterlands of Bordeaux, you can find good light reds to the north on the Loire in such places as Chinon and Bourgueil, or south in the Rioja district of Spain, or east in Italy the light-bodied Bardolino or Valpolicella. But for Americans perhaps the most logical trade-out from Bordeaux is to California, where the Cabernet Sauvignon, the great grape of Bordeaux, produces the best red wine of California, ordinarily somewhat fuller than the typical red of Bordeaux, but with some of its characteristic elegance.

Experiment in blue. Those are the most widely employed alternatives to the most widely sought-after wines. But it is interesting to note that in trading up among the Popular Names you have put yourself in roughly the $5.00 to $10.00 price class, which overlaps the Pale Blue Chips, which begin at about $8.00. So it is a natural progression, over time, for the wine drinker to move from prime reliance on the Popular Names at any level to the greater range of experience available among wines of the Blue Chip class. It can be said that this marks the transition from an apprentice to a journeyman in wine.

But if this is a logical and natural step, it is also a complicated and forbidding one—and that, of course, is why the Popular Names remain popular. Even the names Montrachet or Chambertin sound expensive, and if they are hyphenated to some other name, as they certainly will be in their lower price range, one feels that familiar sense of insecurity in not knowing whether the hyphenation is to a vineyard or a village (and even if he knows that, not knowing whether the wine in question is overpriced). The problem among Bordeaux is similar: It is difficult to remember whether a given Médoc is a Second Growth or a Fourth, to keep clear the distinction between La Mission-Haut-Brion, Laville-Haut-Brion, and Latour-Haut-Brion, or to separate Château Haut-Bailly from Haut-Batailley.

If you are in a restaurant, all you can really do is bull ahead. If you want to ask a question, ask it. You can then either believe the answer or ignore it as seems appropriate. If you make a mistake, you will have learned something. If the results are too awful, you can order something else, with or without a price concession from the management, and charge the expense to education. The important thing is to begin drinking the great and fine wines of the greatest regions in order to learn what they offer and how to buy them.

Once again it can be seen that it is much easier to begin your study of complicated place names in the privacy of your home, with your wine

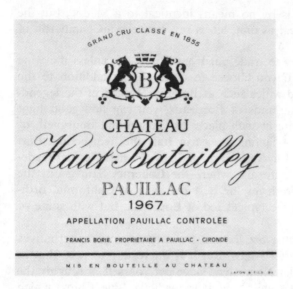

books at your elbow and your objective the purchase of a few bottles or a case from the local merchant, than in a restaurant when you are under the gun.

But you should have learned enough by now to know that ignorance in some degree is the normal human estate in these affairs, that the price of a wine gives at least some rough indication of its quality, and that a blunder in good grace is a better indicator of *savoir-faire* than clumsy posturing.

✽ XIV

THE PERILS AT THE POINT OF SALE

✽

That completes our survey of the normal alternatives the mind might weigh in searching for value among the various categories of wine. Each person would play the game differently, of course, depending on his preference and experience. But what should be clear by now is that under the impact of growing demand the game of wine is becoming very much more complicated. Strategies of trading up, trading down, trading over, or trading out call for more knowledge, experience, and thought than the blind buying of a bottle whose label says "Chablis" or "Pommard" or "Mouton" or "Chambertin"; and playing the market in the finer wines is by no means simple or free of risk.

It takes either a lifetime of learning or a photographic memory to keep straight the ranking of any but the finest vineyards of either Burgundy or Bordeaux. No one could possibly remember the names of all the good shippers, much less the exporters, importers, and wholesalers. There is less incentive to cheat and confuse on the Rhône or the Loire, but there are also more totally unfamiliar names—which may represent good value or rubbish. And in places like Châteauneuf-du-Pape on the Rhône and Muscadet on the Loire, where the wines are coming into strong demand, the confusion and deception have begun.

In the early 1950s, as the wine trade began moving into new territory, Frank Schoonmaker, the wine expert, conceived the idea of putting his seal of approval—"A Frank Schoonmaker Selection"—on a bottle of wine from a little-known region, thus offering the buyer his name and considerable skill as a guidepost. In the years since, a number of others have followed suit, although not all of them have Mr. Schoonmaker's qualifications.

There is no doubt that selections by a competent expert offer value to the ordinary buyer of wines that he would not be able to seek out for himself. But there is a law of diminishing returns in such matters. The number of people "discovering" wines has increased much faster than the number of wines to be discovered. Furthermore, just as in the case of a shipper's wine, when a certain level of demand has been created at a certain price, it must be met, in bad years as well as good. "A Joe Blow Selection" may be better than the general average in a bad year, but still may not be much. Furthermore, if Joe Blow's selections are being heavily promoted, and demand for wines bearing Mr. Blow's seal is expanding markedly, it is not always possible, even in good years, for him to maintain previous standards.

So recommendations are only as sound as the man who makes them, and in some cases not that.

Inevitably, in wines as in Wall Street, the successful employment of any buying strategy, however sound or even brilliant it may be in concept, comes in practice to depend on the man with whom you are dealing for the merchandise. If he is very good, he serves as your counselor and guide, sharing his experience, identifying pitfalls, giving you information you need to make your buying strategy work. If he is incompetent or dishonest, then you must either get rid of him or employ a counterstrategy to compensate for his defects.

Let us assume that you are seated at a table in the Restaurant Imaginaire on the East Side in New York. The place has three stars (out of a possible four) in the *New York Times Restaurant Guide*. You have eaten there twice before, once with considerable satisfaction, once on a Saturday night when the wait was somewhat long, the service rushed, and the food a bit cold. (But that perhaps reflected your poor judgment in going to a three-star place on Saturday night.)

The maître d', ruddy and Gallic, appeared to recognize you on this, your third go-round, and ushered you to a good table without seeming to expect a large bribe. Good sign. The decorations are a bit more fancy, a bit more "decorated," than you would see in a typical small, family-run French restaurant. This place has begun to make it, and it shows.

Success is reflected also in the price of the food, $6.50 to $10.00 for an entree. The wine list is handwritten, which is either a good sign or an affectation, you can't be sure. There is a handful of obligatory master-pieces to give the list tone, but the prices cluster in the $12.00 to $15.00 range. This is a modestly good sign. They haven't lost their heads.

The other couple with you are personal friends who have come to regard you as a great gourmet (in the country of the blind, the one-eyed man is king), so to live up to your reputation, after a mental check of the money in your wallet, you suggest that the group all order the food together and get an extra-good bottle of wine to go with it. The waiter rec-ommends the *gigot,* and after an uneasy moment you recall that *gigot* means our old friend, leg of lamb. The company agrees to lamb, and lamb calls for red Bordeaux. You look on the wine card under Bordeaux Rouge (red) and locate a Château Kirwan for $17.00.

The château name you recognize, or anyway you think you do. Is it a Second Growth indicating good value at the price, or is it just something unknown with a me-too tag that some importer is pushing? You reach for the memory. It doesn't come.

The waiter is young, red-haired, charming Breton accent, quite unsure of his English—obviously just got off the boat. And contrary to what most Americans think, young Breton peasants, however beguiling their accents, have ordinarily never tasted a fine wine, much less a great one. (They usually left Brittany because they couldn't find a job.)

You attempt without success to ask him if this is a Second Growth. (Your French is worse than his English.) Is it a good wine? "Oh yes, 'sgood, very good," he assures you, unconvincingly.

As gently as possible you ask if the maître d' could come over. Is this a Second Growth? you ask.

"No, sir," without hesitation, "Third Growth."

He is either bluffing beautifully or he knows his stuff.

Then a pause. He is neither volunteering nor concealing, just waiting for your next move.

We are having *gigot* tonight, you say, uttering the word now with cas-ual knowledgeability. We want something, uh, extra nice. If you were choosing, would you have the Kirwan?

Slight pause, head cocked, while he, too, makes a calculation of the money in your wallet and the purpose on your mind, and perhaps, instinc-tively, whether he could expect to see you again. "You want something *special?*" he probes. You nod. "For *me,* Château Petrus. This is *good* wine. You will like it. We do not even show it on the list."

He makes a slight, authoritative gesture as though to take the list from you. The matter is closed. He has decided. You hesitate fractionally, then

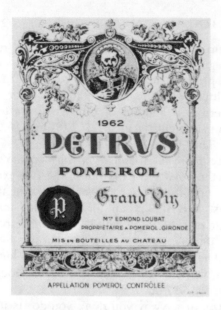

let him have the list. Fine, you say, nodding firmly, displaying your best command presence.

The vulgar question of price has not been discussed.

The wine is gorgeous, best you've had in a year. The meal is an enormous success. The check, including tip, comes to $112.50, $56.25 a couple, considerably more than you meant to spend, and if you bother to look closely the wine alone cost $32.00. So home you go, substantially poorer, a little tiddly, but proud and happy. Your reputation as a connoisseur has been greatly advanced. You have shown yourself a successful gambler, a judge of human character as well as wine, a Leader of Men.

Two basic principles apply to this situation.

First, wherever possible, *don't be a customer, be a client*. The ancient Greeks divided the world into two classes of people, Greeks and barbarians. Greeks were relatives and friends, to be cherished and protected. Barbarians were strangers, enemies, to be plundered and sometimes murdered. The men who deal in wine are artists in some ways, or close to it, but in other ways they are very definitely businessmen, or worse, in a tough and risky game, and there is never enough of the good stuff to go around.*

The maître d' at the Restaurant Imaginaire had seen you before; he

* A vivid interpretation of this rule was offered on a television talk show some years back. Craig Claiborne, the food editor and author, and Clifford Weihman, head of the Chevaliers du Tastevin (and author of the foreword of this book), were being interviewed. The interviewer asked, "What is the best restaurant in New York?" Claiborne responded with a knowledgeable analysis of several of the top ones. When it was Weihman's turn, he said simply, "The best restaurant in New York is the restaurant where you are the best known." The restaurant, in short, where they care enough about you to offer their best.

might hope to see you again. You asked an intelligent question, suggesting not only sophistication but prosperity, and flattered his own knowledge. So he shared with you his limited stock of excellent wine. Had you been a barbarian from Nebraska it would not have been so.

There is an apt analogy here to Wall Street. It is alleged, and not wholly without justice, that the brokerage fraternity gives the hottest tips and the best services to the huge "institutional" investors—mutual funds, insurance companies, pension funds—rather than to the small individual investor. And small wonder. From an institutional order, a broker can make $30,000 for no more work than it takes to make $30.00 on an order from little old you.

The second basic principle is this: *Deal as high as you can.* Real knowledge of wine is rare; it takes a lifetime to acquire; and once acquired commands a high price. The man who has knowledge is more likely to be the owner or manager, the proprietor, sommelier, or maître d', than simply a waiter or a clerk. And here, again, if you are a client and not simply a customer, you are in better position to command thoughtful service from the top.

Another useful principle is *specialize.* It is said that Prince Philip Mountbatten, when he inspects a ship of Her Majesty's Navy, will casually ask, "What is the storage capacity of your tanks?" The officer showing him around stutters a few times and says, "About 60,000 gallons." To which Prince Philip replies blandly, "Oh really. I had the impression it was 43,476." They check, and, of course, it is 43,476 to the gallon.

Nobody can know everything, but by learning a little and leading from strength, he can know enough, and give the impression of knowing more than he does. No ordinary drinker of wines can have expert knowledge of everything available. But he can learn quite a lot about one narrow segment, and by so doing be in position not only to move confidently in that segment but to command respect elsewhere.

Now for actual situations:

A great restaurant. For most of us the time to visit a truly great restaurant such as Twenty-one or Père Bis is on company business with an expense account, or else on vacation with a propensity to squander. A truly great restaurant will, by definition, have a truly great wine list (although frequently they will offer you a pony version, listing only a few wines, to save time and embarrassment. You can get them to bring the big one if you feel equal to it).

In a truly great restaurant you should expect your order to be taken by the sommelier—the keeper of the cellar. This will be a man who knows wines and knows how to match foods and wines. But take note. If you are a stranger, a barbarian, he may be inclined to push off some of his outdated stock on you, before it goes completely over the hill. He figures you won't know the difference, and he can't afford to let it spoil. He has to make a living just like you. By the same token, even if you are a dear friend and valued client, it is to his financial advantage to recommend the most expensive wine in the place to you, since, as indicated in Chapter XI, he works on a percentage of the gross.

If the sommelier is busy and it is a big place, you may be waited on by his young assistant. It is unlikely he knows as much as the boss. He is learning the business, but hopefully he will know enough to help you. If there is doubt, and it seems worth it, you can go over his head.

As to the merchandise, for anyone with even a modest knowledge of wines just glancing through the wine list of a great restaurant is an adventure. Here are the great vineyards, the ones you read about in books. Here are the finest vintages, including legendary ones out of the past. Here are the aristocrats among shippers and importers, the proudest, oldest names. Here, also, will be the lesser wines, chosen in the practical realization that not everyone can afford Romanée-Conti every night. These are likely to be well chosen and well kept, too (with the proviso noted above that even when they have guessed wrong they must still get rid of it, as they must when a wine is past its prime).

Perhaps more than anywhere else, in a great wine list you are offered "pure" exposure to the alternatives offered by the Spectrum of Possibility. To the extent that it can be done by careful buying and handling, the human risks and variables have been canceled out, and you can have anything the vineyard offers in its finest form. All it takes is money, and either the knowledge to choose correctly or the courage to ask for help.

The fine and the would-be fine. In a fine restaurant as opposed to a great one, or, alas, in one that merely wishes to pass itself off as fine, you lose the sense of exhilaration that comes from working at the very top, and you lose the simplicity, too. The names of the very greatest vineyards fade into those of the near great, the hyphenations, the look-alikes. The finest years are replaced by the next finest, the aristocrats of the trade by the bourgeois. If you deal with a man who calls himself sommelier, he will have the rigging: big brass key (purportedly the key to the cellar, although the actual door will have a cylinder lock), silver tastevin dangling around his neck—and in the pretentious places he will use it to taste the wine with clumsy ostentation. But he may or may not be a true member of his craft. More likely you will be dealing with the captain, the maître d', or the waiter himself, and how much he knows will be the question.

The problems of choosing wine from a list of this sort differ in no radical way from those of choosing it from the list in a truly great restaurant. But the human variables are wider, the uncertainties more numerous, the chance of a fine experience less, and the possibility of a mediocre one proportionately greater.

By the same token there is more of a challenge, a "game" quality, to the encounter. It is easier to get great wine in a great restaurant, if you can afford it, than it is to get really good wine in a restaurant one or two notches down the scale. If you do get first-rate wine there, you will have accomplished something.

If you are a *client,* obviously you will know what kind of place this is and what kind of people these are, and will have had some experience working with their list. If you are only a customer, you will not know, unless you have a recommendation from a friend you trust, or there is a clearly favorable review in the press that has not had time to grow stale or go to their heads.

If you are completely uncertain about the quality of the place and the merits of the list and there is no source of guidance at hand, then consciously or unconsciously you are likely to adopt a defensive strategy. You will scan the list for old friends you can count on: a Tavel from d'Aqueria, a Fumé from Ladoucette.

You might trade up to a classic or near classic, with a château bottling that means something, counting the extra cost as insurance. You could trade down a notch to a shipper's wine (particularly if you know the shipper), which if never great is not likely to prove a total disappointment. Or you might trade out to California, to a label representing an adequate wine if not a great one.

There is a tendency among these restaurants also to adopt the "pony" list. This can be a great convenience. It can also be a means of pushing unheard-of, mediocre wines on which the management takes a gigantic markup. There is a restaurant in a suburb near New York, carrying four stars, which in addition to the most arrogant rudeness on Saturday night (at least to barbarians) uses a pony list to palm off truly third-rate merchandise.

The murky mid-zone. As we have tried to make clear, the geographic mid-zone is the source of most of the greatest wines. The economic mid-zone of restaurants is not. Here you slip from hyphenated vineyards and

village wines to the regionals, the shipper's wines, and the châteaux you never heard of from regions you don't respect. Here the odds are quite good that the help will be almost totally incompetent—mumbling the red-wine-with-red-meat rule—although chances of actual thievery are less: the stakes aren't high enough and they are not sophisticated enough to know how.

Here in the restaurant mid-zone there is a widely held view that selling wine is unprofitable and should be discouraged. The money lies in hard liquor, so this line of reasoning goes, and if they bring you wine, you will not only order less hard liquor, but will sit around a long time, sipping and talking, using up valuable table space.

The strategy in these places is to bring you your first cocktail as soon as possible after you sit down, then try to get you to order a second and maybe even a third. Then, finally, the food is brought on and hopefully you will be too potted to do anything but gobble it up and leave.

Obviously, in a restaurant where they really don't want to bring you wine at all they are not going to take much interest in what is on the list, and they will mark the prices up high enough to discourage buying. It is in these places that the markup runs upward of 300 per cent.

Fortunately, not all restaurateurs of the mid-zone feel this way. Every once in a while you come across a restaurant, often a small one, as a rule where the owner himself is the chef or maître d', where the proprietor knows wine, loves wine, has chosen and tasted every entry on his list, and is as proud of them as if they were his children. This will often be a French restaurant, or an Italian place of quiet success where the proprietor has gone beyond the obligatory Chiantis and Soaves.

The handling of most wine lists in the mid-zone presents relatively little challenge. If the list is small and good, you can hardly go wrong. If it reflects a thoroughgoing lack of interest in wine or desire to sell it, then if anything on it represents value for the price, it will largely be an accident.

Here, again, the general rule is to go for the names you know, unless you have reason and guidance to trust the others.

There is currently a growing tendency among restaurants at all but the highest levels to sell "carafe" wines. A carafe for these purposes is either a pitcher or a flask or just an empty bottle into which the wine is poured from a larger container, usually a gallon jug. These are likely to be California wines or modest French ones, and may represent good value, particularly since the people with you may be so charmed by drinking wine from an unlabeled carafe they won't know or care whether the wine has a fancy name.

There is also a trend in some restaurants that are quite sophisticated in wine, including even some fine ones in Paris, to offer what might be called "house brands." As in the case of a shipper's wine or a "Frank Schoonmaker Selection," or the house brand of gin or scotch in your local liquor store, the management finds an unnoticed product of more than usual merit, makes a purchase on favorable terms, and with no advertising expense to cover is able to offer the customer good value at a thoroughly competitive price. The customer, meanwhile, is often following no landmark other than his confidence in the management.

A note is also in order about wine-by-the-glass, usually ordered when you are eating alone, or if only one person at the table wants wine (or if *she* orders fillet of sole and *he* orders spaghetti with marinara sauce). Except occasionally in a particularly conscientious French or Italian restaurant, wine sold by the glass invariably comes from a gallon jug of California wine kept under the bar. (If the wine *is* imported, that is a very good sign, and you should probably go back to that place.)

Sometimes, in an eminently third-rate restaurant, the quality of wine served by the glass can be a real shocker, the product of dumping offbrand merchandise at bargain prices by some shoddy wholesaler. But usually it is pretty good, either the "popular priced" California wines like Gallo or Roma or Petri, or, if you are lucky, the "Mountain Red," "Mountain White," or "Mountain Rosé" of Inglenook or Louis Martini.

The profit on bulk wine sold by the glass or carafe is enormous, and smart restaurant operators will sometimes push wine-by-the-glass or carafe over wine in bottles. A gallon of California wine of reasonable quality will cost the restaurant around $4.00. There are perhaps thirty glasses of wine to a gallon. At $.75 a glass, that would yield a gross of $22.50, and a net of $18.50, or more than 400 per cent. There are ten three-glass carafes to a gallon. At $1.50 each this would yield a gross of $15.00 a gallon and a net of $11.00, or close to 300 per cent.

The shipper's lists. At many restaurants at the lower levels of eating and drinking, and sometimes even in restaurants at fairly high levels, you

will notice a curious sparseness to the list, a certain monotony. It is almost invariably printed on just two facing pages; the pages are usually not very large. The type face and layout in one restaurant will bear a curious resemblance to the type face and layout of similar lists in other restaurants, some of them hundreds of miles away. The covers may even be identical. The categories of wine will be neatly and symmetrically presented, Red Bordeaux, Red Burgundy, etc., and there will be only two or three entries, each at a different price level, under each category. All the Bordeaux are usually from one shipper, all the Burgundies from the same one, or one other, all the California or New York wines from a single producer. The names are usually well known but not of top quality.

This is a shipper's list, or, more precisely, a wholesaler's list. One particular wholesaler has persuaded the restaurateur or his chef or head waiter, perhaps for a price concession or as a matter of convenience (or maybe a little bribe), to let him stock and maintain the cellar. The shipper selects the wines and prints the list, and the list includes wines from those suppliers with whom he in turn has been able to make favorable deals.

There is nothing scandalous about such a list and nothing exciting. It offers no chance to ascend to the highest levels of drinking, or even to come upon a satisfying little surprise. But neither, by the same token, is there much risk of descending to the lower levels of dreadfulness. This list is ultimately predictable.

Being such, it takes the sport out of the game. It robs you of the chance to test your skill. But the wine you choose from such a list might well be the wine a prudent man would have chosen in any case from a longer list in the murky mid-zone, given the difficulty of appraising the other merchandise.

The bottom fringe. Once or twice a year, depending on how you live and whether you travel, you will wander into a restaurant where you are in real trouble, winewise at least. The list is very possibly a shipper's list. The wines might be of fairly good quality, on paper, anyway. But the list is smudged, dog-eared, and fly-specked—possibly only an annex to the menu itself. The premises are seedy. The waitress or whatever is not notable for style or cleanliness. If it is a small motel in the Rocky Mountains, your waiter may also be the chef, room clerk, janitor, and owner of the joint.

You have stumbled into a place that got talked into putting in a wine cellar bigger than they needed—if they needed one at all—a long time ago, possibly when it was just opened and the Good Luck ribbons were still on the baskets of flowers. Or it is an establishment that did well once but now is headed down the hill. In any case, relatively few people order wine, so the stock they have does not move, and your problem is to get something drinkable and not spoiled.

The simplest thing is to order beer. Or you could order Champagne and get the reputation of a big spender. Champagne has enough alcohol in it to be harder to spoil than most still wines, and is usually handled with a certain reverence even in the worst places. Also, they sell enough Champagne from time to time to turn the stock—at New Year's, or when a truck driver has a wedding anniversary. But if you are simply dying for a bottle of still wine, the least risky thing to do is to *reverse your normal buying strategy*. Instead of betting *against* the crowd, bet *with* them. You try to figure out, either by hunch or by asking, what is the biggest seller they have (if they have one). The assumption is that if the regular customers keep ordering a wine, it can't be too bad, and if the stock keeps moving, it is the least likely to be spoiled.

The rule "When in doubt, Beaujolais" *could* be valid here, provided the available Beaujolais is respectable enough to have been drinkable when it was bottled. Ordering a big-volume, hard-to-spoil California wine might be the best thing you could do, or the least bad. But perhaps the smartest thing would be just to order an extra martini, followed by a beer.

The general principle that applies here has application in other places, too. In any establishment it is a good idea to ask yourself what sort of place this is and then do your choosing somewhere *in the general range* of what they do the most of, on the assumption that that is what they understand and handle the best. (In other words, the place to look for value is off the beaten path, but not too far off—as they say on Wall Street, "Don't fight the market.") Even in the case of the Restaurant Imaginaire, the special wine the maître d' offered was not on the wine list, but it clearly was tuned to the palates and purse of his best and most regular customers. In run-of-the-mill restaurants the general rule is that people are likely to spend for their wine about the price of a single meal. If the average meal in a restaurant costs around six dollars, people will generally spend about six dollars for the bottle of wine to go with it.

That completes our survey of the problems of buying wine in a restaurant, which are more difficult than those of buying wine in a store. But it is by no means easy to get good value in wines from a store, even from your friendly local merchant. It could be said *particularly* from the friendly local merchant.

What the Vintners Sell . . .

Omar Khayyám, the mathematician-poet of eleventh-century Persia, like scores of poets before and after him, wrote verses in praise of wine. In one of his quatrains Khayyám inquired:

> I wonder often what the vintners buy
> One half so precious as the stuff they sell.

We are not concerned here to speculate whether our wine merchant finances a Rolls-Royce or a Romanée-Conti or a tempting young mistress

with the profits from his trade. Our interest is solely to persuade him to
part with some of his reasonably precious stuff for a not wholly unrea-
sonable price.

The range of options among wine stores is approximately equivalent
to that among restaurants.

The great merchants. It is not possible to say with certainty who is a
"great" merchant and who is not. Some are merely big. Others have great
names they no longer live up to. Others are doing a great job but have not
yet won the reputation they deserve. Some do a magnificent job for the
man for whom cost is no factor, but no better than average, if that, for the
man who has to worry about mortgages, grocery bills, and the like.

Among the retailers at the forefront of the American wine trade
today, names that come immediately to mind include Sherry-Lehmann in
New York, the Berenson Liquor Mart in Boston, Burka's in Washington,
D.C., Green's Wines and Spirits in Atlanta, the Armanetti chain in Chicago, Martin's Wine Cellars in New Orleans, Harry Hoffman Liquors in
Denver, John Walker in San Francisco, and the wine departments of Jur-
gensen's grocery chain in southern California.

When you walk into a great wine store, you are walking into a wonderland of wine. If labels mean anything to you, the feast for the eye alone
is worth the trip. As in the wine list of a great restaurant, on the racks
of a great merchant the classics of the world are spread before your gaze.
Except that here you are looking at the *actual* labels and bottles, the veritable substance. If they offer a jereboam of Lafite '47, there it is in
awesome actuality, like a priceless Soong Dynasty bronze.

If you went there to buy a bottle of innocent Beaujolais, you can simply pay up and leave, knowing the price you paid is probably fair, and the
odds that the merchandise is sound about as good as you can get—assuming, of course, you paid an adequate price in the first place. (The pattern
of demand being what it is, even a very, very great merchant must offer the
lower-priced items, and, indeed, promote them.) If you want to do more
than buy a Beaujolais, you could easily spend an hour browsing, wondering, weighing. It is very educational to browse alone, lovingly studying the
bottles. But if you have a serious purchase to make for a special occasion,
unless you have done your homework very thoroughly you can use a
guide. Clerks at Great Stores may or may not be Great Clerks, the help situation being what it is, but they should certainly be a cut above average,
and if you get to know one, and trust him, you can become his client.

Gilbert Cross, one of the authors of this book, once went into Sherry-
Lehmann to buy a bottle of the best Montrachet they had on display
(about $13.00 at the time, upward of $25.00 today) to sample it as part of
the research for this book. He was planning to drink it with a plain roast
duck. As it turned out, the clerk who waited on him was William Leedom,
who himself has written a book about wine, and a good one (*The Vintage*

Wine Book). When Leedom heard that a bottle of glorious Le Montrachet '61 was to be drunk with a *plain roast duck,* his face assumed a look of gentle anguish, and he tactfully sought to persuade Cross to take a lesser (and cheaper) bottle. Mr. Leedom could not have known, of course, that this bottle was to be drunk not simply in pursuit of pleasure but in the quest for Truth.

Leedom no longer works for Sherry-Lehmann. If he did, it would obviously be a great advantage to become his client and receive not only value but enlightenment. But even at a great store not every clerk is a William Leedom, and not every transaction is as masterfully handled as that one. Another time, Cross went into another of the Great Stores—it might as well remain nameless—to buy a bottle of Beaulieu Vineyard Private Reserve from California (then about $3.00, now about $6.50). The bottle was there, but it was hard to find, neglected on a back shelf, sitting on its bottom rather than lying on its side as it should have been. When the bottle was opened, it proved to be spoiled.

California wines, especially the more unusual ones, were not the main thing they dealt with in a Great Store in those days, not the main thing they cared about. Once again, buy where the volume is, don't fight the market. And recognize that in the wine market as in the stock market nothing is for sure.

Becoming to any extent the regular customer of one of the great wine merchants, or merely asking to have your name put on his mailing list, entitles you to the enormous privilege of receiving and fondling his catalogue.

To someone who has not acquired the taste for it, the fascination of a wine catalogue is a little difficult to explain.* It has some of the reminiscent charm that a list of old and well-remembered telephone numbers would have for a bachelor, along with the irresistible fascination of a list

* The wine catalogue of John Walker & Co. of San Francisco is reproduced in the Appendix of this book.

of mysterious new ones. It has the magnetism that today's financial page has for a heavily committed investor, along with the nostalgia of one of twenty years ago, recalling ventures past. A behaviorist psychologist would probably say that just reading the name of a well-loved wine in a catalogue provides in rudimentary degree the same sensation that drinking it would —the taste buds begin to tremble slightly, like those of one of Dr. Pavlov's dogs.

As the eye runs down the lists of vineyards and vintages, shippers and prices, the mind does quiet little calisthenics, not aggressively and decisively as when the actual purchase is at hand, but gently, musingly, just sort of staying in practice and savoring the game.

For those of a literary inclination there is pleasure, too, in reading the endless changes that can be rung on a relatively limited number of modifiers. One marvels at the nuances that permit a not wholly dishonest use of some of the same superlatives to describe a $20.00 wine and a $2.00 one.

Of course, the catalogues have a practical purpose, too. You can do a better job of shopping and comparing at home at night than you can when you are shifting from one foot to the other in the store and wasting the time of the clerk. You don't have to look at a bottle to buy it thoughtfully. If it happens, as it very often can, that your neighborhood does not boast an excellent or even an adequate wine merchant, you can have the wine shipped to you by one of the great merchants. And for all the charming art work and graceful prose, you will find the great merchant ruggedly competitive in price with your local liquor store—that is how he grew. And there is usually a further 10 per cent discount when you buy by the case.

We also noted earlier that there are significant price differentials between good merchants, particularly among the finer wines. So you can use the catalogues not only to play the great merchant off against his local competitor—with the odds heavily favoring the great merchant—but also to play one merchant off against another, with the odds decisively favoring you. In addition, the great merchants hold sales two or three times a year, during slack periods, with further savings of 10 to 30 per cent.

Thus, if a large merchant is undercutting your neighborhood dealer in price by a significant margin, if you get a further savings buying by the case, and a still further savings during a sale, either you will be getting the same wine for up to 50 per cent less, or, more likely, you will drink oftener and better for not much more money.

The mail-order houses. The problem of buying good wine locally being what it is, particularly in the Great American Heartland, some wholesalers have developed a mail-order service independent of any retail outlet. Thus, if a Caterpillar tractor executive of Peoria, Illinois, has developed a taste for fine wines while traveling on the company expense account in New York or San Francisco or Paris, but finds he cannot get those wines when he returns to Peoria, he gets in touch with one of the mail-order wholesalers and thereafter buys his wine from their catalogue. Doctors, lawyers, and businessmen from all over the Midwest have used mail-order dealers to provide them with acceptable wine.

The big-volume stores. There is no clear-cut dividing line between the handful of merchants who unquestionably deserve the title "great," and the much larger number of stores that do a high-volume business and offer good merchandise. Sometimes it is just a matter of antiquity: the Great Merchant got there first. Sometimes it is a question of market slot: the Great Merchants stress the premium merchandise. Some of the others put main emphasis on medium-priced lines.

The big-volume stores fall into two categories: first are the stores built around one man who knows and cares about wines and knows how to sell, and has parlayed these elements into a large and profitable business. These operations nearly always began as an ordinary neighborhood liquor store, and in a surprising number of cases developed near a college or university. Even though professors are underpaid and students broke, the existence in this volume of reasonably sophisticated taste and cosmopolitan interest has been enough to justify the effort to stock and sell decent wine. Once a reputation in wines begins to grow, business comes in from considerable distances.

Irving Padnos of Chicago built his excellent store and impressive business on this basis. The early core of his wine trade came from the University of Chicago. Nearly every college town or suburb of any size boasts a wine merchant, and usually a prosperous one, of superior quality.

A large and flourishing wine department can be operated very profitably in conjunction with a discount liquor department: each operation pulls in volume to feed the other. Some of the wine-liquor dealers in California operate on a scale and in a style that would put a major supermarket to shame.

The second category of big-volume store is the wine shop associated with a department store, where department store methods of buying and merchandising have been systematically applied to wine. The growth of these operations has been more planned and less Topsy-like than that of the independent big-volume stores, but they offer the same advantages, which in turn are substantially the advantages offered by the Great Merchants: a large and varied inventory handled by people who, hopefully, know what they are doing, and prices and promotional methods designed to draw business away from neighborhood stores.

The style of operation varies from store to store among the big-volume operators. Some resort to highly intensive promotional methods. In some cases a store such as Astor Wines and Spirits in New York City will offer the average, ordinary buyer of wine a greater choice of merchandise in his price range than one of the Great Merchants will. By the same

token, here, too, a large proportion of the stock any big-volume merchant carries must meet the public demand for a wine in the two-dollar range. The cheap Sicilian and Portuguese and Chilean wines sitting in baskets on the floors of these places are just as bad here as anywhere else. The difference is that the clerk is more likely to tell you so, if he is any good, particularly if you have made yourself his client. And he can offer you fine and great wines if you want them.

Some of these stores publish catalogues. Others buy large display ads in the newspapers, offering dozens of wines, which serve the same purpose.

Often the big-volume operators will develop their own house brands of wine (and whiskey, too) which offer good value at the price. One of the most ambitious programs of house branding is conducted by the wine department of Macy's department store in New York. There, virtually every wine listed on our Spectrum of Possibility is offered under the Macy's house label, and usually offer excellent value at their various price levels. In this case, Macy's has become its own shipper and wholesaler as well as a major merchant, and it seems likely that other very large operators will follow this trend.

The neighborhood store. Once again, there is no sharp dividing line between your neighborhood liquor store and one of the big-volume merchants; as we have noted, if a neighborhood store does a good job, he fairly rapidly becomes a big-volume operator.

But in general it can be said that your friendly local liquor store is no more likely to sell you a decent bottle of wine than your friendly local hash-house is. Probably less so, since the point-of-sale and point-of-drinking coincide in a restaurant, so the management is more likely to know more about the taste of its clientele.

The fact is that the average local liquor store owner, like the proprietor of the average local restaurant, too often does not care very much about wine and knows less. Wine is an afterthought. He makes his money on the hard liquor. In recent years, however, it has been the fashion for the wholesaler's representative to persuade the owner of a local liquor store that it will tone up the joint, and make more money, too, if he puts in a big wine display. And he means a *big* display. Almost literally, he sells it by the yard. He explains to the merchant that if he displays a lot of wine, particularly in fancy, sloping racks with expensive labels showing, it will make people think he knows a lot about the subject, so they will be more likely to buy.

The salesman explains that since wine is not fair-traded the markup can be as high as he wants it. However, since as we noted a heavy proportion of the general demand for wine is in the below-four-dollars range, if he wants a high markup he must put in thoroughly shoddy merchandise— off brands of easy names.

Here, again, the client-rule applies. It does not take many visits, many purchases, many conversations, to learn whether a merchant knows what he is doing. If you wander into a strange store, you can test him with a few questions. Sometimes he will be refreshingly candid and tell you he doesn't know a damn thing about wine; more often pride and a desire to appear professional will impel him to bluff it stubbornly. So you had better be sure you know the answers before you ask the questions.

Don't ask him "What shall I have with the lamb chops?" He's likely not only to make a recommendation but to go over and get a bottle of something-or-other and try to sell it to you on the spot. Ask him some fairly obvious questions about the merchandise itself, and see what he does with them: Is Liebfraumilch good wine? How do I know I can trust this Chablis? What do you think of so-and-so (a wholesaler you know to be shoddy)? What's the difference between Pouilly-Fuissé and Pouilly-Fumé?

If he gives you good answers, then swing over hard and ask some toughies, so he will respect you and give you good service. Is this a Third Growth? Did you hear about the new appellation they have down in Pouilly-Fuissé? Do you carry Barolo? Do you have any rosé from that place next door to Tavel—you know, what's-its-name?

But even without a talk with the clerk or the owner, a look around will tell you a great deal. Do you see old friends among the bottles—the growers and shippers you know to be sound? Or do you see $1.86 specials in the big wicker baskets, the off-beat shipper, the wholesalers you know to be junk dealers?

Before long you can quickly detect the basic marketing strategy of a store. Some stores stress the tried-and-true "brand names" of the more reliable (and expensive) shippers, and train their clientele to look for that. Others, by contrast, show imagination and boldness in trading out to unknown places, depending on the client's trust in them to move the merchandise. Others, in more affluent sections, will trade judiciously up among the Popular Names to the superior vineyards and villages, and trade down from the immortals into the Pale Blue Chips, depending, once again, on the client's faith in them to sell the goods.

If there is any doubt about the quality of the place, here again you must switch to a rigorously defensive strategy. You could trade down to one of the popular-priced wines from one of the well-known producers of California—Gallo, Roma, Almadén. A bottle of Gallo Paisano or Almadén Mountain Red will give you a happier experience than a fake Pommard— and these cheaper California wines are so filtered and stabilized it takes real talent to ruin them. Or you can gamble and trade up a bit, to the higher-priced Chablis or Pommard or Beaujolais the salesman told him he ought to stock, too. But don't go up too far. If you buy a fine label in a wretched store, the chances are formidable that the bottle has been there longest of all and the wine has spoiled.

It is because of the risks and inadequacies of dealing at the local level that the fine merchants and mail-order houses have developed such a tremendous business. But all is not lost in the neighborhoods. Some percentage of the local dealers today—perhaps 5, perhaps 15 (but certainly not as much as 30 per cent)—range from the merely adequate to the truly excellent.

The reason is always the same: The proprietor knows about wines and cares about wines and takes the trouble to do his job right. Very often the proprietor of a store that does a good job of wines comes from some background—Italian, Hungarian, Greek, Jewish, or good old American exbootlegger—in which he was exposed early enough and thoroughly enough to wine not to fear it and to be able to work with it.

But even with an excellent neighborhood store it is essential to get to the boss whenever you can. The help situation everywhere is desperate. The boss can advise you what to have with your dinner tonight, and sometimes can tell stories from firsthand acquaintance about the French aristocrat who grew the wine he is about to sell you—and he may offer you a famous bottle from a small stock in the back room that he recently purchased from the estate of a rich man. His clerk might be able to do little more than take your money.

If you live in one place for a long time, you come to rely on one or two outlets for your wine. But if you move to a new place, or travel, it can be an adventure and an education to visit a number of stores and compare them. You can get ideas of new wines to try, and develop a keen sense for the ebb and flow of the market place as it responds to the steadily rising demand for good wine.*

---

* See Appendix for specific advice on how to choose a wine merchant.

THE VIEW FROM THE CELLAR

❧

Those, then, are the principal sources of wine at the point-of-sale, their major characteristics, and some of the tactics that can help you in dealing with them. Every case differs, obviously, and nothing guarantees success in every instance, although a growing skill as a "trader" is both helpful and fun.

But, to reiterate one basic generalization: The effort involved, the risk involved, the knowledge required to buy a *single* bottle, hardly makes the game worth the cork. From a good source, at least in a restaurant, the price even of reasonable assurance of quality is often $10.00 or $15.00. The price of a genuinely delightful experience can be much, much more.

So anyone who is serious about enjoying wine of superior quality at reasonably frequent intervals is sooner or later forced to the conclusion that the "overhead" of study and effort required to purchase wisely on a current basis is inordinate, and the risks too great. It makes more sense to accumulate an inventory of sufficient size to justify the time and effort required to maintain it. On Wall Street, buying for inventory and drawing from it is called "making a market." In wines they call it starting a cellar.

To own a wine cellar does not necessarily mean that you must phys-ically possess a musty hole in the ground. Your "cellar" can be a closet or a cabinet or a trunk. It can mean space in a storeroom or warehouse loaned or rented to you by your merchant. (The charge is usually about twenty-five cents per bottle per year.) It will more than likely start with a few bottles resting in a rack on the sideboard of your dining room. The important point is that you are no longer buying hastily, under pressure, for immediate consumption. You are buying at leisure, with an eye to the future, in sufficient volume to justify a little extra thought and effort, shopping for bargains and price fluctuations. If your start is very small, so much the better. There will be less risk of expensive mistakes. As the value and pleasure of keeping a cellar grow on you, the odds are your cellar will grow, too.

If you have your own cellar and buy shrewdly over time, a wine that might cost you $30.00 to $50.00 in a restaurant or $15.00 to $30.00 at retail might cost only $6.00 to $10.00. Or, if you have bought wisely a few years earlier and put the wine away, you might have one of the lesser classifications, barely distinguishable from a great one, for $3.00 or $4.00 a bottle.

If there is no decent merchant in your neighborhood or your town, you can assure yourself a steady supply of wines as good as you want them, with the advantages of economy, variety, and quality that come from dealing with a great merchant by mail. You can get the catalogues of three or four merchants and "arbitrage" the difference between their lists. You can club together with friends to split a volume order or speculate on a few cases of a promising vintage on the Bordeaux market.

If you are working with a cellar, it will tend almost automatically to sharpen your knowledge of the relatively limited group of wines that fit your taste and market slot, and thus increase your competence in buying for every occasion. At the same time you will have the basis for a program of steadily widening your knowledge, occasionally ordering a mixed case of wines you have never tried before—obscure wines from developing districts. If you spot a winner, you can rush back—and you should waste no time—and order more before it is gone. (But don't tell the merchant how much you like it. If you do, he may raise the price.)

If you have a cellar of whatever size, you are far more a client to any merchant than you were before, and not just any client, but a respected client, almost a colleague. He will give you time and thought. He will look for bargains for you.

If you keep a cellar you can, if you choose, maintain a cellar book, showing what you bought and when, when it was opened, and how it turned out. This way you can trace a wine as it develops and have a better chance to catch it in its prime. If you keep good records, your experience will count for more, and your knowledge of vineyards and vintages will leap ahead.

In tasting and comparing the contents of your cellar your palate will also leap ahead in discernment, and you will find your taste in wines moving up the scale. And with a cellar available you will have more cause to entertain at home and to explore and learn about the food as well as the wine side of *la haute cuisine*.

A cellar in whatever form should be cool, ideally 45° to 60°. If the cellar temperature is more than 70°, the wines will mature more rapidly.

But even at this temperature wines can be kept without hazard for several years; a higher temperature can even be an advantage in bringing an immature wine to its prime. In a closet or actual cellar, white wines, which age faster, are usually kept at the bottom, where it is cooler, red wines above.

The temperature should also be relatively constant. Frequent temperature changes will ruin wine. The cellar should be dry, dark, and preferably not subject to jarring every time the elevator door closes or somebody runs up the stairs. However, absolute darkness is not mandatory. The light that is certain to ruin wine is direct sunlight. The amount of light that reaches a corner of your living or dining room would do no harm.

As to fittings, every department store, hardware store, or specialty cookware store today offers wine racks of metal or wood for sale. Wooden wine cases, if you can find them, can also be stacked to make a rack. If you are handy, adequate wooden racks are not hard to build. Frank Prial, the wine columnist for the New York *Times,* reported in mid-1975 that the suburban-farm catalogue of Sears, Roebuck, listed at around $25 a wrought-iron wine rack, holding seventy-five bottles, which might have sold for $75 to $100 in a department store.

If money is no object and space is available you could purchase a ready-made vibration-free, insulated wine cellar, with controlled temperature and humidity, holding hundreds of bottles, for up to $5,000. A cheaper approach is to find an old refrigerator and put your good wines in there. It will hold about fifty bottles at a temperature, at a low setting, of around 55°. A local appliance store might be able to give you the name of a family that has just bought a new refrigerator and would be glad to give you the old one if you are willing to haul it away.

In the Appendix are descriptions by their owners of the wine cellars and wine tastes of New York *Times* Food Editor Craig Claiborne, and of Paul Child and his wife, Julia Child, of "French Chef" fame.

Not many people will ever command the capital and expertise (and the space) to support one of the veritable museums of wine that have marked the connoisseur in eras past. But it does not take many bottles, resting, waiting, watched, and loved, in a closet or on a shelf, before you become a full-fledged member of the club, privileged to enjoy "that most beguiling of the minor pleasures," a worthy player of the game of wine.

Appendix

THE SPECTRUM OF POSSIBILITY
(For Dry Table Wines)

Category of Wine

		See Page
Rosé	TAVEL (Rhône)	96
	ANJOU (Loire)	91
	GRENACHE ROSÉ	
	(California)	141
	CALIFORNIA ROSÉ	135
Light-bodied Red	BARDOLINO (Italy)	120
	VALPOLICELLA (Italy)	120
	HAUT-MÉDOC (Bordeaux)*	28, 41
	RED GRAVES (Bordeaux)	31
	CALIFORNIA "CLARET"	134
	PINOT NOIR (California)	141
	ZINFANDEL (California)	141
Fuller-bodied Red	ST.-ÉMILION (Bordeaux)	34
	POMMARD (Burgundy)	71
	BEAUJOLAIS (Burgundy)	76
	CÔTE DE NUITS	
	(Burgundy)*	65, 78
	CHIANTI (Italy)	114
	CÔTES DU RHÔNE (Rhône)	97
	CHÂTEAUNEUF-DU-PAPE	
	(Rhône)	96
	RED HERMITAGE (Rhône)	94
	CÔTE RÔTIE (Rhône)	94
	CABERNET SAUVIGNON	
	(California)	141
	CALIFORNIA "BURGUNDY"	134
	CALIFORNIA "CHIANTI"	134

On the following pages are listed separately the entries on the Spectrum of Possibility from each of the seven major wine districts discussed in this book.

* Oversimplification: Some wines of the Haut-Médoc are full-bodied; some wines of the Côte de Nuits are light-bodied. See discussion of Burgundy versus Bordeaux on pages 53–55 in text; see comparative table on page 85.
NOTE: Classifying California generic wines by character is at best an approximate matter, since the character of a California "Chablis" or a "Rhine" or a "Burgundy" can vary greatly according to the producer, and sometimes according to the batch from which the wine was bottled.

THE SPECTRUM FOR BORDEAUX

	Basic Spectrum	Secondary Listings
Fuller-bodied White	—	White Graves
Light-bodied Red	HAUT-MÉDOC* RED GRAVES	(Bas-) Médoc
Fuller-bodied Red	ST.-ÉMILION	Pomerol
(Sweet Dessert Wines) †	SAUTERNES	Barsac Cérons

See pp. 25–36 for description of the Bordeaux wines. See pp. 41–51 for detailed discussion of the wines of the Haut-Médoc.

THE SPECTRUM FOR BURGUNDY

	Basic Spectrum	Secondary Listings
Light and Delicate White	CHABLIS POUILLY-FUISSÉ	—
Fuller-bodied White	MEURSAULT MONTRACHET	White Corton
Light-bodied Red	—	—
Fuller-bodied Red	POMMARD BEAUJOLAIS CÔTE DE NUITS*	Volnay Côte de Beaune Red Corton

See pp. 62–78 for description of the wines of Burgundy. See pp. 78–87 for detailed discussion of the Côte de Nuits.

In the comparison of the red wines of Burgundy with those of Bordeaux on pages 53–55 we indicated that while the wines of Bordeaux are on average lighter than those of Burgundy, some relatively light Burgundies are in fact lighter than some of the fuller Bordeaux. The table on the next page shows the relative fullness of the finest wines of the Haut-Médoc of Bordeaux and those of the Côte de Nuits of Burgundy. In the scale of fullness, big, "manly" Chambertin of Burgundy is arbitrarily rated 100 and light, delicate Margaux of Bordeaux at 25, and the greatest of all, Lafite and Romanée, side by side at the golden mean of 50.

---

* Oversimplification: Not all the wines of the Haut-Médoc are light-bodied; not all the wines of the Côte de Nuits are full-bodied. See table on next page.

† The sweet dessert wines are not actually a part of the Basic Spectrum, but are essential to any listing of the major wines of Bordeaux.

	Bordeaux (HAUT-MÉDOC)		*Burgundy* (CÔTE DE NUITS)	
			Chambertin	100
Very Full				
			Vougeot	85
	St.-Estèphe	60	Échézeaux	60
Medium Full	LAFITE	50	ROMANÉE	50
	Mouton	45		
	Latour	40	Bonnes Mares	40
			Musigny	35
Light				
	Margaux	25		

THE SPECTRUM FOR THE LOIRE

	Basic Spectrum	*Secondary Listings*
Light and Delicate White	MUSCADET SANCERRE POUILLY-FUMÉ	—
Fuller-bodied White	VOUVRAY*	Saumur*
Rosé	ANJOU	—
Light-bodied Red	—	Bourgueil Chinon

See pp. 89–93 for description of the wines of the Loire.

THE SPECTRUM FOR THE RHÔNE

	Basic Spectrum	*Secondary Listings*
Fuller-bodied White	—	White Hermitage
Rosé	TAVEL	Lirac
Fuller-bodied Red	CÔTES DU RHÔNE CHÂTEAUNEUF-DU-PAPE RED HERMITAGE CÔTE RÔTIE	—

See pp. 93–97 for description of the wines of the Rhone.

* Also sparkling.

THE SPECTRUM FOR THE RHINE BASIN

	Basic Spectrum	*Secondary Listings*
Light and Delicate White (Dry)	MOSELLE	—
Fuller-bodied White (Dry)	RHINE ALSACE	Frankenweins
(Sweet Dessert Wines)*	MOSELLE RHINE ALSACE	—

See pp. 97–106 for descripton of the wines of the Rhine Basin.

THE SPECTRUM FOR ITALY

	Basic Spectrum	*Secondary Listings*
Light and Delicate White	SOAVE VERDICCHIO	—
Fuller-bodied White	ORVIETO	Frascati Lacrima Christi
Light-bodied Red	BARDOLINO VALPOLICELLA	Lambrusco
Fuller-bodied Red	CHIANTI	Barbera Barbaresco Barolo

See pp. 114–122 for description of the wines of Italy.

THE SPECTRUM FOR CALIFORNIA

	Standard Wines	*Varietal Wines*
Light and Delicate White	"MOSELLE" "CHABLIS"	JOHANNISBERG or WHITE RIESLING
Fuller-bodied White	"RHINE WINE" "DRY SAUTERNE"	PINOT CHARDONNAY
Rosé	ROSÉ	GRENACHE ROSÉ
Light-bodied Red	"CLARET"	PINOT NOIR ZINFANDEL
Fuller-bodied Red	"BURGUNDY" "CHIANTI"	CABERNET SAUVIGNON

See pp. 134–136 for description of the standard wines of California.
See pp. 140–143 for description of the varietal wines.

* The sweet dessert wines are not actually a part of the Basic Spectrum, but are essential to any listing of the major wines of the Rhine Basin.

A GUIDE TO MATCHING

The chart opposite indicates the broad affinities between foods and wines as described in Chapter VI, "The Categories of Affinity." The list below provides citations of more detailed discussions of the matching needs and problems of various categories of food. Most of the citations are from Chapter VIII, "Cherchez la Sauce."

THE CATEGORIES OF AFFINITY

THE WINE   THE FOOD

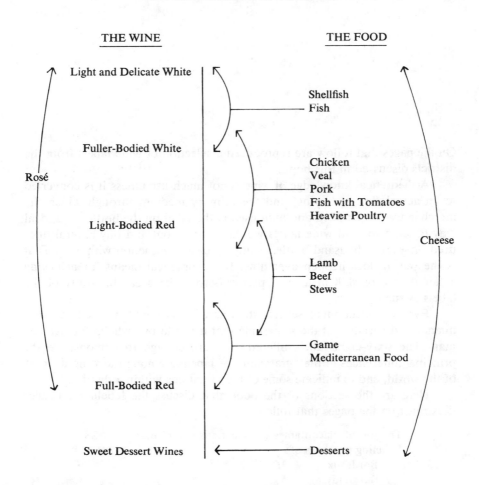

Light and Delicate White

Shellfish
Fish

Fuller-Bodied White

Chicken
Veal
Pork
Fish with Tomatoes
Heavier Poultry

Light-Bodied Red

Cheese

Lamb
Beef
Stews

Game
Mediterranean Food

Full-Bodied Red

Rosé

Sweet Dessert Wines   ←   Desserts

AN ALBUM OF LABELS

On the pages that follow are reproduced a selection of wine labels from the districts discussed in this book.

A theoretical knowledge of wine is not much use unless it is converted to an actual skill at buying, and the primary medium through which the merchandise is identified and appraised is the label on the bottle. The ideal way to learn to read wine labels would be to go out and buy several hundred or several thousand bottles, studying each transaction with care. That is the way it does happen over time. But a practical means for achieving a fair degree of skill in a brief period is to make a careful study of the labels as such.

Even a collection of several thousand labels could not reflect every nuance and variable, at the same time that it would overwhelm the average man. The sixty-eight labels offered here are enough to demonstrate the principal differences in the "grammar" of labeling among the wine districts of the world, and to indicate some of the variations within a district.

Here are the sections of the book that discuss the labeling practices illustrated on the pages that follow:

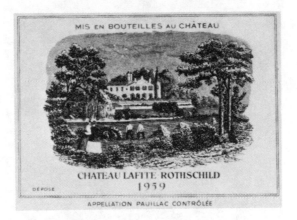

The wine of Château Lafite-Rothschild in the commune (village) of Pauillac in the Haut-Médoc region of the district of Bordeaux is generally acknowledged to be the greatest red wine of Bordeaux and one of the two greatest red wines in the world, comparable only to Romanée-Conti of the Côte de Nuits in Burgundy.

Château d'Yquem, owned by the Marquis de Lur Saluces and located in the region of Sauternes, a few miles south of the Haut-Médoc, produces the finest sweet white dessert wine of Bordeaux. Its only peers are the great sweet dessert wines of the Mosel and Rhine rivers in Germany.

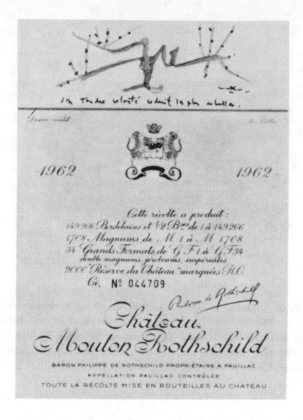

On these two pages are shown the labels of the other four First Growths of Bordeaux, all of them red wines. Château Mouton-Rothschild, owned by another branch of the Rothschild family, is also located in the commune of Pauillac, not far from Château Lafite-Rothschild.

Château Margaux is situated in the commune of Margaux, a few miles south of Pauillac, but still in the Haut-Médoc. Margaux also produces a dry white wine, the Pavillion Blanc de Château Margaux.

Château Haut-Brion, owned by the American financier Clarence Dillon, is situated not in the Haut-Médoc like the other First Growths, but in the region of Graves, just south of the Haut-Médoc. Like Château Margaux, Haut-Brion also produces a white wine, Haut-Brion Blanc, which is generally considered the best *dry* white wine produced in Bordeaux.

Château Latour is also located in the commune of Pauillac, along with Lafite and Mouton. In Bordeaux the appellations contrôlées on the labels of even the finest vineyards designate either the commune or the region of origin, not the vineyard. When the appellation contrôlée law was drawn up, it was felt that the institutions of classification and château bottling of Bordeaux were guarantee enough that a wine was authentic. In most of Burgundy, by contrast, where ownership of the vineyards is divided, the appellation for the finest vineyards extends to the vineyard name itself.

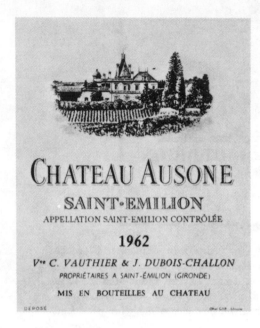

Château Ausone of the St.-Émilion region of Bordeaux was named for the Roman poet and consul Ausonius, who was born in Bordeaux around A.D. 310 and according to tradition once owned the vineyard that now bears his name. The wines of St.-Émilion fall into two groups, the wines of the limestone slope and the wines of the gravelly plateau. Château Ausone produces the best of the "wines of the slope."

Cheval Blanc means "white horse," but Château Cheval Blanc of St.-Émilion has no connection with the scotch whisky of the same name. Cheval Blanc produces the best "wines of the plain" on the top of the St.-Émilion plateau.

Château Petrus is the finest vineyard of the region of Pomerol,
north and west of St.-Émilion. Because the name Petrus was originally Latin, not French, the final
"s" is sounded, even in French.

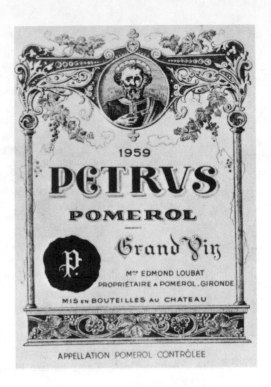

Château Beychevelle is located in the commune of St.-Julien in the
Haut-Médoc region. Beychevelle was designated a Fourth Growth in
the classification of 1855, but the management of the vineyard has been
excellent, and the wine now sells at a higher price than many Second
Growths.

Château Cos d'Estournel, a Second Growth of the Haut-Médoc, is located in the commune of St.-Estèphe, just north of incomparable Pauillac. The wines of St.-Estèphe are rich in tannin, which makes them harsh in their youth but gives them exceptionally long life. Thus, the wines of Cos d'Estournel are likely to be found in collections of very old wines.

Château La Mission-Haut-Brion of the region of Graves is located across the road from the great First Growth, Château Haut-Brion. La Mission-Haut-Brion makes very good wine, but not the equal of that of its famous namesake. There are a dozen vineyards, all told, in the region of Graves that have added Haut-Brion to their names, just as a number of vineyards of the Haut-Médoc have borrowed Lafite, in various spellings, or Latour.

Château Beaumont of the Haut-Médoc is not a Grand Cru Classe, a Great Growth, but a Cru Bourgeois Supérieur, a Superior Bourgeois Growth, a lesser although still good classification (and one more likely to be within the price range of the average buyer). A careful reading of the label indicates that Château Beaumont is located in the commune of Cussac. However, Cussac is not a famous name, so the wine goes to market under the better-known regional designation of Haut-Médoc.

The Château Fourcas-Hosten of the commune of Listrac in the Haut-Médoc is also classified a Cru Bourgeois Supérieur, but the label does not bother to mention it, and instead merely stresses the regional appellation, Haut-Médoc.

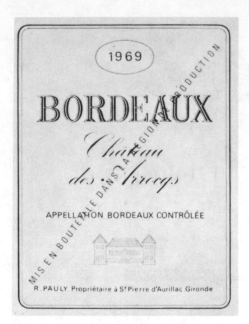

The "lowest" appellation of origin is a district appellation: Bordeaux, Burgundy, Loire, Rhône. The only lower designation would be simply *vin rouge,* red wine, or *vin blanc,* white wine, indicating a *vin ordinaire.* On the label opposite, a château name is given, as it often is on cheaper wines, but it has little meaning since the wine deserves only the district appellation Bordeaux. The statement *"Mise en bouteille dans la région de production"* means that the wine was put into bottles in the region where it was produced, which means precisely nothing.

Here is the label of what is known as a "shipper's wine." The wine was selected and blended by the well-known shipper of Bordeaux, Barton and Guestier. Aside from the district appellation on the label there is nothing to indicate the origin of the wine. The only assurance of quality is the reputation of the shipper himself. In this case the shipper has even given a "brand name," Prince Blanc, to the wine. This makes it easier to advertise, and to develop a "brand preference" on the part of customers.

An alternative to a "shipper's wine" is an "importer's wine." Here are two wines of Bordeaux selected and sold under its own label by the importer Dreyfus Ashby of New York. The St.-Julien represented by the label shown at right is a "communal" wine, since it bears the designation only of its commune of origin, St.-Julien in the Haut-Médoc, with no château (vineyard) identified. It may well be a blend of wine from several vineyards of that commune.

The label at right represents a "regional" wine, since it carries only the name of the region of St.-Émilion, to the east of the Haut-Médoc. The communal St.-Julien is a notch higher on the appellation scale than this regional St.-Émilion, and therefore presumably a better wine. A novice buyer might have trouble remembering that, particularly since each wine invokes the name of a saint and the two saints are easy to confuse. However, the price of the wine usually reflects the difference.

BURGUNDY

The wine of the vineyard of Romanée-Conti is considered the finest red wine produced in Burgundy, the only one comparable to that of the great Château Lafite of Bordeaux. The entire vineyard, consisting of only 4.5 acres, is owned by one concern, the Domaine de la Romanée-Conti, which was the first in Burgundy to practice the equivalent of château or estate bottling. The language *"Mise en bouteille au domaine"* indicates that the wine was bottled at the estate.

The greatest white wine of Burgundy and generally considered the greatest *dry* white wine in the world is Le Montrachet. As is the case of virtually all the great vineyards of Burgundy, the vineyard land of Montrachet is divided among a number of owners. The Marquis de Laguiche is one of the largest and one of the best regarded. The shipper in this case is Joseph Drouhin, one of the most respected in Burgundy. His name on the label is a further indication of quality. Dreyfus Ashby is one of the finest importers in New York. The combination of the name of a great vineyard, the name of an excellent grower, the name of a reputable shipper, and the name of a respected importer certifies a very fine wine at a *very* high price.

The Domaine de la Romanée-Conti includes other parcels of vineyard land in the Côte de Nuits. (A *domaine* is a property, a holding, and thus can consist of one piece of land or several.) Here is the label of the *domaine* for the wine of La Tache, a near neighbor of the great Romanée-Conti itself, and another fine and expensive wine.

Another highly regarded *domaine* is that of the Compte Georges de Vogüé. Bonnes Mares is located about three miles north of the great Romanée cluster in the commune of Chambolle-Musigny. The Compte de Vogüé is also the largest owner in the vineyard of Musigny nearby, where he produces a white wine, Musigny Blanc, as well as the famous red.

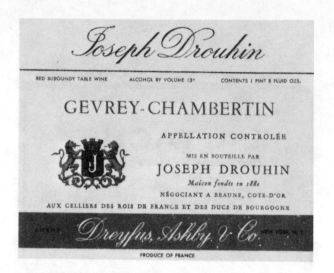

The house of Drouhin, founded in 1880, ships a great many Burgundy wines besides the great Montrachet of the Marquis de Laguiche. The label above is that of Chambertin-Clos de Bèze, one of the greatest red wines of the Côte de Nuits (where virtually all the greatest reds of Burgundy are grown).

Here is the Drouhin label for the much less splendid "communal" wine of Gevrey-Chambertin. Gevrey is the township within which the great Chambertin vineyard is located. Following Burgundian custom, it has hyphenated the name of its greatest vineyard to its own, and the wine of the whole commune, whatever its quality, is thus entitled to go to market under the name Gevrey-Chambertin. The Drouhin label proudly asserts that its wines are "for the cellars of the Kings of France and the Dukes of Burgundy."

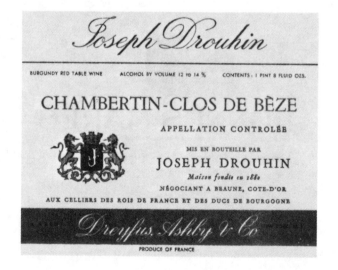

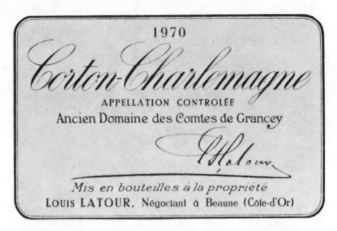

Another shipper of the highest standing is Louis Latour, whose firm was founded in 1797. Latour is the principal owner of the famous white wine vineyard of Corton-Charlemagne, reputed to have been planted by the Great Charles himself. As the label indicates, the Latour holding in Corton-Charlemagne was once in the hands of the Counts of Grancey.

Still another fine shipper is Joseph Faiveley. Here is his label for the vineyard of Musigny. It will be noted that the appellation on this label is that of the vineyard itself, not the commune or region of origin, as in the case of the best wines of Bordeaux.

One of the best-known institutions of wine in Burgundy is the Hospices de Beaune, a charity hospital which for the past five hundred years has been receiving bequests of fine vineyard land from well-off Burgundians. The Hospices sells the wine produced on its holdings to support its charitable activities. The wines are sold at an auction held each year in the city of Beaune. The prices for which the wines are sold tend to set the price levels for all the wines of Burgundy for that vintage. The wine represented by the label at the top came from a parcel in the commune of Corton in the Côte de Beaune originally donated by a Dr. Peste. It was purchased at the auction by the importer Frank Schoonmaker, who then had an appropriate label printed. The wine that sold under the label below was purchased by the importer Dreyfus Ashby, which had its own labels printed. This wine came from a parcel in Beaune donated by a Maurice Drouhin, presumably from the same family as the shipper Joseph Drouhin.

Both labels above are for wine of the same vineyard, Les Grands Épenots of the commune of Pommard in the Côte de Beaune (the more southerly of the two slopes of the Côte d'Or). The wine represented by the first label was bottled by the grower, Madame Bernard de Courcel. The second label does not even mention a grower, so was presumably purchased in barrel and bottled by the shipper, Louis Latour.

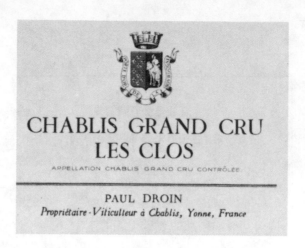

At the top of the page is a label from Les Clos, one of the best of the Grands Crus, or Great Growths (vineyards), of Chablis, the northern-most region of Burgundy. The wine comes from the parcel of the vine-yard owned by the grower Paul Droin. The label does not indicate estate bottling, but Droin may simply not have bothered to mention it; or perhaps the shipper bottled the wine. The second label is for Chablis Premier Cru, First Growth, the next grade down. In this case no vineyard is mentioned, much less a grower. This may mean that the wine is a blend from several First Growth vineyards (which can pro-duce a better-balanced wine in a risky region like Chablis). The ap-pellation contrôlée regulations of Chablis provide for this practice. Unlike those of the Côte d'Or, farther south in Burgundy, the appel-lations for Chablis do not mention specific vineyards but refer only to their classifications: Chablis Grand Cru, Chablis Premier Cru, Chablis, and Petit Chabls (small hablis).

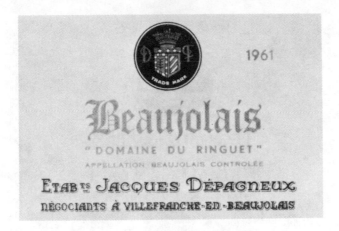

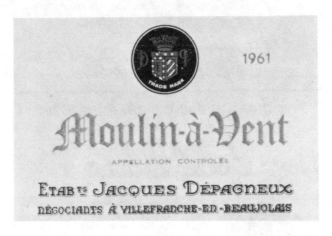

Shown above are the labels of two categories of Beaujolais from a
single shipper, Jacques Dépagneux. The one at the top carries the
regional appellation Beaujolais. The name of a vineyard is given, although it is not of great significance. The second label carries the appellation of Moulin-à-Vent, the best-known village of Beaujolais. The
eight finest villages of Beaujolais, including Moulin-à-Vent, have been
given the right to send their wines to market under their own appellations. But because everybody is expected to know what Moulin-à-Vent
is, the label does not mention that it is indeed a Beaujolais. This can
be confusing to an inexperienced buyer.

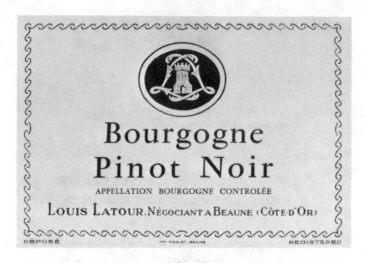

On this page are two labels carrying the humblest appellation of Burgundy, the district appellation, Bourgogne. However, the label at the top, from the shipper Louis Latour, also names the grape from which the wine was made, Pinot Noir. This practice is being increasingly followed in Europe as well as California. The second label, from the shipper Joseph Drouhin, also names the grape, Pinot Chardonnay, the white wine grape of Burgundy, and assigns a "brand name" as well —Soleil Blanc, White Sun or White Sunshine. (This might remind some Americans of White Lightnin', which of course it does not resemble at all.)

The Loire

The labels of the other districts of France are both less difficult and less interesting to decipher than those of Burgundy and Bordeaux. There is not the elaborate classification system of Bordeaux, nor the intertwining of growers and shippers and hyphenations of Burgundy; nor are there the world-famous names and the pressures to forge or imitate them. The label at the top of the page represents a Pouilly-Fumé from far upriver on the Loire, produced by the most important grower of that region, de Ladoucette. The de Ladoucette label is well worth looking for, although there is now a premium price attached to it.

Directly across the river from Pouilly-Fumé is grown the white wine of Sancerre, somewhat lighter and drier than Fumé, less widely available, and, being less known, less expensive. The best Sancerres come from the town of Chavignol, just east of the village of Sancerre.

This label is from the increasingly popular wine of Muscadet, far downriver at the mouth of the Loire. The Muscadets are divided into two groups: the Côteaux de la Loire, the slopes of the Loire, and a group of villages on the Sevre and Main rivers to the south. This wine comes from the second area, as the appellation indicates. The wine was bottled *sur lie,* that is, directly off the lees, or heavy sediment that a young wine throws in barrel. This is supposed to yield a better, more flavorful wine, and is language to look for on the label of a Muscadet. The name of the *domaine* in this case has little market significance. The name that counts is the name of the highly regarded importer.

The Rhône

This label is from Châteauneuf-du-Pape, the increasingly popular red wine of the lower Rhône. The shipper is Chanson, a shipper of Burgundy to the north, who lets it be known that his cellars (*caves*) are "an ancient bastion of the fifteenth century at Beaune."

As the better-known wines of the Rhône, including Châteauneuf-du-Pape, have tended to become overpriced under the pressure of growing demand, there has been increasing market interest in the good and plentiful wines bearing the simpler appellation, Côtes du Rhône, slopes of the Rhône.

The rosé of Tavel, across the river from Châteauneuf-du-Pape, is considered by many the best rosé of France, and therefore the best in the world. Château d'Aqueria is one of the largest and most reliable producers of Tavel. As in the case of de Ladoucette of Pouilly-Fumé, this is a name worth looking for; here, too, there is now a premium price attached to it. As prices have increased for all the wines of Tavel, there has been a shift of demand to the lesser-known village of Lirac, nearby, whose wines are similar, and to the rosés of Anjou on the Loire.

The Rhine Basin

The wines of the Mosel, Saar, and Ruwer rivers, the most northerly of
the fine wines of Germany, are so similar in characteristics that they
usually carry the single designation "Mosel-Saar-Ruwer." This wine is
from the Scharzhofberg vineyard in the village of Wiltingen on the
Saar River, one of the very greatest white wine vineyards in the world.
It is so famous the label does not bother to mention the village name,
as is the normal custom with the better German wines. Since all the
fine wines of the Mosel-Saar-Ruwer are made from the Riesling grape,
the grape variety does not need to be mentioned on the label, as it usually is on the labels of the Rhine, farther south. The wine is an *Auslese,* a sweet wine whose grapes were selected bunch by bunch. The
Scharzhof is a manor house which has been owned for several generations by the Egon Müller family, which also owns most of the vineyard. The language Original Kellerabfüllung indicates estate bottling.

A wine from the famous vineyard of Schloss Johannisberg in the Rheingau, another of the finest vineyards of Germany. *Schloss* means "castle" and is the equivalent of "château." Schloss Johannisberg is owned by the Metternichs, one of the oldest of the noble families of Germany. The wines of Schloss Johannisberg are made in various grades, as indicated by the color of the seals on the label. Red is the lowest grade, followed by green, pink, orange, white, blue, and gold. This label bears the red seal, as indicated by the word *Rotlack*. Wine-growing is so risky in the northern vineyards that a vintage year is important on any German wine.

This wine comes from the Schönhell vineyard in the village of Hall-garten in the region of the Rheingau. The wine is made from the Riesling grape, and is a very sweet one, *Beerenauslese,* made from individually selected grapes. The black eagle insignia, surrounded by the initials V.D.N.V. is the seal of the Verband Deutscher Naturwein-versteigerer, German Natural Wine Sellers Association, a certification that the wine is "natural," that is, no sugar has been added during fermentation. *Korkbrand* means that the cork is branded with the name of the vineyard, an indication of authenticity to look for.

During the German occupation of Alsace after the Franco-Prussian War of 1870, the fine vines were rooted up and the vineyards turned over to making ordinary wines to blend for Liebfraumilch. During both World Wars the lands were heavily fought over and some of the villages destroyed. Because of this history of disruption, no adequate classification of the vineyards of Alsace exists and the appellation contrôlée laws apply loosely at best. Thus the primary designation of an Alsatian wine is the name of the grape from which it was made, and the name of a good shipper is more important even than in Burgundy to certify the quality of the wine. This wine is a Riesling from the well-regarded shipper Hügel, who is located at Riquewihr, one of the two best wine villages of Alsace.

Italy

One confusing fact about the wines of Italy is that its best wines, which are very good, and its humblest, which are not, often go to market under the same name. This is true of the plentiful and popular Chianti. At right are two labels of better-quality Chiantis, which are shipped not in the romantic, straw-covered flask called a *fiasco,* but in square-shouldered bottles of the Bordeaux-type. The best Chianti comes from the Classico zone, and bears the seal of the Gallo Nero, a golden cockerel on a black background with a red border. An aged Chianti is called a Riserva. This is also a designation to look for. The producers whose labels are shown here are the Marchesi Antinori and Conti Serristori. A half-dozen other producers of superior Chiantis ship their wines to the United States.

ESTATE BOTTLED

Fattorie dei Marchesi *Lodovico e Piero Antinori*
Firenze *Italia*

VILLA ANTINORI
Chianti Classico
DENOMINAZIONE DI ORIGINE CONTROLLATA

CLASSIC
CHIANTI
RED WINE
S. ANDREA IN PERCVSSINA
ANTICA FATTORIA DI NICCOLÓ MACHIAVELLI
S. CASCIANO VAL DI PESA · FIRENZE
SV. CONTI SERRISTORI S.p.A.

Another difficulty with the wines of Italy is that there is no regular pattern to the use of names. Chianti is a region. Soave, above, is a village. Verdicchio, below, is a grape. The Soave whose label is shown was shipped by Bolla, a major shipper of the wines of the Verona area, where Soave is grown. Aside from the better Chiantis, which are products of large estates, a considerable proportion of the other Italian wines that come to the United States come under the label of a major shipper. Other important shippers include Bertani, Bertoli, and Ruffino.

Italy has only recently adopted strict laws of geographic origin, comparable to the French appellations contrôlées. The first laws of Denominazione d'Origine Controllata were passed in 1963 and went into effect in 1967. The "classic" area producing the white wine of Verdicchio consists of several towns which carry the *denominazione* Verdicchio de Castelli Jesi. This is the name to watch for. The nearby areas, producing lesser wines, are entitled only to use the name Verdicchio.

CALIFORNIA

These labels represent the two principal categories of table wine produced in California. Gallo Hearty Burgundy is one of the latest successes of one of the most successful wine marketers in the world. It is a popularly priced "generic" or "standard" wine, named for a well-known category of European wine (which it may or may not resemble), blended to suit the taste of a carefully researched and chosen market segment, with nothing on the label other than the name of the producer to certify either the origin or the quality of the wine. (It is worth noting that the forebears of the Gallo brothers were winegrowers in the province of Piedmont in Italy.)

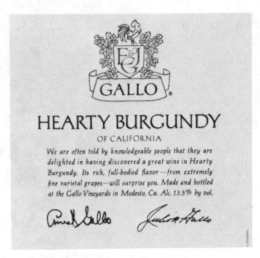

This is the label of a California "varietal" wine, so called because it is named for the primary grape variety from which it was made, in this case the Cabernet Sauvignon grape of Bordeaux, which yields the best red wine of California. The producer of the wine is Beaulieu Vineyard in the Napa Valley, one of the best-regarded producers in California's most famous winegrowing area. The notation of estate bottling means not only that the wine was bottled at the winery where it was made, but that all the grapes in it were grown on lands adjacent to the winery. Georges de Latour, for whom this bottling is named, was a Frenchman who founded Beaulieu Vineyard in 1900. He was related to families prominent in wine in both Burgundy and Bordeaux.

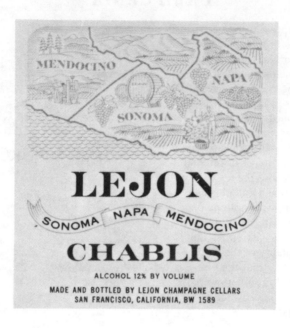

Some of the best bargains in sound if simple wine to be found anywhere are the "jug wines" of California, sold in gallon and half-gallon
bottles. Both premium- and standard-wine producers market jug wines;
the premium producers usually charge a premium price, which is sometimes deserved and sometimes not. Some of the jug wines affect Italian
names and styles. Others merely carry simple generic names. (*Tavola*
is not an exotic wine region of Italy. It means "table." *Tipo* is not a
characteristic or a trade name. It means "type." Thus Tavola Red is
"table red," and Tipo Chianti means "Chianti-type.")

The two labels above represent "proprietary" wines, blended products
with made-up names. There is a growing trend toward development of
proprietary wines in Europe as well as California. A proprietary name
is a "brand name" which can be profitably promoted. Also, the quantity
of a blended wine can be increased as demand increases, while the
quantity of wine from a specifically named place is obviously limited
by the area of that place. One risk for the buyer of proprietary wines,
however, is the fact that a producer will sometimes offer a superior
product until he establishes a good market position, and then cut back
the quality.

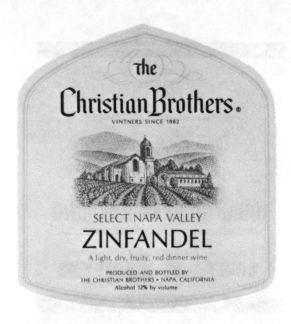

The two labels on this page and the lower one on the page opposite represent the "Big Three" among the premium wine producers of California. Together they market more wine annually than all the rest of the premium producers together. Each one offers a "full line," including standard as well as varietal wines. The wines are popularly priced and do not attain the levels of excellence of the best of the medium-sized and small producers.

Here are the labels of some of the better-known among the medium-sized producers of premium wines in California, all from the Napa Valley. Among long-established producers, Louis Martini and Beaulieu Vineyard are especially well regarded. The cask designation on the Inglenook label, like the Private Reserve designation on the Beaulieu Vineyard label on page 325, has no special meaning under the law, but depends for its significance on the reputation of the bottler. Robert Mondavi, a member of the family that has operated the Charles Krug Winery since 1943, established his own winery in 1964 and has since won a very high reputation for his wines.

A vintage year is important to look for on the label of a bottle of California wine for three reasons: First, as in the case of most European districts, the quality of the wine does vary from year to year. Also, in the case of a red wine, the year of production indicates whether it is old enough to be drunk at all. In California as in most other places the demand for wine is so great that often the wine of a fine vintage will all be drunk within three or four years of fermentation, whereas it might not actually have been "ready" for several years after that. In addition, a vintage year on a California label provides extra assurance as to quality. When a vintage year is indicated, the wine in the bottle must be at least 95 per cent from the year noted and 75 per cent from the place noted.

Here are two more relative newcomers to the marketing of California wines who have established excellent reputations in a remarkably short time. The Mirassou family has been producing premium wines in bulk to be sold under the labels of other producers for five generations, and only recently has begun selling wine under its own name. Joseph E. Heitz was for ten years a wine maker in California wineries. In 1961 he went into business for himself, not as a grower, but as a buyer of grapes and a "finisher" (aging, blending) of wine made by other people.

These are the labels of two of the "little vineyards" of California, small, individualistic, family operations, very much in the old European tradition. Most wines of little vineyards are good to excellent; some are considered overpriced. Most are very difficult to buy outside of California.

HOW TO CHOOSE A WINE MERCHANT

Choosing a wine merchant partakes of many of the hazards of choosing a wife: luck plays an important part; one man's nectar could be another man's vinegar; and what seems heaven in May can prove a drag in September. However, while courtships are less intense in the wine game, divorces are easier and less expensive to arrange. And in wine as in matrimony the quiet rewards of a good relationship persist through many years.

Initially, most people settle on their wine merchant in a random way. It is usually the fellow located next to the drugstore or close to the commuter station or near the office. Then there is a certain amount of trial and error. If the clerk was rude or refused to cash a check or the wine was disappointing, your business moves to the man down the street. Or if you are giving a particularly splendid bash and the stock of the local outlet does not equal the occasion, you shop around until you find somebody with a bigger inventory; then, impressed with the greater resources at the new place, you go back and the fellow next to the drugstore gets his feelings hurt.

As your palate improves you may also find yourslf becoming restless with the local outlet. Then when you stumble across a new place, you are likely to go in and prowl about, eying the merchandise, while the man behind the counter wonders if you are a stick-up man, maybe, or a federal agent.

One argument for starting a modest wine cellar is that it intensifies and organizes the search for a good merchant, usually resulting in a decisive upgrading of your source of wine. Sometimes you will discover that a mere three blocks away is an absolutely superb merchant; and here you have been wasting all that time on a mediocrity. (One of the authors of this book lived three years in a community before he discovered that an outstanding merchant was located fifteen minutes from his house.)

The real challenge comes when you move to a completely strange town and are faced with the need to locate from scratch a merchant qualified to supply your growing habit. The best way to work is to get a referral. If you know a first-rate merchant in the place you are moving from, see if he knows someone, or knows someone who might know someone, in the place where you are going.

Too often, however, the search has to start all over again, usually as a more or less "random walk." But this time don't settle for the first place you come to. Scout around. Cruise a bit. Be hard to please. When you like the look of somebody's inventory, try to find out who the top man is and test him and draw attention to yourself with some challenging questions. If you like the answers, become a client, not a customer, as quickly as you can.

Word of mouth is a useful if imperfect guide. If you meet a man who knows wine, ask him where he buys it. The people who run those little shops selling fancy cookware and offering instruction in French cooking might have some tips. The man who runs a specialty grocery store may also know wines (in some states he sells it) or he may not. A call or letter to the office of a local wine wholesaler or importer might yield some excellent recommendations. He has salesmen who call personally on every store worthy of attention. But the wholesaler or importer feels no particular obligation to please you, so he may or may not be courteous, or even reply. And be sure that you go to a responsible organization whose name appears on bottles of highest quality. There are plenty of junk dealers in the business whose advice would be worse than worthless.

If there is a local chapter of the Confrérie des Chevaliers du Tastevin in your area, or the Wine and Food Society, they will obviously have some notion of who the better merchants and wholesalers are. (And if you do contact them, they might even invite you to join their group. Wine freaks love to discover a soul mate.) If there is no listing of these organizations in your telephone book, the national offices can tell you if there is a local chapter. They are: Wine and Food Society, 50 East Forty-second Street, New York, N.Y. 10017, and Confrérie des Chevaliers du Tastevin, 236 East Forty-sixth Street, New York, N.Y. 10017.

The food editor of the local paper may know something about wine and wine outlets. On the other hand, she may be a strictly home economics type. Even so, she might have in her files the name of the man who runs the local food-wine group.

In every major downtown center there is at least one merchant who deals in fairly large volume with good wines, and these people usually advertise in the newspapers. You may decide to give all your business to the downtown store, particularly if he sends out a catalogue. But beware. If you are extremely rich and want to place a five-thousand-dollar order, you can probably count on respectful service. If you are Joe Schmo from nowhere, the attention may be scaled down accordingly, along with the merits of the merchandise.

There is an organization called the Wine and Spirits Guild of America, whose membership consists of about forty of the finest merchants in the country. A letter of inquiry to its executive secretary, Mr. Al Butler, 1275 Glencoe Street, Denver, Colo. 80220, would determine whether there is a member of the guild in your area. However, while many of the finest merchants do belong to the guild, others do not. Membership is limited to two merchants in any given area and some excellent people have chosen not to belong.

Another organization of merchants who pay special attention to wine is called Les Amis du Vin, The Friends of Wine. Its head office is at 4701 Willard Avenue, Washington, D.C. 20015, and they would no doubt be happy to tell you who their members are. But Les Amis du Vin, like the *vignoble* of Burgundy, is very democratic. They admit anybody who applies. Thus a membership in Les Amis is not the same credential as one in the guild.

Another means of developing good leads would be to write to the offices or agencies that publicize the better European wines and ask them for the names of exceptional merchants in your area. Most of them maintain what are called "key account lists" of people who deal in considerable volume with the better grades of merchandise. And with their need to stay on good terms with their clients or sponsors these organizations are a bit more likely than a wholesaler or importer to deal courteously and conscientiously with the general public. Here are the names of several of these groups: Bell & Stanton (Bordeaux and Alsatian wines), 909 Third Avenue, New York, N.Y. 10022; Irving Smith Kogan & Co., Inc. (French Champagne), 850 Third Avenue, New York, N.Y. 10022; German Wine Information Bureau, 666 Fifth Avenue, Sixth Floor, New York, N.Y. 10019; and the Italian Trade Commissioner, One World Trade Center, Suite 2057, New York, N.Y. 10048.

If you are especially interested in Bordeaux wines, let us say, there would be an obvious advantage in writing to the Bordeaux people.

There is no magic formula, but time and diligence usually deliver results. The challenge of discovering a good merchant is really only an extension of the challenge of picking out the bottle itself. Taken together they comprise a major element of the endless fascination of the game of wine.

THE WINE CATALOGUE OF JOHN WALKER & CO.

As noted in Chapter XIV one of the benefits of doing business with a great wine merchant—or even a very large one—is "the enormous privilege of receiving and fondling his catalogue." However, as we also observed, for someone who has not acquired the taste, the special charm of a wine catalogue is a little hard to explain.

The best approach, obviously, is not to try, but to let the reader experience it for himself through firsthand exposure. But a really good wine catalogue is often a sizable tome, impractical to reproduce here.

An outstanding exception is the annual "Special Offering" of John Walker & Co., which finds its way to the public each season through the medium of a display advertisement on two full pages of the West Coast edition of the *Wall Street Journal*. On the pages that follow is reproduced in its entirety the John Walker "Special Offering" of October 24, 1974. The prices quoted here obviously will not be current at the time the reader sees them, nor would the wines offered necessarily be still in stock (nor would federal law permit anybody outside of California to send for them). But here reflected in pure essence is the product of all the good and great vintages of recent memory, and some before that, the legendary place names going back a thousand or more years, and the names of individuals and organizations who are proud inheritors of an art and tradition that stem from the earliest beginnings of civilized man.

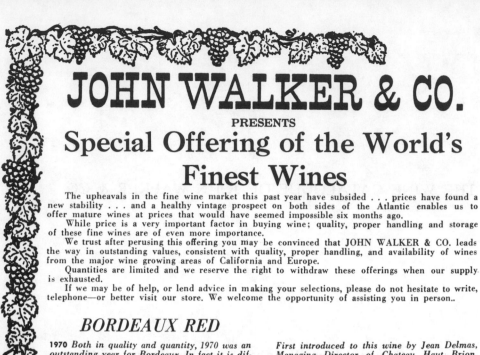

JOHN WALKER & CO.

PRESENTS

Special Offering of the World's Finite Wines

The upheavals in the fine wine market this past year have subsided . . . prices have found a new stability . . . and a healthy vintage prospect on both sides of the Atlantic enables us to offer mature wines at prices that would have seemed impossible six months ago.

While price is a very important factor in buying wine; quality, proper handling and storage of these fine wines are of even more importance.

We trust after perusing this offering you may be convinced that JOHN WALKER & CO. leads the way in outstanding values, consistent with quality, proper handling, and availability of wines from the major wine growing areas of California and Europe.

Quantities are limited and we reserve the right to withdraw these offerings when our supply is exhausted.

If we may be of help, or lend advice in making your selections, please do not hesitate to write, telephone—or better visit our store. We welcome the opportunity of assisting you in person..

BORDEAUX RED

1970 *Both in quality and quantity, 1970 was an outstanding year for Bordeaux. In fact it is difficult to fault any of the Great 1970s. They are full, round wines for the most part, often with an early appeal; and yet most have the reliance, stamina and resource to develop well for many years to come.*

The wine drinkers of the world have quickly recognized the intrinsic excellence of 1970 in Bordeaux—the best year since 1961—and have clamored for them.

After you peruse our list of 1970s we are confident that you will agree it is the most comprehensive offering of these Great Wines to be found in America—AT PRICES THAT CANNOT BE MATCHED.

	CASE PRICE
100 CHATEAU DE LA VIELLE CLOCHE, Grand Cru, St. Emilion	39.50

M. A. Leveque, the owner of this Chateau, has made a fine wine in the traditional manner for more years than we can remember. Situated as it is in the township of St. Emilion itself (the most prestigious site) its wines are sturdy, yet with a delicate breed of their own.

101 CHATEAU CAP DE HAUT,
Moulis, Haut Medoc 39.50

Chateau Cap De Haut is situated besides the well known Chateau Maucailou in Moulis, Haut Medoc. The owner of this tiny Chateau, covering 4 hectares, is Monsieur Claude Bobinau. This wine has a delightful bouquet and mellowness, characteristic of Moulis.

102 CHATEAU ROC ST. MICHEL,
St. Emilion 39.50

103 CHATEAU LA ROSE
TRINTAUDON, Haut Medoc 42.50

This noble vineyard has recently been replanted under the supervision of Professor Teynaud of the University of Boreaux faculty—a man who ranks among the foremost oenologists of the world.

105 CHATEAU PICQUE CALLOU,
Graves 49.50

First introduced to this wine by Jean Delmas, Managing Director of Chateau Haut Brion. Typical Graves—good body—priced well under its true class.

106 CHATEAU GREYSAC, Medoc...... 51.50

A "sleeper"—from an astonishingly fine Medoc vineyard proudly owned by Georges Hereil, creator of the Caravelle airplane and now Honorary Chairman of Chrysler-International. His dedication to excellence is reflected in this long-lived noble wine.

107 CHATEAU DE PEZ,
St. Estephe 52.50

An elegant wine, with good balance and a well-knit flavor. Color is good and the wine—with good development potential—is already pleasing.

108 CHATEAU SIMARD,
St. Emilion 52.50

37½ acres which produce an excellent St. Emilion. 1970s developing a clean Bordeaux nose—an even wine with discreet flavor and firm on the palate. Medium color, rather light acidity, developing well.

109 CHATEAU BELLEVUE,
. St. Emilion 54.50

A Grand Cru St. Emilion of only 15 acres. Well situated and the producer of a full bodied wine which ages well. The 1970 is one of the best years for this vineyard.

110 CHATEAU DASSAULT,
St. Emilion 59.50

111 CHATEAU CLINET, Pomerol 69.50

Only some 18 acres in size, producing some 2600 cases annually, one would hardly think its wine would gain world renown, yet Chateau Clinet has won over 15 of the world's highest awards for fine wines. This is a wine with a big nose, faintly reminiscent of violets, and a full, yet velvety, body.

112 CHATEAU CISSAC,
Haut Medoc 67.50

A Cru Burgeois of only 5 acres. Ideally situated among illustrious neighbors. Highly rated by Harry Waugh. "This chateau should be rated among the 2nd or 3rd classified growths."

113 CHATEAU BOUSCAUT,
Graves 79.50
This wine reached great heights in 1970 under the direction of Wine Master Jean Delmas, Managing Director of Chateau Haut Brion.

114 CHATEAU PAVIE,
St. Emilion 74.50
In 1855, 18 vineyards of St. Emilion were classified as 'First Great Growths'. These include Ausone Cheval Blanc, Figeac and this vineyard—Pavie. A glory in 1970.

115 CHATEAU CLOS RENE,
Pomerol 69.50
One of the few Pomerols left from the famous 1970 vintage.

116 CHATEAU L'ANGELUS,
St. Emilion 79.50
The great French restaurants of Paris and New York clamor for L'Angelus because of its softness, fruitiness and deliciousness. Hard to come by because of intense world demand.

117 CHATEAU LA LAGUNE,
Haut Medoc 74.50

118 CHATEAU CANTENAC BROWN,
Margaux 89.50
3rd Classed Growth of Cantenac-Margaux, Medoc, which, unlike some others, still deserves its 1855 rating. Produces a red wine of typical breed and finesse.

119 CHATEAU CLERC MILON
ROTHSCHILD, Pauillac 89.50
Not far from Chateau Mouton Rothschild in Pauillac, there is a small but excellent vineyard, Clerc-Milon, which was classified 'Grand Cru' in 1855. Baron Philippe de Rothschild, aware of its excellence, acquired the vineyard several years ago to bring out its full potential. It was under the Baron's supervision that this superb 1970 was nurtured.

120 CHATEAU DUHART MILON
ROTHSCHILD, Pauillac 89.50
Adjacent to Chateau Lafite, sharing the same proprietor, Baron Elie de Rothschild. Elegance and depth are beautifully harmonized.

121 CHATEAU MOUTON BARON
PHILIPPE ROTHSCHILD,
Pauillac 109.50

122 CHATEAU BRANE CANTENAC,
Margaux 89.50

123 CHATEAU LEOVILLE LAS
CASES, St. Julien 99.50

124 CHATEAU BEYCHEVELLE,
St. Julien 99.50

125 CHATEAU CALON SEGUR,
St. Estephe 99.50

126 CHATEAU DUCRU
BEAUCAILLOU,
St. Julien 99.50

127 CHATEAU PICHON
LONGUEVILLE, LALANDE,
Pauillac 99.50

128 CHATEAU COS D'ESTOURNEL,
St. Estephe 99.50

130 CHATEAU LYNCH BAGES,
Pauillac 119.50

131 CHATEAU PAPE CLEMENT,
Graves 119.50

133 CHATEAU TROTANOY, Pomerol..150.00

1969 *Carefully selected and said to be the vintage that knowledgeable Frenchmen will drink. The wines of the bigger Chateaus are displaying excellent character and breed and are definitely vins de garde, or lay-away wines. The smaller Chateaus are on the lighter side and may be enjoyed now and for a few years hence. Like the wines - the prices are very attractive and make the 1969s excellent values.*

134 CHATEAU LA MISSION HAUT
BRION, Graves 199.50

135 CHATEAU CHEVAL BLANC,
St. Emilion 249.50

129 CHATEAU HAUT BRION,
Graves 249.50

136 CHATEAU LATOUR, Pauillac 329.50

137 CHATEAU MARGAUX, Margaux...279.50

132 CHATEAU LAFITE ROTHSCHILD,
Pauillac 349.50

138 CHATEAU MOUTON
ROTHSCHILD, Pauillac 379.50

Baron Philippe de Rothschild is proud of the bigness, power and beautiful balance of his 1970 Mouton. Certainly one of the greatest of his post-war years.....

139 CHATEAU PETRUS, Pomerol 399.50

140 CHATEAU CLINET, Pomerol 51.50
Only some 18 acres in size, producing some 2600 cases annually, one would hardly think its wine would gain world renown, yet Chateau Clinet has won over 15 of the world's highest awards for fine wines. This is a wine with a big nose, faintly reminiscent of violets, and a full yet velvety body.

141 CHATEAU SIMARD, St. Emilion.... 49.50

142 CHATEAU SIRAN, Margaux 44.50
This vineyard is owned by the Proprietors of Pichon-Lalande and is cared for 'in the same tradition.

143 CHATEAU LYNCH BAGES,
Pauillac 79.50

144 CHATEAU MOUTON BARON
PHILIPPE ROTHSCHILD,
Pauillac 84.50

145 CHATEAU LATOUR, Pauillac 199.50

146 CHATEAU MOUTON ROTHSCHILD,
Pauillac 249.50

147 CHATEAU LAFITE
ROTHSCHILD, Pauillac 259.50

148 CHATEAU PETRUS, Pomerol 259.50

1968 *Likely to be overlooked as a vintage. The great vineyards listed below, through selection and reduction of total quantity, have been able to provide truly excellent wines and are ideally suited for present drinking. Here are some giants of Bordeaux that can be consumed now at a price much below the value of the intrinsic excellence you will experience.*

149 CHATEAU HAUT BRION, Graves.. 99.50
A wine of quality and finesse, even better than the 1960.

150 CHATEAU CHEVAL BLANC,
St. Emilion 79.50
Penetrating bouquet and full flavored.

151 CHATEAU PETRUS, Pomerol 109.50
Outstanding, soft and velvety.

152 CHATEAU BELLEVUE,
St. Emilion 51.50

153 CHATEAU GREYSAC, Medoc 49.95

154 CHATEAU L'ANGELUS,
St. Emilion 72.50

155 CHATEAU LA LAGUNE, Medoc ... 79.50

156 CHATEAU PAVIE, St. Emilion 74.50

157 CHATEAU SMITH HAUT
LAFITE, Graves 69.50

1967 *Called the stepchild of 1966 — just as 1962 was the stepchild of 1961. But as stepchildren often do—they become a joy.
1967s are fine, fruity, quicker to mature and offer the same unexpected charm for early drinking that fortunate wine buyers found in the 1962 vintage. The present "sleeper" vintage of the 1960s.*

158 CHATEAU LATOUR CARNET,
    St. Laurent 67.50
159 CHATEAU YON-FIGEAC,
    St. Emilion 69.50
160 CHATEAU BATAILLEY, Pauillac .. 72.50
161 CHATEAU MOUTON BARON
    PHILIPPE ROTHSCHILD,
    Pauillac 99.50
162 CHATEAU PRIEURE-LICHINE,
    Margaux 82.50
163 CHATEAU COS D'ESTOURNEL,
    St. Estephe 89.50
164 CHATEAU PICHON LONGUEVILLE,
    LALANDE, Pauillac 99.50
165 CHATEAU PALMER, Margaux 149.50
166 CHATEAU HAUT BRION,
    Graves 179.50
167 CHATEAU LATOUR, Pauillac 179.50
168 CHATEAU CHEVAL BLANC,
    St. Emilion 199.50
169 CHATEAU MARGAUX, Marguax ...199.50
170 CHATEAU MOUTON
    ROTHSCHILD, Pauillac 249.50
171 CHATEAU PETRUS, Pomerol 299.50
At recent tasting—this wine was judged the best Petrus since 1961 — A real collector's item.
172 CHATEAU LAFITE ROTHSCHILD,
    Pauillac 279.50
173 CHATEAU PICQUE CAILLOU,
    Graves 49.50
A typical Graves - Good body - Priced well under its true class. Perfect for current drinking.
174 CHATEAU YON-FIGEAC,
    St. Emilion 74.50
175 CHATEU BATAILLEY, Pauillac ... 79.50
176 CHATEAU PAVIE, St. Emilion 82.50
177 CHATEAU L'ANGELUS,
    St. Emilion 79.50
178 CHATEAU BOUSCAUT, Graves 69.50

1964 *The 1964 vintage is now expressing itself, particularly at the famed and great vineyards. Here are wines you can enjoy now, with the happy knowledge that they will still prove delightful years hence.*

179 CHATEAU MOUTON BARON
    PHILIPPE ROTHSCHILD,
    Pauillac 109.50
180 CHATEAU LA MISSION HAUT
    BRION. Graves 159.50
A big confident wine—as imposing as a trumpet-call among the delicate flutes of the other red Graves. Because of its fine balance 1966 Chateau La Mission Haut Brion is at its most elegant.

181 CHATEAU HAUT BRION, Graves..279.50
182 CHATEAU, Margaux 279.50
183 CHATEAU CHEVAL BLANC,
    St. Emilion 299.50
184 CHATEAU LATOUR, Pauillac 299.50
185 CHATEAU PETRUS, Pomerol 399.50
186 CHATEAU LAFITE
    ROTHSCHILD, Pauillac 479.50
187 CHATEAU HAUT BRION, Graves..269.50

1966 *A great, great claret year—a worthy successor to the classic 61's— and an excellent precursor to the '70s. In the grand tradition—beautifully balanced. Long lived. Rapidly disappearing off the market.*

188 CHATEAU MARGAUX, Margaux ...299.50
189 CHATEAU LATOUR, Pauillac 329.50

BORDEAUX

Rarities

When experienced buyers seek the rare and old vintage wines, PRICE is secondary— PROPER HANDLING is always the most important factor. In like manner in our seeking out rare wines, we followed the same pattern—all the wines listed below have had special care—kept under constant temperature control and rarely moved. They are irreplaceable and in LIMITED QUANTITY.

BOTTLE
PRICE

196 CHATEAU TALBOT,
    St. Julien, 1961 .... 22.50
197 CHATEAU AUSONE,
    St. Emilion, 1955 .... 34.50
198 CHATEAU CHEVAL BLANC
    St. Emilion, 1949 .... 64.50
199 CHATEAU CHEVAL BLANC,
    St. Emilion, 1952 .... 45.00
200 CHATEAU CHEVAL BLANC,
    St. Emilion, 1955 .... 59.50
201 CHATEAU CHEVAL BLANC,
    St. Emilion, 1959 .... 59.50
202 CHATEAU CHEVAL BLANC,
    St. Emilion, 1961 .... 59.50
203 CHATEAU HAUT BRION,
    Graves, 1952 .... 47.50
204 CHATEAU HAUT BRION,
    Graves, 1955 .... 49.50
205 CHATEAU HAUT BRION,
    Graves, 1959 .... 52.50
206 CHATEAU MARGAUX,
    Margaux, 1947 .... 59.50
207 CHATEAU MARGAUX,
    Margaux, 1952 .... 50.00
208 CHATEAU MARGAUX,
    Margaux, 1953 .... 59.50
209 CHATEAU MARGAUX,
    Margaux, 1955 .... 59.50
210 CHATEAU MARGAUX,
    Margaux, 1959 .... 57.50
211 CHATEAU MARGAUX,
    Margaux, 1961 .... 57.50
212 CHATEAU PETRUS,
    Pomerol, 1953 .... 75.00
213 CHATEAU LATOUR,
    Pauillac, 1952 .... 50.00
214 CHATEAU LATOUR,
    Pauillac, 1953 .... 59.50
215 CHATEAU LATOUR,
    Pauillac, 1955 .... 59.50
216 CHATEAU LA MISSION HAUT
    BRION, Graves, 1955 .... 39.50
217 CHATEAU MOUTON
    ROTHSCHILD, Pauillac, 1952.. 59.50
218 CHATEAU MOUTON
    ROTHSCHILD, Pauillac, 1955.. 62.50
219 CHATEAU LAFITE
    ROTHSCHILD, Pauillac, 1957.. 45.00

"Advance Offering"

BORDEAUX RED—1971

As often happens, the harvest following a great vintage year goes unnoticed. This was true with 1962 following the great 1961 vintage: 1967 following the highly acclaimed 1966; and now the 1971s following the much heralded 1970s.

We all remember the rewarding 1962s and 1967s. While the 1971 harvest was small, selected vineyards produced outstanding wines—in some instances even greater than their 1970 counterparts.

Our selection limited us to only four wines—all of which we are extremely proud.

CASE PRICE

529 CHATEAU MARGAUX, Margaux 249.50
An excellent wine with elegant bouget and mellow body—truly the most feminine of the great red wines.

530 CHATEAU CLERC-MILON
ROTHSCHILD, Pauillac 109.50
This 1971 vintage is the second production under the auspices of Baron Philippe de Rothschild. 1970 was excellent, but 1971 looks even better, with the character of the Great Mouton Rothschild.

531 CHATEAU MOUTON BARON
PHILIPPE ROTHSCHILD,
Pauillac 109.50
Definitely a greater and longer maturing wine—with more bouquet and finesse than the 1970s.

CASE PRICE

532 CHATEAU MOUTON
ROTHSCHILD, Pauillac 279.50
A very low yield harvest of surprisingly high quality. Wine connoisseurs agree it will be a greater and longer lived wine than the great 1970. Available in Magnums (2), Double Magnums (4), Jeraboams (6), Imperials (8).

BORDEAUX RED—1973

The 1973 vintage was a bountiful one. The wines were fruity, soft, with fine bouquet. In Bordeaux they compare 1973 with the 1962s, which were certainly most satisfying. One should be quite selective in the purchase of this 1973 vintage. We have thus far purchased only TWO wines—both exceptional quality.

CASE PRICE

533 CHATEAU MOUTON BARON
PHILIPPE ROTHSCHILD,
Pauillac 109.50
1970 was an abundant year in the Medoc District. Because of the high percentage of Cabernet Sauvignon grown in this vineyard it is rated one of the best of '73.

534 CHATEAU CLERC-MILON
ROTHSCHILD, Pauillac 109.50
Situated between Chateau Mouton Rothschild and Chateau Lafite Rothschild, this wine has both characteristics of its famous neighbors.

---

190 CHATEAU MOUTON
ROTHSCHILD, Pauillac 349.50

191 CHATEAU LAFITE
ROTHSCHILD, Pauillac 399.50

1962 *Quick to mature, the excellent 1962 clarets are appreciated by connoisseurs because they carry their full quota of completeness to the wine-drinker who wants to enjoy a great wine today, and not a decade hence. Few '62s can be found in Bordeaux today, because they have been spoken for by appreciative wine drinkers throughout the world.*

192 CHATEAU MOUTON
ROTHSCHILD, Pauillac 349.50

193 CHATEAU LAFITE
ROTHSCHILD, Pauillac 349.50

194 CHATEAU LATOUR, Pauillac 479.50

195 CHATEAU MOUTON
ROTHSCHILD, Pauillac 499.50

BORDEAUX—WHITE

CASE PRICE

220 MOUTON CADET, Blanc 1972
Baron Philippe de Rothschild..... 43.09

221 CHATEAU OLIVIER,
Graves, 1969 .... 53.46
Dry, Excellent and very popular Graves.

222 CHATEAU LARRIVET-HAUT
BRION BLANC, Graves 1969...... 67.50

1959 *Was hailed as the "vintage of the century". Those that survive are glorious, extremely expensive, and will excite wine-lovers everywhere. We do not have many of them to offer and we list them below.*

223 CHATEAU CARBONNIEUX,
Graves, 1969 .... 75.06

224 CHATEAU LA TOUR
BLANCHE, Sauternes, 1970 .... 69.50

225 CHATEAU DE MALLE, Grand
Cru Sauternes, 1970 .... 72.25
Owned by the first cousin of the Lur-Saluces Family of famous Chateau D'Yquem - one of the great values of Sauterne.

226 CHATEAU COUTET, 1st Grand
Cru de Sauternes, 1969 .... 72.25

227 CHATEAU VOIGNY,
Sauternes, 1970 .... 59.50
Superb example of rich Sauternes.

228 CHATEAU SUDUIRAUT,
Sauternes, 1967 .... 79.50

CASE PRICE

229 PAVILLON BLANC du
Chateau Margaux, 1972 .... 78.30
This is the only white wine produced by the famous Chateau Margaux in Bordeaux. It is a dry white wine of exceptional flavor and bouquet, with fine character and finesse.
VERY LIMITED PRODUCTION.

---

230 CHATEAU D'YQUEM,
Sauternes, 1966 ....249.50

CASE PRICE

231 CHATEAU HAUT BRION
BLANC, Pessac Graves, 1970...229.50
A small portion of Chateau Haut Brion is dedicated to the production of an exceptional dry white wine—the best of Bordeaux, and one of the great white wines of the world. Limited Supply.

HALF-BOTTLES

There is a joy in adventuring among many different wines—and the easiest and most economical method of embarking on this Odyssey is to acquire half-bottles. There are 24 instead of 12 experiences with every case. Here are some choice selections to launch you on your adventure among the vineyards of the world.

RED WINES

CASE PRICE

232 CHATEAU LA ROSE
   TRINTAUDON, Haut
   Medoc, 1970 .... 53.00
233 CHATEAU PICQUE CAILLOU,
   Graves, 1970 .... 56.00
234 CHATEAU GREYSAC,
   Medoc, 1970 .... 55.00
235 CHATEAU DE PEZ,
   St. Estephe, 1970 .... 56.00
236 CHATEAU SIMARD,
   St. Emilion, 1970 .... 56.00
237 CHATEAU PAVIE,
   St. Emilion, 1970 .... 78.00
238 CHATEAU LA LAGUNE,
   Haut Medoc, 1970 .... 93.00
239 CHATEAU DUHART MILON
   ROTHSCHILD, Pauillac, 1970.. 93.00
240 CHATEAU L'ANGELUS,
   St. Emilion, 1970 .... 83.00
241 CHATEAU LYNCH BAGES,
   Pauillac, 1970 ....138.50
242 CHATEAU LATOUR CARNET,
   Haut Medoc, 1967 .... 71.00
243 CHATEAU LATOUR CARNET,
   Haut Medoc, 1966 .... 79.50
244 CHATEAU GRUAUD LAROSE,
   St. Julien, 1967 ....103.00
245 CHATEAU BRANE CANTENAC,
   Margaux, 1970 ....123.00
246 CHATEAU MOUTON
   ROTHSCHILD,
   Pauillac, 1967 ....253.00
247 CHATEAU MOUTON
   ROTHSCHILD,
   Pauillac, 1970 ....383.00
248 CHATEAU MARGAUX,
   Margaux, 1967 ....183.00
249 CHATEAU LAFITE
   ROTHSCHILD,
   Pauillac, 1967 ....283.00
250 CHATEAU LATOUR,
   Pauillac, 1966 ....303.00
252 CHATEAU HAUT BRION,
   Graves, 1961 ....503.00
253 CHATEAUNEUF DU PAPE,
   Clos de le Oratoire, 1969 ..... 52.50
254 GEVREY CHAMBERTIN,
   Louis Jadot, 1970 .... 82.08
255 BEAUNE THEURONS,
   Louis Jadot, 1969 .... 77.76
256 VOSNE ROMANEE,
   Louis Jadot, 1969 .... 99.36
257 COTE DE NUITS VILLAGES,
   Louis Jadot, 1969 .... 60.48
258 NUITS ST. GEORGES,
   Louis Jadot, 1970 .... 98.28

259 BROUILLY, Chateau de la Chaize,
   in 18 oz Pichets, 1972 .... 69.50

What is a pichet? It is a handsome 18 Oz. bottle that represents a useful midpoint size between the usually insufficient 12 Oz. half-bottle and the standard 24 Oz. full bottle. When it is "dinner for two" you can feel generous about your wine drinking and yet avoid the possible waste of a full bottle.

WHITE WINES

260 MACON BLANC,
   Louis Jadot, 1972 .... 49.50
261 MACON LUGNY, Les Genievres,
   Louis Latour, 1971 .... 49.50
262 CUVEE LES AMOURS,
   Pinot Blanc, "Hugel" 46.59
263 CHATEAU VOIGNY,
   Sauternes, 1970 .... 59.50
264 BRAUNEBERGER JUFFER,
   Spatlese, Qualitatswein
   mit Pradikat,
   S. F. von Schorlemer, 1969 .... 66.50
265 MAXIMIN GRUNHAUSER
   Herrenberg, Spatlese,
   C. von Schubert, 1969 .... 72.50
266 OCKFENER BOCKSTEIN,
   Spatlese, Dr. H. Fischer, 1970 .. 69.50

MAGNUMS—Equal to 2 bottles

CASE PRICE

267 COTES DU RHONE,
   La Vieille Ferme, 1972 .... 38.50
268 CHATEAU LA ROSE,
   TRINTAUDON,
   Haut Medoc, 1970 .... 46.00
269 CHATEAU PICQUE CAILLOU,
   Graves, 1970 .... 53.00
270 CHATEAU GREYSAC,
   Medoc, 1970 .... 55.00
271 CHATEAU SIMARD,
   St. Emilion, 1970 .... 56.00
272 CHATEAU PAVIE,
   St. Emilion, 1970 .... 78.00
273 CHATEAU L'ANGELUS,
   St. Emilion, 1970 .... 83.00
274 CHATEAU DUHART MILON
   ROTHSCHILD,
   Pauillac 1970 .... 93.00
275 CHATEAU LYNCH BAGES,
   Pauillac, 1970 ....138.50
276 CHATEAU PICHON
   LONGUEVILLE LALANDE,
   Pauillac, 1970 ....133.50
277 CHATEAU MOUTON
   ROTHSCHILD,
   Pauillac, 1970 ....383.00

THE WINES OF BURGUNDY

After the 1973 harvest there were broad smiles on the faces of all the Burgundians. This vintage finished their fifth successive harvest without a bad year—1969 thru 1973—the first time in over fifty years!

The 1969s—an exceedingly great year, quite in the class of the fabulous 1961, deep colored, rich, everything that fine Burgundies should be. We know of no better way of testifying to the true excellence of the 1971 red Burgundies than to simply quote Frank Schoonmaker's recently issued Vintage Report: "A fabulous and extraordinary year, unlike anything we have seen since 1947 . . . sadly, because of hail and torrential rains many small growers along the Cote lost half their crop while their neighbors, a few hundred yards away, were completely unscathed. Those who were spared may well give us some of the best Burgundy of our generation—big, splendid wines, slow to mature and certainly of long life, conceivably even better than the 1961s which is anything but faint praise."

1970 and 1972 were good wines—fruity and quick to mature.

The 1973 vintage was large and the wines good —not outstanding, but very drinkable, pleasant and quick maturing.

SELECT WELL AND YOUR LOVE OF BURGUNDY CAN ONLY INCREASE!

BURGUNDY RED

CASE PRICE

278 BEAUJOLAIS VILLAGES,
Louis Latour, 1971 .... 39.50

279 BEAUJOLAIS, Louis Jadot, 1971 ... 47.50

---

280 BROUILLY, Chateau de la
Chaize, 1972 .... 45.90

As in each preceding year since 1969, the wine seems to have grown in stature. We think this 1972 vintage is the best we have had thus far, full bodied—rich in tannin— ready to drink now, and will improve within the next two years. To avoid disappointment we urge early acquisition.

---

281 COTE DE BROUILLY,
Chateau Thivin, 1971 .... 45.90

282 PERNAND VERGELESSES,
Louis Latour, 1970 .... 49.50

283 CLOS DE COUCHERAUX,
Louis Jadot, 1969 .... 71.28

284 VOLNAY SANTENOTS,
J. Matrot, 1970 .... 64.50

285 BEAUNE-THEURONS,
Louis Jadot, 1969 .... 73.98

286 BEAUNE-THEURONS,
Louis Jadot, 1970 .... 73.98

287 CHAMBOLLE-MUSIGNY,
Louis Jadot, 1970 .... 82.82

288 BEAUNE-BRESSANDES,
Louis Jadot, 1969 .... 80.46

289 GEVREY CHAMBERTIN,
Louis Jadot, 1969 .... 73.98

290 GEVREY CHAMBERTIN,
J. Faiveley, 1969 .... 72.95

291 GEVREY CHAMBERTIN,
J. Faiveley, 1971 .... 99.50
One of the outstanding wines of 1971. A big, full-bodied wine, slow to mature—worth seeking out for its breed and elegance.

292 VOSNE ROMANEE,
J. Faiveley, 1969 .... 84.50

293 VOSNE ROMANEE,
Louis Jadot, 1969 .... 95.58

294 BEAUNE CLOS DES URSULES,
Louis Jadot, 1969 .... 94.50

295 NUITS SAINT GEORGES,
Clos de la Marechale,
J. Faiveley, 1969 .... 89.50

296 NUITS SAINT GEORGES,
Les St. Georges,
Henri Gouges, 1970 .... 82.50

297 CORTON, Vigne Au Saint,
Louis Latour, 1970 .... 92.50

298 CLOS DES CORTONS,
J. Faiveley, 1966 .... 99.50

299 CLOS DES CORTONS,
J. Faiveley, 1969 ....109.50

300 CORTON POUGET,
Louis Jadot, 1970 ....124.20

301 CORTON CLOS DU ROI,
Prince de Merode, 1970 .... 99.50

302 CORTON,
Bonneau du Martray, 1971 ...... 99.50

303 CLOS DE TART,
J. Mommesin, 1970 ....109.50

304 CLOS DE VOUGEOT,
J. Faiveley, 1969 ....139.50

305 BONNES MARES,
Louis Latour, 1970 ....149.50

306 CHAMBOLLE MUSIGNY,
Amoureuses,
Comte G. de Vogue, 1969 ....249.50

307 CHAMBOLLE MUSIGNY,
J. Faiveley, 1971 ....109.50
Famed Burgundy from the town that also produces Musigny and Bonnes Mares. Not as exalted, but endowed with similar finesse and distinction. A real bargain for a big 1971 Burgundy.

308 MUSIGNY,
Comte G. de Vogue, 1967 ....249.50

309 CHAMBERTIN CLOS DE BEZE,
J. Faiveley, 1971 ....249.50
Clos de Beze considered even superior to Chambertin itself—on the same exalted level as Musigny and Richebourg. This is our selection AS THE BEST of the Great 1971 Burgundies.

DOMAINE DUJAC
S. C. E. Seysses Pere & Fils

Domaine Dujac, consisting of six vineyards, was purchased by the family of J. Seysses in 1969—the last major purchase of a great Burgundian Domaine in our lifetime. Totally devoted to the making of fine Burgundy in the traditional manner, these rare wines deserve your careful consideration.

CASE PRICE

310 MOREY ST. DENIS, 1969 .... 89.50
311 CLOS ST. DENIS,
Premier Cru, 1969 ....129.50
312 CLOS DE LA ROCHE,
Grand Cru, 1970 ....139.50
313 BONNES MARES,
Grand Cru, 1970 ....169.50

VINS DOMAINE de la ROMANEE-CONTI

We are proud of our collection of the Domaine de la Romanee-Conti wines—we believe it is the most comprehensive collection held under a single roof. Unfortunately though, our Domaine inventory is not inexhaustible, and suggest that those true wine lovers of these Great Burgundies act swiftly, so as not to be disappointed by prior depletions.

BOTTLE PRICE
FIFTHS
315 ECHEZEAUX, 1969 .... 15.95
316 ECHEZEAUX, 1970 .... 19.50
317 GRANDS ECHEZEAUX, 1965 ... 12.95

318 GRANDS ECHEZEAUX, 1969 ...	19.75
319 GRANDS ECHEZEAUX, 1970 ...	23.75
320 LA TACHE, 1966	34.50
321 LA TACHE, 1969	34.00
322 LA TACHE, 1970	34.00
323 RICHEBOURG, 1965	13.95
324 RICHEBOURG, 1969	30.75
325 RICHEBOURG, 1970	30.75
326 ROMANEE ST. VIVANT, 1970 ..	30.75
327 ROMANEE CONTI, 1970	78.50

	BOTTLE PRICE
MAGNUMS	
328 ECHEZEAUX, 1970	39.50
329 GRANDS ECHEZEAUX, 1970 ...	47.50
330 LA TACHE, 1966	69.75
331 LA TACHE, 1969	69.75
332 LA TACHE, 1970	69.75
333 RICHEBOURG, 1969	61.95
334 RICHEBOURG, 1970	61.95
335 ROMANEE ST. VIVANT, 1969 ..	57.95
336 ROMANEE ST. VIVANT, 1970 ..	61.50

	BOTTLE PRICE
JERABOAMS	
337 ECHEZEAUX, 1970	79.00
338 GRANDS ECHEZEAUX, 1970 ...	95.00
339 LA TACHE, 1970	139.50
340 RICHEBOURG, 1970	125.00
341 ROMANEE ST. VIVANT, 1970 ..	125.00
342 ROMANEE CONTI, 1964	300.00

Ten Percent discount by the case, or mixed cases, with the exception of Romanee-Conti.

BURGUNDY WHITE
CASE PRICE

343 SAINT AUBIN BLANC, Raoul Clerget, 1967	39.90
344 MACON BLANC, Louis Jadot, 1971	47.50
345 LA FORET MACON VILLAGE, Joseph Drouhin, 1970	43.09
347 BEAUJOLAIS BLANC, Louis Jadot, 1971	57.50
348 SAVIGNY LES BEAUNE, Louis Jadot, 1970	62.10
349 CHABLIS LA FORET, Vocoret, 1971	59.50
350 CHABLIS LES CLOS, Vocoret, 1971	67.50
351 MEURSAULT, Louis Jadot, 1971	85.86
352 POUILLY FUISSE, Joseph Drouhin, 1971 ... ••••••••	75.7!
353 POUILLY FUISSE, Louis Latour, 1971	75.49

354 CHATEAU DE MEURSAULT,
Comte de Moucheron, 1971 .... 89.50
Bottled at the Estate—this great white wine is one of the very few allowed the use of the name "Chateau." This honor is deserved thru a particular control and selection.
Made from grapes grown exclusively on the Estate of the Count de Moucheron. It is only sold in bottles after being made and cared for in the Chateau's own cellars.

355 PULIGNY MONTRACHET,
Clavoillon,
Domaine Le Flaive, 1971 .....119.50
At a recent tasting, this elegant Puligny Montrachet finished No. 1 against such celebrated vineyards as Batard, Chevalier and Le Montrachet. An outstanding value!

356 CORTON CHARLEMAGNE, Louis Jadot, 1969	145.26
357 CORTON CHARLEMAGNE, Bonneau du Martray, 1971	109.50

358 BATARD MONTRACHET, Domaine Le Flaive, 1971	199.50
359 CHEVALIER MONTRACHET, Domaine Le Flaive, 1971	249.50

360 CLOS BLANC DE VOUGEOT,
ler Cru,
L'Heritier-Guyot, 1971 ....134.46

Clos Blanc de Vougeot is one of the rare vineyards of the famed "Cote de Nuits" that produces great white wines. Its wines have been celebrated since the time of the monks of Citeaux, and one finds in the archives of the village of Nuits that the wines of Clos Blanc sold for the same prices as the wines of Clos Vougeot during the 17th and 18th Centuries.

Not only is this wine of rarity and interest, but it is beyond question an outstanding example of an exceptional white Burgundy imported only in great vintage years. The proud owner of the vineyard, L'Heritier-Guyot, has shipped only a small quantity of this "collector's item" to the United States. Each bottle bears its individual identifying number.

	BOTTLE PRICE
361 MONTRACHET, Domaine de la Romanee Conti, 1965	19.95
362 MONTRACHET, Marquis de Laguiche, 1967	24.56
364 MONTRACHET, Marquis de Laguiche, 1970	27.79

THE WINES OF THE RHONE VALLEY

With the ever increasing prices of Bordeaux and Burgundy wines, wine lovers are looking more and more to the Rhone Valley for quality wine at reasonable prices. We recommend that strong consideration be given to these big, full-bodied, robust reds and the long lived whites as today's best wine values.

Rhone Red

CASE PRICE

365 COTES DU RHONE, La Vieille Ferme, 1972	34.50

Quoting from
The CRAIG CLAIBORNE JOURNAL

"We found a red wine that is honest and dry and clean to the palate. From the Rhone Valley—bottled at the vineyard called La Vieille Ferme—it is excellent and the equal, we feel, of the much better known and neighboring Chateauneuf-du-pape, which it resembles.
In our experience as wine merchants we think this is the best red wine value under $3.00 we have ever found—buy early while supply lasts!"

366 COTE ROTIE, Dervieux Thaize, 1969	69.50

CHATEAUNEUF DU PAPE,
CASE PRICE

Clos de le Oratoire, 1969 ..... 52.50
With the inflated prices of the Rhone wines, especially Chateauneuf-du-Pape, which in some cases have advanced approximately 100% within the past 90 days, we believe this Estate Bottled Chateauneuf - du - Pape, Clos de le Oratoire, which Andre Simon lists in his book as one of the best available, is an exceptionally good buy.
Early acquisition is suggested as the supply is limited.

Rhone White

CASE PRICE

367 CHATEAU CONDRIEU, Coteaux de Vernon Georges Vernay, 1970 ....125.00
Interesting and unusual white wine of the Rhone Valley, produced some thirty miles South of Lyon. Its terraced vineyards planted to the Vioginer grape are as steep as Cote Rotie nearby, and their output is absurdly small. Almost all of this is consumed locally and in the famous Restaurant de La Pyramide (Point) at Vienne. Often faintly petillant or sparkling when young—golden in color—fruity—with a special and distinctive bouquet—among the scarcest of all French wines.

WINES OF THE LOIRE

367 MUSCADET, Domaine de L'Hyverniere, 1971 ... 37.69
368 QUINCY, G. Meunier-Lapha, 1971 .... 49.50

A pleasant, spicy, dry white wine from the village of this name, on the River Cher, not far from Bourges, in central France. Quincy is not unlike a very dry Sancerre or Pouilly-Blanc-Fume.

369 POUILLY FUME de Ladoucette, Chateau du Nozet, 1971 .... 57.13
Chateau du Nozet produces one of the world's finest white wines—the Pouilly Fume of Ladoucette Freres located in France's famous Pouilly-sur-Loire region. Production extremely limited.

ALSATIAN WINES

The Alsatian wines are usually named after the grape from which they are made, such as Sylvaner, Riesling, Gewurztraminer, etc. Their distinguishing characteristics are flowery fragrance, relatively dry but fruity. The wines of F. Hugel are generally acknowledged as the best of Alsace.
CASE PRICE

370 PINOT BLANC, "Hugel" 36.50
371 SYLVANER, "Hugel" 38.77
372 RIESLING, "Hugel" 48.06

SPANISH WINES

CASE PRICE

373 CUNE, Rioja Clarete, 1970 ..... 32.50
Imported exclusively for John Walker & Co. by Frederick Wildman & Son. We consider this medium bodied, well balanced claret, with amazing character, the finest value in the wine-world today.

ITALIAN WINES

Many wine drinkers are now turning to Italy to provide good wines at a modest cost. Our selections in this offering represent the best values we have been able to locate from Italy.

RED WINES
CASE PRICE

374 BARDOLINO, Classico, Estate Bottled, Fratelli Poggi, 1970 ...... 32.40
375 VALPOLICELLA, Dinominazione Di Origine Controllata, P.A.S. Produttori Associati Soave 32.40
376 CHIANTE CLASSICO, Fattoria Di TIZZANO, Riserva, Estate Bottled, Donominazione Di Origine Controllata, 1968 ...... 43.20
377 NOZZOLE, Chianti Classico, Estate Bottles Riserva, Denominazione Di Origine Controllata, 1968 .... 45.90
378 BARBARESCO, Vino Tipico Delle Langhe, Denominazione Di Origine Controllata, Alfredo Prunotto, 1965 .... 78.30
379 BAROLO, Vino Tripico Delle Langhe, Denominazione Di Origine Controllata, Alfredo Prunotto, 1966 .... 70.20

WHITE WINES

380 ORVIETO, Dry, Barberani & Cortoni 35.10
380 FRASCATI, Vigneti di COLLE Portella, Estate Bottled, A. De Sanctis & Figli, 1970 ...... 35.10

THE WINES OF GERMANY

The 1971 vintage in the Rhine and Moselle areas will be remembered as one of the outstanding vintages of this century. What is more important, the 1971 wines were very good to superb to extremely great in EVERY part of the German wine country.

Even tho the great 1971s have advanced approximately 40% from the opening prices, our large inventory permits us to offer these superb estate-bottled wines at liveable prices. While the 1972 and 1973 vintages in the Rhine and Moselle were above average in quality, there were very few great wines (Spatlese and Auslese); no dessert wines (Beerenauslese and Trocken-beerenauslese)—resulting in heavy demand for these great '71s—few if any will be left at the end of the year.

For best values in current drinking we particularly commend the 1969 and 1970 Rhines and Moselles that are offered here at prices that cannot be acquired elsewhere. Our advice is to buy the '69s and '70s for drinking now and keep the '71s to be enjoyed later. YOU WILL NOT REGRET THEIR ACQUISITION.

German Rhine

	CASE PRICE
381 NIERSTEINER GUTES DOMTHAL, Qualitatswein, Villa Eden, 1972	34.50
382 RUDESHEIMER ROSENGARTEN, Qualitatswein, Villa Eden, 1972	34.50

Highest quality Regional Rhine Wines from the firm of Hermann Kendermann—OURS EXCLUSIVELY.

	CASE PRICE
383 JOHANNISBERGER KLAUS, Qualitatswein, 1970	39.50
384 SCHLOSS VOLLRADS, Schlossabzug, Red Silver Cap, 1970	41.50
385 SCHLOSS VOLLRADS, Kabinett, Blue Cap, 1970	56.56
386 SCHLOSS VOLLRADS, Kabinett, Blue Cap, Qualitatswein mit Pradikat, 1971	74.50
387 SCHLOSS SCHONBORN, Johannisberger Klaus Riesling Spatlese, Qualitatswein mit Pradikat, 1971	69.50
388 SCHLOSS JOHANNISBERGER GRUNLACK, Spatlese, Qualitatswein mit Pradikat, Furst von Metternich, 1971	76.50
389 HATTENHEIMER NUSSBRUNNEN, Kabinet, L. Von Simmern, 1970	49.75
390 HATTENHEIMER NUSSBRUNNEN, Kabinet, Qualitatswein mit Pradikat, L. Von Simmern, 1971	69.50
391 HATTENHEIMER NUSSBRUNNEN, Spatlese, L. Von Simmern, 1970	69.50
392 HATTENHEIMER NUSSBRUNNEN, Spatlese, Qualitatswein mit Pradikat, L. Von Simmern, 1971	92.50
393 ELTVILLER SONNENBERG, Qualitatswein, L. Von Simmern, 1970	47.50
394 ELTVILLER SONNENBERG, Kabinett, Qualitatswein mit Pradikat, L. Von Simmern, 1971	59.50
395 ELTVILLER SONNENBERG, Spatlese Feine, Schloss Eltz, 1969	76.50
396 STEINBERGER, Qualitatswein, Orig. Abf. Staatsweinguter, 1970	42.50
397 STEINBERGER KLOSTER EBERBACH, Spatlese, Qualitatswein mit Pradikat, Orig. Abf., Staatsweinguter, 1971	72.50
398 FORSTER JESUITGARTEN, Cabinet, Orig. Abf. Dr. Von Basserman-Jordan (Palatinate), 1970	54.50
399 FORSTER JESUITGARTEN, Spatlese, Orig. Abf. Dr. Von Basserman-Jordan (Palatinate), 1970	69.50
400 FORSTER JESUITGARTEN, Cabinet, Orig. Abf. Dr. Von Basserman-Jordan (Palatinate), Qualitatswein mit Pradikat, 1971	62.50
401 FORSTER JESUITGARTEN, Spatlese, Orig. Abf. Dr. Von Basserman-Jordan (Palatinate), Qualitatswein mit Pradikat, 1971	82.50

	BOTTLES ONLY
402 NIERSTEINER KRANZBERG, Beerenauslese, Erz. Abf. Qualitatswein mit Pradikat, Franz Karl Schmitt, 1971	25.00
403 STEINBERGER RIESLING, Cabinet, Beerenauslese, Orig. Abf. Staatsweinguter, 1959	49.50

German Moselle

	CASE PRICE
404 BERNCASTLER RIESLING, Villa Eden, 1971	32.50
405 PIESPORTER GOLDTROPFCHEN, Villa Eden, 1972	34.50

Exclusive shipment of the highest quality Regional Moselle Wines from the firm of Hermann Kendermann—

OURS EXCLUSIVELY

	CASE PRICE
406 OCKFENER BOCKSTEIN, Cabinet, Dr. H. Fischer, 1970	42.50
407 OCKFENER BOCKSTEIN, Spatlese, Dr. H. Fischer, 1970	62.50
408 OCKFENER BOCKSTEIN, Cabinet, Dr. H. Fischer, Qualitatswein mit Pradikat, 1971	59.50
409 OCKFENER BOCKSTEIN, Spatlese, Dr. H. Fischer, Qualitatswein mit Pradikat, 1971	72.50
410 PIESPORTER GOLDTROPFCHEN, Spatlese, Qualitatswein mit Pradikat, Erz. Abf. Weingut Freudeureich, 1971	54.50
411 BERNKASTELER SCHLOSSBERG, Kabinett, Qualitatswein mit Pradikat, Erz. Abf. Weingut Meyerhof. 1971	52.50
412 BERNKASTELER SCHLOSSBERG, Spatlese, Qualitatswein mit Pradikat, Erz. Abf. Weingut Meyerhof. 1971	62.50
413 BRAUNEBERGER JUFFER, Spatlese, Qualitatswein mit Pradikat, S. F. von Schorlemer, 1971	76.50
414 GRAACHER HIMMELREICH, Kabinett, Joh. Jos. Prum. 1970	52.50
415 GRAACHER HIMMELREICH, Spatlese, Joh. Jos. Prum. Qualitatswein mit Pradikat, 1971	87.50
416 GRAACHER HIMMELREICH, Auslese, Joh. Jos. Prum. Qualitatswein mit Pradikat, 1971	104.50
417 WEHLENER SONNENUHR, Kabinett, Joh. Jos. Prum. 1970	54.50
418 WEHLENER SONNENUHR, Auslese, Joh. Jos. Prum. Qualitatswein mit Pradikat, 1971	119.50

419 SCHARZHOFBERGER,
   Egon Muller, 1970 .... 52.50
420 MAXIMIN GRUNHAUSER,
   Abtsberg, C. von Schubert, 1970 .. 42.50
421 MAXIMIN GRUNHAUSER
   HERRENBERG, Spatlese,
   C. von Schubert, 1970 .... 67.50
422 MAXIMIN GRUNHAUSER
   HERRENBERG, Auslese,
   C. von Schubert, 1970 .... 99.50
423 MAXIMIN GRUNHAUSER,
   Abtsberg, Kabinett,
   Qualitatswein mit Pradikat,
   C. von Schubert, 1971 .... 76.50
424 MAXIMIN GRUNHAUSER
   HERRENBERG, Spatlese,
   Qualitatswein mit Pradikat,
   C. von Schubert, 1971 .... 99.50
535 MAXIMIN GRUNHAUSER,
   Abtsberg, Auslese,
   Qualitatswein mit Pradikat, 1971 ..119.50
536 MAXIMEN GRUNHAUSER
   HERRENBERG, Auslese,
   Qualitatswein mit Pradikat, 1971 ..129.50

538 BERNCASTLER DOCTOR,
   Spatlese, U. Graben,
   Dr. H. Thanisch, 1970 ...... 179.50
539 BERNCASTLER DOCTOR,
   Spatlese, U. Graben,
   Dr. H. Thanisch,
   Qualitatswein mit Pradikat, 1971 ..239.50
540 BERNCASTLER DOCTOR,
   Auslese, Qualitatswein mit
   Pradikat, U. Graben,
   Dr. H. Thanisch, 1971 ....299.50

	BOTTLES ONLY
541 WEHLENER SONNENUHR BEERENAUSLESE, Orig. Abf. Joh. Jos. Prum, 1969	66.50
542 WEHLENER SONNENUHR BEERENAUSLESE, Orig. Abf. Joh. Jos. Prum, 1959	69.50
543 MAXIMIN GRUNHAUSER HERRENBERG TROCKEN- BEERENAUSLESE, Orig. Abf. C. von Schubert, 1959	65.00

California Wines

THE WINES OF CALIFORNIA are finding their rightful place in the finest wine cellar collections of the world. Recent auctions attest to this, as the rare old California vintages attract as much interest as their European counterparts. While much good wine is made in favored Valleys of California, the exceptional quality varietal wines are in short supply. As the new plantings of California wines grow slowly to a producing maturity, we still look for the current vintages to lay down or enjoy now.

At today's current European prices, we suggest that you take a good look at the values now presented in our Premium California Wines. We are proud to offer this collection of the bounty of California's finest wine growing areas.

ALMADEN VINEYARDS, Los Gatos
SPECIAL SELECTION VINTAGE WINES

	CASE PRICE
414 GAMAY BEAUJOLAIS, 1971-72	46.98
415 PINOT NOIR, 1971-72 (m)	46.98
416 CABERNET SAUVIGNON, 1971 (m)	46.98
417 PINOT CHARDONNAY, 1971-72 (m)	46.98
418 JOHANNISBERG RIESLING, 1971-72	46.98

(m) *Available in Magnums.*

BEAULIEU VINEYARDS, Rutherford (Napa)

	CASE PRICE
419 BURGUNDY, 1971	29.70
420 CHABLIS, 1972	29.70
421 GAMAY BEAUJOLAIS, 1972	32.40
422 RIESLING SYLVANER, 1972	32.40
423 JOHANNISBERG RIESLING, 1972	43.20
424 JOHANNISBERG RIESLING, Spatlese, 1972	54.00

This magnificent late-picked Johannisberg Riesling is in the true tradition of a German Spatlese—yet it is uniquely a Napa Valley product and should be judged as such.

425 CABERNET SAUVIGNON *(Limited)*, 1971	48.60
426 PINOT CHARDONNAY, 1972	48.60
427 PINOT NOIR, 1970	48.60

BEAULIEU VINEYARDS

	BOTTLE PRICE
428 CABERNET SAUVIGNON, 1965	8.00
429 CABERNET SAUVIGNON, 1967	7.00
430 CABERNET SAUVIGNON, 1969	8.00
431 CABERNET SAUVIGNON, Private Reserve, 1965	14.00
432 CABERNET SAUVIGNON, Private Reserve, 1967	10.00
433 CABERNET SAUVIGNON, Private Reserve, 1969	6.50

—Limited Supply—

DAVIS BYNUM WINERY, Healdsburg (Sonoma)

CASE PRICE

434 SAUVIGNON BLANC, 1973 .... 37.80

THE CHRISTIAN BROTHERS, St. Helena (Napa)

CASE PRICE

439 CABERNET SAUVIGNON 37.80
440 GAMAY NOIR 35.10
441 PINOT NOIR 37.80
442 PINOT ST. GEORGE 43.20
443 PINOT CHARDONNAY 43.20
444 PINOT NOIR, Special Selection, Lot 12-0-7, Bottled Dec., 1970 .... 37.80

FETZER VINEYARDS, Redwood Valley (Mendocino County)

CASE PRICE

445 CARMINE CARIGNANE, Mendocino, 1972 .... 27.00
446 ZINFANDEL, Ricetti, Mendocino, 1972 .... 51.84
447 ZINFANDEL, Bin-42, Mendocino, 1972 .... 37.80
448 PETITE SIRAH, 1972 .... 51.84
449 CABERNET SAUVIGNON, 1971 .... 54.00
450 BLANC DE BLANCS, 1972 .... 27.00

FREEMARK ABBEY WINERY, St. Helena (Napa)

CASE PRICE

451 JOHANNISBERG RIESLING, 1971 .... 43.20
452 PINOT CHARDONNAY, 1971 .... 64.80
453 PINOT NOIR, 1969 .... 59.40
454 CABERNET SAUVIGNON, 1970 (Limited Quantity) 64.80

HEITZ CELLARS, St. Helena (Napa)

CASE PRICE

455 BARBERA 36.18
456 BURGUNDY 29.70
457 GRIGNOLINO 31.86
458 CHABLIS 25.38
459 PINOT BLANC, 1971 (Lyncrest Vineyards) 37.80
460 JOHANNISBERG RIESLING, 1972 .... 42.66
461 PINOT CHARDONNAY, Lot 2-11, 1971 .... 81.00

LLORDS & ELWOOD WINERY, Santa Clara County

CASE PRICE

464 CABERNET SAUVIGNON, Cuvee 6, Bottled Summer, 1972 .... 54.00
465 PINOT NOIR, Cuvee 8, Bottled Summer, 1972 .... 48.60
466 JOHANNISBERG RIESLING, Cuvee 5, Bottled Winter, 1972 ..... 45.90
467 CHARDONNAY, Cuvee 5, Bottled Spring, 1972 .... 45.90

ROBERT MONDAVI WINERY, Oakville (Napa)

CASE PRICE

482 CHENIN BLANC, 1973 .... 32.40
483 FUME BLANC, 1973 .... 48.60
484 JOHANNISBERG RIESLING, 1972 .... 48.60
485 CHARDONNAY, 1972 .... 70.20
486 GAMAY ROSE, 1972 .... 29.70
487 GAMAY, 1972 .... 35.10
488 ZINFANDEL, 1971 (Limited Quantities) 48.60
489 PETITE SIRAH, 1970 .... 48.60
490 PINOT NOIR, 1971 .... 56.70
491 CABERNET SAUVIGNON, 1971 (Limited Quantity) 64.80
492 CABERNET SAUVIGNON, 1970 (Limited Quantity) 78.00

BOTTLE PRICE

493 CABERNET SAUVIGNON—UNFINED, 1966 .... 15.00

A limited quantity of the first great Cabernet Sauvignon, made by this fine winery, and thought by many to be the finest.

CHATEAU MONTELENA, Calistoga (Napa)

CASE PRICE

494 JOHANNISBERG RIESLING, 1972 .... 59.40
495 CHARDONNAY, 1972 .... 64.80

California Wines (cont.)

J. PEDRONCELLI WINERY, Geyserville (Sonoma)
CASE PRICE

496 CABERNET SAUVIGNON, Private Stock, 1967 .... 53.46
A fully matured Cabernet Sauvignon—ready for drinking, full flavored and a bargain at this price.

RIDGE VINEYARD, Cupertino
PRICE CASE

497 CARIGNAN, Coast Range, 1971 .... 40.50
498 ZINFANDEL, Coast Range, 1972 .... 35.10
499 CABERNET SAUVIGNON, 1971 (Limited Quantity) 108.00

SONOMA VINEYARDS, Sonoma County
CASE PRICE

506 JOHANNISBERG RIESLING, Spatlese, 1972 .... 54.00
Winemaker Rodney Strong is proud of this Spatlese and justly so. We recommend it to the lovers of German wines. (Limited Supply.)
507 PINOT CHARDONNAY, 1971 .... 64.26
One of the most sought-after Chardonnays in California—a superb wine combining a subtle, silky texture—complex intriguing bouquet, and a rich lingering taste. (Limited Supply)

SOUVERAIN CELLARS, St. Helena (Napa)
CASE PRICE

508 BURGUNDY 40.50
509 ZINFANDEL, 1971 .... 45.90
510 GREEN HUNGARIAN, 1972 .... 35.10
511 JOHANNISBERG RIESLING, 1972 .... 54.00
512 PINEAU SOUVERAIN, 1971 .... 40.50
513 PINOT NOIR, 1972 .... 56.70
514 CABERNET SAUVIGNON, 1971 (Limited Quantity) 70.20
515 PINOT CHARDONNAY, 1972 .... 64.80

SUTTER HOME WINERY, St. Helena (Napa)
CASE PRICE

516 PINOT NOIR, 1971 .... 40.50
517 ZINFANDEL, 1971-72 (Deaver Vineyard) (Limited Quantity) 40.50

OAK CREEK VINEYARDS, Napa County

This select Napa Valley wine, made exclusively from Cabernet Sauvignon grapes, comes from a small family-owned vineyard. Situated halfway between the town of Rutherford and Oakville, on the west side of the valley, Oak Creek Vineyard lies in the heart of this famed wine-growing region.

It has been our privilege to offer our customers, on an exclusive basis, this rare estate bottled Cabernet Sauvignon, starting with the 1969 vintage, continuing through the 1970 vintage, and unfortunately ending with the 1971 vintage. However, at this writing the 1969 and 1970 vintages are in private cellars and are certainly considered "COLLECTOR'S ITEMS."

This offering of the 1971 wine will be the last produced by this famous winery. We feel that this will certainly be a COLLECTOR'S ITEM and we offer our customers this exceptional opportunity to buy this wine at a special saving.

It is our considered opinion that while quantities last this will be your best opportunity to put away a special Selection 100% Cabernet Sauvignon in any quantity for the next few years.
CASE PRICE

518 CABERNET SAUVIGNON, 1971 .... 66.00

CHAMPAGNE—CALIFORNIA
SCHRAMSBERG, Calistoga, Calif.
BOTTLE PRICE

523 BLANC DE BLANCS, 1972 .... 7.75
524 CUVEE DE GAMAY, 1972 .... 6.75
525 BLANC DE NOIR, 1970 (Very Limited) 10.00
526 CREMANT—Demi Sec 6.75

(Available Nov. 15, 1974)

C'EST BON, Los Gatos

C'EST BON CHAMPAGNE, naturally fermented in the bottle—an excellent value for wedding receptions.
CASE PRICE

527 C'EST BON, Brut 32.50
528 C'EST BON, Extra Dry 32.50

CRAIG CLAIBORNE'S WINE CELLAR

In 1973 Craig Claiborne, food editor of the New York *Times* and author of numerous cookbooks, decided to build a new kitchen onto his house on Long Island. The plan included such convenient touches as a nine-foot "island" in the center with work surfaces of wood, plastic, and marble (for pastry), a Chinese professional wok range, a counter full of electric appliances, each with an individual outlet; stainless-steel double refrigerators, and a walk-in pantry. (The space occupied by the old kitchen is now a bar, where guests may help themselves.)

The remodeling also provided Mr. Claiborne with an opportunity to install a new wine cellar, twelve feet underground, beneath a well-insulated sauna, temperature-controlled (57°) and dehumidified. Two walls of the cellar are lined with hand-made redwood racks, constructed by a neighbor, capable of holding up to five hundred bottles, with spaces for half-bottles and magnums as well as those of regular size. In the cellar also is room for storing liquor, cordials, and preserved foods such as salami, *confit d'oie* (goose), and sauerkraut. The cellar can also be used for Sunday lunch or supper, with guests seated at an oval-shaped table on an English pub bench and stools.

When the cellar was complete, it was necessary for Mr. Claiborne to expand substantially his collection of wines to fill it. This he did in late 1973. Not many people are faced with the opportunity and challenge of buying nearly $2,000 worth of wine all at once. However, the basis on which Craig Claiborne did this illustrates one man's approach to wine. Here is what he had to say about it at the time*:

* "A Good Wine Cellar for $2,000," *Travel & Leisure,* February 1974.

I am convinced beyond argument that there is no miracle formula for furnishing a wine cellar or a wine closet. There are too many factors involved. One of these is that the wines of any given European shipper are not available universally in this country. Similarly, numerous excellent wines of small production are available in California but not in the rest of the country. Thus a description of my present collection of 500 bottles is intended to serve only as an example of what can be done to put together a personal cellar for just under $2,000.

There are endless modi operandi for setting up a wine collection. The final judgment depends on individual taste and one's pocketbook.

I have heard of wine cellars devoted exclusively to the wine of Bordeaux; others that contain nothing but the wines of Burgundy. In selecting the wines for my new cellar, there was a definite forethought to make it international, although there are many interesting wines from various countries that are missing—the wines of Hungary, Australia, Russia, Yugoslavia, to name a few. As time passes, these omissions will be remedied. One of the nicer features of a wine cellar, however, is its fluctuating nature. A wine cellar that is static is a museum and who needs cobwebs?

Among my treasures I count a dozen or so bottles of Nuits-St.-Georges Argilières 1966 and Les Corvées 1969. I selected these for sentimental reasons as well as excellence. Nuits-St.-Georges was the wine I drank when I first became aware of the glories of Burgundy. The bottles are among the most expensive of my new purchases and are currently priced at about $11 and $12.50 a bottle.*

There are two wines in the cellar that I consider of uncommon interest because they are "champagne types" and remarkably inexpensive. Yet, they compare favorably to some of the best-known bona fide champagnes of France. They are called Boyer Brut and Le Duc Blanc de Blancs and are priced at $4.99 a bottle.

Approximately one fourth of the wines in my cellar hail from California. Another fourth are of Swiss, Italian, Spanish, and German origin. I wanted the wines from Switzerland not only because they seemed to be reasonably priced, but because I have a certain nostalgia for the wines I drank in my middle youth—the dry white Fendant, the full-bodied dry red Dole.

The wines of Alsace, Germany, and Italy were chosen for their excellence and because there are certan foods that go best with these wines. My German wines include Mosels such·as Bernkasteler, Piesporter, and Zeltinger; wines of the Rhine such as Rudesheimer and Hochheimer. Among the Italians are Barbaresco, Barbera, Barolo, Bardolino, and several Chiantis.

The bulk of my wines—about 50 per cent, in fact—are of French

* Prices noted are as of late 1973.

origin and are mostly the wines of Burgundy and Bordeaux. The wines of Beaujolais are heavily represented, for Beaujolais, to my mind, is just about the most serviceable of French wines—all things considered, including cost. And there are numerous bottles of Châteauneuf-du-Pape, a Rhône wine.

There is a current attitude among wine snobs that only novices prefer the wines of Burgundy to those of Bordeaux. Given a limited choice, I prefer the Burgundies, so maybe I'll never make the first team—or do I mean that's what makes horse races? The white wines of Burgundy are made from the Chardonnay grape and, in my opinion, the finest white wines produced abroad or in America derive from the Chardonnay or Pinot Chardonnay grape. Many of these wines are modestly priced, and the discovery of a good bottle is well worth the search.

In earlier days, I "speculated" on great wines such as a Château Margaux 1959, and I reaped—on paper, at least—something like a thousand per cent profit within a ten-year period. While this is very comforting, I seriously doubt that I will ever again speculate by buying the finest wines of Burgundy and Bordeaux, unless I become, in some unforeseen fashion, wildly rich. There are several reasons for this. As the least informed wine enthusiast must know, the values of all wines throughout the world, and particularly the great châteaux of Bordeaux, have escalated on a heroic scale so that a 1970 vintage First Growth such as Château Latour now sells for $36.95 a bottle, while even a Fifth Growth such as Château Lynch-Bages of the same year retails for a "modest" $13.50.

Will anyone please tell me what grand occasions occur in life when a bottle of wine (my long-held Château Haut-Brion 1961, for example) that costs nearly $90 is appropriate? I haven't had a coronation in my house in a good long while, and I feel that champagne is infinitely more festive for weddings and birthdays than any still wine, red or white.

There is another, to me, wholly related case in point. And that is the American institution known as the cocktail hour. It is as thoroughly a part of the national scene as malted milk, apple pie, and T-bone steaks. And it thrives most in precisely the large and small metropolitan centers where wines are frequently part of the bill of fare. My friends are educated, interesting, concerned, and sincere, and on any Saturday evening the cocktail hour flourishes in my home. Guests and chefs alike have free access to the open bar. If most of the guests have drunk a couple of martinis prior to the meal, to serve a bottle of wine of enormous cost would—to my mind—be distinctly absurd. A simple white wine, a Pinot Chardonnay, for example, or a good red Beaujolais, would be more judicious. Europeans, who have a far longer history of wine use, are content with their *vins du table* or country wines for ordinary occasions.

It is my opinion that the subtleties and nuances in wine are far more involved than those of food. It is easy to elaborate on the cheeses that are the most interesting to my palate. It is simple to specify preferred brands of sardines or rice or olive oil or imported pasta, but wines are another ball game.

I have friends who pale at the thought of a sweet wine. *Any* sweet wine. On the other hand, to my taste, a well-chilled Sauternes (a genuine Sauternes from France and not the dry California wine that mistakenly bears that name) is one of the glories of the world *provided* it is drunk with pure foie gras.

Taste in wine is enormously subjective, and to build a collection, you should taste for yourself.

THE WINE CELLAR OF PAUL AND JULIA CHILD

In the house of Mr. and Mrs. Paul Child of Cambridge, Massachusetts, as in millions of households across America, the lady of the house takes care of the cooking while the man of the house looks after the wine. But the Childs are by no means a typical American household. The man of the house, Paul Child, began learning about and enjoying wine as a young man in Europe many years ago, and continued during a career in the U. S. Foreign Service. The lady of the house, Julia Child, not only cooks to the obvious satisfaction of Paul Child, but by way of her books and public television has put her culinary skills at the service of millions of other Americans who wish they could eat and drink as nicely as the Childs do.

The Childs' wine cellar is not pretentious or extravagant; they are not that kind of people. But it is well chosen, well loved, and skillfully and often used. It offers good Clarets of the 1950s and fine Burgundies of the 1960s, along with a representative selection of German wines.

Unlike the proprietors of many cellars, Paul Child does not bother to keep a "cellar book," recording in detail what wines he bought and when, when he drank them, with whom, what he thought of them, and so on. Rather, he uses a large piece of illustration board (the kind available in art stores) on which he writes in pencil the names and vintages of the wines he buys, along with a number for each bottle, 1, 2, 3, 4, 5, etc. When he drinks a bottle of that wine, he erases a corresponding number. When all the numbers are erased, that means the lot is gone. He then erases the name of that wine and writes in a new one.

At the time this book was going to press, Frank Prial, the wine columnist for the New York *Times,* had dinner with the Childs in Cambridge and wrote a column about them, describing in particular Mr. Child's unu-

Region	Wine	Year	1	2	3	4	5	6	7	8	9	10	11	12	13	CH	Notes
BORD	Château de Pichon-Longueville (Pauillac)	'53	1	2	3	4	5	6	7	8	9						
BURG	Pommard Rugiens (Bouserole)	'52	1.	2	3	4	5	6									
BORD	Château Palmer	'64	1	2	3	4	5	6	7	8	9						
BURG	Clos de Vougeot	'64	1	2	3	4	5	6	7	8	9						
BURG	Clos-Vougeot (Olivier)	'62	1	2	3		[66]	1	2	3	4	5					(Wonderful)
BORD	Château Lynch-Bages (Pauillac)	'64	1	2	3	4	5										
BURG	Grands Échézeaux	'64	1	2	3	4	5	6	7	8	9	10	11	12	13		
BURG	Clos des Epenots (Pommard)	'64	1	2	3	4	5	6	7	8	9	10	11				
BORD	Château Lafite-Rothschild	'66	1	2	3	4	5	6	7	8	9	10					(total!)
BORD	Château Léoville-Barton	'66	1	2	3	4	5	6	7	8	9	10					(total!)
BURG	Musigny (Olivier)	'62	1	2	3	4	5	6									(very good)
MOSEL	Graacher Himmelreich (Spätlese)	'67	1	2	3	4											
BURG	Chevalier-Montrachet (Seylou)	'68	1	2	3	4	5	6	7	8	9	10	11				
BURG	Corton-Charlemagne (Drouhin)	'69	1	2	3	4	5	6	7	8	9	10	11	12	13		
MOSEL	Piesporter Goldtröpfchen (Feinste Auslese)	'64	1	2													
ALSACE	Gewürztraminer (Grand Reserve)	'69	1	2	3	4											
ALSACE	Riesling (Brandlüft)	'69	1	2	3												
RHINE	Schloss Vollrads	'70	1	2	3	4	5										
LOIRE	Muscadet sur lie (Métereau)	'73	1	2	3	4	5	6	7	8	9	10	11	12	13		
BORD	Graves (Graville-Lacoste)	'67	1	2													

sual chart for recording his wines. Coauthor Gilbert Cross wrote Mr. Child to ask for more details. He responded not only with an explanation of his chart and a hand-rendered sample of same, but with a description of the arrangements of his *cave* (cellar). Cross sent Mr. Child a further list of questions. Back came another detailed and spirited reply. Following are Paul Child's account of his wine chart and wine cellar, along with his answers to the other questions put to him:

That wine chart referred to hangs on the wall next to our kitchen here at home. It is made of a sheet of heavy, white illustration board, 28″ high and 20″ wide. Its upper half is devoted to red wines, the lower half to whites. The left-hand columns are vertical sections of ruled lines drawn with black ink, which enclose the wines from geographic areas. Examples: Burgundies, Bordeaux, Champagnes, etc.—or Alsaces, Rhines, Arbois.

From left to right: the first column is ¾″ wide. (*Beau* for Beaujolais, or *Burg* for Burgundy.) The next vertical section to the right is 4″ wide, enough to accommodate such longer words as *NUITS, Clos des Grandes Vignes, (Olivier)*, or *MUSCADET sur lie (Métaireau)*. The final ¾″ column is for the individual years, such as: '62 or '71.

The rest of the chart takes up thirty-six spaces, each ⅜″ square, arranged in horizontal "boxes," like a crossword puzzle. The horizontal lines in the upper half of the chart (red wines) are ruled in red ink, and the lower half (white wines) are ruled in blue ink. On the right-hand side of the chart (the numbered boxes), the vertical lines are also either red or blue, as appropriate.

Ideally, there should have been both a wider and a longer chart, but I started this chart in 1961, am used to its limitations, and don't want to take the time to redesign and redraw it.

All the names of the wines and their years, as well as the number of bottles in the *cave,* the boxed-in numerals (e.g., 1, 2, 3), are written in pencil. The ink lines never change, but the penciled words are necessarily changed from time to time as certain names are added, or dropped, or as numbers come and are erased. That way the chart can tell us at any time what's in our cellar.

I used to keep 3-by-5″ cards filled with information, but they became burdensome because the temptation to fill empty spaces with words instead of with wine became silly, so I stopped. Now if I do want to put in information I pencil on my chart just one word, such as "lousy" or "great!" Now and then I want to add more information, so I pencil in above the numbers in quite small letters something like this: "Potentially excellent, but keep to at least 1979."

Obviously this system is not perfect, but it suffices for me, and is a simple, workable system. It is not for display.

The wines in my cellar are stored in two rooms, one for reds, one for whites. I have a thermometer in each *cave,* which stays around 60°. Each has a chair. Small tables in the main cellar outside are used for opening cases and boxes. Gins, whiskeys, rums, cordials, etc., are upstairs in a pantry. My two *caves* are totally unpretentious, but they work for me. The wines are arranged like bookshelves, except that the shelves are divided into "boxes" also: each division on the shelves holds twelve bottles. The inside dimensions of each division are 12″ deep, 14″ wide, and 10″ high. The bottles can be slid out and in easily. The bottles are laid in corks-end-first, bottoms out. This makes it easy to read labels. On the front edge of the floor of each division is stuck a length of Scotch drafting tape, on which is marked with a black felt marker the name of the bottles. These tapes are for quick visual reference when I am standing several feet away. The tapes are easily peeled off if I want to change names or positions.

I use the same chart system for our house in Provence, except that the chart in Cambridge is twice as large. In our smaller Provence house we have room for only half the number of wines.

Question: *How often have you replenished your cellar in the past?*

I have·replenished our various cellars in the houses where we've lived in many locations, and what seems like countless times. The cellars at five different epochs in Washington, plus Paris, Marseille, Bonn, and Oslo, as well as fourteen years in Cambridge and Provence, all have been re-plenished often. It's impossible to answer the question, "How often have you replenished your cellar in the past?" The replenishment is constant. It may mean two cases of Brouilly '73 purchased last month, or it means eight cases of assorted wines still going strong after two years. It can mean a case of excellent Spanish Rioja Alta '59 recently told me about by a dealer. There's also the single bottle-gift of Beaune, Clos de la Roche, 1921 (collection of Docteur Barolet). It's waiting, waiting for an auspi-cious occasion. And I cannot mention without sadness the three prestigious bottles which a recently widowed friend gave to us in remembrance of her husband.

How much does the merchant guide you in making your choice, and how much do you lead him?

Wine merchants necessarily vary in their knowledge. During the "lives" in various European countries, I have been guided largely by my own experience. (When I was much younger I lived in Italy and France for six years, between 1925 and 1931.) There have been our knowledge-able friends, our experienced sommeliers and chefs, and, latterly, in Cam-bridge, an experienced, sophisticated, and charming wine merchant named Joseph Moreno has become a friend and guide for us both.

Does Mrs. Child participate in the decision about what wines to buy, or do you simply decide what to do?

We participate in all our decisions as nearly as possible: food, wine, television, work, writing, photography, travel, etc., etc. We of course discuss books and catalogues about wines and food, but—in the end—what happens on our tongues, through our own tasting, is what determines what we buy.

How long have you had what could be described as a wine cellar of any sort?

"What could be described as a wine cellar of any sort" depends on each individual's conceptions. One finds himself in a semantic bog at once, because, what Mr. X describes seldom looks like Mr. Z's preposterous (or magnificent, or unhealthy, or reasonable) wine cellar. Therefore I have made my choice: My cellar is "any of several kinds of wines, numbers at least thirty-six bottles, stored anywhere in an enclosed area, no warmer than 68°, not colder than 55°, kept in a dark place, not moved until moved, stored on their sides, produced from grapes, being naturally fermented, having an alcoholic content between 10 and 13 per cent; age, color, nationality, taste, being matters personal and not matters of fiat or decree."

When and how did your interest in wine begin?

I began storing wines in 1946, in Washington, when my wife and I returned from China-Burma-India after World War II. My interest in wine began in Italy, in 1925, where I lived as a tutor of two boys, whose father and mother were musicians, Americans (and wealthy), and interested in wines and food. So was I, but my purse and my interest in owning wines had to wait another twenty years for fufillment.

It seems clear from what you write about it that your house in Cambridge came complete with cellar. Did you buy the house with a wine cellar in mind?

Our house was built in 1870 by Josiah Royce, the Harvard philosopher, who died in 1916. There have been several owners since then. The house came with a cellar, but not with a *wine* cellar. One of its basic utilities was a big coal furnace. By 1961, when we bought the house, an oil-burning furnace had been installed. One of the first changes I made was turning one part of the cellar into two wine "cellars." These were large coal bins, so: out with black coal dust and cobwebs! Clean up! Whitewash! Put up lights! Shelves! The whole enormous cellar has stone walls, is seven feet underground and about three feet above the ground. The floor is made of cement. Four days ago here the outdoor temperature was 94°, but the two wine-cellar thermometers read 68°. The cellar temperature changes very slowly, both winter and summer.

A wine cellar, therefore, was *not* one of the reasons for our choice. A big kitchen was primary; also large rooms for photography and painting, music, "regular" books in one place and cookbooks in another for Julia, as an office and work place, guest rooms, bathrooms, etc. Only then came, "What shall we arrange as an adequate place for our wines?" There was some competition with a laundry, fireplace wood storage, trunks, garden tools, a workshop for me, etc. But those Victorian houses were designed for grandparents, parents, children, and domestics, thus there is almost a superfluity of space.

Did you have to make any modifications to convert your ordinary cellar into a wine cellar?

I enclosed those original big coal-bin places, using Cel-O-Tex. I also hung a door in each, installed lights, built the wine-shelf sections, put a thermometer in each room, and added things like a roll of masking tape, a black felt marker, and—for neatness—a pair of scissors.

How do your friends keep track of the contents of their cellars?

Most of my friends have better memories than mine. I have one friend who puts a marker on each bin. (The markers are plastic numbers.) Then he files numbered cards corresponding to each type of wine. He has to paw through the box full of cards when he wants to find whatever data is written on the cards. He changes information on each card in order to keep track, by scratching out or adding to the cards. When any card gets too filled up with scratches-out, or information, he makes a new card and throws away the prior one.

Do you ever regret that you do not have a record in a book, going back many years, of what wines you drank, with whom, etc.?

Most of our friends who like wine, and who use it constantly, don't seem to be those who keep record books about the late-departed wines. In fact, it has never occurred to us nostalgically to read about what we once drank, and with whom, and where, and why. We do remember a good many notable wines, and the meals that were consumed with friends, but perhaps we are among the future-hopers, rather than the past-day nostalgics.

What is the purpose of the chair in each of your caves?

You may well ask! I dragged a chair into my *cave* once, to reach up to fix an electric fixture. It just stayed there because I found it was useful for putting things on—things like boxes, tools, paper-and-pencil stuff, wine baskets, jackets, other objects. . . . Now and then I put myself on it for a brief rest. I must confess: These two chairs could just as well be *out* as *in,* but they joined my wine *caves* years ago and now I'd feel deprived if they weren't there.

When you pick out a wine, do you consult the chart, then go to the cellar and get it? Or do you go down and choose the wine, then record the transaction on the chart?

Usually, when we're planning a meal if it's something special, we discuss the wines to be served in relation to who's coming. "If we're going to have a dessert, why not serve so-and-so? Yes, but remember the last time, last year, we gave them a Suduiraut '67, so why, next time, why not that Château Rayne-Vigneau '62, or even our Sigalas Rabaud '55?" Then we check our chart to make sure we have two bottles left. In other words: We do not consult the chart first—we consult each other. *Then* comes the chart consultation, and finally, the transaction is recorded. Of course it works both ways: Perhaps I'm working in the cellar at my workbench, making something, and I'm too lazy to consult Julia two floors above, or even one floor above where the chart is, so I go into one of the wine *caves,* and see all those bottles, and I come up with a surprise for tonight's dinner—and hope to remember to erase that number from our chart.

Is there a temperature problem in your cellar in Provence?

In Provence I store wines in a half-underground, small cellar, known as *Le Cabanon,* originally used as a storage place for tools and wood, put up by some unknown peasant at least a hundred years ago. It has an earth floor, stone walls, one tiny arrow-slit-type of window, high up open to the air. So far I've had good fortune, having had no disasters—though I do not know why. It seems probable that God is not particularly interested in whether or not my little wine cellar does well or ill. We built our house in which we live in 1964. *Le Cabanon* is a very short stone's distance from the house.

One or two characterizing details on your house in Provence might be interesting. Is it very old, historic, etc.?

Alas, sir! It's neither old nor historic—but give us time. If they now call our Cambridge house The Royce House since he up-and-died, maybe they may change its name to The Julia House once we've popped off.

The house in Provence has a long living room with centrally located fireplace. The kitchen walls are covered with pegboard, painted blue, with doors, shelves, closets painted dark green. Hung on the kitchen walls are Julia's tools of her trade (pots, pans, whisks, knives, etc.). The floors are all red tile. There's also a gas stove, a sink, work tops for cutting. Refrigerator. Three windows.

One bedroom for guests, a studio-bedroom for me, an "office"-bedroom for Julia's writing work. One and a half bathrooms. Two outside terraces, each with a small tree, one a mulberry and one an olive tree—we sit under our terrace trees for most of our meals. There are olive trees everywhere. A neighbor down below has vineyards and vegetables. Flowers are all around us (this is an area where most of the local peasants grow roses, as a crop, for use as scent in the perfume industry). Our roof tiles are spotty old red tiles.

We work—writing, painting, photography, cooking-experimentation.

When we are in the United States or elsewhere, we lend our Provence house to friends who are writers, painters, musicians, professors, Foreign Service pals, etc., who need a quiet place to work or rest. It is always full. The shutters are dark green. It is quiet. . . .

Sorry about the historic and aged-romantic quality. However, it is full of life, interesting people doing something. There are two San Francisco chef-friends there right now, as I am writing this.

INDEX

Figures in italics indicate where the main
information on the subject will be found.